Orby Shipley

Principles of the faith in relation to sin

Topics for thought in times of retreat

Orby Shipley

Principles of the faith in relation to sin
Topics for thought in times of retreat

ISBN/EAN: 9783337161750

Printed in Europe, USA, Canada, Australia, Japan

Cover: Foto ©Lupo / pixelio.de

More available books at **www.hansebooks.com**

PRINCIPLES OF THE FAITH

IN RELATION TO SIN

TOPICS FOR THOUGHT IN TIMES OF RETREAT

ELEVEN ADDRESSES
DELIVERED DURING A RETREAT OF THREE DAYS
TO PERSONS LIVING IN THE WORLD

WITH AN INTRODUCTION ON THE NEGLECT
OF DOGMATIC THEOLOGY IN THE CHURCH OF ENGLAND

BY
ORBY SHIPLEY, M.A.

LONDON
C. KEGAN PAUL & CO., 1, PATERNOSTER SQUARE
1879

[*The rights of translation and reproduction are reserved.*]

Contents.

INTRODUCTION.

On the Neglect of Dogmatic Theology in the Church of England vii

Eve of Retreat.

ADDRESS ONE.

Introductory Address 3

First Day of Retreat.

GOD THE GREAT FIRST CAUSE IN RELATION TO SIN.

ADDRESS TWO.

God the Creator of Man 30

ADDRESS THREE.

God the Redeemer of Man 54

ADDRESS FOUR.

God the Sanctifier of Man 84

Second Day of Retreat.

MAN THE IMAGE OF GOD IN RELATION TO SIN.

ADDRESS FIVE.

Man Created by God 112

ADDRESS SIX.

Man Purchased by God . . 140

ADDRESS SEVEN.

Man Inspired by God. 173

Third Day of Retreat.

GOD IN UNION WITH MAN IN RELATION TO SIN.

ADDRESS EIGHT.

The Incarnation of God 204

ADDRESS NINE.

The Sacrifice of the Cross 236

ADDRESS TEN.

The Sacraments of the Church . 265

End of the Retreat.

ADDRESS ELEVEN.

Concluding Address . . . 295

Introduction.

ON THE NEGLECT OF DOGMATIC THEOLOGY IN THE CHURCH OF ENGLAND.

THE present work is offered, with much diffidence, to English Churchmen, with a double purpose: first, as an humble contribution towards the study of certain portions of theology, dogmatic and practical; and secondly, as an ethical effort to probe some of the deeper levels of conscience through the media of the higher truths, facts and mysteries of the Christian Religion.

It is, moreover, published as an experiment to discover, in an age impatient of first principles, and under ecclesiastical circumstances not favourable for calm thought, what amount of sympathy and acceptance may be afforded to a treatise which, however superficial, is based upon dogmatic principles, and however imperfectly, seeks to illustrate them from Catholic practice. Although it has taken the familiar form of Addresses to persons living in the world, and though it aspires only to supply such persons with Topics of thought in times of Retreat, yet the book is, substantially, a theological treatise. *Principles of the Faith in relation to Sin* shews the result of an attempt to popularize certain features of Catholic dogma, through the connection between a common humanity and the most practical question in manhood, on the one side, and some of the higher and deeper realities of Christian faith and practice, on the other.

Before, however, these truths, facts, and mysteries of Religion, become subjects of practical consideration, it may be well to inquire, with such brevity as the questions allow, into certain topics of an introductory character. The position and prospects of Dogmatic Theology, for example, and the reasons which may be given for the neglect of its study, at the present day in the Church of England are of importance in the Revival of the Faith. The consideration of these points will include a discussion of some of the difficulties which attend the production of works of dogma; into some of the causes of the neglect of dogma; and into some of the results of such neglect. Each of these points will be treated in the like manner in which the Christian doctrines and practices have been treated in the following volume. They will be discussed more with a view of stimulating thought upon assured positions, than with the intention of indicating all that may be offered for the reader's consideration—in short, suggestively rather than exhaustively.

I. The production of works on dogmatic theology must, as a rule, be confined to those who believe in theology, dogmatically. Practical experience in the domain of religious literature alone relieves the statement from a charge of being a truism; for practical experience alone discovers that many writers ignore this rule. The rule, however, is sound. Whatever further qualifications may be required in authors of dogmatic works, this one is essential. Such writers ought to accept the faith as external to themselves, and objective in itself. They ought not to disbelieve in theology as a dogmatic science. They ought not to originate, nor to elaborate, a creed or a system of belief subjectively, from their inner consciousness; nor, again, to receive that divine teaching only which most nearly concurs with their private opinion, or with their own foregone conclusions. In a word, they ought, and in harmony with them their readers ought, simply to bow before the teaching of Revelation, so far as it may be obtained, on the authority alone of the Church.

Hence, it is neither to the Liberal clergy, nor to Evangelical ministers that we must look for works of dogmatic theology. However competent they may be personally, by talent or culture, by gift or acquirement, to deal with theology in the abstract; or, however learnedly they may be able to treat other divisions of the sacred science, historical, critical, exegetical, or even devotional, both classes should abstain from the region of pure dogma. The Broad Church man, as a fact, does not believe in the principles of dogmatic theology, under any conditions. The Low Church man believes in its principles, only so far as they commend themselves to the believer's individual judgment. We are, therefore, restricted in our search for modern works on Christian dogma to the labours of the third main section of the existing Church of England—the Catholic party. And the production of such works by the Catholic priesthood of the present day is, from the circumstances which surround the Revival of Religion in our communion, attended with great and exceptional difficulties.

Two reasons are sufficient, perhaps, to show the truth of this remark.

The first reason is this. The more exact and dogmatic

teachers, the more cultured and theological minds, the incomparably greater intellects of the old Tractarian party, with one grand exception, have either passed away to their reward; or, have retired from the conflict, disheartened by their inability to realize their ideal of a Church in the Anglican obedience; or, one by one, have been called to labour in another portion of CHRIST'S Vineyard. But, more than this is true, notwithstanding that the fact may be concealed, or indeed, in some quarters, is boldly denied. Since, and in addition to, the death, disappointment, and secession to the Latin Church, of the eminent divines in question, a perennial stream of younger men—less able indeed, but only less able than their teachers—with not infrequent instances of men of maturer years and of higher standing in the Church, has flowed from the Anglican to the Roman communion. This stream has never ceased. Sometimes it has flowed with a greater volume, sometimes with a less: and though at one time a faint prospect of a partial intermission was apparent; yet, at the present moment, the flood-gates have again been opened. This is not the place to inquire into the reasons of this marked increase of secessions, especially of the large number of the laity who submit to the obedience of Rome. One only need be named, which of itself is more than enough to account for our late heavy losses: namely, the deliberate and voluntary surrender of their spiritual and God-given jurisdiction, by the entire bench of Bishops, into the hands of the secular and non-Christian power; and all that results from such a surrender. These younger men, however, contained within their ranks many who possessed learning, ability and power sufficient to have placed them in due time in prominent positions, and some in the very forefront, of the Catholic Revival, as thinkers, writers, or workers. But—they have been lost to us. Of course, it may be replied, the numbers of this ecclesiastical exodus are small: but, the aggregate of the clergy also is small from whence the exodus proceeded; and personal influence and weight cannot be estimated by numerical averages.

It will be observed, that the causes of this transference of allegiance from one communion to another is not now the point in debate—but rather, the result of the transference; and that, in one direction only, namely, the serious loss of power to the Anglican obedience. As a fact, account for it as we can and minimize it as we may, and of course, without any desire to depreciate those in the English Church from whom these comparatively few great men severed themselves, the vacant places of the latter have in no wise been refilled.

The same may be said, with obvious qualifications, of the many hundred of less distinguished converts who have been individually reconciled with Rome. And, although it may be freely granted that clergy of considerable capacity in various ways have, in GOD'S providence, been raised up for the Church's edification and guidance; no person with any knowledge of both generations would venture to affirm, that the younger men of the Anglican priesthood of the present day are comparable with the elder Tractarians.

Here it may be allowed to speak of the Tractarian party as a whole, however the individual career of any unit of the party may have terminated. The later generation have had their work to do, and have done it nobly and with self-sacrifice. But, the work cannot fairly be said to have been as great in itself, nor to have been done in so artistic a manner, nor to have been done with equally good materials, as that of the earlier generation. Origination is very far indeed in advance of mere improvement, or even of consistent development; and moreover, certain of the best traditions of the older school — notably their respect for Authority, however misplaced, and their intense realization of and desire for Unity—have been either recklessly ignored or cynically abandoned by the newer. Taken as a whole, then, the original Tractarian party was a scholarly, gentleman-like, philosophic, cultured, thoughtful body of divines and students. Even with an experience of only one half the period of the Movement, it cannot be said that these are pre-eminently the characteristics of the Neo-Tractarians, again, taken as a whole. A decided deterioration has taken place in the party, which is apparent to all who stand a little aside from the whirl of ecclesiastical events and exercise their judgment without prejudice, and is caused by a mixture of good and evil. The Revival has become more democratic: and it is injuriously affected by the unscrupulousness and low tone of the widely read and so-called "Church press." The results of this deterioration are not less apparent. The present party of action do not possess the genius, nor the intellectual strength, nor the powers of the former school of thought. Their tone and culture are not of the same calibre. They fail to exercise a like authority with the logical and masculine minds of their own, or of any other party. And, with a very few brilliant exceptions, they do not so much as touch with personal influence the outside world—at least in the upper orders of society. Indeed, the theory has been loudly proclaimed, if not ingeniously conceived, to meet the self-evident inconsistency of leaders who do not lead, and of authorities who will not counsel, and of moral forces who decline to act, that, under existing circumstances, it were better for the Movement that there should be a multiplication of minor points of attraction and secondary centres of work, rather than one authority of commanding influence and of acknowledged power.

The same truth, indicated above, is unconsciously admitted by an unexpected testimony which is beyond a suspicion of interested motives. It is inferentially admitted in articles, speeches and conversation, by the oft-repeated, and it may be added, silly boast—which, however, is far from being founded in fact, and is open to a cruel retort if it were—that, since the days of the earliest and most distinguished converts, few persons or none of intellectual vigour or of theological acquirement have submitted to the claims of the Roman Catholic Church. It would be inconvenient in this place, though possible, to quote names in disproof of this statement: but a general disclaimer, even from those who have been deprived of the co-operation of their brethren, is all that is needful to meet a vague and indefinite charge. And that some disclaimer was demanded from those who would deal generously with friends that have parted from us, and truthfully and with self-respect even in polemical controversy, both others and myself have long felt.

The second reason for the difficulties which attend the production of works of dogmatic theology, is not less obvious than the first. It is, however, far more hopeful for the future of the Oxford Movement, as the agent of the counter-Reformation in the English Church, as the adversary of Protestant opinion, and as the restorer of one aspect of Catholicism to the English people. The elder Tractarians were emphatically a school of thought. The younger Ritualists—to use a conventional, but inexact term well understood —are not less decidedly, as has already been hinted, a party of action. There is no necessity to compare, to the disparagement of either division of the historical High Church party, the respective work of each phase of the Movement. Both the theoretic and the practical phases of the Catholic Revival are valuable. Both have fulfilled, in different ways, the object of their existence. Both have supplied a want which the modern Church of England could not, or, if she were able, did not otherwise supply. And if the intellectual world, at an early date of the Movement, was forced to respect the master-mind which influenced, and still influences, English thought, in a manner and to a degree which none other attempts nor expects to influence it; yet, the outward aspect of ecclesiastical England has been changed by the action of a later generation, to an extent which it was impossible to predict beforehand, and which, as an after-result, has fallen nothing short of revolutionary. It is possible, indeed, that the results in both spheres of labour have, to an extent, been affected by secondary causes, to which it is only just to give due weight. Abstract thought, in all metaphysical topics, was less widely than now developed in England thirty or forty years ago. Hence, a single intellect of commanding genius effected, perhaps, more in those days than it would have effected, had it appeared when thought had become more active and more diffused. Again, a spirit of reform in abuses, and of improvement in method and detail, not less than of inquiry into principles, has been infused, during the same period, into every human organization in the land. This fact may be remarked, amongst others, in social and political circles, in the relations between capital and labour, in trade and manufacture, in law and education, in civic bodies and in charitable institutions. Hence, again, Religion, in a communion where authority is unhappily in abeyance, and even in its divine relations, could not expect to escape, and has not escaped, the effects of the prevalent spirit of investigation and change.

Yet, after all that may be said by enemies in the way of detraction, or may be allowed by oneself on the score of justice, this result has been secured by the later phase of the Tractarian Movement. In the course of a short half-century, a National Church, which once willingly severed itself from the tradition, example and authority of the centre of Christendom, and which has since made no corporate effort for Re-union, but rather has departed wider and wider from the spirit of Unity, has been revivified from a deathlike torpor and indifference to a condition which the world beholds— and beholding, strives to counteract. The Church of England in the nineteenth century has been restored to a comparatively healthy condition of existence, in spite of the passive opposition, at the least, of those in positions of authority both in Church and State, and of the active and ceaseless opposition of almost every form of Public Opinion which can either make its voice heard, or its hand felt. Such restoration has been effected by the influence and labour of the second order only of the ministry, and the hearty co-operation of the faithful laity, of that party in the Church which is by turns abused and imitated, scorned and followed, prosecuted and in word commended—the historical High Church party.

However the fact may be explained, or whatever attempts are made to explain away the fact, such a re-organization, under similar conditions, is simply without a parallel in the history of the faith. A believer in Christianity must allow that it could not have been effected apart from the direct inspiration, without the personal work of GOD the HOLY GHOST.

The evidence of this fact is not far to seek. It need only be mentioned in outline. Witness the church building and restoration; the extension of the Episcopate; the development of Foreign Missions; the revival of Convocation; and the enormous amount of middle-class and lower-class education that has been originated or completed by Churchmen, in the last five-and-forty years. Witness the re-opening of churches in the week; the restored daily Offering of the holy Sacrifice; the improved ceremonial both in the Mass and in the Hours of Prayer; and of the adoption and naturalization amongst us of other forms of devotion of the Catholic Church (*e.g.* the comparatively modern office of the Three Hours Service on Good Friday, and the Stations of the Cross in Lent), during the same period. Witness, again, the frequent, habitual and wide-spread use of the Sacraments of Penance and the Holy Eucharist; the note-worthy development of Retreats and parochial Missions; the establishment of permanent works of corporal Charity, of Sisterhoods, large and small, and of religious Societies, Confraternities and Guilds, almost without number. Witness, lastly, the deep and intelligent interest which the laity take in the Catholic Revival—both men and women, and specially of the great middle-class which the Church had entirely lost, as well as of the uppermost and lowest classes on which she has ever retained a hold—and the active part which they play, with time and money, in works of self-denial, devotion and piety.

In the face of such evidence to a revival of practical work in the Church of England—work which, it may be repeated, has been effected by the High Church party, and it is painful to own, in antagonism to all legitimate ecclesiastical authority —it were unwise and unreasonable to expect from its originators and agents, any equivalent action in the world of thought. Indeed, there has been, to a like extent, no such equivalent action. Not that the Church party has not availed itself of the use of the press, as a missionary agency for the propagation of the faith. On the contrary, it has employed the press to a larger extent, perhaps, than either of the other two parties at present included within the comprehensive embrace of the Establishment. This may be proved by a reference to the records of the publishing trade; and is seen in the number and variety of the works which are issued. Of course, the numbers of any given book, or of the works of any given author, which may be sold offers no criterion of the literary activity of a party, specially of one situate as the High Church party is situated. From the nature of the case, the works of English Catholics do not command the double sale which is secured, in different ways, by those of the Low Church clergy and of Roman Catholic divines. The works of the latter circulate amongst both Anglicans and members of their own communion—*e.g.* the invaluable and unequalled spiritual books (with all their peculiarities) of the late Father Faber. The works of the former—*e.g.* of Bishop Oxenden, of whom it is advertized that the aggregate sale of his books exceeds two million copies—circulate amongst both Evangelicals and Nonconformists, within and without the Church.

But, especially of late years, though the Tractarian school has produced works of value and of permanent interest in many fields of theological inquiry; it cannot be said that, since the early days of the Movement, it has exerted an influence in the domain of pure intellect comparable to the radical change which it has effected in the entire life of the Church as an external organization, or in the inner life of Churchmen as moral and accountable beings. This fact, though it be true of all, is observable in the field of dogmatic theology, perhaps more than in any other. For example— to go to the root of the matter. In spite of our constant reference to Christian doctrine and Christian duty as factors of the neo-Reformation, there does not yet exist in the language an exhaustive dogmatic Catechism of the Faith, nor a complete Manual of Moral Theology, for the use of members of the English Church. We have to turn to the French or Latin. And if we pass to other divisions of theology, in spite of our respect for GOD'S Word written, and of our appeal to primitive Christianity, whilst other schools of thought have issued their own special comments (such as they are) on Scripture, or have published their version of the history of Christianity; after a weary waiting of upwards of twenty years, the Catholic party are only in possession of a fragment (worthy though it be of its venerable author) of a Commentary on the Bible, and a philosophic History of the early Church is still amongst the *desiderata* of the future. We have to turn, again, to the Latin or the German.

This avoidance of dogmatics is not caused by the absence of intellectual, or of theological power. There have been, and still are, many priests, not to speak of cultivated laymen, of the High Church party, who are, or were, capable to produce intellectual work that would live. But here, as in many other aspects of the Revival, the want of any practical organization, and consequently of division of labour, and the setting the right man to do the right work; the want of a leader who could and would command, and consequently of followers who were compelled to obey—in short, the absence of authority—has been calamitously felt. Of course, the Church, or its representative, the episcopate, is the authority to which Catholics would naturally look for such direction. But this is an authority to which the bishops, unhappily, have taught us not to look. And, for any other authority, inferior though it may be to that of the Church's living voice, yet, still possessed of value, the Catholic party has long looked in vain.

The result of this want of authority is apparent. Men of ability and talent, self-guided and without combined unity of purpose, have chosen their own line of thought, and have either practically followed it or not, according to their own good pleasure. They have either refrained altogether, though well qualified, to take action in the republic of letters; or they have acted at hap-hazard, or as their natural gifts and tastes prompted them, even though unqualified. They have over-stocked the literary market with certain kinds of products, which form the luxuries of religion; and have failed to supply souls, hungering and thirsting after its essentials, with the necessities of the supernatural life. They have become disappointed in their realization of the claims and position of the Church of England; and hence, have turned their minds away from divinity, and applied themselves to secular subjects in which they have become distinguished. They have squandered their talents upon earthy and party politics—in support of eminent individual politicians, or in defence of important political measures. They have devoted themselves to unlovely, but engrossing, questions of religious controversy—sometimes on high and worthy themes, sometimes on those that are unworthy and low; or they have frittered away their time on the yet more unprofitable result of newspaper articles, criticism of those in authority, pamphlets on many subjects, and letters on all. They have studied and written on history, biography, philosophy, philology, science, poetry, art, nature, classical literature, mathematics. They have cultivated nearly every branch of human knowledge—but one. The higher branches of dogmatic theology they have not cultivated.

If we will be at the pains to estimate the work of the majority of the ablest clergy of the High Church party, we shall perceive another cause which tends to produce the same result. Whether it be self-chosen—for such men usually gravitate towards centres of life and action ; or be forced upon them externally—for they are generally transplanted from quiet country parsonages ; their labour is found, as a rule, located in towns, and the agent is always found worked at high-pressure. It is almost physically impossible for the ordinary type of an Anglican priest to perform more than he actually succeeds in doing. Any person who is conscious of what the life of such an one involves, will feel no surprise at the result which is here described. How can it be expected of the head of an ecclesiastical organization, or of the founder of a London Mission, or of a laborious parish clergyman, or of an over-taxed Confessor, or of the ceaseless preacher or conductor of Retreats, or of the active attendant at committees and councils, any more than of the mere controversialist, or the political partizan, or the priest who is absorbed in secular pursuits, that he shall be willing if he be able, or that he shall be able if he be willing to devote time and thought, study, prayer and meditation, in the interests of pure theology, and in a form which may instruct or edify others ? It would be too much to expect this of any, save in the exceptional case of a great mind that seldom is created. In the meanwhile, dogmatic theology languishes in the Church of England of to-day.

Nor is it only in the Church of England, nor is it from the neglect of writers in her communion only, that dogmatic theology languishes. The whole stream of English theological, or semi-theological works, during the past many years, has drifted, if not in an anti-dogmatic, at least in a non-dogmatic direction. The yearly supply of books which may be catalogued in literary records under the heading of "Religion," and which make divinity their subject-matter, is large almost beyond belief, and certainly beyond experience. But, it is noteworthy, apart from a few books of devotion, a few books of sermons, and some of the inevitable annual volumes of the Bampton and other lectures—but few of which attract more than a transient attention—how small is the proportion of works now published in divinity which are even professedly dogmatic in form. No doubt, works of standard value—monographs chiefly, on the outskirts of theology proper, apologetic or exegetic, legal or liturgical, critical or controversial, proceed from the pens of dignitaries, professors, scholars, and others : and these deservedly command respect. But the books that are written for and are eagerly devoured by the thousands of the theology-reading public, are those which avowedly ignore the science of theology, or whose authors possess but a feeble grasp of its sacred principles and practice.

For instance: take but a cursory glance at the topics of some of the more popular works of the class under consideration, which have issued from the press during a few past years. A novel aspect of the mystery of the Divine Life on earth, from a humanitarian and rationalistic stand-point. A realistic and photographic description of CHRIST'S actual physical career in the gorgeous and changeless East. Picturesque and brilliant word-paintings of historical and geographical Christianity, done in the language and thought of the day, to prove that events, however miraculous, always repeat themselves and that no scene in one age is without its counterpart in another. Disquisitions on the origin of the Gospel-story, and theories more or less plausible on Supernatural Religion, usually based on the opinion that such origin and such religion is not divine. Commentaries on Scripture, only not entirely borrowed from German semi-infidel writers, Lutherans, and Calvinists. Cultivated and refined essays on religious subjects, by avowed liberals in religion and open sceptics. Discussions on the Last Things, by authors who have sought to discredit things that are past, and to cast doubt upon things that are present. Controversial tractates against the doctrines of the Church of Rome, founded on the facile principle of the infallibility of private judgment; or, in favour of the latest phase of Neo-Protestantism in Germany, built upon the entirely gratuitous assumption, that the position of the Alt-Catholics was originally, or is now, in the days of its decadence, identical with that of the Anglican communion. And efforts, in a pamphlet, serial or other form, to be freed from the awful realities of Death, and of the Judgment to follow, by attempting to shew, or by suggesting without any proof, that, after all, this life may not be, and probably is not the only, perhaps is not the chief stage of man's moral education, probation and trial to which he will be exposed.

These, and such as these, are the topics of the literary works which captivate the public ear at the present day in the Church of England. And if it should happen, that these books are put forth with the adventitious interest secured by first withholding the author's name, and then betraying it to the world as a profound secret; or, are published with the keener attraction, that the writer's position in Church or State gives a piquancy to his attack on Catholic principles, to his defence of a Protestant schism, or to the enunciation of heresy in high quarters; or, are written by those—be they political or clerical writers—whose earlier and un-retracted works, or whose later and un-absolved action ought to have caused them to keep discreet silence when moved to *pose*, in a different attitude, as defenders of the faith—then, in such a case, their popularity becomes unbounded.

The authors of such works, be they Churchmen or Nonconformists, the authors whose works thus become popular, are little likely to enrich the Church or to benefit Religion by the production of laborious, thoughtful, philosophic books of dogmatic theology. And, hence, as these authors are representatives of a large proportion, if not of the majority of the producers of popular modern books which may be registered under the title of "Religion," the study of dogmatic theology, with contemporaneous commentaries, does not thrive.

II. The neglect of dogmatic theology in the Anglican communion at the present day is referable to many causes. Some of these causes are related more closely to the Church than to ourselves, and some are connected more nearly with ourselves than with the Church. As this Introduction is less concerned with the action of a corporate organization than with the way in which we, individually, are influenced by such action, it will be well to state the former causes without much comment, even if we discuss the latter somewhat at greater length.

The isolated ecclesiastical position which the Church of England deliberately assumed in the Christian family in the sixteenth century, is the first and foremost cause of the neglect of dogmatic theology within its borders. No opinion, it may be observed, is here expressed either on the expediency, or on the right, of a National Church thus to sever itself, at the dictation of any earthly authority, from the rest of Christendom. Such a right is here taken for granted, even if the expediency of measure be questioned. We are pledged to the position, and have to argue upon it. But, we are not pledged to all the results (nor indeed to any given result) which flow, or may be supposed to flow from this position of the Church to ourselves. And one result of our isolation in Christendom, which all must combine to deplore, is the loss of the temper and spirit of dogmatic theology. This loss is beyond controversy a reality. Explain it as best we may, we cannot explain away one of its effects—namely, that few comprehensive and scientific works of dogmatic theology have been produced by the post-Reformation divines of the Anglican Church. Indeed, none have been produced which in scope and character are comparable to the *Summa* of S. Thomas Aquinas. And this is the more noteworthy, because the isolation of our position, if loyally accepted and honestly carried to its legitimate conclusion, imperatively demanded such theological works for the special use of the Church of England. If the production of these works was not required to teach the instructed, it was required to instruct their teachers.

The original compromise, which nearly all shades of Churchmanship concur in declaring to be the basis of the re-establishment of the Anglican Church in the sixteenth century, is another cause. This compromise aimed at the creation of an autonomous body, visibly out of communion with the remainder of Catholicism and not less decidedly separate from all forms of mere Protestanism, a body which still claimed the features, the power and the authority of a Christian Church. It involved the adoption of the judicious mean—as its promoters persuaded themselves—between superstition on the one hand and infidelity on the other. It also secured the happy combination—as explained by its apologists—of Apostolic order, Evangelical liberty, and Gospel truth. To this compromise, whether in the results which followed or in the effects which were anticipated, we are committed not more than to any other outcome of our isolation in the family of faith. But, there ensued from its acceptance a balancing of opposite, if not antagonistic opinions. The avoidance of any extreme judgment, even when such judgment might be necessitated as a legitimate conclusion from acknowledged premisses, was encouraged. And the failure to lead any revealed doctrine to its legitimate conclusion was considered a venial fault, if not an actual virtue. The atmosphere generated by such a compromise, from the nature of the case, must have influenced those who were nurtured in it. Even if this atmosphere were not prejudicial to the spiritual life, it certainly has been proved to be unfavourable to the cultivation of dogmatic theology.

The subsequent ecclesiastical declension from the original compromise in faith, worship and practice, more or less extensive as the isolation became developed or as its remedy became hopeful, is a third cause. The compromise itself was not, of course, the lowest position to which a National Church could fall; and, indeed, was patient of a Catholic interpretation. But, the like cannot be affirmed of any positive declension from it. The declension in question began, perhaps, at the time of the Great Rebellion. After a short-lived improvement in ecclesiastical affairs at the Restoration, the declension from a higher position to a lower was again obvious, under the influences which were imported at the Revolution. But, at the very time of the greatest revival in religion which England has ever witnessed, the declension has once more been developed to an extent which has almost, if not altogether severed the Anglican obedience from a just claim to Catholicity. And this phase of the declension has been effected through the voluntary action of the existing episcopate in the year of grace 1874. It has been caused by their transference of spiritual jurisdiction to the civil power, and by their consequent acceptance of secular judgments in ecclesiastical causes.

Moreover, this declension has been followed in former days by no corporate effort for re-union with Western Christendom; whilst at the present day any individual action to this end is promptly and rigorously discouraged. It has been relieved by no synodical action whatever tending to perfect the Anglican system on its own principles; by no legislation on the part of Convocation; and by few personal efforts. It has been restrained by no authoritative reaction; nor has any authoritative rectification of even the worst features of the original compromise been so much as attempted. If these results be observable in all stages of its career, they have been more evident to ourselves in the later history of the English Church than in its earlier stages. As a continuation of former causes of the same issue, they make the assent to dogmatic truth, on the basis of ecclesiastical authority, one degree more difficult; and hence, they make the neglect of the study of dogmatic theology in the Church of England one degree more easy.

The combined result of this isolation, compromise and declension is the last cause, connected with the Church, which need be here named. The total abeyance of legitimate authority in the English Church—of spiritual authority which a person of Catholic instinct and of ordinary intelligence can recognize—is the death-knell of the study of dogmatic theology. On so wide a subject only a few words can be said in this place. But, it may be affirmed without danger of disproof, that, beyond the range of the Creeds, and even for their interpretation on most points, there exists in the Anglican communion no tangible basis of certitude in religion. There is no living ecclesiastical authority to which any actual appeal can be made for the assurance of faith: nay, the Church of England herself nowhere claims the gift of infallibility—but rather, inferentially disclaims it. There is no living authority, be it personal or official, be it individual or corporate, for the settlement of doubt. There is none, neither Court Christian, nor Court of Appeal, nor Provincial Convocation, nor National Synod, even for the final condemnation of heresy. It is true, of course, that theological error is, or has been condemned;

that doubts may be, or are removed; that individual souls, under every disadvantage, do hold the faith. But, none of these effects ensue from the exercise of legitimate Church authority. They are the result whether of controversial argument, or of personal influence, or of private judgment, or of hereditary belief. Individual opinion reigns supreme. The principle of authority is ignored by one section of the Church, is derided by another, is misapplied by a third. Under such conditions, it were impossible but that dogmatic theology should be relegated by English Catholics to neglect.

The last is the most important of the above-named four causes. Indeed, it includes the three earlier reasons for our neglect of dogma. It almost necessitates amongst us the absence of doctrinal precision in belief, or even in the expression of opinion. Attention will be drawn to this topic at a later point in this Introduction. In the meanwhile, and keeping in mind the questions of isolation, of compromise, of declension, and of want of authority, three additional causes may be considered in relation to ourselves. They are as follows: first, the view which we take of the ecclesiastical status of the Anglican communion; second, the estimate we form of our present position as English Churchmen: third, our attitude towards the Catholic Church at large.

1. It is not easy to say what may be the view which the majority of educated persons, whether priests or people, take of our connection with the Christianity of the past; nor yet, indeed, with that of the future. But, it may be assumed that, whatever estimate be formed of either position, it will materially affect our relations towards dogmatic theology at the present time.

Our connection with the Church of the future is both too involved and too uncertain a question to be discussed in this place: neither is it pertinent to the subject under consideration. It need only be said that, on this point and to a large extent, the best and noblest traditions of the old Tractarian party have been abandoned, and even that the original programme of the Ritualist section has been ignored by a younger generation. This is true, whether or not either party were possessed of any organized plan of operation for Catholicizing the English Church. It is true, both of the published words and of the private aspirations of a majority of the High Church school, as well as of its most influential members. But, the teachers of the Neo-Tractarians, whether individual priests or self-constituted and public organs of opinion, have gone beyond the stage of ignoring their own earlier and purer aspirations, and of abandoning the old traditions of others. By constant efforts to this end, they have almost succeeded in stifling the yearnings for Re-union which once inspired and refined the party as a whole, and in turning love into hate. Such yearnings, indeed, and the causes which prompted them, formed the sole justification to the High Church party for its efforts after a counter-Reformation ; and the end in view supplied it with a watchword. But now, the desire for Re-union, if it still fitfully exists in some minds, has been unhappily leavened by principles which are essentially those of Protestantism—namely, the elevation of private opinion into the seat of judgment, to act as arbiter between the dictates of an individual belief and the decrees of a Catholic Church. And the hope for the future visible unity of Christendom, in cases where in spite of general antipathy it still lingers, is held in concert with a vague assumption, that in any such re-union we have nothing to lose, nothing to repudiate, nothing to regret ; but rather, on the principle that " to him that hath shall be given," that we have all to gain. Such a hope is carelessly forgetful of that other and more awful principle, which is applicable to individuals and to Churches alike, that "from him that hath not shall be taken away even that which he seemeth to have." And being so forgetful, it incites its possessor to hold that, whatever may be our relation to one division of the great Christian family, in regard to the other portion, we ought to assume the attitude of a mature friend at length reconciled, rather than, in view of our history and many imperfections, to take the position of a penitent, though once rebellious child.

The opinion of an ordinary Churchman of average intellect, on our ecclesiastical status, would appear to be this. The Reformation, avowedly, did not originate a new Church in this realm of England. But, in the sixteenth century, by a series of acts into which it were wise, perhaps, not to inquire too critically, and by agents of whose motives and characters it were, certainly, wise to speak as little as possible, the Church of England emerged from the heart of Western Christendom an ecclesiastical organization, perfect and complete. This theory possesses an amount both of poetic sentiment and of practical utility which makes it attractive to several classes of minds. The idea recalls an old heathen mythological tale. It is not unlike the actual plan proposed by the originators of the first Canterbury Settlement in New Zealand, who desired, not to create a new colony, but to transport to the antipodes an integral segment of the old country, with its material civilization intact, its traditions, its habits, its laws and its customs

So, the average Anglican. He is wont to conceive of the Church of the Tudors, though by what means it so became he pauses not to ascertain, as a Church which was fully equipped for its mission against the World, and fully prepared to lead souls to Paradise. He believes that, although the English Church were not infallible, it could teach nothing that was false ; that, though it were not impeccable, it could do nothing that was wrong. He holds that, by some unexplained Divine right or gift, it inherently or by acquisition possessed its own powers of autocratic government, legislative and executive; and that it was competent to rule itself and to decide upon all points of faith and practice for its children. Moreover, he perceives, as a fact beyond question, that it has issued its own Articles of Religion, has compiled its own vernacular Liturgy, and lives under the authority of its own disciplinary customs. As this transcendental organization originated, in its present form, in Tudor times, so has it descended with occasional vicissitudes in its history, which always eventuated in its improvement, until our own day. As such it is the object of the firm belief and the devoted labour of multitudes—and justly so ; for, without some ideal to believe in and work for, no true religion is possible.

Can this ideal be considered one that is real and true? Will it stand the test of stern lessons of history which, by some of its most zealous advocates, is reckoned as the twin-sister of theology ; or of the eternal verities of faith ; or of practical experience, to which all can appeal? Our holy Mother is depicted as the personation of an ecclesiastical body, perfect and entire in all its parts ; furnished with a system of doctrine founded on the faith once delivered to the Saints, with an incomparable liturgy understanded of the people, and with a code of morality in accord with the sanctions and inhibitions of Holy Writ. Such is the picture drawn. But, certain questions may be fairly asked of the artist, in explanation of his design. Are these integral portions of a true Church, even in combination, of themselves and alone able to bear the weight that is laid upon them? Do they exhaust even the outward elements of which a Church, that is entire and perfect in all its parts, must be composed? That these notes of the Anglican Communion, as they may be considered, fail to bear the burden forced upon them will be evident when they are further examined, upon principles of faith which all will admit, and facts of history of which any one may be assured. That they are not exhaustive of Catholic elements of ecclesiastical perfection must be allowed, if they shall be proved hereafter to fail in the preliminary trial.

Take the three above-named criteria in order; and examine them briefly, and with the fewest possible examples, by the touchstone of faith and by the light of experience.

In the matter of discipline, the state of the English Church, for a period of three centuries, has been simply chaotic. It is hard to say under which of the two political systems, which have obtained since the Reformation, the condition of the Church may be considered least unhealthy. At one time within the memory of man, her discipline was enforced by state law, even to the altar-steps, by penal statutes. At another, as during the last fifty years, her discipline has ceased to be exercised, because its employment is practically prohibited by civil law. Under both systems the Church of England has groaned. But, she has endured both. Hence, at one period of her history and as a National Establishment, the Anglican Church was forced to communicate political and conscientious Dissenters, before they could enjoy their civil rights as British citizens. At another, in the person of her Deans and Bishops and under the authority of Courts of Law which decide on her discipline, she has voluntarily communicated with continental Protestants, and American schismatics abroad, and has actually invited and communicated avowed heretics, Socinian or other, at home. At one time, by the union of the Church with the State, she constrains all English subjects to appear before her altars, if they desire to enter into married life; and at another, she is powerless to prevent the Sacrament of Matrimony from being sacrilegiously administered to members of alien religions or of no religion; and her blessing from being profanely bestowed upon her own members who have been divorced by the civil law, and are by her accredited ministers re-married.

Of course, the reason of these anomalies in practice—which it must be remembered are typical only of a large class and not exhaustive—is obvious, the want of discipline. And the want of discipline is caused, in part and to a large extent, by the subjection of the Church to the State—a subjection against which the Church does not rebel. As loyal members of the Church, we may accept this double-edged cause, argumentatively. As a fact, we are committed to it. But, we are not committed, in practice, to the results which ensue from this cause. These are condemned by loyal members. At the same time, this further result cannot be denied in argument, and should be acted upon in life. If these causes and consequences are admitted to exist in one of the three outward elements of a Church theoretically intact in its organization, the ecclesiastical status of that Church is not in the position in which it is assumed to be.

In the domain of worship, the attitude of the English Church, for a period of three centuries, has been that of imitator or debtor. In her public offices she has either unconsciously followed the tradition of antiquity, or she has been openly indebted to the Latin Church for ceremonial details and adjuncts of the divine office. Of late years, indeed, she has followed Catholic ceremonial, whether continuously employed or with a restored usage, under the ban of unpopularity and persecution. But, under evil report or under good report, she has followed it. And she has been forced thus to follow. The constitution of the Anglican service-books, both in their source and in their original use, presupposed and necessitated a traditional following of customary forms; it did not anticipate a critical investigation of unwonted usages. This has become so generally acknowledged, save by those who are pledged to opposition, that it were needless to argue the point at length. The Book of Common Prayer contains the *minimum* of ceremonial order which is lawful in the Anglican obedience. What may be the *maximum* of ceremony is not now the question. It was admitted by an adversary years ago, in the *Quarterly Review*, in allusion to the saying of Matins and Evensong, that without supplementing the letter of the rubric, a clergyman could get neither into his surplice, nor out of the vestry. It is declared by colleagues, at the present day and at a hundred altars, in reference to the traditional mode of saying Mass, that without a similar course of action ceremonial adjuncts, of primary importance and in use from the very first, cannot be employed. Two adjuncts only, out of many, need be particularized, which were undoubtedly instituted by CHRIST Himself in the Upper Chamber—Unleavened Bread and the Mixed Chalice. These, whether legal or unlawful, are plain additions to the letter both of the text and rubric of the Prayer Book. They are additions equally with the practice of turning to the East at the recitation of the Creed, or the ascription of Glory to GOD before the Gospel. In short, the supplementing from tradition, and the interpretation and guidance from a living use, in the ritual of the Book of Common Prayer, is a necessity common to all parties in the Church and to every clergyman.

Of course, in union with all others, we accept the Prayer Book loyally, and we legally interpret its laconic directions and augment them from the tradition of the Church. One great difference, however, between our position and that of many others is this: that, whilst they take similar liturgical liberties and declare the ceremonial which they supplement to be perfect ; we candidly admit the imperfection and inadequacy of the letter of the Anglican offices, by the fact, to the extent and at the time of our making the improvements. In both cases, however, and on all hands it is allowed, that the ecclesiastical status of the English Church, in relation to its liturgy and other offices, is not so complete and self-contained an ideal as the average Anglican is disposed to contend.

In questions of dogma, the position of the English Church during the like period and up to the present day, and judged by the highest ideal which we can conceive in practice, has been one of absolute imperfection and positive shortcoming. Here, at the outset of this stage of the inquiry, it may be well to observe that such an avowal is made with frank loyalty to the Anglican communion, which only falls short of an illogical and unreasoning belief in her perfectibility and infallibility. The Anglican formularies may be honestly accepted without the recipient being debarred from seeking external aids to faith, from wheresoever and from whomsoever such aids may be found. This liberty not only may be used in a devout and chastened spirit, but must be employed, if the inquirer would attain in belief to the measure of the stature of the fulness of CHRIST. For, to attain such stature, it is demonstrable to affirm that the authorized formularies of the English Church, as they exist, are entirely insufficient. No doubt the Creeds are included in the authorized formularies which we have accepted : and in a general way and so far as they teach whole truth, they are sufficient when held of faith for salvation. But, even the Creeds are presented for our acceptance by the English Church on a principle which falls short of the highest —namely, on the conformity of their contents, as an abstract fact which may be intellectually proved, with Holy Scripture —not upon the divine authority of the Church. And that the Creeds are of themselves insufficient for the attainment of the entire fulness of faith, is admitted by the Church herself. It is admitted by the fact of her having formulated a large number of other theological statements, external and supplementary to the Creeds. These statements fall far short, indeed, of the authority of the Creeds ; but they have been published authoritatively. In conformity with them the clergy are pledged to teach ; or rather, to speak more exactly, in opposition to them the clergy are prohibited from teaching. And the license which the Church thus indicates on questions of faith her loyal members are bound to assert—namely, that though the Creeds are final as to the points on which they dogmatize; yet, that they are not exhaustive declarations of faith which may not be supplemented.

Into this endless discussion it is almost impossible to enter without being drawn into a vortex of argument. But, following the line of treatment above adopted in the cases of discipline and ceremonial, it may suffice to lay down a single principle, to illustrate it by a two-fold example, and to leave both instance and theory to be conducted by the reader to their logical conclusion.

It is admitted, even by our opponents, that the Church of England, so far as she teaches dogmatically, holds and must hold to the teaching of Universal Christendom on all points that are not specially treated by her authorized formularies. If the Anglican communion be a Church, and if a continuity of faith in the pre-Reformation and ante-Reformation Churches be maintained, this point is essential. Of course, the Church of England holds to the teaching of ancient Christianity on many points also which are treated in her formularies. This is only another way of saying, that on many points the direct teaching of her formularies and those of other parts of Christendom are in harmony. But, we are concerned chiefly with the first-named division of truth. And the principle enunciated is not only true when applied to dogma, but also is true when applied to morals and ritual, though in different ways and with varied results. This development of the principle, however, is denied by many who yet accept its soundness in abstract terms, or even when developed to questions of doctrine. But of doctrine, it is almost axiomatic, that the Anglican Church now holds what the Church of England held in mediæval times, and what the Catholic Church held in primitive times, saving only on such questions as she has definitively expressed her judgment for the purposes of modification, limitation, expansion, or denial.

If this principle be admitted, the terms at the outset employed by the theory of the average Anglican, namely, that the system of doctrine dogmatically asserted by the Church of England was perfect and complete, are abundantly justified. If this principle be denied, the Anglican obedience is involved in the charge that, for three centuries, her doctrinal teaching has fallen short of the Catholic faith. For instances of such shortcoming and imperfection, it may suffice to point the reader to two questions which combine both faith and works. In the first place, the Church of England has failed to provide positive dogmatic teaching on a Sacrament of the

Church, which possesses distinct Apostolic and Biblical authority, and of which her children, at their latest hour of life and at their sorest human need, have been cruelly and recklessly deprived—the Sacrament of Unction. In the second place, on a practice which in itself involves a life-long blessing, which is conformable with natural instinct, is the inevitable result of the doctrine of the Communion of Saints, and has the authority of some of the earliest and of all the greatest Fathers of the Church, the Church of England has preserved a painful and even an ignoble silence—the Invocation of Saints. The Last Sacrament of the Church, whether theoretically or practically, is treated by her formularies in a series of negations only by the Church of England. No office has been appointed for its administration; and certain denials of its claims, nature and outward form are alone predicated of it in the Thirty-nine Articles. Whilst, of the Christian privilege—for none affirm that Invocation is a duty—to ask the prayers of the holy dead, no direct and affirmative teaching is to be found in the Anglican obedience. The faithful are only warned against a certain "Romish doctrine concerning . . . Invocation of Saints," which the Twenty-second Article fails to enunciate, and which, it may be truthfully added, learned men have failed accurately to discover. A loyal Churchman may accept the negations in regard to Unction, and may reject the abuses attributed to Invocation: and yet, in either case respectively and for the edification and benefit of his own soul, he may honestly seek in principle and apply in practice "a more excellent way," in the custom and belief of the Catholic Church.

If this estimate be just and in accordance with facts, the view maintained by the majority of educated Anglicans on the ecclesiastical status of the English Church must be pronounced to be wrong in theory, and to be out of harmony with the teaching of history. If in the matter of discipline, during the last three hundred years, the state of the Church of England can be truthfully described in itself as chaotic; if, again, in the domain of worship, during the same period, her attitude has been that of imitator and debtor in relation to Western Christendom; if, lastly, in questions of dogma, the position of the ante-Reformation Anglican communion, in comparison with the faith of Christendom, has been one of imperfection and shortcoming—then, in any one of these cases, and much more in any two or in all three of them, it cannot be justly affirmed and historically defended, that her status is that of an ecclesiastical body, perfect and complete in all its parts. Neither can it be pretended, that the condition of an organized communion which is here depicted offers any decided encouragement to its members to cultivate the study of dogmatic theology.

2. The next cause which may be mentioned as tending to the neglect of dogmatic theology amongst Anglo-Catholics is the estimate which many of them form and express of their own spiritual position in the Church of England. They do not appear to be assured of their position; or rather, they seem prepared to share it with others. They do not hold that they are, of right, exclusively the true teachers, or that they are the only faithful expositors of Catholic faith and practice; but are willing, if not anxious, to divide with others their claim to such exposition and teaching. This ecclesiastical liberalism, this religious laxity, of course, is wholly in accord with the spirit of the age, which is impatient of any exclusive and absolute claims to truth or right. The doubtfulness of their spiritual position, or a desire to share it with others, is not exhibited, however, by English Catholics in favour of Western Christianity, in which case something might be urged argumentatively in favour of their theory. Rather, it is paraded in favour of other theological systems of doubtful, or, of more than doubtful orthodoxy within the Establishment, in support of which, from a consistent Catholic stand-point, nothing can be urged. There are those amongst us who are never wearied of declaring, and there are those who are content, without inquiry, to repeat the cuckoo-cry, that the High Church party is but one of the two great historical parties, or that it is one of three existing schools of thought, in the Church of England. They affirm that both parties, or that all three schools, legitimately find a place within her obedience; and, moreover, that it is positively beneficial to the boasted comprehensiveness of the Anglican communion that it should be composed of two, or even of three constituent elements—to use well understood terms—High, Low, and Broad Church.

A more suicidal, a more unfaithful, it may even be said a more anti-Christian opinion, on the part of those who make pretence to hold the Catholic faith and to teach Catholic truth upon authority, can hardly be conceived. This theory of the English Church finds continual expression in the so-called "Church newspapers" of the day. These papers are either the organs of opinion, without specially asserting it, of a considerable body of upper-class and educated High Church people; or, on the strength of a large circulation amongst a lower and less educated class, elect themselves organs of the Catholic party without in reality being so. The fallacy which they propagate, by the force of re-iteration, has become imbedded in the minds of many, as almost of axiomatic certainty. This fact is shown from the frequency with which the fallacy is met in published letters, speeches, and statements of those who read such organs of opinion and are either avowedly or hypothetically influenced by them. A single quotation, and that not the strongest which might be made, is sufficient to establish a charge of the essentially anti-dogmatic character of much that is publicly taught by " Church newspapers " of the present age. Nearly three years ago there appeared in one of the two papers above alluded to, which is professedly Catholic in its sympathies and tone, a leading article on " the Situation " of that day. The writer of this article—whether priest or layman—was neither afraid nor ashamed to describe a possible future for the Anglican communion, as that of " one great Church in which there were two schools *legitimately* acting and reacting upon each other to their *mutual* advantage." The same line of thought, apparently, underlies a second leading article in the other contemporary High Church newspaper, published during the present year, on the foundation of "Keble College." The writer of this article declares that "it is the answer to misgivings or interested prognostications about the Church" to remember "the sort of criticism which might be passed . . . on English political institutions." And an apology for the Anglican compromise in religion is found by the writer in the existence of a similar " compromise between opposite and inconsistent principles of [civil] government." The above editorial views are hazarded with reference to the High Church and Low Church elements in the Established faith: but the like remarks are also not uncommonly heard in regard to the third party which has more recently established itself, perhaps permanently, within the obedience of the Church of England. Such is the current teaching both of the more moderate and of the more advanced sections of Churchmanship at the present day. And such is the teaching which Anglo-Catholics accept, if not with complacency, at least without a murmur. Is it too much to declare, of such teaching, that it is distinctly subversive of all dogmatic theology?

This topic is worthy of further thought. The opinion in question may be said to be, in theological language, heretical in its tendency. Had either the originators or the reproducers of this opinion been content to affirm, and to deplore whilst they affirmed, the historical fact, the results of which they almost elevate into a principle, no objection could have been raised against the assertion, and no notice need have been taken of so harmless a statement. It might have been truly said, and with regret, that from the days of the Reformation there ever had been, and there still existed two, or indeed three separate and hostile systems within the bosom of the Establishment which struggled for the mastery. From this historical fact, as against fresh political enactments and constant legal prosecutions, a defencible position might be assumed. It might be argued that any one of the three schools, even the most unpopular at any given moment, might appeal to precedent for a peaceful solution of its principles and to fair-play for its practice, apart from persecution by either of the other two schools. It might even be urged, with self-evident conditions, that the action and reaction of one rival school upon another would prove beneficial to that one of the two which was most Protestant. These opinions might have been uttered, and no objection need have been made, nor any result have ensued. But our new Catholic teachers have not been content to state historical facts and to draw demonstrable conclusions from them. These false prophets, with those that blindly follow them, have positively gloried in their shame, and in the disgrace in the eyes of Christendom of their holy Mother Church. They have publicly declared, not only that such antagonistic parties exist within her communion; but, that the compromise by which the Anglican communion was created demands their existence. The rival parties (they say) exist; and their existence is emphatically good. They have affirmed that the two opposite schools of thought, which as a fact teach two opposite forms of belief under the shelter of a single Church, are *legitimately* found within a common obedience, and that they act and react upon each other to their *mutual* advantage.

If I may venture to speak for myself, it has never been my good fortune to ascertain on what Catholic principle such a position is based; nor to have met with any person, outside the *coteries* which enunciate such a view, who pretended that the principle underlying it was Catholic. Without professing to admire a dull, heavy, uncritical, unintelligent uniformity of belief, and whilst being fully alive to the value of inquiry, discussion and argument in religious questions, I cannot but feel that to such variation and discussions there must be some limit in the direction of authority. But, practically, the opinions above quoted, and others which have not been quoted, place no limits within the bounds of private judgment. For what limitation can be claimed by one who admits the equal right of High, Low and Broad Church opinion to a legitimate position in the Anglican communion? What bounds can be conceived, if it be so much as entertained that High Church and Low Church doctrine can act and react upon each other, with mutual advantage to both divisions of the Anglican obedience ? In such pronouncements I cannot but realize an utter absence of all Catholic principle. They abandon every principle of Church authority.

Of course, the like words on the lips of non-Catholics are intelligible, if not consistent. It may be understood that an honest Broad Churchman can legitimately accept the enforced, if uncongenial relationship of High Church and Low Church neighbours, on the ground that nothing in this world, not even his own form of scepticism, is assured beyond the possibility of doubt. Or, he may, indeed, reasonably hold that Liberal opinions must in the end convince both the bigoted and benighted Catholic, and the shallow and half-educated Evangelical. He may mentally allow either uncertainty, or time, or both combined, to do their work. He may even believe that the action and reaction of superstitious reverence for authority on the one hand, and of a partial and inconsistent belief in authority on the other, may prove of advantage to his own deliberate denial of both. So too, the position of the conscientious Low Churchman is intelligible, if not defensible, from his own point of view. A devoted and holy Evangelical may legitimately tolerate the presence of the High and Broad schools of thought, on the ground that, as he thinks, Gospel-truth by the grace of GOD must eventually prevail over both the dogma of the semi-Papist and the unbelief of the semi-Infidel. He may even conceive that, as an ensample of self-sacrificing submission to authority, or as a warning of the results of a repudiation of Revelation, the two parties which are antagonistic alike to themselves and to his own school, may both act and react with advantage to the Church. But, it is impossible to understand, on any intelligible principle worthy of the name, the position of the nominal Catholic which is under consideration. It is impossible for a consistent Catholic to accept, or even to tolerate, much less to defend and to glory in the defence of the co-equality of right of all three schools of thought in the Church of England. Such an exercise of private judgment inferentially denies the claims of the Anglican communion to be Catholic. It inferentially affirms of those who hold to such an opinion, that they believe Catholic truth on a principle which falls short of its belief upon authority.

But more than this may be admitted. One may understand the existence of *bonâ fide* schools of thought within the legitimate boundaries of any given party in a Church ; or, in any given Church, weakened by the presence within its bounds of discordant parties. The friendly, or even the bitter disputes of the old Dominican and Franciscan controversies, or those between the regular and secular clergy, in the middle-ages, in the Roman Catholic Church; or, the controversies current between the so-called extreme and moderate men of the Catholic party in the Church of England, are intelligible in principle, if not defensible in practice. So also, are the opposite theories of various parties or of single theologians in the Church at large, on dogmatic questions held as pious opinions or as allowable theses, at a time when the Church has not spoken decidedly and thus closed all legitimate controversy. On all hands and on both sides such variety of opinion starts from a common basis, seeks a common end, bows to a common authority.

But, for myself again, I fail to see any authority, end, or basis, which is common to all three antagonistic parties in the distracted Church of England. I fail to see any community of faith or practice, in those points which necessitate the existence of hostile parties within her boundaries, and which tend to make her obedience, at the present day more than at any former time, a city of confusion and discord, rather than a temple of peace and unity. For, to cast aside for a moment the conventional terms of an unreal unanimity, in what terms may be described the three conflicting parties which strive for the mastery in the existing Church of England? To speak plainly, they are severally the Sacramental, the anti-Sacramental, and the Liberal parties : in other words, the Catholic, the Protestant, the Infidel. Everything, or nearly everything, short of the veriest elements of the faith—and sometimes even the essentials of the faith—which the first party clings to and upholds, the second casts aside and denies, the third ignores or despises. Nor, if the first and second schools agree in many points of a common Christianity—in many more than is usually supposed—can this with truth be declared of the third. Indeed, the opposite must rather be admitted of the last ; namely, that the Broad Church school has less in common with either the High Church or the Low Church parties than is usually supposed : it may be almost said that, in principle, it has more in common with unbelievers than with the faithful of either school.

This is not the place to enter into details, though details might freely be given. But, an intelligent and unbiassed observer, who stands outside each of the three parties alike in the Anglican obedience and has mastered the principles of all of them, could do no otherwise than arrive at this conclusion.

He would affirm that three distinct religions are content to abide within the boundaries of the Church of England—distinct in their system of belief, distinct in their theory of worship, distinct in their practice of Christianity. He would be justified in making this assertion, although the three parties in the Church accept the same Articles of Religion, use the same Book of Common Prayer, and hope for the same reward in the exercise of the Christian virtues. But, in the face of these facts, which can be denied by none, our organs of Church opinion are constantly preaching the comprehensive compromise of the Anglican Establishment; the legitimate existence of two opposite schools of thought or three distinct parties within her borders; the mutual or the several advantages which both or all in turn derive from the action and reaction of the others. If this indeed be so, nothing could be more fatal, nothing could be more condemnatory to the claim of the Church of England to be considered Catholic. If it be not so, nothing could more decidedly prove the un-Catholic and anti-Catholic views of those who assume to be the organs, and who are the public teachers, of the Catholic school of thought.

There is no need of entering, and I have no intention to enter, in this place, into a consideration of any results which flow, or may be supposed to flow, from holding to principles opposite to those of the current organs of opinion. I am content to state but one result which ensues from assenting to principles in conformity with them—namely, its effect upon the reception of dogmatic truth. It is not difficult to see the effect, which is indisputable, on those who utter and on those who accept such an estimate of the position of the Catholic party in the Church of England. The result is simply the abandonment of all dogmatic teaching which is founded upon the authority of the Church. It elevates private opinion into the seat of judgment. This result, in the question under consideration, is only a single instance of a principle in action which, it is much to be feared, has attained considerable force amongst professing Catholics in the English communion. Late years have witnessed the growth of a school of thought in the Catholic party which actually, if not avowedly, has abandoned authority in favour of private judgment. Such a growth is observable not only in matters of practice, for instance, in regard to Fasting Communion, but also in some questions of principle: indeed recently, in questions of vital principle, such as that of the Eternity of the Punishment of the lost. That the school at present is small may be allowed; but it cannot be denied that it is able and energetic, nor that it possesses peculiar powers for disseminating its views broadcast over the Church of England. The school in question has done much and done well for the faith. But the remembrance of former good and valued work, the evidence of a brilliant defence of friends, and the literary and logical annihilation of adversaries, should not blind us to an obvious degeneracy in principle, nor to the grafting of false principles upon those that are true. Nor should those who labour for a common cause object to, or take amiss, a friendly warning from former co-adjutors, when further combination for a common weal seems hopeless—least of all those whose work to a large extent consists, as mine never has consisted, in contemporary criticism. But, whether friends and fellow-labourers take such warning ill or well, it seems to be the duty of one who thinks he perceives fatal rocks ahead to sound the alarm. And, unless he misreads the signs of the times, a serious warning is greatly needed, lest the Catholic party unconsciously fall into giving an intellectual assent to certain, and only to certain definite theological propositions apart from the entire circle of faith. We are, indeed, in considerable danger of being influenced, if not of being led, by those who may fairly be called Catholic-Rationalists; that is to say, by a rationalizing school of Catholics who, accepting the major part, though by no means the complete scheme, of Catholic belief and practice, accept it only as being in conformity with private opinion, not on the basis of the authority of the Catholic Church.

3. In the third place, the attitude which is assumed by a considerable portion, perhaps by a majority, of Anglicans towards the Catholic Church of the West, is a fruitful source of our neglect of positive dogmatic teaching.

Here, one who proposes to treat this subject, with freedom and truthfulness, must feel that he stands upon the edge of a volcano which is by no means extinct. In treating it, he must be prepared for severe criticism, which is not the worst fate that can befal a writer; and also, perhaps, misconstruction even from friends, which is more hard to bear. Both these results may be anticipated in this case, because friends seem to me to act in a manner the opposite to consistent; and because one object in view in these strictures is to make such inconsistency obvious, even to those who are guilty of it. For, there are few points of doctrine, true or false, which may not be held; there are scarcely any matters of practice, however exaggerated, which may not be used in the Anglican obedience by a High Churchman, provided only that he avoid any suspicion of what is known as "Romanizing." In order to secure the confidence of ordinary Anglicans, and to preserve it when secured, a layman and much more an ecclesiastic must more or less positively yield to the prevailing anti-Roman mania. This mania—for no other word equally well explains the phenomenon—which at one time reached a portentous height, now appears to be somewhat subsiding. Yet, he who would succeed in any work for his Mother Church must be either absolutely free from all sympathy with, or discreetly silent upon the position and claims of the Holy Roman Church, if he be not honestly antagonistic to, or actively hostile to her. But, let him only accept unreservedly the shibboleth of certain sections of Anglicanism, and he may believe anything, he may practise anything, to the fullest extent permitted by private judgment in a Rome-ward direction.

For instance, to take a few examples: A priest or layman may openly fraternize, in person or on paper, with the Alt-Catholics, with heretical Easterns, or with any other form of Greek or Latin schism. He may perseveringly seek to revolutionize continental Christianity, in divers parts of Europe, whilst avowedly making known only the principles and worship of the Church of England. He may actually engage at home in a combined effort for the destruction of the cherished ideal of the majority of Churchmen, however much they may grumble at some of its results—namely, a Religion established by Law. He may speculate in either Oriental or Occidental systems of philosophy, to the extent of endangering his belief in Christianity; or, he may seek to break down almost the last remnant of popular Religion which exists amongst us—which, as such, ought to be cultivated and regulated as a Christian feast rather than lowered into a day of pleasure or improvement only—the English respect for the LORD'S Day.

As a clergyman, again, he may celebrate the English rite in a Greek church; although the Orthodox Eastern appraises Anglican orders almost at the like value at which they are popularly estimated in the West. He may affirm and teach Calvinistic tenets on the importance if not the necessity of instantaneous and sensible conversion: or, he may deny the Catholic doctrine of the Eternity of Punishment. He may disregard, in his own person, the world-wide law of fasting reception; and may either directly teach others to do the like, or indirectly encourage the same by permitting late celebrations of the Eucharist, apart from any effectual prohibition of late communions in his church. He may minimize the importance of the place which confession holds in the sacramental system of the Church; and without actually declining to do his duty, he may seldom or never advise any person to frequent the Sacrament of Penance. He may himself omit, and even publicly deprecate, the employment by others of certain usages of Christian symbolism which have secured Catholic acceptance. He may satirize, insult and defame his ecclesiastical superiors; calmly withstand his own bishop or silently ignore the requirements of canon law; and beyond the dictates of his own will, obey no existing, visible, or external authority in either Church or State. In a word, he may be guided in faith and duty, by his own private opinion only. He may do, or not do anything; he may believe, or fail to believe anything—but one. The average English Churchman, in order to live a quiet life in the Anglican obedience, must be free from suspicion of the unpardonable offence alone of sympathy with the Apostolic See.

This is the one only sin which will not be forgiven in the average Anglican, be he layman or priest. Once let a stigma be affixed, whether true or false matters little, that a man be disposed to Romanize (as the term is employed), and for all practical purposes of good work for the Church of England, his death-warrant is signed. Nay; even if it be currently believed that he declines to take a conventional view of the *differentia* between the two Churches of England and Rome, and elects to exercise his own independent powers of thought and argument upon them—his influence, if he possess any, and his labour, in his own line of work, practically ceases in the Anglican obedience. His sphere of usefulness, however humble, for the future is restricted to labour in company with the few—for there is yet a remnant of consistent Anglo-Catholics—who are too generous, too fearless, or too logical to be influenced by the present anti-Roman mania. And yet, with strange absence of principle, all "dallying with Rome," so-called, is not forbidden to an Anglican. Indeed, to a large and yearly increasing extent, much "imitation of Rome," however veiled, is encouraged. Only, it is essential that the moth should be attracted to the flame on a right principle of self-destruction; and that the victim must not revolve in unwonted convolutions. The layman must be careful to employ the accepted means and methods of the majority of his co-religionists. The priest must use a certain discreet phraseology which will neither shock those in authority, nor indicate too definitely his meaning to those under authority. Both must believe and act within certain limits, which are not always easily recognized beforehand, nor at any time are clearly defined; but which are of inflexible rigidity when once imposed, and cannot be overpassed without producing prompt and sometimes decided results.

For instance, again, take a few examples, which may be confined to the case of the clergy: An Anglican priest may write and speak and pray in favour of the Re-union of Christendom; but, at his peril, even when carefully refraining from committing others, does he seek to take action, private or corporate, to this end. He may adopt almost every article of faith in the Council of Trent: but, he must accept it as Catholic, not as Roman doctrine. He may employ almost every detail of Western ceremonial: but, he must call it the ancient custom of the Church of England—the venerable Use of S. Osmund of Salisbury. He may place seven pendant lights before an altar untenanted by the Sacred Presence: and he must esteem the non-symbolical usage (as was once apologetically said), "so truly Eastern, you know." He may receive penitents with closed doors in his vestry, or in his own house: though, if he presumes to hear confessions, as they are wisely heard abroad, openly in the church, he is energetically condemned. He may burn incense, if it be not used in the authorized Latin manner: he may bow at the *Gloria*, if he kneel not with the West at the *Incarnatus est*. He may "incline" in the Liturgy with Sarum, but not "adore" after consecration with Rome: or he may "elevate" as high as the one enjoins, but not as high as the other permits. He may speak of the Sacrament of Unction which the English Church does not use, though not of the Sacrament of Penance, which she still employs: and may freely speak of attending at Matins, though only speak in confidence of assisting at Mass. He may invoke the Saints obliquely, but not directly: and may say the *Confiteor* in the Missal, but not the *Ave Maria* in the Hours. He may keep Thursday after Trinity Sunday, so long as he calls it not *Corpus Christi:* and may observe the feast of the Conception of our Lady, so long as he calls it not Immaculate. In brief, he may hold to anything, he may do anything, provided that he can persuade others that the action and belief are not "un-English," and can deceive himself that neither his faith nor his practice are a "slavish imitation of Rome."

It is needless to affirm that the temper which is illustrated by this insularity and exclusiveness is repudiated by many loyal members of the Church of England. Personally, I have no sympathy whatever with such a temper. But, it is of more importance to remind the reader that this spirit is by no means in harmony with the best traditions of the old Tractarian party. No doubt the early Tractarians were alive to the claims and assertions of the See of Peter; and when occasion required, frankly and boldly gave vent to their Anglican sentiments and opinions. But their line of thought and action, as a party, towards Western Christendom was more defensive than offensive. It may be admitted indeed, that one or two distinguished clergy have always had, or had up to their time of death, unconquerable Roman antipathies; though their method of controversy on behalf of Anglicanism was different from the present mode of argument. But, the whole tone of the Oxford Movement, its main purpose, in the means it employed, and in its final earthly cause, might have been indicated and was comprised in a single word—Re-union. Not to speak of the manner of conducting controversy, the difference in principle between the pro-Anglicanism and the anti-Romanism of the elder Tractarians and of the younger Ritualists respectively, may be described by the algebraical terms *plus* and *minus*. The former ventured to criticise Western Christendom with the earnest hope and wish for Re-union strongly developed. The latter loudly "abuse Rome" without any apparent wish or hope of Re-union—indeed, with the hope, and even the desire deliberately cast aside. The difference between the two schools is a difference not of detail, but of principle; not in degree, but in kind. It is comparable to Augustinianism based upon the doctrine of grace; and Calvinism apart from the grace of the sacraments. The loving, charitable, forbearing spirit that above all things sought to fulfil the desire which was dearest to the Sacred Heart of JESUS—the desire for Unity—has departed from a very wide circle of professing High Churchmen. It has been replaced, though it may be hoped not to an equally wide extent, by a hard, bitter criticism of, and even a revengeful antagonism to the centre of Christendom. The two tempers cannot be contrasted more completely than by comparing the well-known lines of the saintly John Keble with the refined cynicism of the *Guardian* or the almost savage hostility of the *Church Times*. The spirit of the early Tractarians has been succeeded by an opposition which is based to a large degree upon individual susceptibilities; by an opposition that spares neither person nor thing, neither belief nor practice, which emanates from the Church of the West, or which gravitates towards it from the Anglican obedience.

This is not the place to prove, what however is demonstrable, that there is an "imitation of Rome" which is not "servile," but filial; and that, in many cases and on many topics, Anglican imitation is not only legitimate but indispensable. It is not the place to show that an open, bold and honest following of the mighty Mother of the West is not only compatible with absolute loyalty to the daughter Church, but is essential. It is essential if that daughter would arise, as she is emerging, from the state of degradation in both belief and practice into which the LORD of both Churches has allowed her to fall.

Here it may be sufficient to indicate an actual danger to true faith in the midst of which we live; and to suggest a possible cause for some of the ills from which we suffer. We live in an age which has liberated itself from nearly all external authority. We are suffering as a Church from neglect of dogmatic theology: a neglect which, if not remedied by the Church of England, it needs no prophet to predict, will prove fatal to her Catholicity. I take the liberty to contend, in opposition to much teaching of a popular sort, that such freedom and such neglect are caused, in part, by the attitude which we present towards the most authoritative and dogmatic of Churches —an integral, though divided portion of which we still actually are. We endanger true faith by our hostile relations towards the Church of Rome. And why? Because in everything upon which the Church of England has not definitely pronounced otherwise, the complete circle of Catholic belief held by the Church of Rome is binding upon us. Of course, the like principle applies to ritual and morals: but, with these developments we are not now concerned. We are, however, deeply concerned with matters of faith: and in the absence of anything comparable to an expression of infallible authority in the Anglican obedience, we are bound to respect and defer (subject to the above named conditions) to the teaching of Western Christendom. This reaches us with the nearest approximation to authoritative teaching of which we are conscious in our present isolated condition. And it is because the High Church party, as a party, is impatient, even to unreasoning irritability, of anything that approaches to external authority, that we are so hostile to the authority of Rome. We fail to accept anything, we fail to do anything, simply upon authority. In all things we are an authority to ourselves.

In my humble judgment, nothing tends more to stimulate self-satisfaction, and to sap the principles of divine authority, than the estimate which Anglicans form and express of the Roman obedience. A torrent of detraction, misrepresentation of facts, gratulation over supposed failure, and even personal and individual abuse of the Church of Rome, of members of that communion, and of all that is distinctively Roman in Catholic faith, worship and practice, issues week by week and year after year from the Church-press. It is presumably read by many who on principle ought to disavow all connection and all sympathy with such tactics. It certainly penetrates to the lower and uneducated classes of the Church party by the combined force of cleverness and cheapness, of accepting popular prejudices and unscrupulously utilizing them. The constant perusal of these attacks, ostentatiously made under the cover of speaking as an acknowledged organ of Church opinion, must issue in one of two effects. Either they make the reader despise all outward authority and uphold any form of private judgment; or they cause him to loath a system which I will not say needs, but is patient of such support, and to be attracted by an impulse of generosity to the system which is subjected to such unworthy and un-Christian treatment. As these attacks are certainly popular, it is probable that the first result generally ensues. In any case they tend directly to the neglect of dogmatic theology, to the lowering of all legitimate authority, and to a breach of divine charity. None, upon principle, can affirm that these attacks on a Church of CHRIST are defensible. Few would venture to affirm that, in practice, they are even politic.

One excuse only, for it is no justification of this course of conduct can be made. Whilst it explains the action of individuals, it is made at the expense of the consistency of the party. The excuse is alluded to here, lest any should imagine that it were either forgotten, or intentionally overpast. In order to account for the obvious change of front which has been made by the High Church party in its relations to the Church of Rome, men point in unworthy triumph, as more than a justification of their new position, to the Vatican decrees on Papal Infallibility. We may fairly place on one side the false and even childish deductions that are made by educated Catholics, on the infallibility of the Pope in ways and on topics not recognized by the decrees, and even on his supposed impeccability. It is enough to argue upon the theological terminology of the decree itself: and taking the accepted meaning only, and without expressing any opinion on its truth or error, we are led to inquire what may have been the attitude which the old Tractarian party assumed towards the decrees of the General Council of the Church of Rome which preceded that of the Vatican? The answer is explicit. The Tractarian party, in the persons of its chief members, have ever been willing to entertain and even to advocate the question of Re-union on the basis of the decrees of Trent, authoritatively explained. What may be the present opinion of the disorganized body which has developed from the early Tractarians it is not easy to affirm, inasmuch as there are no accredited leaders to express a common opinion. But those who are wont to speak on its behalf are accustomed to claim a legitimate descent in faith, at the least, from the distinguished leaders of the Oxford Movement; and hence, presumably, they accept this opinion as their own.

If this be so, there appears to be no escape from the following dilemma. The Tractarian party, both past and present, have been willing to accept, with authoritative explanations, the dogmatic decrees of the Council of Trent. These decrees could have been accepted on two principles only; namely, on that of private opinion, or, on that of authority. If the Tractarian party accepted the Council of Trent as the expression in faith and morals of their own private judgment, the like sentiment might reasonably move them to reject the decrees of the Council of the Vatican. But, if they were prepared to receive the decrees of the Council of Trent upon authority, it is difficult to understand on what principle they could decline to discuss and to labour for Re-union, with the like conditions as before, on the basis of the Vatican decrees. In truth, though it requires some courage to say so, the question of Re-union now occupies exactly the same position, logically, as it occupied before the Vatican Council—at least, from the point of view of the early Tractarians. That it presents a different aspect, subjectively, to many pious and learned minds, may be admitted. But, objectively, it does not. The two Councils, of Trent and of the Vatican, were equally œcumenical. Their decrees have been equally received with that subsequent "moral unanimity," by the entire Roman Catholic world, which some divines desiderate as a note of Catholicity. The only logical deduction which can be drawn from the unwillingness of the present High Church party to advocate what the former High Church party were willing to adopt, as illustrated by its organs of opinion, appears to be this. The younger Ritualist school believe in a Church and accept communion with a Church, because in faith and morals that Church teaches doctrines which they personally hold to be true. The Catholic principle, however, is the converse of this: namely, to believe in Catholic dogma and to adopt Catholic practice, because the Church teaches them—that is, on the authority of the Church. The elder Tractarians were influenced by the latter principle. In the forgetfulness of this principle consists the inconsistency of the excuse of the younger Tractarians for their abandonment of a desire for the Re-union of Christendom.

The prevalence of this rationalizing opinion, that we submit to the Church because we personally believe what the Church divinely teaches, is at the present moment extensively diffused. To its influence may be directly credited the hostile attitude towards Western Christendom which the Catholic party has of late unhappily assumed. To its effects may be attributed indirectly the absence amongst us, which cannot be concealed, of dogmatic teaching in questions of faith. For, why should not private judgment be critical, even when opposed to the teaching of a Church? And how can that theology be dogmatic, which is accepted by individual minds solely as the expression of their own private opinion?——As, however, I proposed merely to take a cursory view of this important topic, and desired only to instigate other and more competent thinkers to gauge our ecclesiastical position accurately; and as such a view, be it never so imperfect and faulty, has now been taken, at this point I dismiss the third and last cause which has been named for the neglect in the Anglican communion of dogmatic theology.

III. Some results of the neglect of dogmatic theology in the Church of England now demand attention. They are obvious in the wide-spread ignorance which prevails on most religious subjects and pervades all classes of society amongst English Churchmen. In this case typical evidence alone, in as brief a space as may be and in a very few instances, will be offered in support of the position which is here assumed. Moreover, in order to avoid a breach of charity, and so far as it is possible, all personalities will be avoided by the suppression of names. Of course, this plan will detract somewhat from the point of the illustration. But, under any circumstances, the mere statement of results which are apparent to all who watch the course of events, is of secondary importance to a statement of the causes which may be mitigated if observed. In such an inquiry, also, it is of less moment who may have been the person that displayed any given want of theological knowledge, than that such ignorance was actually displayed. And, if certain well-known instances are mentioned, they will be quoted, not for the purpose of re-slaying the slain, but because they are types of a large experience.

It is almost impossible for a clergyman to examine a class of children on religious knowledge, or to prepare confirmands for their first Communion, without perceiving evidence of the fact under consideration. If he for a moment travel out of the beaten track of catechetical question and answer, he becomes conscious of dense ignorance on principles of the faith, sometimes incredible, sometimes ludicrous, always lamentable. It is a question, whether such ignorance would be displayed by the children either of Nonconformist or of Roman Catholic parents?

A more intimate acquaintance with more educated adults, oftentimes the disciples of that intellectual culture which is now so widely preached, and which has to a large extent usurped the place of religion, confirms the evidence previously obtained. Such an acquaintance may be obtained either by personal intercourse, or by letter. The evidence may be derived from discussions or conferences, either on controversial questions which unhappily divide England from the residue of Western Christendom, or on questions of morals which are almost elementary in casuistry. But, in any case, the result is the same. The average Anglican adult has emerged indeed from his infantine stage, but he has not developed in his knowledge of theology.

Neither can this estimate be confined to the youth of the present day, nor to the adult layman. The same observation of facts is forced upon the attention of those who are called upon to "hear sermons" from average English clergymen; who glance at the contents of "Church newspapers," especially of the correspondence columns; or whose duty it may be to attend meetings of clergy or laity, even of the less anti-dogmatic school of thought, at Congresses, Conferences, or more private gatherings. Readers or listeners are often surprised and concerned at the theological blunders that are made, whether by professed teachers or by amateur apologists; at the dogmatic fallacies that are gravely enunciated; at the un-Catholic statements that are deliberately uttered, and when uttered, eagerly defended; and even at the actual heresy which is sometimes unconsciously declaimed.

In the case of sermons, it is possible that a cause for this experience, amongst a portion of the clergy, may be found in a miserable scandal which, seemingly of wide prevalence, has of late been deservedly exposed. There would appear to flourish a systematic and, whether in buyers or sellers, a most immoral trade in sermons, lithographed and otherwise manipulated to deceive the guileless. These sermons are written to order by facile laymen, "Non-conforming brethren," or clergy—as has been lately proved in a court of law, and grievous as it is to own to the fact—of not unblemished character, who thus prostitute their ability and power for good. Amongst much for which Catholics have little cause to be thankful to the *Guardian* newspaper, their gratitude for assisting in the exposure of this humiliating clerical scandal is certainly its due.

The like gratitude from Catholics, however, is as certainly not due to the *Guardian* for the course which it adopts, year by year more extensively, in regard to the regulation of its correspondence columns. In truth, from its powers of production, and from its large circulation amongst the upper-middle classes, the letters which appear in that paper—and not only in that paper—have become a serious theological misfortune in the current history of the party. This opinion has not been formed without sufficient experience of many years' standing. Although the usual formula that "the Editor is not responsible for the opinions of his correspondents" does not appear in print above the letters in the *Guardian*; yet, this fact is abundantly evident from an inspection of their miscellaneous contents. Were it otherwise, the editorial intellect and conscience must be of superhuman capacity and power for the mental assimilation of the contrarient and diverse opinions and views to which he gives publicity. It is a question, however, whether or not the Editor of a professedly "Church paper" ought not to be, and is not morally, responsible at least for the dogmatic statements which appear by his direct permission in his columns? The question is not merely a hypothetical one. For, within the last few months burning questions have been discussed by letter-writers in the *Guardian* with the utmost laxity of theological supervision, and with a license which approaches to doctrinal libertinism. Notably these topics, amongst many more, have been discussed, the majority of them in hastily written communications, and some of them disfigured by ill-digested or half-digested theories—the doctrine of the Objective Presence, Reservation of the Blessed Sacrament, Non-communicating Attendance, Habitual Confession, Eternal Punishment, and the Invocation of Saints. On these points, the average clerical and lay mind has poured out itself at considerable length, in letters signed with name, initials, or *nom de plume*. Many of these letters contained heretical propositions distinctly stated. In some of them, heresy was latent under a cloud of assumed philosophy. With one or two or three exceptions, in each order, the writers certainly had no claim to be distinguished, either in theology or in the realms of thought. And yet, their questionable, or more than questionable teaching has been scattered far and wide in country parishes and town homes, under the indirect but potent authority of the Editor of the *Guardian*. As a rule, the more fluent and "moderate" contributors are supreme in such controversies—the contributions of the more thoughtful or "extreme" writers having an inevitable tendency to gravitate towards the waste-paper basket. That this is no imaginary picture is proved by the experience of many. One instance may suffice by way of evidence. In the recent discussion on Invocation of Saints a carefully prepared paper, with authorities from the Fathers which supported the Catholic doctrine, was sent to the *Guardian* by an accomplished theologian of recognized standing in the Church. The letter did not appear in print: and on a remonstrance being made, the writer was editorially rebuked, first for "sending pamphlets," and then for being "surprised" that the *Guardian* could not "make room for them."[1]

If we ascend higher in the scale of intelligence, or into regions that ought to be higher than that of newspaper letter-writers, or average laymen or clergymen, the evidence of current ignorance of theological questions, both within and without the range of doctrine, becomes the more positive.

It is well known that in the ecclesiastical law-courts, the counsel for the defence of the doctrine and discipline of the Church of England do not depend upon their own unaided powers of argument or stores of knowledge. They have to be inspired and instructed by clerical experts. Under existing

---

[1] As these sheets are passing through the press, further evidence on this topic has appeared, which more nearly and directly affects the question of the neglect of theology in the Church of England. It may be premised, that the *Guardian* has had cause to complain of late years at being overpowered with letters on subjects of popular religious interest. Questions of mere Ritualism will, alone and in a week's time, produce correspondence enough to fill a whole number, or more, of the paper. But when topics of deeper importance than "posture and gesture" are discussed, when questions which demand learning and thought and mental power are suggested for discussion, the flow of correspondence suddenly ceases. A writer who signed himself "Speculator"—but whose signature failed to conceal his personality from those who were acquainted with his writings—published a most interesting letter, of two columns' length, on "the Science of Comparative Religion" on September 11th, 1878. It was suggestive of even more interesting letters on details of Professor Max Müller's opening course of the Hibbert Lectures, from some at least of the multitudinous letter-writers of the *Guardian*. "Speculator" promised to disclose his name if his "letter attracted the smallest attention." He was forced to make good his promise—for his letter did attract, literally, the smallest attention, though by no means on its merits. A fortnight later, "Speculator" again wrote in his own name, as a single letter—beyond one which corrected an error in a question of fact—had been alone contributed by the readers of the *Guardian* to this momentous controversy. Those who recognized the initials of this solitary answer would expect the letter to be able and full of thought. Both letters will be laid under contribution further on in these prefatory remarks.

circumstances of the neglect of the study of ecclesiastical law, there is nothing surprising in such a division of labour, but much that is of advantage to the Church. Of course, it occasionally happens that the inspiration lacks something of being plenary; and in such a case, a counsel has been known to pause and to await further instruction from the ecclesiastic, on the name and use of one of the simplest of the eucharistic vestments. Most ably have certain clergy, learned in the law, performed their un-recognized labour of love. Yet, on a noteworthy occasion, in an important suit, both clerics and counsel were powerless to offer any argument before the court for the Catholic use of symbolical light in divine service. It may be questioned whether or not a similar want of familiarity with the elements of ship-building, or of the laws of navigation, characterizes the efforts of advocates in the Admiralty Court, as occasionally appears in Court of Arches? But, it may be said that the custom of burning tapers or lamps in the daytime, "for the purpose of giving light," is as universal in the divine service of the Catholic Church for symbolical purposes as the use of lights, at night and for utilitarian purposes, is common in the practice of navigation.

Of course, the House of Commons, when it ventures to discuss ecclesiastical questions, is a fruitful field for the display of theological ignorance. It may be doubted, however, whether without special attention to the point, persons are conscious to what extent such ignorance is displayed, or to what amount of it the House will submit, on the assumption of those who presumably, or on their own shewing, are better instructed than their neighbours. Though almost unequalled amongst representative bodies, for discussions on most subjects within its limits of action, Parliament fails ignominiously when it essays to legislate for the Church. On a recent occasion, an educated layman, a sound member of the Church of England, a public-school boy and university man and member for his county, one who boasted of theological acquirements, at least to acquaintance with his "Hooker," made a singular exhibition of such knowledge on the floor of the House of Commons. In the course of debate he took occasion to attack the sermon of a clergyman which had been preached before a gathering of fellow-clergy. The *Times* of the following morning contained a summary of this legislator's conception of "blasphemous fables and *damnable* deceits," which were unbefitting a loyal clergyman to advocate, and which required the strong arm of the law to restrain him from preaching if he were not loyal. Passing by the misquotation of the Thirty-first Article, which once probably he had learned by rote, it may be well to state some of the many points which this champion of the Anglican Church held up to Parliamentary obloquy, and to the obloquy of the world outside Parliament. Ten points in all were advocated in the sermon, as points to be regained by the Church of England through her devoted priests. Among them were these—Liberation of the Church from the tyranny of the State; Freedom in the Election of Bishops; Reform of Convocation; Abolition of secular Judgments in spiritual Suits; Restoration of the Religious Life; and daily Celebration of the Holy Communion. These points amongst others were gravely, and even warmly, stigmatized by the Member of Parliament as "damnable deceits." Neither in this opinion did he stand alone. He was eagerly supported by another professed High Churchman, who was also a County Member, and who entirely concurred with him. But not one Churchman in Parliament was sufficiently brave to stand up, not on behalf of the inculpated sermon, but of the Church's rights and privileges. It may not be out of place to add one fact in regard to the after-action of the Member first spoken of. In a late debate on the Bill for relieving the Church of the custody of her own grave-yards, this gentleman was prepared to advocate the "rights" of a non-Christian Chinaman who may desire to utter words of faith and hope and love over the remains of a deceased comrade, in the consecrated burying grounds of the Church of England.

If we pass from the lower House of Parliament to the lower House of Convocation, the same evidence of the neglect of dogmatic theology haunts us. In the Convocation of either Province, the want of theological precision and accuracy, in much that is cardinal in the faith and practice of Christianity, is painfully obvious. It is, perhaps, more than usually apparent when the proctors for the clergy and the official members leave the ordinary routine of legislative work, and pronounce upon subjects which presuppose a certain amount of scientific theology to discuss at all. For example, the utterances of the clergy, on recent occasions in the Jerusalem Chamber on the Burial question, on the Sacrament of Penance, on the question of Vows and Sisterhoods, on Liturgiology and the Revision of the Lectionary, would not, in the case of some of the speakers, have disgraced the General Assembly of the Presbyterian Kirk, or the Wesleyan Conference. Nor, in this relation, must one fact be forgotten, of the nature of a continuous action, the result of which even now affects the character of the Lower House from a dogmatic stand-point, and may affect in the future the character of the Church from a like point of view. A Company of learned men, appointed by a Committee of Convocation, has been for years past engaged in the sacred task of revising the authorized version of the Holy Scriptures. This Company is to a considerable extent composed of those who own no obedience to the English Church, who are external to her system, and are, in fact and although distinguished for intellectual gifts, heretics and schismatics of many denominations. There seems to be little doubt that future controversies on dogmatic theology, when they turn upon the authority of texts from the vernacular Bible, will be argued in reference to the volume which is now in course of translation. This fact, beyond the serious position to which it commits the Church of England in the future, is suggestive of no very high standard of belief or knowledge in dogmatic theology on the part of the Convocation of Canterbury.

From the priesthood we may turn to the episcopate, in order to enquire, whether the like evidence of a want of theological acquirement meets us here also. It is much to be feared that it may. A Bishop, somewhat advanced in years, was lately reported to have said, at the anniversary gathering of a Theological College that, in his youth, special preparation for Holy Orders there was none. Perhaps a like frank avowal might be made by other occupants of the bench, who have not done so much as the Bishop in question to repair in afteryears the theological shortcomings of his early life. It is certain that many a priest of the same generation, and in spite of the much or the little which has been effected by Theological Colleges, of a later generation also, could affirm the same. Perhaps, too, much that is deplorable in the opinions and actions both of our superiors and equals may be credited to the same cause. However this may be, a well-known Bishop, with fair pretentions to criticism and scholarship outside the pale of theology proper, may be cited as an instance in high quarters of the neglect of scientific knowledge in matters pertaining to his vocation. The case is so familiar, that did it not aptly illustrate the present argument in three distinct branches of theology—ceremonial, history and doctrine—an apology would be due for its repetition. But, in an official investigation into certain assumed irregularities by the inferior clergy, his lordship betrayed a want of familiarity with all three branches which was remarkable. He mistook an Antiphon to be sung before the *Magnificat*, which appeared in the English Kalendar, for the name of a Saint or the title of a Festival. Without a suspicion of irony, the Bishop solemnly asked a priest, how he was wont to keep the Feast of *O Sapientia*. In order to be quite exact, it may be added that the question was as follows: "2058. Do you on December 16th celebrate the Communion differently in regard to a Festival called the 'O Sapientia'?" (*First Report of the Ritual Commissioners*, 1867.) The liturgical blunder is obvious. What represented the hagiography of the question in his lordship's mind, would be an interesting speculation. But, it might at least have been supposed that the Bishop's dogmatic instincts would have suggested to him that the invocation, *O sancta Sapientia, ora pro nobis*, would have been equally heretical, or equally profane to a true Catholic, or to a staunch Protestant respectively.

An apology might also be demanded for the recital of another and last instance of the absence of theological acumen in exalted positions, were it not for the gravity of the occasion, the importance of the error, and the rank of the object of criticism. The unhappy notoriety which, under a succession of episcopal referees or assessors, the Judicial Committee of the Privy Council has earned for itself during the last quarter of a century, is well-known. In a series of ecclesiastical suits it has been guilty of theological misquotations, misstatements and mistakes—to speak only in a guarded manner—more than sufficient to have discredited any actual secular Court which did not pander to popular prejudice, and any so-called spiritual Court whose existence and preservation had not become a political necessity in order to sustain State tyranny over the Church of England. Indeed, a Nemesis seems to follow its pronouncements; and an almost certain fatality to await its decisions upon theological topics. Those *dicta* which the Judicial Committee are most anxious to dignify with an assumption of learning and a display of authorities, are usually those in which the Judges, whether legal or ecclesiastical, expose their profoundest ignorance. Of these cases, the Ceremonial Mixture of Water and Wine in the Eucharist, and the use of the Surplice in conjunction with the Vestments in the Mass, are two only of the latest instances.

Perhaps the lowest depth in theological ignorance to which a judgment of the Final Court of Appeal in matters ecclesiastical has been known to sink, is one to which two Bishops had the rashness to affix their signatures. In a momentous spiritual cause, in relation to the highest act of Christian worship, the Supreme Court some years ago deliberately affirmed that, for a given time—namely, during the legal use of the Second Prayer Book of Edward VI.—our Liturgical office was free from any Consecration Prayer. In other words, the Primate and the Premier Bishop of the Anglican Obedience, as Assessors to the Court, were committed to the statement, that for the like period in the history of the National Church there was no valid Eucharist in her communion, there was actually no consecration in the Celebration of the Holy Eucharist. It might have been thought that the contrary would have been "well-known" even to Lord Macaulay's (theological) "school-girl." But in order, again, to be quite exact, it may be added that the affirmation of the above position was made in the celebrated appeal case of Liddell *v.* Westerton. The judgment, as "concurred" in by the above-named ecclesiastics, and for which they were responsible, contained these words in reference to the Second Book of Edward : "that the Prayer for the Consecration of the Elements was omitted, though in the present Prayer Book it is restored" (*Mr. Moore's Edition of the Case*, p. 179, footnote). Who discovered the blunder ; how it was cancelled ; the terms into which the sentence, after delivery, was changed ; and the casuistry of the question which, in an "authorized" edition and without avowal of change, substituted the amended for the original statement—need not be here considered. The evidence which has been afforded of some of the results of the neglect of dogmatic theology in the Church of England may fitly culminate in and be closed by the present palmary instance of the want of theological instinct in high quarters.

Although further discussion on this topic is not strictly pertinent to the neglect of dogmatic theology in the Church of England, yet I am desirous to offer some remarks on two more points. The first is the almost total decay of dogmatic theology in certain sections of society in England as a nation: and the second is the absolute extinction of dogmatic theology in one community abroad. Indirectly, indeed, these considerations are suggestive to ourselves of the possible, if not probable results of our own neglect of dogma.

I. Of the lower orders of society and of their acquaintance with the elements of dogmatic theology, from a lack of evidence, I do not propose to speak. Of the great middle class, there is evidence sufficient to make an inquirer morally convinced, even if he lacks positive evidence, that dogma, as we understand the phrase, is not largely cultivated by Protestant Nonconformists. It cannot be affirmed that during the last three centuries Dissenters have been morally forced to leave the Anglican Establishment, by dogmatic exactness of faith in the teaching of the Anglican obedience. And yet, it is, I believe, demonstrable that about one half, if not more than one half of the English population are avowedly external to the Established Religion. Amongst this moiety of the country, it can hardly be said that dogmatic theology is largely cultivated. In the upper classes the decline of positive dogma, even in its most elemental form, is unhappily apparent to one who is sensitively alive to its features or indications. And it is to this side of the question that I would confine the following observations.

Even to one in middle life who can recall only a score of years' experience, the aspect of society in relation to Christian dogma has become changed in a marked manner. This is obvious in many more ways than can here be described. But, it is not too hasty a generalization to declare, that outside avowed circles of the many-sided religious world, the average position of persons moving in society are in their sympathies, if not anti-Christian, at least non-Christian. This generalization on society at large is supported by the result of inquiries amongst certain well-defined sections of the upper-class English world. It is proved from evidence derived from political life which, perhaps as a whole, can lay claim to the greatest intellectual vitality which exists in England, down to the type of an average gentleman, without any definite calling or profession who, probably, represents the lowest form of English upper-class intellectuality.

The average English gentleman, of course, with a wide margin for almost numberless exceptions, yet as a specimen of his class may, indeed, make pretensions to Christianity in the abstract, or in his family circle, or amongst his poorer neighbours in the country. But, when he is relieved from external pressure, or becomes absorbed in society in London, he leads the life of a civilized heathen; refined and cultured, perhaps, more or less according to circumstances, but certainly not living, in any sense of the term, a supernatural life in the realization of another state of existence. A picture of the average political character has been conveyed to me by a distinguished member of many years' experience in the House of Commons. This gentleman, himself a Liberal in religion, once assured me that, with a few exceptions which may be counted by units, and which are notorious to every person, the large majority of those representatives of the people who are returned to serve as Members of Parliament, have ceased to believe in dogmatic Christianity. There still smoulders, indeed, an element of Protestantism in a proportion of the House, chiefly amongst the elder members of the Conservative party, which duly exhibits itself and flares-up on due provocation. On a noteworthy occasion—the debate upon the Public Worship Regulation Bill—the scene in Parliament amongst the country-gentleman party was something outrageous of all decency, and beyond the belief of any who had not witnessed it. But, amongst the younger members of the House, the members who in the course of events hereafter are destined to govern the country, or who will have to act as her Majesty's Opposition, there exists either a distinctly hostile attitude against Revelation, or a supercilious indifference to all that savours of the supernatural. My informant, on reflection, could recall the names of no member of a younger generation, on either side of the House, of actual power, or of the slightest promise, who would probably take a definitely Christian part in the politics of the future.

The like observations are, of course, forced upon inquirers in the wide, and ever increasing section of society which either is, or assumes to be, scientific. The medical world, although it is pre-eminently remarkable for its obedience to many of the dictates of practical Christianity, in works of temporal mercy, is not so remarkable for the cultivation of the temper and spirit of dogmatic theology. The artistic world, again, with a marvellous drawing towards the principles of religion, as a rule seems to miss the highest development of true æstheticism, in the submission of sense to faith, and in the obedience of reflected or bestowed power to the Source and Origin of all form and beauty, of all light and knowledge. It is the testimony of an experienced man of letters, that in the profession of literature it is not easy to find writers who are capable of making any defence for the faith, or indeed who take sufficient interest in dogmatic Christianity to induce them to make the effort. And the same sort of evidence may be obtained of the sympathies of the large divisions of society which fill the higher levels of trade, business, manufacture, or mercantile life. Whilst of the professions of the army, navy, and civil service, it cannot be said that they produce many noteworthy and intelligent defenders of the creed of Christendom.

There are, however, two centres of religious life from which those who are jealous for the supremacy of dogmatic theology might justly look for support. I mean the two great metropolitan churches (speaking civilly) of S. Paul's Cathedral, London, and of S. Peter's, at Westminster. It may be worth while to inquire, what part these centres respectively play, whether positively or negatively, in the question which we are now considering? What may be the result, to an observant spectator, of the work of influential types of both these spiritual corporations—of the teaching of a prominent member of the one, in favour of dogmatic religion; and of the efforts of the authorities of the other, in opposition to dogma?

For some years past, whenever occasion has offered, it has been one of the greatest of intellectual and spiritual treats which may be enjoyed to enter S. Paul's of a Sunday afternoon three or four times a year, and to listen to the eloquent words which proceed from a distinguished preacher there. Time was when, perhaps, the divine in question held the first or almost the first place amongst Anglican preachers. Both matter and manner; voice, gesture and outward appearance; the outline of the sermon and its details; its point and the arguments by which the point was elaborated and driven home—all these elements of perfection combined to produce a realization of a typical English Master in Israel. These were the days in which the preacher taught his hearers from written notes only, or without a manuscript. Then, one could almost see the working of the mind and could almost perceive the marvellous elaboration of the argument, as it flowed forth in logical sequence and in language which could hardly be improved by the most critical. Since those days, early friends and former pupils who would desire to live on the recollection of the image of a noble ideal, have become conscious of a change. What has been the cause of change need not here be considered. But, it certainly is not that the charms of eloquence and style and manner are absent. Nor, perhaps, is it that the matter, or the arrangement, or the development has sensibly deteriorated. It is true, that the sermons in question, almost from the necessities of the case, are now delivered from a book. And, it may be true, that old admirers become over-critical, and desiderate for their idol a supremacy which shall ever be perceptibly in advance of all rivalry: or even, indeed, that the attitude itself of friendly critics may have undergone a change more or less decided.

In one point, however, I venture to be bold in making an estimate of the position which these sermons assume towards the subject-matter of the present introductory remarks. Argumentative and persuasive, orderly and logical, able and masterly as they may be allowed to be and are, it is a reasonable question, whether or not they satisfy a craving for the due proportion of faith in dogmatic theology? Whilst fully allowing, then, all their unequalled powers of attraction to thousands, and not forgetting that they absorb the attention of a very mixed assemblage, the questions force themselves on the minds of some of their hearers—What definite points in dogmatic theology, beyond of course the elements of Christianity, such as the Divinity of CHRIST, do these sermons teach men and women who are bound to believe that " before all things it is necessary to hold the Catholic faith"? Or, what definite points in practical theology do they thereby and in consequence enforce on men and women who are equally bound to believe that "faith without works is dead"? Do they instruct persons living in the world "which be the first principles of the oracles of GOD"? And do they, as the legitimate result of accepting such first principles, force such persons to practise one of them, namely, "repentance from dead works"? In a word, do they tend to make their hearers truer Catholics as well as better Christians: do they not only convince their hearers of sin, but also bring them to their knees in the confession of it? I would prefer to allow others, with greater experience, to answer these questions, rather than to answer them myself. But, so far as an estimate may be formed from personal experience, and from inquiries from others, it cannot be affirmed of the sermons at S. Paul's that they obviously produce these effects. If this be a true estimate, to the like extent to which they fail in producing these results, to the same degree do they fail in counteracting the prevailing neglect of dogmatic theology.

Of course, as a rule and at the present time, the sermons which are delivered from the pulpit of S. Peter's, Westminster, are infinitely less marked by Catholic dogma and discipline than those which are spoken beneath the dome of S. Paul's. It is needless, in proof of this opinion, to do more than refer to a late series of sermons under the somewhat doubtful title of "Eternal Hope" which, since they were preached in the Abbey, have circulated in some ten-thousand copies over intellectual England. But, another series of lectures has been more recently delivered in the Chapter House of Westminster, which afford a striking instance of the point that we are considering. It is true, indeed, that the Chapter House was employed for this purpose by the consent of the Board of Works (a fact which is in itself suggestive of grave thought): but it was thus employed with the approval, and also at the request, of some at least of the authorities of the Abbey. To this series I desire to draw attention. The lectures are called, after the name of their founder, the Hibbert Lectures: their subject-matter is the Science of Comparative Religion: the present course was the introductory course of the series; the first lecturer was Professor Max Müller: and they were delivered under the patronage, amongst others, of dignified members and office-bearers of the Church of England.

In drawing attention to the object and purport of these Lectures in relation to the neglect of dogmatic theology, it may be wise to quote the judgment alone of others more capable than the writer to form a just opinion upon them. Three statements only need be premised.

Firstly: The general drift of the Lectures may be gathered from the following words of one who has studied them. They assume, says a writer who signs himself E. F. W. in the *Guardian* of September 18th 1878, for their "basis a principle utterly destructive of Christianity—*viz.*, that all religions are the natural outcome of the workings of the human spirit: it denies the supernatural at the outset; and thus, a condemnation of Christianity already lurks in the fundamental principle of a science of comparative religion."

In the second place: Admittance to the Lectures was obtained by means of tickets supplied to those who made application for them. The subject proved to be so popular, in certain circles, that each lecture (it is said) was spoken twice on the several days of delivery. A crowded and attentive audience was usually present. The audience (it has been reported) included but few of the leaders of thought, and fewer still of clergymen or other teachers of religion; but a fair proportion of ordinary-looking persons, both men and women, of the average Church or Chapel-going class, were present, who appeared to realize (naturally enough) that the lecturer often spoke far above their power of understanding.

Lastly: After quoting various definitions of Religion, the lecturer supplies his own—of which he asserts that, though it is not exhaustive and is open to objections, "the kernel of it is sound." According to Kant (he says) "religion is morality. When we look upon all our moral duties as [though not because they are] divine commands, that constitutes religion." Fitche, however, "takes the opposite view. Religion (he declares) is never practical and was never intended to influence our life. . . . Religion is knowledge." Again: according to Schleiermacher, "religion consists in our consciousness of absolute dependence on something which, though it determines us, we cannot determine in turn." On the contrary, according to Hegel, religion "is, or ought to be, perfect freedom; for it is neither more nor less than the Divine Spirit becoming conscious of himself through the finite spirit." Once more: by Comte "we are told that man cannot know anything higher than man; that man, therefore, is the only true object of religious knowledge and worship." But Feuerbach "destroys even that last of idols, man; he thinks that selfishness is the only natural motive of human actions." "The essence (he contends) of all religion is covetousness, which manifests itself in prayer, sacrifice and faith." The lecturer, having previously assured his hearers that "religion is not a new invention," gives the following as his contribution to its terminology, by quoting from his own lectures on the *Science of Religion:* "Religion (says Professor Max Müller) is a mental faculty which, independent of, nay, in spite of, sense and reason, enables man to apprehend the Infinite under different names and under varying disguises." ("On the Growth and Origin of Religion;" in the *Contemporary Review*, May, 1878.)

The following quotation contains the more important parts of a letter on "the Science of Comparative Religion," which appeared in the *Guardian*, September 11th, 1878, and was signed "Speculator." The extracts have been verbally contracted, and some entire passages have been omitted.

"In the discourse preached at S. Paul's, before the Lambeth Conference, by the Bishop of Pennsylvania, a reference is made to the above-named subject. Bishop Stevens regards the new science hopefully. He reckons it as among 'those outside forces necessary to give Christianity a world-wide equipment for its world-wide conquest.'

"I believe that this opinion will be found correct. But, in order that such a result may be obtained, there will be need of watchfulness; and I would entreat a consideration of some of the dangers, as well as the benefits, which are likely to arise out of the study of comparative religion.

"On the advantages it is needless to dwell. All truth, except the mere knowledge of evil, must be a gain to humanity; and Christians ought always to welcome truth, from whatever quarter it may come.

"But the professors of this science appear to occupy a position, which, if not untenable, must be difficult to keep. They assume that it is possible to judge a religion without having any fixed standard by which to judge it. I am at a loss to understand how in this case they can have a right to call any given creed good or bad. And, as a matter of fact, it will be found that these philosophers do for the most part really assume the existence of a standard, whether that standard be Deism, or Pantheism, or a sort of semi-Christianity.

"Again, they take for granted that the non-Christian creeds and their adherents will be treated unjustly by Christians, but justly by sceptics. Here, also, we have an assumption which I cannot allow to be necessarily a correct one. Surely a real desire to do justice to the good features of heathenism was manifested in the writings of S. Clement of Alexandria, and of others of the great Alexandrian school. In our own century a similar disposition is apparent in the works of Windischmann, Neander, J. H. Newman, John Keble, Maurice, Döllinger, De Broglie, J. B. Morris, Monier Williams, and many more. But it is not easy to name a more harsh and uncharitable estimate of Mohammed than that of the sceptics Voltaire and Goethe. How different is the generous (possibly over-generous) treatment of the man and his teaching by the truly Christian Möhler!

.   .   .   .   .

"But it is important to observe that the manifestoes of the Professors of this new science fall naturally into two classes. One class (whether the stand-point of the writers be logically tenable or not) simply makes statements, and does not introduce into its books any attacks upon the Catholic faith. The other class does introduce these attacks, and often in such wise as to call for remonstrance. These authors are perpetually saying to us Christians, 'Do be just to the creed of every non-Christian teacher.' The demand is a perfectly fair one. But can it be thought unreasonable if we in turn should say to them, 'Do be just to the creed of Christendom'?

. . . . .

" Bishop Stevens singles out one author in connection with the science of comparative religion. This can hardly be a matter of surprise. The high and well-merited reputation of Professor Max Müller renders it natural that he should be thus selected: nor could any student, who was at all attracted to these subjects, dream of putting on one side contributions to its study so important as those furnished by this eminent lecturer.

. . . . .

" Into the criticism of the Professor's *Introduction to the Science of Religion* I will not enter, however mistaken and unjust may seem to me to be some of its representations of Christian dogma. But a more recent manifesto from the same pen is before me. On my table is lying the June number of *Macmillan's Magazine*, containing the first part of one of the Hibbert Lectures of Herr Müller.

. . . . .

" The lecture is in itself so deeply interesting and suggestive, that to comment even on some of its *obiter dicta* would occupy several columns of your paper.

. . . . .

" In that long and ceaseless duel between those who love to look at matters in the abstract and those who prefer to study them historically, we find that Herr Müller is coming forward as an enthusiastic supporter of the cause of the former. Be it so: by all means, let each side have its say. To me, perhaps from prejudice, the utterances of the Professor sound like the trite objections of a Walpole and a Madame du Châtelet. To those assaults upon the value of history I *read* the replies, as a schoolboy, in the pages of Professor Smyth; and I *heard* the replies, as an undergraduate, uttered in the weighty and manly tones of Thomas Arnold. If I say—and I do say it—that those accents still linger in my ears, and that they seem to drown the objections of Professor Müller as something poor and weak, I trust there is at least one member of the Chapter of Westminster who will not on that account reckon me among the heretical and the profane.

" But let this pass. There is no fear whatever in the England of to-day that historic studies will perish. Least of all can this peril be deemed a serious one within the precincts of the great University, of which Herr Müller is so conspicuous an ornament.

. . . . .

" Such men [*i.e.*, students and teachers of Greek philosophy, from the days of Chaucer and the Cambridge Platonists to the present age] would make great allowance even for Pantheistic error on the part of heathens living amidst the defilements of a gross polytheism. They would listen calmly to an eulogy on such a thinker as Heracleitus. They would make their own the often-cited words of S. Clement of Alexandria; that Greek philosophy was 'a gift of Divine Providence,' and 'an education for Christianity.'

" But they are also Christians. They know that they are sinners. They also know that they are wholly unable to atone for their sins. They believe that One has died for them, to reconcile them to an offended

Maker. Was that One a mere man like themselves; only a creature? Or, was He their Creator, God of God and Light of Light? This was the real question at issue when the ancient Councils met. It cannot possibly be a frivolous one. Neither can it be a futile one—if there be a God; if He has given us a revelation; and if that revelation is, in its fundamental ideas, intelligible.

"It is true, that much which is saddening passed at the Council of Ephesus. It is true, that the earlier career of Cyril had not been worthy of the work which he was called upon to execute. . . . But none the less does it remain also true, that at Ephesus the work of Cyril was, in the words of Neale, 'in spite of whatever infidel or schismatical historians may choose to call it, a noble defence of the perfect Divinity of our Redeemer.' The counter-watchword of Nestorius ran thus :—'Anathema to him who shall say that Emmanuel is true God.'

. . . . . .

"The whole question turns upon this—' Is the doctrine of the Incarnation a truth or a fable?' I must not pause to quote the passage in which Arthur Hallam calls that doctrine 'the most powerful thought that ever addressed itself to a human imagination.' But, I will venture to borrow a few sentences from pages 119, 120, of Mr. Leslie Stephen's *Freethinking and Plain-Speaking* :—

'Christianity, as it is understood by Ultramontanes or by ultra-Protestants, implies a body of beliefs of unspeakable importance to the world. They may be true, or they may be false, but they cannot be set aside as perfectly indifferent. . . . To say that such dogmas matter nothing, is to imply that they are not true; for the only alternative is that God sent His Son upon earth to proclaim to His creatures the awful realities of their position; to tell them how to escape His wrath, and how to do His will; and that, for all practical purposes, He might as well have let it alone. The dogmas are true, or they are immoral.'

"With Bishop Stevens, I am anxious to learn all that can be learnt concerning the most important non-Christian creeds. Professor Max Müller is able, I doubt not, to teach me a great deal concerning them, and I wish to treat his convictions (when I can really make them out) with all respect. He says, most truly, that human thought is not always progressive, but often retrograde. And here is the way in which he illustrates this position :—

'Ephesus, in the sixth century before Christ, was listening to one of the wisest men that Greece ever produced, Herakleitos; while a thousand years later the same town resounded *with the frivolous and futile wranglings of Cyrillus and the Council of Ephesus.*'

"This language of arrogant contempt for the creed of Christendom was uttered in the Chapter-house of the Abbey of Westminster; and at least one great journal seems to treat it as an excellent joke. Gibbon wrote his, very similar, sarcasms in his study. For the present, I say no more. But even the most insignificant person may be justified in offering a protest on behalf of millions, who will, he knows, sympathise deeply with his remonstrance."

II. There is, perhaps, no more complete instance, in the present day, of the absolute extinction of dogmatic theology in any organized or semi-organized body, than is exhibited by the Socialist community abroad. The results at which they have arrived, in both an undogmatic and anti-dogmatic direction, may be taken as a warning of the possible results of a neglect of dogma, if such neglect be carried to its legitimate conclusion. The following quotation is taken from a leading article which appeared in the *Economist*, June 15th, 1878, and was entitled "The American Socialists." The political and religious opinions of the community are so intermingled, that the introductory remarks of the writer are necessary to explain the extract which appears at the close of the article. That extract deserves the careful attention of the reader, being connected more directly with religion than politics, and being a frank avowal of an almost entire absence of belief, written by a Social Democrat himself. It is, says the writer,

"It is extremely difficult, perhaps, impossible, to estimate with precise accuracy the strength of the Socialist party in the United States. The distances there are too great, the centres of action too numerous, the sources of information too varied for any final opinion to be quite safe or quite satisfactory to the observer's mind. We are, however, bound to say that as yet the tendency of the public mind in this country is to underrate, instead of overrating, the force of the new movement. The current idea in England is, we believe, that a country in which more than half the white population derive their subsistence from the ownership of the land, in which every adult male has a vote, and in which education is universal, cannot be in any serious danger from communistic theories, and this idea is doubtless in the main well-founded. If the Socialists rebelled as a body against the authority of the United States, they would be crushed by physical force almost as easily as in Germany. If they attempted to override the general law, or even the law of any particular State, they would be defeated by bodies of men quite as earnest as themselves, and much more numerous. But we do not feel certain that it is beyond their power to possess themselves by legal voting of some one particular State, in which event they would, under the Constitution, hold a sort of entrenched position, and we do feel certain that the sect includes a great number of convinced followers, that it is supported by still greater numbers of the poor, and that its leaders, at all events, hold ideas of the most desperate kind, ideas with which modern society could not co-exist. They are ready to fight if they see a chance, and to fight for objects about which it is impossible for their fellow-citizens to compromise, and on which therefore the struggle, if it ever arises, must be a struggle to the death. This, the thoroughness of Socialism, its total incompatibility with any system whatever, is the main danger, and the extent of that danger depends only on the force the Socialists control.

. . . . .

"This force, even if it is not organised, is formidable, and it may be led and supported by one more formidable still. There is a strong leaven of Socialism in the foreign element within the United States. The Irish, fortunately for order, are not as a body attracted by a movement which their priests pronounce utterly sinful; but there are Polish, French, and above all, German Socialists in every State of the Union. The German Socialists, indeed, must be a very numerous body, quite a perceptible division of the three millions of Germans within the United States. The New York *Tribune*, of 1st June, has devoted nearly a page of its valuable space to a paper read by Pastor Oerter, of the Reformed Church, to a synod of that body, and it is quite evident that this

Church, at least, regards the movement with serious alarm. Mr. Oerter writes with singular moderation, and appears to endorse one main grievance of the Socialists, the inadequate wages paid by capitalists to workmen, but he affirms that the party is large, that it menaces all order, and that its ideas are of the most far-reaching, and, indeed, abominable character. It has leaders, propagandists, and newspapers, chiefly German, and he quotes from these newspapers specimens of the teaching which is abroad. He affirms that the American Socialists differ in nothing from the Socialists of the European continent, that they annually honour the rising of the Parisian Commune, which was celebrated on Sunday, March 17th, of this year by all Socialistic organisations within the Union; that they utterly reject Republicanism as understood in America; and that, like the German Socialists, they insist on the absorption by the State of all capital used for the employment of labour, including specifically all land, on laws compelling all citizens to labour, for a fixed number of hours a day, and on the use of force whenever there seems a chance that force will secure their ends. Mr. Oerter believes on rather weak evidence, that they are also opposed to marriage—we gather from other sources that their creed, or at all events, their teaching, is rather the propriety of divorce by consent than any prohibition of marriage—and that they are absolutely hostile, not only to any existing creed, but to the religious idea itself. Upon this point he has strong testimony to produce. The hostility to religion must be very deep and very pronounced when the organ of an American party subjected to no oppression can indulge in language like that of the New York *Volks Zeitung* only four months ago. The readers of the *Economist* are not likely to be injured by any language Socialists may use, and we therefore give the following extract from a leader in that journal of 12th February, 1878, which marks the severance of the party from Christianity, and, indeed, from any religion ever known among men, much more sharply than any words of ours could do. Indeed, if we were to attribute to Socialists the views which they here attribute to themselves, we should be accused of inventing falsehoods in the interest of capitalists:—

'Our opponents assert that Social Democrats are enemies of all religion and do not believe in a God. Now, this reproach, as terrible as it may seem to some, is not altogether without foundation. Yes, we Social Democrats are opposers of everything that falsely is commended to the deluded masses as religion. We do not believe in a Supernatural Being, we do not believe in a Personal God, in an avenging and recompensing Almighty, Omniscient, All-wise God, who, in his goodness and mercy, in spite of his omnipotence, can permit millions of men on earth to languish in the hard bonds of slavery and subjugation, while, on the other hand, a few without their own merits live in revelry and rioting, feed on the sweat of the suppressed and disinherited, and laugh at human misery. We Socialists do not pull at the triumphal carriage of the priests. We do not take reason captive. We do not want to believe, but to conceive. We are not so ignorant as to resign to these clerical lords our claims on temporal enjoyments for fabricated manna of Heaven. We are not stupid enough to believe that there is a life after death, where justice will be exercised, and where each one is rewarded according to his merits. And as we are not so stupid as not to believe all this; as we do not allow ourselves to be lulled asleep by the old "denial-lullaby—the Eiapopeia from Heaven," just on this account we demand justice on earth; for this reason we demand our portion of enjoyments and temporal fortunes, out of which these hypocrites would like to cheat us, in order that their portion might become all the larger. As we are free from all erroneous notions, we try to establish the "kingdom of heaven on earth." We do not want to know anything about a Heaven after the finished earthly misery; we readily leave that to the "angels and the sparrows." And because we have no religion and do not believe in the God of the ruling class, we do not submit in humility to the Divine order of the universe, and do not acknowledge any superiority by birth as created by God, nor do we acknowledge the power of the purse.'

"The danger in that series of blasphemies does not lie in the fact that they are blasphemous, for their utterance in a form like this only shocks Americans, who might be attracted by the revolt of the party against economics, but in the relation between the blasphemies and the 'modern' spirit, always so powerful in the Union. The essence of religion as taught in the Union, is resignation. The essence of progress is discontent. Consequently, religion is false, and should be put down. That syllogism has evidently made way in the States, and, adopted as it is by a party which appeals to the whole proletariat, it threatens institutions whose strongest defence has from the foundation of the Republic been the religious feeling of the people."

The last topic to be annotated in this prefatory Introduction is that of authority in the English Church, viewed from the standpoint we have taken—namely, as one great cause, perhaps as the greatest of the causes which have been mentioned for our neglect of dogmatic theology, when authority is absent, obscured, or ignored.

Authority in the Church is a topic which it is more difficult to treat suggestively and briefly—or, indeed, to treat at all under existing circumstances—than some others that have been already considered : and for many reasons. It is difficult, because there is so little common ground for agreement amongst Anglicans upon the question of authority from which to begin an inquiry. It is difficult, because there is little exaggeration in saying that no two Anglicans can concur upon the need of possessing authority, or upon the value of acting upon authority. It is difficult, because few Anglicans can determine the form which authority should take, if it be needful to the Church ; the limits of legitimate authority, should it be exercised in the Church ; the attitude which we ought to take towards it, when authority is duly exerted ; and the nature and extent of the authority which is either claimed or exercised over her members by the Church of England. These difficulties are neither fanciful nor unreal. Indeed, they are so overpowering, that I only purpose, in this place, to examine what others say upon the subject ; to state the logical results which flow from current opinions ; and to note the effect which ensues from the absence of certitude, personally, to myself.

There are some persons amongst us, whether clergy or laity, who boldly deny the need, or even the benefit of visible and external authority in the Church of GOD ; who look to individual inspiration from the Holy SPIRIT for guidance into all truth. These take simply a personal view of the case; they hold that all Christians are not only priests, but prophets before GOD. There are other persons who ignore individual authority; who will not pass beyond the definite limits of recognized authority; who look exclusively to authority which is external to themselves and comes to them altogether from without. These take solely an official aspect of the question, apart from all Christianized individuality. There are others, again, who combine the subjective and objective views; and whilst they believe that the Church has spoken once for all, believe also that each individual soul must, by means of grace, give an inward assent to such pronouncements of the Church. These are eclectic in their opinions: they are eclectic in whatever proportions they commingle the integral parts of Church authority and individual responsibility, in a composite whole. There are others who advisedly assert the fallibility of the Church Militant; who only admit the infallibility even of a General Council that proceeds on principles the validity of which themselves are the judges; who declare that, in the last resort, appeal not only may, but must be made to individual opinion. These, whatever else in theory they may hold of Catholic truth, believe practically in the infallibility of private judgment. There are others, once more, who, in the absence of any definite guidance upon authority, add to some combination of two or more of these systems, speculations from their own imagination. But none of the classes which have been named, and only a comparatively few English Churchmen submit their private judgment to the self-contained position, that the living voice of a Living Church is of authority to Catholics; and that whenever and however she is moved by the HOLY GHOST to speak, they are bound to be obedient to her teaching. It may not be easy to accommodate this position to all the facts and all the opinions to which we seem to be pledged; but there is no doubt that such a position is elementary and almost axiomatic in the holy Religion of CHRIST.

Lest it should be thought that no proof can be produced of the existence of such varied opinions amongst English Churchmen at the present day, the following extracts will show that evidence may be given on behalf of at least one of the positions above named. The quotations are taken from a small volume entitled *Essays on Spiritual Subjects* (Calcutta: Smith), printed in India during the past year, and published anonymously. The book only came to my knowledge after the above words had been written. It therefore only incidentally corroborates to my mind previous impressions. But, for others it supplies documentary evidence of opinions which are not always accessible, in a tangible form, for purposes of exact inquiry: and hence, I avail myself of permission to quote from it. Although its authorship cannot be mentioned, I have reason to believe that the opinions which it contains are shared by some at home who exercise a wide and considerable, and for their work's sake a most just influence, both intellectually and religiously. They are held, also—and this fact makes the author's opinions all the more dangerous—in common with the very highest Sacramental doctrine known to the Anglican communion, and by those who employ all the essentials of the highest type of ceremonial Worship of which the Anglican communion is patient. It may be presumptuous for the writer to question the views of such fellow-labourers in the Church. But, if the views to be quoted are sound, truth will profit by renewed attention having been drawn to them: if the views be unsound, truth will benefit by even a feeble warning against them having been made. Moreover, the opinions of these eminent men will not be criticized. Extracts will be given from the work in question; and such remarks only will be added as the case appears to demand.

The subject-matter of the Essays from which the following extracts are taken is "the Voice of the Church." The writer begins by saying:

"Whilst it is very general now for men to appeal to the Voice of the Catholic Church, considerable indistinctness exists in the minds of many, as to what that voice is to which they appeal, and how it is to be heard. The Church is confidently declared to be infallible by many who have not carefully considered what they mean by the word Church, and who are consequently forced, by Ultramontane arguments, either to accept erroneous doctrines, or to make contradictory statements. This paper is an attempt to consider briefly what is meant by our profession of belief in the infallibility of the Catholic Church, and how we can hear her voice.

"In the first place, then, when we say that we believe the Catholic Church to be infallible, we do not mean that that portion of it which exists on earth, *i.e.*, the Church Militant, is infallible, so that we are sure to receive the right faith if we follow the majority of its members, or even of its bishops and priests.

"The whole Catholic Church comprehends, not only the Church Militant, but also the Church Triumphant, and it is to the decisions of the whole Church that we look for infallibility.

"The Holy Spirit indwells in the Church and secures to it immortality and infallibility; but the Church Militant cannot monopolize these gifts. Our apostles, our fathers, our doctors, have not died and bequeathed to successors the gift of the Holy Spirit. They have departed, indeed, from our sight, but they live for evermore.

"They are still part, and the most important part, of the Body of Christ, and a voice of the Church in which they should have no share, would be but a pretended utterance of the Holy Ghost, a voice not of the whole Church, but only of part of it. When a General Council is summoned, they are invited to it. The inspired writers of the Holy

Scripture give their testimony as speaking the words of infallible truth. The fathers and doctors testify respectively to the belief of the Church in their own days, and give the traditions which they received and the deductions which, by the aid of the Holy Spirit, they have ventured to form. And the voices of all these, as expressed in their writings, are of more authority than their successors who are present in the body and speak with the mouth. And the greater their antiquity the more value we assign to their testimony, because they were closer to the source of apostolic unwritten tradition.

"If these be not summoned and their voices [be not] heard, the council is not a General Council, and its voice is not the Voice of the Catholic Church. The decisions of such a council we dare not accept. To do so would be to accept a part of the Church as the whole—a member of the body for the whole Body." (pp. 41-43.)

It is not needful to follow the author into the defence which he makes of his position. In the above quotation, he asserts the fallibility of the existing Church Militant; and apparently allows the infallibility of the Apostolic Church only because there then existed no Church Triumphant. He asserts the infallibility of the whole Church, Militant and Triumphant, at the present day; although he permits himself to contemplate a course of action by the whole Church in counsel which it would be morally impossible for a General Council to take. He claims for the Church Triumphant— without giving any reason for the claim, and whilst ignoring the Expectant Church—the most important part of the Catholic Church; and for the dead voices of the sub-Apostolic fathers and doctors a position of higher authority than the living voices of their successors in all ages, however august or eminent. He pronounces the written words of the Apostles to be infallible : but, he fails to point to the authority which declared them to be "words of infallible truth," and which delivered them as such to the custody of the future Church of all ages. He claims infallibility for the whole Church : but, he fails to indicate the authority which exhibited and declared such infallibility to the faithful of all ages, in the form of constitutions, canons and creeds. In both cases of course, the author has fallen short of a complete theological statement, by having omitted to say that the Creeds of Christendom were imposed and that the Book of Life was accepted by the Church of all time future, upon the authority alone of the Church at a certain date. This Church we call the Church Militant : this authority we deem to be infallible.

But, this is not all which the author asserts. He opens out a wide field of inquiry on another topic, which in this place can only be stated. The further we live from the source of "unwritten tradition" the less likely (he seems to think) are we to secure the truth ; and the condition of the

Church of to-day in regard to doctrinal certainty, has sensibly deteriorated and is deteriorating, in an ever increasing ratio, from its condition in the Apostolic age, in the primitive ages, in the ages of faith, in the latter ages. Indeed, we have now reached a period in the history of the Church when the objective certitude of faith resolves itself into a subjective opinion of the infallibility of private judgment. This the writer appears to allow, though the statement is not made with theological precision, in the following passage :

"It will, perhaps, be urged that this doctrine we have set down of the fallibility of the Church Militant, throws us back upon the Protestant position, that each individual is for himself the final judge in matters of doctrine.

"Unquestionably, the responsibility of accepting or rejecting the true faith does rest with each individual, and a Catholic can no more free himself from this responsibility than a Protestant. If a time comes when he has to choose between orthodoxy and heresy, he cannot escape the choice or put it upon the Church; since the very question at issue is 'Which is the Church' . . . The difference between the Protestant and Catholic positions is not as to the final appeal, which must inevitably be to the conscience of each individual, but as to the mode of arriving at the decision." (p. 51.)

The essay is thus concluded :

"Alike, then, we reject the Protestant and Ultramontane position; the Protestant as wanting in humility, the Ultramontane in faith. There exists, no doubt, in the heart of man a craving for exact [super] natural certainty in religion, and it is upon this craving that the great argument of the Ultramontanists is founded. But it does not seem to be the will of God that this craving should be supplied in this life, any more than the craving after any other part of perfection.

"This claim of earthly infallibility is, of course, in harmony with the claim of the Roman Church to perfect outward unity; but it is inconsistent with the Anglican tenet that the outward unity of the Church has been destroyed. The Romanist desires to have all the promises of God perfectly fulfilled at the present time on earth, and teaches that the Church Militant is still perfect in unity, and perfect in faith. But, we maintain that the promises of God are not broken because man's sin has brought divisions and error into the Church. The divisions in the Church are a patent fact, and error follows as a necessary consequence of divisions. We profess a belief in the sanctity of the Church as well as her unity; but as that sanctity is imperfect, so is the unity, and so by consequence the teaching.

"The undivided Church gave us councils and decisions which we may safely trust and follow : the divided Church gives us synods and doctors whose decisions may guide (but not command) us, until such time as God of His goodness shall grant us again a General Council whose decisions, being in accordance with the teaching of the Church from the beginning, may be safely accepted by all true Catholics." (pp. 52-53.)

The existence of these manifold, these antagonistic views, any one or more of which may influence our opinion, makes it a matter of grave difficulty to arrive at a trustworthy

NEGLECT OF DOGMATIC THEOLOGY. lxvii

judgment on the question of authority in the Church of England. There is no practical, there is no theoretic agreement, amongst professing Catholics. The laity follow the view of some ecclesiastic to whom, for the moment and in general so long as he concurs with their opinion, they yield for the most part an informal and partial obedience; although in some cases the obedience which is exacted is definite and severe. The clergy as in all subjects, so in this, are divided widely in opinion amongst themselves. No two priests, who may be asked at hazard for an expression of opinion, co-incide in giving a like judgment, or even in many cases a judgment which, when reduced to practice, or at the time for action, is consistent with itself. The presumable leaders of the High Church party, and the great majority of their followers, persistently depreciate any authority that issues from the Church which is pre-eminently dogmatic in character, and whose accredited priesthood, as a rule almost without an exception and on all points of primary importance in Christianity, speaks but one voice with unfaltering precision. The Anglican Church itself is silent upon the topic—silent, that is to say, beyond a mere statement of theoretic principle that "the Church hath . . . authority in controversies of faith;" silent, in the expression and enforcement of such authority, when controversies of faith practically abound, which cry aloud—but cry in vain—for any decision from the Church's divine voice.

These are hard facts which possibly may be capable of explanation; but, they cannot with truth be denied. They are facts which demand consideration from thoughtful men. They are specially important to those who are anxious to bow to legitimate authority in doctrinal matters where it be established; but who seek to be independent thinkers in the absence of any authority which avows itself. They are important also to all who live, as many of us live, in the presence of opinion which either discourages speculation where authority is silent, or which fails to carry such speculation, apart from rightful authority, to its logical conclusion. The consideration of these facts suggests to a thoughtful mind who searches for truth irrespectively of the results to which truth will lead him, an inquiry into the position which visible and external authority occupies in the Church of GOD. And the following amongst other similar questions force themselves upon his conscience and await therefrom an intelligent reply:

Is there a real and true basis of authority in the Church of England? Of what elements is this basis composed? Where does it reside? What are its notes; or how may it be recognized? Again—granted that there be such a basis of authority —How can we approach to it; appeal to its decisions; listen to its teaching; conform ourselves to its voice divine? As a matter of fact, apart from mere opinion—Are there any assured truths outside the creeds of Christendom, and beyond the elements of Religion which the Church of England teaches upon authority; or which she teaches as of obligation? If such there be—What are these assured truths, categorically? Again: Are we bound to believe in the Anglican Church as an infallible authority, even though she asserts no actual claim to such an attribute: or, as an authority which enunciates infallible truths, although she (through her representatives) declines to be considered infallible? Or, if she be infallible and if she teaches with certitude, in what documents has the Church of England directly or inferentially declared her infallibility; or through what channels or agencies does she profess to promulgate infallible truth? Or, once more: Is there any body corporate, or any united voice which, without claiming absolute infallibility, yet approximates to authoritative power or utterance sufficiently definite to claim legitimate authority over members of the Anglican obedience?

These are some of the many momentous questions which force themselves on minds harassed and perplexed by the present position of external and visible authority in the Church of England. The temper of mind which proposes these questions is faithful. It is faithful, because it presupposes the acceptance of the principle that underlies them all. That principle takes for granted, as a primary truth of Revelation, the crucial question of all—the question over which our present anomalous position now casts a portentous gloom—namely, Is there any such thing in Religion, is there any such power in the Church of GOD, as authority? And if there be, in what does it consist, and where does it abide? The above questions are in no sense captious or inopportune. They are meant to suggest the application of an indisputable principle to a condition of ecclesiastical affairs in the midst of which, as a fact, we live. They are in no wise intended to place devout souls in a difficulty, and to leave them there with no help to extricate themselves. They are not meant to create doubts, whilst making no effort to supply their solution. No. They are genuine questions, however feebly expressed, which have occurred, and which will occur again to genuine searchers after truth, in the old paths of the Catholic Faith. As such, and with all humility, they are commended to the consideration of those to whom these lines are addressed, and of those to whose attention these lines may be directed. That the questions are capable of receiving an answer which shall be deemed satisfactory to some, I do not allow myself to doubt. That some of them may be answered in a manner to persuade many, I am assured. But, in order to answer these questions honestly and fairly, one must estimate the existing position of the Church of England, in relation to herself, to her members, to the State with which she is in full union, to the Catholic Church from which she is unhappily divided. And looking at these relations at the present time, and speaking only for myself—although I might speak for some others like-minded, whether they be many or few—I, personally, am obliged, sorrowfully and with much sadness, to make this avowal. I feel convinced that these questions, or the major part of them, not only on the part of dogmatic theology but in regard to the Catholicity of the English Church, ought to receive a definite and positive answer from every priest and from every intelligent layman in the Anglican obedience. But, I am powerless to give a reply to them. I am powerless to give a theological and practical answer which shall be logical to men and truthful before GOD. I am powerless to give an answer which, without accommodations that would be unfaithful, shall be even self-satisfying to one who earnestly desires to be loyal to the English Church, and which still less can prove satisfactory to the hostile, to the critical, or to those who are the conscientious victims of honest doubt.

In conclusion. It is with no Quixotic or vain idea of being able to counteract the wide-spread ignorance of theological questions, or the current neglect of dogmatic theology which prevails, that the present Addresses are published. It will be admitted that a difference exists between feeling a consciousness of a want, and feeling a capacity to supply it. I desire to anticipate any objection which may be made to the following work on the ground of presumption. The Addresses are not intended for the instruction of any who have had, or who ought to have had, a theological education, whether laity or clergy. They are meant, rather, for the edification of average and intelligent English Catholics, men and women, living in the world. As a fact, they have been delivered, during a Retreat, to the class of persons named. The substance of them has been for years before the mind of the writer. In various forms, at different times and to different hearers, the Addresses have been spoken during the last London Mission; again, as Lenten Meditations; and, also in part, before the inmates of an Anglican Convent. Previously to each repetition with a different intention, the Addresses have been rewritten; and absence from England, in Rome and North Italy during the past winter and spring, gave the author the opportunity of quiet thought for the purpose of finally reconsidering the subjects treated, and of transcribing his manuscript notes for the press. This is mentioned in order to prevent a charge being made of precipitancy in dealing with the deep questions involved in the present book: and although the writer is fully conscious of much want of knowledge on the topics discussed, he cannot rightly be blamed for a want of thought in the composition of the following pages.

Of course, no effort has been made to exhaust any topic which is treated in the present volume. If only what the writer has been led to say may induce the reader to take further steps for the study of any one or more definite points in question, a great object in view will have been attained. It is true that a difficulty exists in pointing to books which may tend to supply the prevailing deficiency of dogmatic teaching, fully and with accuracy. It has unhappily been the wont of authors to take the Thirty-nine Articles of Religion as a basis, directly or indirectly, for theological inquiry. But, whilst much valuable matter may be extracted from treatises on the Articles; yet, it has to be extracted incidentally, from theological surroundings of controversy or apology which are distinctly unfavourable for accepting the truth with simplicity, or upon faith. The early Tractarians, and some of their descendants have, of course, done much and done well to teach first principles of the Truth to the modern English Church. But, of all the works of these distinguished men, perhaps a book of the late Archdeacon Robert Wilberforce, on the *Doctrine of the Incarnation* (Mozley), has done more than any other to open the minds of an elder generation to the central verities of Religion, and to instigate its readers to a fresh departure on their own account, both upwards and outwards. From the fact that this work was allowed to remain for some years out of print, a younger generation has not benefited so largely as their predecessors from the perusal of its philosophic and theological pages. The volume is now happily once more reprinted in a cheap form: and any reader of these words who has not studied the book, is advised to master it.

Three points only need be added. The first is this: that the remarks which have been made in the following pages on one aspect of the question of the Eternity of Punishment, were written before the late miserable controversy was revived—developed and encouraged as it has been by Anglican clergymen. The thoughts which will be found in the Sixth Address, whether or not of any value in the discussion, must be taken as independent utterances on this awful and painful subject. It is a hopeful sign, amongst much that is discouraging, to learn that a second edition of the valuable work of the Rev. H. Nutcombe Oxenham, called *Catholic Eschatology*, in defence of the Catholic faith on this doctrine, is on the eve of publication (Allen and Co.). In the second place: those who may desire to study the question of Retreats from a devotional point of view, are advised to read an Essay by the Rev. T. T. Carter, which originally appeared in the Third Series of the *Church and the World*, and has since been reprinted in the Second Volume of *Studies in Modern Problems* (C. Kegan Paul & Co.). It is entitled *Retreats for Persons living in the World*. There is only one way to obtain a practical knowledge of the subject superior to reading Mr. Carter's Essay—and that is, personally to attend a Retreat. But, even the benefit of this spiritual discipline to the soul will be enhanced by a previous perusal of the Essay. Lastly: the title which has been chosen for the present volume may seem to some persons to be at once too ambitious in itself, and to fall short in performance of the hopes of which its terms are suggestive. On this point it may be sufficient to say, that the title is not meant to be understood exhaustively; that the popular estimate of the First Principles of our Religion appears to be at issue with the judgment of the Author of the Epistle to the Hebrews; and that the inspired explanation of the phrase, quoted at the beginning of this volume from the Epistle, certainly justifies the present use of it, and possibly may enlarge the reader's view of the true meaning of first principles.

In spite of all difficulties which attend the question of authority in the Anglican obedience, I venture to submit my work, with much humility, to the judgment of the Church.

London: ORBY SHIPLEY.
Eve of S. Luke, A.D. 1878.

ERRATA.

Page 95, line 2, *for* of GOD, *read* by GOD.
Page 99, line 9, *for* of GOD, *read* by GOD.
Page 254, line 20, *for* of Angels, *read* of the Angels.
Page 316, line 16, *omit the commas.*

Postscript.

SINCE the above Introduction—which has been some months in writing—was completed, I have felt it my duty to submit to the Catholic Church.

The whole of the present work had passed out of my hands before I became a Catholic. Had this not been so, some things which it contains would, of course, have been differently expressed. But, for its contents I alone am responsible.

The book was written by me as a loyal clergyman of the Church of England. When reluctantly convinced that I could no longer consistently and logically remain in the Anglican communion, I at once left it.

This is not the place to offer to those with whom I have formerly worked, or to whom I once ministered, reasons for my great change ; nor to explain, as I can explain, the circumstances of it. Neither am I able now, amidst the mental suffering caused by my severance from friends who are very dear to me, and from the past which includes upwards of twenty years of service, however unworthy, in the English Church, to state these reasons and to give these explanations with the calmness which their importance demands. The Introduction to the present book will, to an extent, indicate the temper of mind which naturally, perhaps irresistibly, led to my ultimate decision. But I hope, at no distant date, to proceed with another work which has long absorbed my thoughts, and which I had intended to call " An Apology for Doubt in the Present Position of the Church of England."

In the meanwhile, I desire to say, for the information of any who may care to know, that three main causes have forced me to take this momentous step. The first is, that whilst for many years I have held all

Catholic doctrine not distinctly denied by the English Church, I have held it upon a wrong principle, namely, upon private judgment, not upon the principle of authority. In the second place, I have been powerless to realize the authority upon which the Anglican Church presumably taught Catholic truth, or what truths she taught upon authority; what definite and external authority claimed my obedience, or how practically I was enabled to render obedience to such authority. Lastly, I have always endeavoured to believe in the One, Holy, Catholic and Apostolic Church of the Nicene Creed; and have honestly striven to accommodate the evident facts of corporate dis-union with various current theories—whether under the similitude of a branch or a family—of the invisible and essential unity of the mystical Body of CHRIST.

After a gradual upward growth of years towards light and truth, I have been led, by GOD's mercy, to see, 1. that Authority is the true basis of religious faith; 2. that the Catholic Church alone distinctly claims, and actually exercises divine authority; and 3, that positive Unity can only be obtained, for individual souls, by personal submission to the Catholic Church, and by union with the centre of Christendom.

It would not be right to deny that recent Ecclesiastical events have greatly quickened my perception of these truths—especially two.

By the voluntary initiative of the bench of Bishops, a Bill was introduced into Parliament which, in its necessary results as an Act, has committed the English Episcopate to accept and put in force all the decisions in spiritual causes of the Judicial Committee of the Privy Council. The two Anglican Primates having, under the provisions of the Public Worship Regulation Act, appointed a Judge of the so-called Court of Arches, are henceforth, together with their Suffragan Bishops, morally and legally responsible for all the decisions to which that official, their representative, in spiritual suits is bound by the law of England.

Amongst other decisions to which the Episcopate are thus committed are (speaking popularly) these—to a denial of Regeneration in Holy Baptism, to a denial of the Inspiration of Holy Scripture, to a denial of the doctrine of Future Punishment.

I have hoped against hope, for four painful years, that the Anglican clergy would, in some positive and effectual manner, have freed themselves from the spiritual responsibility of remaining in communion with Bishops who are thus committed to distinct heresy. But, the clergy are apparently content to abide, or at the least they still abide, however discontentedly, in sacramental communion with ecclesiastical superiors against whom these charges are admitted.

A more recent event, however, has tended to mature, and even in a measure to precipitate, my decision. The entire English-speaking Episcopate of the Anglican communion has lately, with absolute unanimity, affixed their signatures to a document which pronounces against the practice of the Confession of Sin. This pronouncement, as is well-known, is contained in a "Letter" from the "Conference of Bishops," which was lately "published under authority."

I am fully conscious of certain explanations and refinements which have been made to minimize the authority, the importance and the results of this Letter, which is only not in name and object Encyclical. To these distinctions I desire to give every weight; and some of them are undoubtedly valid. But, after every plea has been admitted, this unhappy fact remains unquestioned. The English Bishops have laid down four propositions on the subject of Confession, upon three of which at least there is certainly a very widespread, and probably an entire agreement between the members of the Catholic school in the Church of England—an agreement in direct and positive antagonism to the Episcopal pronouncement. It is, they affirm, the "deliberate opinion" of their Lordships, "that no Minister of the Church is authorized to require" (in popular language), 1. the Confession of sin before Absolution; 2. to "encourage the practice of habitual Confession"; or, 3. to "teach" that such Confession is a "condition of attaining to the highest spiritual life." (Letter, page 41).

This direct and open attack upon the teaching of the clergy, and upon the practice of the laity of the Catholic party in the Anglican Church, for a period of twenty, thirty, forty years, has been met in neither of the only two ways in which, in my humble opinion, it could be consistently met. It has been neither loyally and obediently accepted as the nearest approach which is possible, under existing circumstances, to an authoritative statement on dogma or discipline by the acknowledged heads of the English Church : nor has it been boldly and categorically denounced as anti-Catholic and untrue. Indeed, individual efforts which, as I can testify, have been made to secure a repudiation of this Episcopal manifesto, at the hands of certain typical High Church clergymen, have signally failed.

Such, in brief, are some of the reasons which caused me, as I believe at the call of GOD, and after much thought, and consultation with others, to submit myself to the authority of the Catholic Church.

I can now fervently, yet not without fear and trembling, thank GOD for having turned my earnest prayer in the hour of doubt—from the Psalm, Judica me, in the Anglican and Catholic versions respectively—into an antiphon of blessed assurance in the time of certitude. "O send out Thy Light and Thy Truth, that they may lead me : and bring me unto Thy holy hill and to Thy dwelling"—has at length become for me, "Send forth Thy Light and Thy Truth : they have conducted me, and brought me unto Thy holy mount and into Thy tabernacles." DEO gratias.

ALL SOULS' DAY, A.D. 1878.

PRINCIPLES OF THE FAITH.

"When for the time ye ought to be teachers, ye have need that one teach you again which be the First Principles of the Oracles of GOD . . . Repentance from dead works, and . . . Eternal Judgment." *Hebrews*, v. 12, and vi. 1, 2.

Eve of Retreat.

INTRODUCTORY ADDRESS.

IT would be an interesting psychological study, for any one person to be able to see, in all their fulness, the dispositions which led any other person to seek GOD in a Retreat. It would be interesting, not merely as a devout inquiry, still less as a matter of intellectual curiosity; but, as indicative of GOD'S inner and hidden dealings, in any given case, with the soul of man. From the consideration of these dispositions, we could not fail to derive both benefit and blessing.

An interesting psychological study in regard to our neighbour, however, in regard to ourselves becomes more. Under existing circumstances, it becomes of the deepest and most intimate importance to the soul. Its solution is almost essential to our welfare if, entering into retreat to consider the First Principles of our holy Faith in relation to Sin, we would come worthily; if, finding ourselves under its influence, searching or soothing as the case may be, we would accept the teaching which our Divine Master has in store for us; if, leaving the World and its cares behind us, so far as may be and for a little space, we would return to the World and its cares refreshed by our temporary absence, and strengthened with the gift which He has specially provided for us individually.

The dispositions spoken of, in all their fulness, which affect others, or which influence self, include both the proximate and remote disposition. They indicate when analyzed, not only the obvious fact that we felt moved, forced by outward agency or inward feeling, and that we took action on the suggestion; but also, the more hidden causes which roused the feeling, or the combination of events which led to the agency. This examination of the origin, source, outcome of our present dispositions will probably show that they are the result of one of three conditions. It may disclose, firstly, the sad and painful story of a single strong passion or master sin, or even of more than one, traced in development downwards to petty omissions of duty, to trivial faults of commission, or to venial sins. It may recall, secondly, the blessed history of a life, from font to altar and from thence to the present time, untouched with the taint of deadly sin. Or, it may record, thirdly, the more common-place features of the majority of the lives of persons living in the world, the sketch of a career neither wholly bad nor wholly good; chequered with equal, or nearly equal, squares of light and darkness; now devoted to GOD, now given to Satan; not entirely free from deadly sin, and still less entirely free from venial; both attracted to good works, and absorbed in works that are not good; to-day drawing nearer to GOD in purity, gentleness, humility, truth, and reality, to-morrow drawing away from Him by self-consciousness, self-pleasing, self-esteem, self-love —in a word, by selfishness.

The revelation of self, or of some other, if we consider the dispositions which influence either, will, therefore, probably take one of three forms. It will disclose a biography of sin. Or, it will reveal a vision of sanctity. Or, it will become an account of the average condition which the large majority of ordinary men and women feel that they occupy, when at the pains to analyze their spiritual position, partly holy and partly sinful.

In all our doings for GOD, and in dealing with souls, it is wise, it is almost essential, it is certainly dutiful to secure the divine co-operation. My efforts to lead, or to give a direction to your thoughts; your willingness to be guided by or to accept my suggestions, will be without avail if unblessed of GOD. His blessing may be obtained, and His co-operation may be secured, by devoutly asking for them. Prayer, then, ought to precede even the Introductory Address in a Retreat; specially a Retreat devoted to the consideration of some First Principles of the Faith in relation to one of the greatest of mysteries in life—Sin. In our meditations, we shall need the presence and inspiration of the Third Person of the Holy TRINITY. It will be the Person of GOD the HOLY GHOST, Who, in the words of the collect, will prevent this and all our doings with His most gracious favour; Who will further our efforts with His continual help; and Who will fulfil our work, begun and continued in GOD'S holy Name, to His greater glory and the good of souls. To the Blessed PARACLETE, the COMFORTER, therefore, let us, in the first place, betake ourselves in prayer. Let us invoke GOD'S HOLY SPIRIT. Let us, as with humility and confidence we may, summon Him to come to us; to abide with us and be in the midst of us; to inform and indoctrinate us; to give to the one lips to speak, and to the other ears to listen to words which may, in the lives of both, bring forth fruit unto holiness, and in the end everlasting life. This we will do, fervently and heartily, by saying together,

Veni, Creator Spiritus:
Come, HOLY GHOST, our souls inspire,
And lighten with celestial fire.
Thou the Anointing SPIRIT art,
Who dost Thy Seven-fold Gifts impart.
Thy blessed Unction from above
Is comfort, life, and fire of love.
Enable with perpetual Light
The dulness of our blinded sight.
Anoint and cheer our soiled face
With the abundance of Thy Grace.
Keep far our foes, give peace at home;
Where Thou art Guide, no ill can come.

> Teach us to know the FATHER, SON,
> And Thee of Both, to be but One;
> That, through the ages all along,
> This may be our endless song:
> Praise to Thy eternal merit,
> FATHER, SON, and HOLY SPIRIT. Amen.

Now, as in the immediate presence of GOD the Only COMFORTER, consider with me:

II.

What cause—be it reason or inspiration—was it, which led any given soul to know itself and to seek its GOD, with the help of these Meditations, and under existing circumstances during the present short season of retirement? With what dispositions have we come? For, it may be taken for granted that we came with some one, definite, special disposition, and not merely to conform to the custom of the Church, which demands a yearly Retreat, public or private; nor yet to the exigencies of a Christianized civilization, under the influence of which we should feel ill at ease if we did not in some fashion, more or less complete, yield to such requirements.

Perhaps, no two souls were wholly influenced by the same reason, or allowed themselves to be guided by the like inspiration. Doubtless many were, in part, thus guided or influenced. But it would be difficult, and might be hazardous, to assign to any single soul the exact cause which alone prevailed. It were safer to say, that it was no simple or self-contained cause. Probably one, or more, or even all of the three following mental postures may have contributed to this end.

I. The first reason, or inspiration, which caused us to seek GOD more closely in retreat, may have been this: the presence in the soul of some one, actual, and definite sin; a sin known to GOD, known to our Guardian Angel, known to our confessor, known to ourself, even if hidden from our neighbour; a sin which, by the help of the Blessed PARACLETE, we would conquer, or at least would lessen in degree, during the present Retreat.

It may be the sin of pride, in some most unlikely of the many forms in which it assails us; not only in pride of birth, position, fortune, personal attractions, in the more vulgar kinds of the sin; but, also, in more refined kinds of pride, such as the pride of influence with others, of acquaintance or friendship with the really great, or even the notorious, of knowledge of the world, or even, knowledge of sin.

It may be sins of thought, when we have broken the force of sins of action, whether in memory, understanding, or will, in sentiments or affections, in imagination or desire: or, sins of word, after those of thought have been abandoned; sins of the tongue, in using exaggerated, boastful, and unreal language, or one of the worst types of gossip—religious gossip, or words of double meaning, capable of conveying impressions not absolutely pure: or, sins of the temper, when sins of thought, word and deed are conquered, even if only the result, in endless forms, of nervous irritability, or of constitutional weakness.

It may be, again, the sin of rebellion against the holy Will of GOD; discontent with our lot in life, though perhaps of our own seeking; quarrelling with our fate, though intellectually persuaded that, if fate was in our own hands, we could on the whole hardly better ourselves or mend our position; yet still, craving after what He will not give us, or in His mercy withholds, and repining at what in His providence He has sent us, or in mercy permits—in our domestic, religious, social, or public life. It may be, I repeat, the sin of rebellion and all that flows from it, want of self-command, spiritual peevishness, devotional distraction, and mental disorganization.

II. The second reason or inspiration, which caused us to seek to know ourselves more perfectly, or less imperfectly during retreat, may have been this: the need of some positive gift or grace in the soul, again known to GOD, to our Guardian Angel, to our confessor, to ourself, and certainly not concealed from our neighbour; a gift or grace which we would acquire, whether wholly or in part, by the will of the Holy PARACLETE, in this Retreat.

Is it one of three sister virtues?

Is it, first, that great virtue in domestic, or social, or even public life, which stands high in the ascetic life; that gift which is almost a Christian grace, and is not far from a supernatural gift; that result which ensues from the chiefest of all human victories, the conquest of self—I mean, the virtue of un-selfishness? Is it the virtue of self-subdual, which seems to contain within itself, and to employ on the behalf of others, the features and qualities of many opposite gifts and graces; which softens every hardness from others, but hardens itself against all softness unworthy of ourselves; which blunts the point of hostile attack, and turns the edge of unkind defence; which minimizes supposed difference, and magnifies real agreement; which makes man's action Godlike, and sees in every creature of His hand, the divine image of GOD the Creator?

Or, is it, secondly, that peculiarly Catholic quality, theologically called, recollectedness? It is collectedness of spirit, which results from a belief in, and the ensuing practice of, the three-fold truth underlying the foundation of the life above nature: 1st, that GOD and the soul are the only two beings in the universe with which we are really concerned; 2nd, that Thou GOD seest me, even me—as if I alone, and none other, had been created—as if I alone, and none other, existed in creation; 3rd, that all things are to be done by man, created, redeemed, inspired—as the only right intention under the joint influence of GOD'S greater glory and the soul's salvation.

Or, is it, thirdly, conformity; oneness, intimate or absolute, of the human will with the Will divine? Is it that supernaturalized virtue which springs from an honest and sincere imitation of CHRIST, the only One of the children of men in .Whom the two wills were both inherently conformed and practically exercised, the only One Who was rightly termed the Son of Man? Is it that gift or grace which makes its possessor live each day of life, of and by and for itself, not forgetful indeed of the day past in warning, but un-reliant on the day to follow as not assured ; which turns trials and disappointments into blessings ; which makes us see with superhuman insight into the permissive Will of GOD that, in our case at least, what is, is best ; and hence, which gives light and colour to what otherwise were colourless and dark, and makes human life to be, not only heavenly by anticipation, but even a true, though faint foretaste of the Vision of GOD in bliss.

III. The third disposition which causes us to make a Retreat is, perhaps, the most difficult to describe, whilst it is the most easy to feel. It may be nothing decided or definite, nothing tangible or obvious which can be named, though its effects are certainly practical, real, and positive. It may be that inconsistent, unhappy, and almost hopeless condition in which many souls find themselves placed, neither wholly dedicated to GOD, nor entirely enslaved by Satan; to-day apparently devoted to things of the next life, to-morrow recklessly pledged to the things of this; not actually outside a state of grace, but never fully in accord with the divine gift; escaping, indeed, deadly sin, but callous to venial ; leading a dull, heavy, average, monotonous, common-place existence of religious respectability, without energy, or fire, or zeal, or enthusiasm for the higher walks of a life of faith in the unseen.

In fact, there may have been no disposition in this case at work within the soul to lead us to retreat. A miracle of grace, to save the soul from death has been performed—however little it may be known to the object of it, and however little it would be allowed in this unbelieving age—a miracle, on behalf of the victim of indifferentism. A miracle has been performed on behalf of one who never feels at ease with his conscience, his confessor, his Angel, his GOD; who never feels worthy to receive communion, absolution, blessing; who never feels prepared for the last great summons and the judgment to follow, when death comes very near indeed to himself as a warning, in the person of a friend : a miracle, to give one more chance to the Precious Blood of effecting a conversion, of securing a penitent, of making a saint.

III.

Such may have been our remote dispositions in coming to retreat—a sin to forsake, or a grace to acquire, or indifferentism to conquer.

What may have been our proximate dispositions?

Is this our first Retreat, the first season of retirement either more or less completely taken from the world and given to GOD and our soul? And are we about to make a spiritual experiment, in order to see what effect, if any, whether positively or relatively good, a brief withdrawal from ordinary avocations will produce on the past by penitence, on the present by self-surrender, on the future by perseverance? Is this our second or third Retreat, the second or third season of retirement, rather more than less completely taken from the world and given to GOD and our soul? And, are we about to renew the spiritual experiment which has proved, on the whole, successful? Is this the last of a series of Retreats—certainly in one sense the last, possibly the last absolutely—which GOD may be pleased to grant to us before He calls us hence to His Seat of Judgment? And have we entered upon the work with a pure intention to confirm a good habit begun, by the help of the HOLY SPIRIT, at a former Retreat; with an earnest desire to complete a conquest over sin, partially conquered by grace in another former Retreat; with an inflexible determination to renew vows made over and over again, in many former Retreats, made in all simplicity, but broken under the force of temptation; and with every wish to secure both will and power to record promises which, in due time, please GOD, shall be scrupulously, even if imperfectly, fulfilled?

In one of these three phases of the spiritual life may be found the proximate dispositions, which influenced the majority of those who in any degree seek edification or light, purification or rest, decision or peace, in this Retreat. But, other dispositions have, in all likelihood, influenced our search. We are here voluntarily severed, for a short space and as completely as possible, from the outer world and its surroundings; from the cares of life and its necessary entanglements; from the ordinary duties of religion, perhaps even of the religious life, and both its distraction and absorption. We have placed ourselves, and hope to continue, in the immediate presence of the Blessed PARACLETE; within the reach of ordinary and extraordinary means of grace; under the influences, at once softening and strengthening, of our holy Faith; and not apart from the legitimate sympathy of created things by real, though unavowed, human fellowship in united spiritual action, and many material aids common to all, for devotion, self-knowledge, and holiness of life.

Certain dispositions, felt alike by all who enter retreat, cannot but be responsible for such results. Are we present in retreat in order to see light in our life, whether in belief or practice, where darkness prevails; or to secure rest and peace, in religion or in the world, where agitation and unquiet have assailed us? Did we come to make a decision when doubt was supreme; or to ascertain GOD'S will when duties, apparently conflicting, seemed and only seemed to point in opposite directions? Have we come hither with an honest and true intention to begin a new account between GOD and the soul, to turn over a new page in our spiritual autobiography, to lead a renewed life of self-dedication, in any one of the three divisions of a Christian's career in which we may be placed, the purgative, or the illuminative, or the unitive way? Shall we decide before we go hence to do, or to abstain from doing, a certain thing; to follow, or to cease from following, a certain course; to begin, or to leave off, a certain habit—such habit, course, or thing being known to GOD, our Guardian Angel, our confessor, ourself?

Or again, have we come here, are we present, shall we depart from this Retreat, only, or chiefly, or to some extent actuated by a lower motive? Is it custom only, good and religious though it be, or a pious fashion never so holy in itself, which has led us hither; or yearning for mere human sympathy, or indeed for supernatural sentiments which fall short of a right intention?

Or once more, to take a different class of causes, is it religious curiosity, or mental culture, or intellectual gratification—in all of which we shall inevitably be disappointed—instead of the good of an immortal soul, and the greater glory of GOD the FATHER?

There is no need to suppose that the proximate cause of the presence of any person in this Retreat, was a bad motive. GOD forbid. It is too early to determine in which class of motives our individual and personal decision may be found. But, it may be hazarded as an opinion, that some of the reasons which have been named, as a fact, influenced the dispositions of the majority of those who have entered into retreat.

IV.

With the larger part of those whom I address, this will not be their first experience of a Retreat. It may be otherwise with some souls; but, with many persons, the yearly Retreat is comparable, both as to intention and in treatment, for regularity and results, to daily or weekly communion, to weekly or monthly confession, and to general or special self-examination of conscience. In any case, much has happened during the past Christian year, of which it is helpful to take some account at the outset of a Retreat, one object of which is to consider certain divine principles in relation to the sin of man. For instance:

I. A whole cycle of sacred festival and fast has passed over our soul. On the Eve of a Retreat, it is at least wise to ask ourselves: What has been the result to the soul, in regard to its most intimate relations, of these religious seasons, whether of penitence or of joy?

II. The seasons of the Church, and all they bring to us, or keep us from, are not the only talents which have been committed to our charge, during the last twelve months. Her public ministrations, accepted generally and applied in particular—in her ancient Hours of Prayer, special offices of devotion, or the offering of the One Sacrifice, with or without reception of holy mysteries—have to be estimated in their spiritual effect. More private ministries, too, and acts of secondary worship, such as examination of conscience, confession of sin, satisfaction offered, resolutions for the future, acts of meditation, the reading of devout books, and other religious exercises—must be weighed in the balance of the sanctuary. What may be the result to our soul, in the past year, of this survey?

III. But the seasons of Holy Church are not all; private acts of devotion are not all: account has also to be taken of another element in the spiritual state of each soul that submits to the discipline of a Retreat. The account must be taken under a two-fold form.

As a fact, and apart from all statement of results, there have been, in the inmost recesses of our soul, strivings with Satan in temptation. These strivings have been unknown to any but self. They were strivings, in which others have not sympathized, in which others could not sympathize. They were strivings, real, severe, prolonged, almost unendurable; which, little as they may tell on our outward intercourse with man, are observed of GOD, have left their mark on the soul, and have prevented us from being spiritually worse than we are. These human strivings, in the temper, even if with none of the success, of our Divine Master's forty days' strife —made against the lust of the flesh, the lust of the eye, and the pride of life—have to be considered.

As a fact, again, and apart from all after effects, there have been, in the soul, wrestlings with GOD for the divine grace. These wrestlings, also, have been unknown to any but self. They were wrestlings in which others did not, perhaps could not, sympathize. They were wrestlings actual, powerful, almost endless, quite exhausting to over-taxed nature, which, too, have left their mark on the soul, and made us, though men see it not, better and holier than we otherwise should have been. These divine wrestlings with GOD, continued even to the break of day, because we would not let Him go, except He bless us as He blessed Jacob of old, have also to be considered.

What result to our souls have these strivings against sin, and wrestlings with holiness, obtained towards our hereafter living a godly, righteous, and sober life, to the glory of GOD'S holy Name?

Take these landmarks in the past year's pilgrimage of life, in their order; and decide with the soul, how far or how little they may apply to our individual and special case.

Firstly: Have we, in every recurring season, placed ourselves in union and sympathy with the divine centre of each festival and fast, as with a living, sentient, self-conscious, and true Person; a Person at once human and divine; the Person of JESUS CHRIST? And did we, or do we, realize that whatever may be said of our holy Faith, whether for or against it, the Christian Religion is eminently, pre-eminently, a personal creed. It is personal, on many grounds; amongst others these: Because the object of our worship is a Personal GOD: the revelation of His will has been made to, and continued by, personal agents: the means of promoting CHRIST'S Church and advancing His kingdom, as a corporate body, are personal; the inspiration of the members of His kingdom and Church is, in endless ways, personal: and the final result of religion, union with GOD in bliss or endless separation from Him in loss, is personal, and will be consummated individually, one by one. Have we realized this truth, as in antagonism to two distinct, and to an extent opposite, theories widely accepted at the present day. Do we hold to the truth as a witness, on the one hand, against the worship of abstract Law and a parody on Nature, outside ourselves as well as outside GOD; and on the other, against the idolatry of an individual acceptance, within ourselves, of the genuineness and authenticity of GOD'S sacred Word written, and of an intellectual assent to our own interpretation of it, apart from the tradition of the Church?

Secondly: Have we, in regard to the public action, or private influence of our Spiritual Mother on the soul, been genuine, honest, and constant, in our relations towards her, both in positive precept and indirect suggestion? Have we omitted or intermitted forms of devotion, religious customs, pious habits, incontinently and without sufficient cause? For instance: Have we been wont to say one of the Hours of Prayer, at mid-day perhaps, only to leave it off, before it has been said long enough to become a spiritual break-water, between the calm of the forenoon and the agitation of the afternoon, for so many lives passed in the world? Have we begun systematic meditation, be it never so brief in time or elementary in form, only to find its practice incompatible with the exigencies of modern daily life: or, early and frequent reception of the Blessed Sacrament, or daily worship before GOD'S Altar without reception, only to find it, in a short time, too large an effort on our spiritual being, or too heavy a strain upon our physical frame?

Again, to take a different side of the devout life: Have we made use of a particular examination of conscience, for a while; to discover only too soon, that general examination is sufficient for the needs of our soul? Or again, to take yet another side: Have we been taught to employ the sign of the holy Cross in divine service, or to kneel at the *Incar-*

natus Est in the Creed, or to pay due reverence to the Sacred Presence on the Altar; to unlearn such Christian practices only too quickly, lest they may be a source of scandal to others, when, in truth, self-consciousness alone causes us to think of any third person to ourself and our GOD?

Or, to pass from the consideration of sacramentals to that of the Sacraments of the Church: Have we come to Holy Communion, time after time, to beg a certain thing from our dear LORD'S hand, a grace for another, a gift for oneself, a blessing for a third, a benefit for a fourth; and when the certain thing has not been granted at once or obviously, have we surceased from asking? Or: Have we come to Confession, time after time, to confess the same sin, of omission or commission, in thought, word, or deed, and the same fall into a little infidelity, trifling neglect of duty, or momentary yielding to temptation; and have we felt contrition, made confession and given satisfaction, time after time, though the sorrow has been perceptibly less fervent, the absolution has been sensibly less welcomed, the amendment has been almost avowedly less honest, real, and lasting?

Thirdly: Have our strivings with the Evil One, and our wrestlings with GOD'S HOLY SPIRIT resulted in any practical effect that we can produce at the bar of conscience; or may offer for the tender verdict of our spiritual guide; or shall dare to bring forward at the Judgment Day, before the presence of Almighty GOD and His holy Saints and Angels? Or: Have we not rather fought till we were tired of fighting, and then given up the fight; have we not prayed till we were weary of importunity, and then given over our prayers: and as an inevitable result, consciously to ourself, knowingly to our confessor, to the grief of our Guardian Angel, and to the loss of favour with GOD, have we not gone backward in religion—for a stationary posture is impossible?

V.

A Retreat is a fitting time to make such inquiries of the soul. Whatever may be our position in religion, whether as a beginner, or as one advanced on our course; whatever may be our attitude towards GOD and His grace; whatever may be the force of our efforts after holiness of life, or the power of attraction in temptation to sin—it is well for the soul to make answer to itself upon these points.

But, a Retreat is a time for more definite and more exact treatment of the soul. Specially is it a time for four distinct religious acts, which involve, 1. Isolation, or the withdrawal of ourself from others; 2. Introspection, or looking inwardly upon self, at the present moment, by self-examination; 3. Retrospection, or a looking backward upon self, in the past, with a view to reparation; 4. Anticipation, or the vision of oneself, in the future, with promises of amendment.

Let us take these four acts in the spiritual life for consideration, in their order.

1st. Isolation: a Retreat is a time for physical separation from others, as well as for mental detachment from self. Detachment from self and separation from others are means of being alone with GOD. Nothing, perhaps, is so unwelcome to the natural man as this—to be alone with GOD. The only fact at all comparable with it, though for opposite reasons, would be to hold intercourse with GOD'S enemy and man's foe, Satan: and this contrast may be imagined from the almost intolerable thought of a soul brought face to face with its own sins, as GOD sees them. Nothing, however, is so sweet and peaceful to a devout soul as isolation from the creature in the actual presence of GOD here, and in the realization of the Beatific Vision hereafter.

True solitude, amongst many persons and whilst living in the world, is only attainable in retreat. The season of Lent, indeed, may be made a counterpart of this isolation, to a certain extent. If not entirely cut off from intercourse with the world, we may be partially relieved of its pressure. We may devote the morning of each day, one day in a week, one week out of the six, to isolation. If not entirely devoted to religious exercises in Lent, yet some home cares may be dismissed, some family and social distractions may be abandoned, some ordinary avocations may be intermitted, on behalf of isolation. But, in a Retreat, severance from others and detachment from the world may be made, for the short space of three days, complete instead of partial. Within such limits, we may gain all from the adoption of isolation, if only we will to gain all. And such isolation, however far it falls short of absolute perfection in practice, coming as it comes periodically, in the midst of modern society, possesses a sobering, health-giving, invigorating effect on the over-taxed soul. It is a merciful dispensation which, for a certain space once in the year, checks our onward course; which moderates the intensity and speed, in this eager, rapid age, at which we live; which makes us tarry awhile and repose after the burden and heat of the day; and which, as it were, in the cool of the evening and in the garden of the Church, places us in the immediate presence of Him Who is invisible, and allows us to listen to words unutterable, spoken by His Voice in the depths of our soul in solitude.

Such are some of the effects of isolation.

2nd. Introspection: a Retreat is a time for self-examination. If not suggested by isolation, the examination of conscience is materially aided by it. Indeed, it is difficult for the soul to be alone with GOD and not to employ introspection. Those who are wont to make an annual Retreat with average devotion, are more or less accustomed to use three sorts of self-examination: the first, a general or life-long examination, extending over the whole field of the past; the second, an ordinary examination made once a day, night by night, or even twice in the day, as well as with more care and exactness before their ordinary confession and communion; the third, a particular or special examination, continued for a certain length of time and devoted to some given topic. Perhaps, save under exceptional circumstances, it is well for the majority of persons living in the world, though not for all who attend a Retreat, if their self-examination be confined to the actual present or to the immediate past; to their position before GOD now, and to their career since their Retreat last year. In any case, opportunity fails us to make more than an effort to this end on the present occasion, even by way of suggestion.

In order to test our conscience, by soundings taken at hazard, consider some of the following elementary questions in the spiritual life, once proposed by a Master in Israel, who has now been taken to his rest. How does this Retreat meet us? As we are, or as we seem to be? As known by GOD, and seen by His Angels; or, as we appear to our confessor, however discerning, and as we disguise ourselves, however intentionally honest? A Retreat helps us to realize our actual position in the life above nature. Are we confirmed in grace; making progress in the spiritual life; seeking a continual state of conversion towards our Divine Master? A Retreat enables us to establish our position; to regain a place that has been lost; to advance upon one that has been gained; to renew all that has gone before. Has the year past been characterized by tepidity; have we been languid, indifferent, or half-hearted; has there been a tendency to sloth, short of deadly sin? A Retreat almost compels us to be more zealous: it reverses the popular maxim, that in religion there can be an excess of true zeal. Has there been a failure in externals, whilst cultivating things within; or have we attended too much to outward things, at the expense of those that are inward? A Retreat tends to equalize the balance between Martha's care and Mary's choice. Have we positively gone backward in the past year; have we fallen into definite sin, even into sin that is deadly? A Retreat gives us power to make a fresh start—and it is one of the marks of progress in the spiritual life, however paradoxical it may sound, to be always making fresh starts: a Retreat gives us power to conquer that which has conquered us, even after repeated confession and absolution—to conquer by means of renewed confession and absolution.

Take one suggestion under this head. In the course of the following Meditations, should spoken thoughts come home to the soul in a new, strange, or unexpected way, in regard to sin, avail yourself of the accident which opens a fresh line of introspection. Make a mental note of the sin, or its development; trace it from source to outcome; follow the feeders which conduct nourishment to it; be led by the suckers which draw support from it; and master its history in the past, as well as its present position in the soul. Such a hint may be taken as an inspiration from GOD, which accordingly is to be utilized.

3rd. Retrospection: a Retreat is a time for reparation. As isolation is suggestive of self-examination; so, in a Catholic conscious of sin in the soul as a result of examination, reparation becomes inevitable. Indeed, reparation is only not essential to be paid to GOD'S offended Majesty—of course, after sin has been treated as the Church commands, after and not before. In this matter, we must not deceive ourselves, nor allow ourselves to be deceived. Much cannot be done, under any circumstances, by the creature to the Creator, in the way of reparation. Still, the less that can be done, the greater becomes the obligation of doing that little. In union with the Person of JESUS CHRIST, little becomes of infinite worth.

Such is the course which the soul who seeks to be true and loyal to its dear LORD, even though it be weak and vacillating, will take in relation to the year that is gone. But, beyond this necessary reparation, if there be a sin once on the conscience, though now by GOD'S mercy forgiven; a sin which the world knows not of, though we can never forget it; a sin which has given tone and colour to the whole previous life, and which to an extent must tinge, or taint, even the renewed life of the future; a sin never altogether absent from memory in times of greatest peace, and painfully present in the hours of deepest penitence—if there be such a sad reality for any single soul, reparation may be made in retreat for this sin also. The saintly David, the man after GOD'S own heart, may with advantage be our model under this spiritual trial. His words must awaken an echo in our hearts; his acts must find a counterpart in our lives: "Wash me throughly," he cried, that is, over and over and over again, "from my wickedness, and cleanse me from my sin."

4th. Anticipation: a Retreat is a time for faithful promises of amendment in the future. This is the second result of introspection to the first, namely, reparation, in the case of a true penitent. It is a wide subject to treat with brevity in an Introductory Address. But this much may be said: In making promises to the soul, its director, or its GOD, for the conduct of our future life, we must ever seek the judicious mean. We shall prove our humility by not aiming, from the low level of an average life in the world, at the highest form of sanctity; though, if we seek not a comparatively high standard, at a standard absolutely beyond our own, we shall rise but little in the life above nature. We shall prove our honesty, earnestness, and devotion, by not promising to do that which we are already bound to do independently of all promises: for obvious duty, after penitence, is taken for granted. In short, we must exercise in this, as in most spiritual matters, Christianized common sense; we must follow the dictates of an enlightened and instructed conscience, as rational beings, as well as pious Catholics.

Each element in this fourfold course of action, will effect some good result on the soul. Isolation will take us out of self; and in solitude will reveal us to ourselves, as if we were another. Introspection will teach us what we have done amiss; and by self-examination will help us to become other than we are, as if we were aiding, not ourselves, but our brother. Retrospection will tell us what we have left undone, and show us how to make reparation for the past, in thought, word, and deed, in sins of commission and omission. Anticipation will enable us to promise in the future to do justly, to love mercy, and to walk humbly with GOD, our neighbour, and ourself. We know, or ought to have learnt, our powers; how to utilize the spiritual force which we possess; where to seek for that gift or grace in which we may be deficient. We know, or ought to remember, our weakness; where we have formerly fallen into sin, or when, or how, or why, or with whom; what may be our chief temptations; how to conquer our master passion or besetting fault. Let us make a mental valuation both of our weakness and of our power; balance one against the other in a spirit of confidence, love, and generosity; and decide to act accordingly as the HOLY SPIRIT may be pleased to inspire us.

This course will ensure, please GOD, that the things which we promise ourselves during this Retreat by anticipation to do in the future, may not require fresh reparation after fresh examination of conscience, when the present shall become the past, and we shall look back, if GOD so permit, in isolation on the coming year, from the standpoint of our next Retreat.

VI.

Two points only remain to be noticed: first, to offer a few remarks on the question of meditation in a Retreat; and secondly to state the subject-matter of the present series of Addresses.

1. What is an Address in a Retreat; how may it be described; how should it be utilized? Negations, perhaps, may convey indirectly to the mind what is a Retreat Address. It is not a sermon: it is not a lecture: it is not an instruction. At least, it is not any one of these, solely and alone. It contains and combines features and elements of all of them:

but it is more than any one, any two, or all three of these varied forms of Christian teaching. The primary object of a Retreat Address is not didactic, mainly or chiefly; is not edification, in the theological meaning of the word; is not, directly, hortatory. The vague term "address," or the non-scientific meaning of "meditation," expresses more clearly the intention with which the following topics for thought will be spoken, and the manner in which it is hoped they will be received.

In accordance with this idea, the present Addresses will be found more or less to declare to some persons certain outlines of Divine Revelation; to build up others in the Catholic Faith; and to encourage all to holiness of life, without which none can see GOD and live. But their principal object is not to present new thoughts for contemplation—rather is it, to recall to the mind old and half-forgotten truths, or to enforce on the conscience old or wholly neglected duties; and having brought them before the soul, to leave them there, to be dealt with as each separate Christian consciousness may be moved by GOD, the Holy COMFORTER, to deal with them.

The chief negation, however, to be remembered and acted upon is this—that a Retreat Address is in no sense a sermon, and must not be treated as if it were. The more part of any religious exercise which can be called a sermon is done by the preacher. Whether previously written, or delivered without manuscript, a continuous stream of thought flows from his lips to the hearts of his hearers; a stream too full, perhaps, of matter, and certainly too rapid in its course, to enable them to dwell, as it flows, upon the subject of the sermon. The listener, indeed, can intellectually receive the words of the preacher, may accept them, will even reject them, instantaneously. But it is impossible for him to meditate upon them at the time; and the usual circumstances which surround the delivery of a sermon do not always encourage meditation afterwards.

The larger part of an Address spoken in a Retreat, on the other hand, is done, not by the director, but by the person engaged in retreat. He who gives the meditation states his subject as deliberately, plainly, and unimpassionedly as he can, and as fully as time permits. He divides and subdivides; gives headings and points; directs thought or suggests it; defines, distinguishes, explains, illustrates in outline; gives a minute plan of his subject—and then leaves it to be completed and worked out in detail by those who follow with attention the lines of the argument. But, he does not attempt to exhaust any question which may be discussed. Indeed, so far is this from his aim, that it may almost be said, the more the director leaves to the capacity of the retreatant to supply, the more effective for the soul's good does the meditation become. Hence, to attend a Retreat Address is a mental exertion far greater than the act of listening to a sermon, for this reason amongst others: because, at its close, the preliminary labour only of the meditation has been done—the real hard work of the act of meditation has to follow. If people leave church at the close of a sermon, they lose next to nothing. If they fail to remain on their knees after a meditation in retreat, they lose nearly all.

A meditation in a Retreat may be described as the thoughts of one person penetrating and permeating the minds of many, growing there, and bringing forth fruit in due season. The speaker's thoughts are uttered aloud: and are addressed to his hearers, to his own soul, or to his GOD. In each case—to GOD, the soul, the hearer—those present make his thoughts their own. His words are listened to with such attention as the retreatant can command; are accepted at the moment without criticism; are mentally stored; and afterwards are brought forth one by one for self-consideration. I say "with attention"; for the thread of the meditation once lost can with difficulty be regained in the same sub-division of the subject: and "without criticism"; for a critical temper is absolutely at issue with the child-like mind of one who enters retreat in order to be taught. They must also be garnered, either by mental or mechanical notes, for the purpose of being recalled, one or more at a time—for closer examination or wider development than is possible at the moment of reception—as each one kneels amongst others in the church, or walks abroad alone with GOD, or retires to the more utter solitude of his own chamber.

To these qualifications, a warning upon one of them need only be added. Above all things of secondary, if not of primary, importance in a Retreat to be avoided, is criticism. Preachers are accustomed to be criticized. Whether or not they are affected by it, they do not escape criticism; they are always prepared for it; they often welcome it. But one who gives a meditation to others in retreat, would fain be free from criticism; not for his own sake, but for theirs. It does not, cannot hurt him; it can, it will hurt them. And freedom from criticism in the director does not mean absence of inquiry on the part of the retreatant: far from it. The more the former is permitted to explain or convince, and to justify or prove to the latter, on matters on which he has unfortunately been obscure, or has failed to carry with him his hearer, the greater is the priest's satisfaction. But this is not what the word "criticism" imports. Criticism, pure and simple, is destructive of sympathy, creates doubts, hinders devotion, encourages self-opinion, stops growth in holiness, and mars a Retreat. Therefore, avoid criticism.

2. A Retreat, to be self-contained, ought to have its own special subject of thought. Sin is the subject of the present Retreat—a large, momentous, and engrossing topic; Sin—considered not as an abstract theological proposition, nor as an important psychological question, nor (again) as an interesting social inquiry, nor (still less) as a mere moral problem: but Sin, as a most intensely practical reality, affecting, by temptation and commission, by repentance and forgiveness, by cause and consequence, in relation to both GOD and man,

the every-day life, the life in every hour, the life beyond the grave, of each individual soul of Christian man or woman. Sin—viewed from the standpoint of certain first principles of our holy Religion, and connected, more or less closely with the case of persons living in the world—such will be the subject-matter of our thoughts. And Sin will be treated under a threefold relation, from three several points of view, bearing upon the like number of divine facts or mysteries of the Faith.

It may be helpful to some minds to be able to examine for themselves, and to ponder beforehand and independently, the formal scheme of thought which will be developed in future meditations. Three being the number of the days of retreat, and three being the number of addresses on each day, it may be convenient to consider day by day each selected mystery or fact, in relation to each several Person of the GODHEAD. This, please GOD, will be attempted in the following manner. The main divisions of the great questions of the Faith will be treated, one on each day of retreat, in this order:

On the first day, the subject-matter will be GOD, the great First Cause;

On the second day, it will be Man, the image of GOD;

On the third day, GOD made Man, the union of the creature with the Creator—all in relation to Sin.

These main divisions will be further subdivided thus:

I. The question of GOD in relation to Sin will be treated with regard, (1) to GOD the Creator; (2) to GOD the Redeemer; (3) to GOD the Sanctifier.

II. The question of Man in relation to Sin will be treated with regard, (1) to Man created; (2) to Man purchased; (3) to Man inspired.

III. The question of GOD'S union with Man will be treated with regard, (1) to the Incarnation of GOD; (2) to the Sacrifice of the Cross; (3) to the Sacraments of the Church.

Each day will thus be devoted to the consideration, under

different aspects, of the doctrine of the Holy TRINITY with reference to the sin of man. Each meditation will be devoted to the consideration of one of the several Persons in the GODHEAD, and of the relations which that Divine Person bears towards man's sin.

Such is an outline of our topics for thought in the present time of retreat.

These are the simple, elementary, and practical truths of our holy Faith, which, GOD helping me, I desire to place before you in this Retreat; and this is the manner in which they will be presented for meditation. In effecting this purpose, it may be repeated, two main objects will be kept in view: first, to recall to the memory old, perhaps half-forgotten, truths in regard to the sin of man; in order, secondly, to recall to the conscience old, perhaps wholly-forgotten, sins in regard to the truth of GOD. It is not impossible, as one result of these meditations, that some truths may be placed in a fresh light to certain minds, and hence appear to be new when they are not; or, that some actions may take a different aspect in the conscience of others, and thus seem to be sinful, when formerly they were held to be sinless. But these will be exceptional cases. As a rule, truths known to be truthful, and sins acknowledged to be not without sin will alone be considered. Indeed, a danger to be avoided on the part of those in retreat is the neglect of the acknowledged and the well-known, because they are such.

In concluding this Introductory Address, I would recall to mind that you are about to examine certain first principles of faith, in regard to one of the chiefest practical mysteries of life—sin. You have come prepared to consider them quietly, deliberately, collectedly. I shall endeavour to place them before you as shortly as I can, consistent with fulness; and as simply, as plainly, and in as practical a form as possible. It will be your part, as my thoughts are uttered, to gather what fruit you may from each address; to take one or more points for further investigation; to work them out individually, according to your capacity, and at more or less length, as they shall prove themselves to be attractive; and to make such firm resolutions from them, suitable to your own personal sin, as GOD the HOLY GHOST shall inspire you to make. You came hither in retreat, for the purpose of meditation. Do not forget that your part in the labour is of greater moment than mine; nor that the work of Another is more momentous than that of either of us. After the power which is given to me, I indeed may supply matter for thought. According to your ability, you can utilize it. But what GOD is pleased to say to the soul, in the stillness and silence of solitude, is infinitely more important than anything that man of himself can conceive, or anything that man can impart to another.

VII.

We will conclude this Address as we began it, with prayer —prayer to the Sacred Humanity of JESUS—in the well-known words, *Anima Christi:*

> Soul of CHRIST, sanctify me:
> Body of CHRIST, save me:
> Blood of CHRIST, inebriate me:
> Water from the Side of CHRIST, wash me:
> Passion of CHRIST, strengthen me:
> O Good JESU, hear me,
> [And grant me . . .]:
> Within Thy Wounds hide me:
> Suffer me not to be separated from Thee,
> [And keep me from . . .]:
> From the malicious enemy defend me:
> In the hour of my death call me,
> And bid me come to Thee:
> That with Thy Saints I may praise Thee
> For all eternity. Amen.

These two prayers, the *Veni Creator* and *Anima Christi*, may with advantage be said, before and after each Address respectively, with a special intention for the object which the worshipper desires to obtain, or wishes to avoid.

First Day of Retreat.

GOD THE GREAT FIRST CAUSE IN RELATION TO SIN.

ADDRESS TWO.

GOD THE CREATOR OF MAN.

IN whatever light we may view Sin in the soul of man now, or in whatever aspect we may be led to regard Sin in the soul of man hereafter, it is well to begin our consideration of First Principles with regard to Man's Sin, by meditating upon GOD.

If we believe in the Church as a divine organization, and in her teaching as the voice of GOD speaking to our conscience; if we believe in our holy Religion as an objective revelation of truth, as a revelation which may be and ought to be examined, but must be received—this plan, to begin our meditation on GOD in relation to Sin, is both Catholic and logical. It is Catholic: for the Church in her teaching, as well as in her ceremonial and discipline, ever begins with GOD and ends with man. It is logical: because, under existing circumstances and with the conditions of Christian faith, worship, and duty, an argument cannot be maintained which adopts the opposite course, which begins with man and ends with GOD. As created beings, we ought to consider the Divine Person, in relation to Whom and against Whom that is committed which we call Sin, before we estimate the human person of him who commits the sin, and is the agent of it.

In all argument, human and superhuman, we need a

foundation upon which to build the edifice of the future; we need a starting-point from which to run the race of the present. In all argument, we must have a result to aim at, or a conclusion to discover. And between these limits we must advance from one stage to another in due order. Theology, the most exact and exacting at once of all the sciences, requires, or rather demands, within the range of its own sacred boundaries, the logical method of all scientific inquiry. Hence, even in the lowest division of theological science, which treats of sin, the mutual dependence between cause and consequence, from outset to result, must be observed. For, the principle of a Revelation and the fact of the Church being allowed, no system of faith exists that is more absolutely reasonable than the Catholic Religion.

We commence, then, with GOD, as the Source and Origin of all: GOD, the Creator, the Saviour, the Inspirer. We conclude, therefore, with Man, as one issue of such source, as one result of such origin; Man, created, redeemed, inspired. Others, indeed, adopt an opposite method. They begin with Man, and hope to end with GOD. They accept the creature, and seek after the Creator. They would gain the unknown through the known. Whatever may be the necessity in some cases, or the benefit in any, of this scientific method outside the pale of Christianity, its value is nothing worth within the obedience of our holy Faith, and there is no excuse even for its employment. Remember the history of the Tower of Babel: and take it as a parable on the effort of the natural man to reach unto GOD by the human process. Remember the inspired account of the Descent of the HOLY GHOST, in Tongues of Fire: and take it as the expression of GOD'S method of teaching the dogmas of faith to man. Hence, in religious matters, ever seek to realize what is to be believed by what has been revealed. Never strive to discover things of heaven by things of earth.

To what end does the opposite and false system of non-Christian argument lead? It leads, in one word, to idolatry.

Idolatry is the result of making man the basis of inquiry and the unit of calculation, instead of GOD ; of seeking to climb from earth to heaven, of striving to ascend from the realization of man to the conception of GOD. By whatever name known, under whatever form of words disguised, and supported by whatever eloquence or force, current theories of rationalistic philosophy are essentially idolatrous. They are reared upon the self-relying evolution of inherent, though created power, whether human or physical: and they are developed into its deification. Stripped of the sophisms of unbelief, and reduced to the language of common sense, these theories, be they in form Pantheistic or Humanitarian, make Nature to be Divine, and GOD to be Man. The philosophic statement, "GOD in everything," necessarily involves "GOD in Man:" and "GOD in Man" legitimately degenerates, for it is a clear descent, into the heresy that "GOD is Man"—developed, perfected, infinitized Man ; Man, magnified and non-natural. GOD, it is said, is Man infinitized—Man, only incomprehensible, eternal, infinite, uncreated, and independent. GOD, it is said, is Man perfected—Man, only more true, more holy, more pure, more beautiful, more just, more loving. GOD, it is said, is Man developed—Man, only omnipotent, omniscient, omnipresent ; in brief, Man, magnified and non-natural. Such is the popular, and to a large extent the fashionable, view of some theories of rationalism. But, theologically, the system which produces such fruit is false.

It were truer to say that Man is GOD, only not developed, not perfected, not infinitized. It were truer; because by, and in, and after the Incarnation of the DEITY, there exists an element of truth in this position. For now, since the GODHEAD has assumed to Itself the Manhood, MAN is GOD, and GOD is MAN. Now, in a sense, at the right hand of the GODHEAD and for all eternity, Nature has been deified, Humanity has been developed, has become perfected, has been made infinite.

But there is no truth in the converse proposition, as it is

popularly held—none. There is no truth in the theory that ever previously to, and now apart from, the Incarnation by the HOLY GHOST of the WORD of the FATHER, GOD was Man, is Man, or could be Man, under any condition of infinity, or perfection, or development. To hold this theory is to deify the creature disguised as an abstraction. All devout souls admit that, however the Supreme Being is pleased to reveal Himself, GOD under any form, in every place, and with all conditions, is to be adored. But to worship, with divine honour, even a created ideal, is idolatry. And the idolatry of human personality, of Man however transcendentally idealized—to one who knows himself as GOD knows him, as his Guardian Angel knows him, as his confessor knows him, even as his neighbour knows him—is of all idolatry the grossest and most debased. To the Christianized intellect, created of the FATHER, redeemed of the SON, inspired of the SANCTIFIER—in any case to the sinner—it is and it is realized to be, the idolatry of self.

We, Catholics, even in thinking about sin, one of the lowest, but not the least needful subjects of meditation, seek to begin with GOD, and hope to end in man. The Catholic theory, as we are taught to believe it, amounts to this: that Man was made in the Image of GOD; in the Image of the GOD-MAN of the future; in the Image of the Incarnated DEITY revealed in time; in the Image predetermined in the ages of ages, in which GOD and Nature, the Creator and the creature, were to become one. Hence, in order to verify the impression, we must possess the seal; in order to estimate the copy, we must realize the original. We must adore the Divine Object in its entirety and completeness, before we can hope to master the partial and incomplete reproduction of the human subject. The absolutely infinite perfection of GOD alone supplies a gauge for the almost infinite sinfulness of man.

II.

If we begin our considerations on First Principles in regard to Sin with a meditation upon GOD, and if, as we believe, our holy Religion is a rational form of faith, it is not unreasonable to inquire somewhat about the Divine Being; about His personality; about His essence, attributes, and operations; about the revelation of Himself to man.

This inquiry may take at least three forms. The first: Who is GOD? The second: What is GOD? And the third: How has GOD revealed Himself? Let us consider these three points in order. They can be here treated only with the concisest brevity.

I. Who is GOD? Theology answers: GOD is a Personal Being, one, sole, and alone. GOD is the one, only Being Who is self-originated, self-existent, self-subsisting. GOD is the one, only Person Who of Himself alone can use the words, or can assume the incommunicable Name, "I Am That I Am." As theologians say—He is, because He is. GOD is the Personal Great First Cause of everything visible and invisible; than Whom nothing is, nothing can be, nothing can be conceived, better or more perfect. He is a Person. And the Personality of GOD consists in His absolute, incommunicable existence—I AM—simple and uncompounded.

II. What is GOD? Theology answers: The essence, attributes, and operations which constitute the Person of GOD. GOD's absolute and incommunicable existence cannot be divided from His Divine Personality. GOD is. He is, because He is. But more may be said on two points. Firstly: God is what He hath. And secondly: GOD is what He doth. In other terms, His essence cannot be divided either from His attributes or from His operations. GOD's operations and attributes are the expressions of His own Divine Personality.

For instance. As theologians say: GOD is what He hath. In other words, when contemplating the attributes of a Divine Personality, it may be affirmed that GOD is not only good, wise, pure, beautiful, holy, loving: but that GOD is

Goodness itself, is Wisdom itself, is Purity itself, is Beauty itself, is Holiness itself, is Love itself. Again, theologians say: GOD is what He doth. In other words, when adoring the operations of a Divine Personality, it may be held that GOD not only acts justly, works powerfully, judges mercifully, speaks and does truly; but that He is Justice, He is Power, He is Mercy, He is Truth.

For the purposes, however, of devout meditation, we may venture in thought to divide what in fact and reality are indivisible: and in order to master even the elements of this side of theology, we must. We must separate the divine attributes from the Personality having; the divine operations from the Personality doing; and both attributes and operations from the Divine Essence which includes them all.

III. How has GOD revealed Himself to man? Theology answers: In many ways, chiefly in three. Firstly; through His Divine Individuality. Secondly; through the attributes and operations of DEITY. Thirdly; through the essential relations of the GODHEAD to the universe, as a Divine Person.

Something has been said of the first two revelations. Of the third, it may be added, that through the essential relations of the GODHEAD, the Divine Nature has been revealed in at least five principal ways; namely, in regard to time, to space, to power, to goodness and knowledge, and to humanity.

1. In regard to time, GOD has revealed Himself as Eternal and Everlasting: always existing and lasting for ever; not like the mortal life of man which has an end, nor like the immortal joy of bliss which has a beginning; without beginning, without end; as not affected or influenced by time. To GOD, the past, the present, the future are unchangeable and are one, as an always existing, all-pervading, everlasting present. GOD is His own changeless eternity.

2. In regard to space, GOD has revealed Himself as Infinite, Incomprehensible, Omnipresent. Infinite: as not subject to any condition or variation; incapable of increase, incapable of diminution; to Whom change or mutability in kind or

degree is impossible. Incomprehensible: not being bound by, nor contained within, any limits in substantial presence, whether in thought or reality, whether by word or act. Omnipresent: because He is in all things by His essence, as the cause of their being; He is in all things by His presence, because all things are present unto Him and open to His sight; He is in all things by His power, because all things are subject unto Him, the supreme Governor, Lord, and Master of all. GOD is all, and therefore is Infinite; GOD is beyond all, and therefore is Incomprehensible; GOD is in all, and therefore is Omnipresent.

3. In regard to power, GOD has revealed Himself as Almighty and Omnipotent: all-powerful in Himself, and powerful over all else and all other. Within Himself, He is absolutely unfettered by and irresponsible to, save in relation to the divine attributes, any necessity or consequence, either within or without Himself; His power is only limited by His will, and His will is only the expression of His power. Without Himself, He can do all things that are implied in the idea of power, though nothing that implies a want of power; all things that are compatible with His attributes, but nothing that presupposes their abeyance; all things that are possible to and consistent with His operations, but nothing that is inconsistent with them, or antagonistic to them.

4. In regard to goodness and knowledge, GOD has revealed Himself as All-good and Omniscient. GOD'S Goodness is supreme and absolute: GOD'S Knowledge is perfect and limitless. In His essential perfection, He is one than Whom nothing better, or holier, or more pure, or more true, or more peerless in beauty, or more boundless in goodness, exists, can exist, or can be conceived to exist. In His absolute knowledge, He knows everything, because He knows Himself, Who is the origin of all knowledge; He knows all things of Himself, Who imparts all knowledge; He knows all things out of Himself, Who made all things, and by Whom all knowledge consists.

5. In regard more especially to the human creation, GOD has revealed Himself as One Whose Divine Will is unchangeable, whether, as theology teaches, it be antecedent or consequent, whether it be efficacious or in-efficacious; Whose Divine Providence is absolute, be it ordained or permissive; whose Divine Predestination of man to grace and glory is certain and immutable.

III.

Thus have we ventured to inquire, though only in a superficial manner, about the DEITY—Who is GOD? What is GOD? How has GOD revealed Himself to man?—GOD, the one self-existent Being; the one, only great First Cause; the One, Living and True GOD, Who has created us in the past, Who preserves us in the present, and Who will judge us in the future, at the last Great Day.

But this inquiry deals only with one side of divine truth in regard to the DEITY. We have to meditate upon GOD, not only as One, but as Three in One, and as One in Three; on GOD the Creator, the Redeemer, the Inspirer; Three Persons, but One GOD.

These words represent to faith and convey to the soul of man the ineffable mystery of the Holy, Blessed and Undivided TRINITY: GOD, One in essence, substance, nature; Three in Divine Personality: One GOD, in Persons Three— 1. the Primordial, Unbegotten, and Everlasting FATHER, the Fount, Source, and Origin of GODHEAD; 2. the Eternally-begotten SON, the Logos or Sophia, the Word, Reason, or Wisdom of the FATHER, the Author and Finisher of Redemption to man, Very and True GOD, GOD and MAN, the MAN-GOD, JESUS CHRIST our LORD; 3. the HOLY GHOST, the COMFORTER or PARACLETE, the Inspirer, Sanctifier, and Advocate, the Cause of holiness to man, everlastingly and eternally Proceeding from Both the Divine Persons of the FATHER and of the SON.

GOD: in Substance One, in Persons Three. Meditate for a moment on these mysteries. GOD, in Persons Three; Co-eternal, Co-equal, Consubstantial; of equal power, dignity, and honour. GOD, in Substance One; a Personal DEITY, GOD blessed for ever. Amen. The SOVEREIGN, SAVIOUR, SPIRIT; FATHER, SON, and HOLY GHOST.

In Substance One. In the bold language of an ancient writer: GOD is infinite in glory; incomprehensible in greatness; super-excellent in power; incomparable in wisdom; immutable in goodness; unspeakable in beneficence. Infinitely good, says another, strong and powerful; invisible, but all-seeing; Himself immutable, yet changing all things; always in action, always in repose; great without quantity and bounds, good without quality, alone and sovereignly good; creating out of nothing, possessing without need, governing without labour, disposing without weariness.

In Persons Three. In the scientific rhythm of the psalm and creed in one, the venerable Symbol known by the name of S. Athanasius: the GODHEAD of each Divine Person of the Holy TRINITY, is all one, the Glory equal, the Majesty co-eternal; Each is uncreate, incomprehensible, and eternal; Each is Almighty, GOD, and LORD. I believe, says a Saint, that, One in Essence, Thou art Three in Persons; True GOD, of a simple Nature, spiritual, incorporeal, uncircumscribed; that there is neither above Thee, nor below Thee; that nothing is greater than Thou art; that Thou art perfect without imperfection, strong without weakness, fulfilling all things without expansion, omnipresent without locality; that Thou art terrible in Thy counsels, just in Thy judgments, impenetrable in Thy secrets, true in Thy words, holy in all Thy works, all blessed and blessed for evermore.

In Substance One, in Persons Three; yet, without confounding the Persons, or dividing the Substance. But we must always remember this further truth, which explains some mysteries and expands others. The ever-blessed Three in One and One in Three hold such divine and heavenly intercommunion, One with Another, and All with Each, that we believe in the doctrine of coinherence, or circumcession. The whole FATHER is in the SON and the HOLY GHOST; the whole SON is in the FATHER and the HOLY GHOST; the whole Blessed PARACLETE is in the Eternal SON and in the Everlasting FATHER.

IV.

There is no greater or more profound mystery than the mystery of Creation. GOD, all true theology declares, is from everlasting. Creation, all true science teaches, is of yesterday. There never has been a time when GOD was not. There has been a time before creation was. For ages of ages creation was not. In the ages of ages GOD was.

GOD was: One in Three; Three in One. One, in nature, essence, and substance; a simple, uncompounded existence; self-originated, existent, subsisting. Three, in Divine Personality; Whose attributes, whether affirmative or negative, we have thought of; Whose operations, divine and human, we have dwelt on. One in Three: the FATHER always begetting; the SON ever-begotten; the SPIRIT ceaselessly proceeding. Three in One: the transcendental relationships of Paternity, Filiation, Spiration, existed for ages of ages and from all eternity. But creation, and the eternal paradoxes which it involved, was of time.

GOD was: one and alone; self-contemplating, self-sufficient, self-absorbed; absolutely perfect in His completeness, absolutely complete in His perfection. He was: a complete and perfect Unity; a pure, free, and undivided Spirit; a simple, uncompounded Essence; dwelling in unapproachable solitude, in still silence, in unchangeful repose; one and alone. Yet creation, and all the relations which it involved between the Creator and the creature, was predestinated before time was.

Why was this condition of silence broken, this phase of repose changed, or this abode of solitude invaded? Why was this estate of perfection and completeness disturbed? Why were fresh relationships created, beyond Paternity, beyond Filiation, beyond Spiration? And why was creation willed outside the ineffable mystery of the One in Three and Three in One? Let us attempt in some measure to answer, with reverence and godly fear, these wide and unfathomable questions.

GOD was good, wise, true, powerful; was pure, beautiful, loving; was just and merciful; was perfect and complete in all the essential and relative attributes of His Divine Personality. He was also perfect and complete, wanting nothing, in His self-contemplation, self-sufficiency, self-absorption. GOD was good: but there was nothing on which to exercise divine beneficence. GOD was wise and true and beautiful: but there was no one to worship and adore His transcendent beauty, His absolute truth, His infinite wisdom. GOD was just and merciful: but there was none on whom to execute righteous judgment, or to show God-like mercy. GOD was powerful and pure: but there was none to dread His awful power, nor any to fear His yet more awful purity. GOD was loving: but there was nought—neither person, nor thing—to feel the warmth of His divine love. GOD was one and sole and alone; in the solitude of silence and repose; complete and perfect. Why was this solitude invaded by creation?

Again: in the absolute attributes of His Divine Nature, GOD was self-contemplating, sufficient, absorbed. Take but these evidences of Uncreated DEITY: His eternity, infinity, and incomprehensibility. GOD was incomprehensible: but, within the bounds of His super-substantial presence, there was none to own Him boundless, supra-local, or clear from all limitation. He alone could contemplate His own freedom from comprehension. GOD was infinite: but, subject to conditions of their own essential imperfection, there was none to pay homage to the infinite perfection of the Divine Being. He alone was sufficient for His own infinite requirements.

God was eternal: but, influenced by past, or present, or future, there was none to yearn after, to seek for, to enjoy eternity. He alone was absorbed in that which had no beginning, and in that which will have no end. God was alone in silent repose. Why was all this sacrificed to creation?

A change took place in the eternal counsels and inevitable decrees of the Unchangeable. It is difficult for human language to explain a divine paradox, or to do more than express the fulfilment of the divine predestination. But it pleased Almighty God to surround Himself with objects external to Himself; with objects made subject to time and space, made subject to imperfection and capable of restoration. It pleased the Self-contemplating, Self-sufficient, Self-absorbed, to surround Himself with objects which owed to Himself their origination, their existence, their protection; with objects which could contemplate Him, be satisfied with Him, and be absorbed in Him. It pleased the great First Cause to surround Himself with objects of love, who could love Him, whom He could love; with objects to whom He might show Himself good, holy, true, beautiful, and pure; with objects who would adore His wisdom, fear His power, respect His justice, crave His mercy. It pleased God—deepest and most inexplicable thought of all—to surround Himself with objects created by Himself, and external to Himself, with which and with whom, eventually, He might become one, in the union of the creature with the Creator. A change took place, and such was the result.

Why? There is, there can be, but one sufficient answer. In order to increase God's glory; that glory which theologians term accidental, and which may be increased; not His essential glory, which is incapable of augmentation. For God's greater glory was creation willed, and all that resulted from creation.

This is creation, from a single point of view. God willed to surround Himself with objects towards which He would bear certain relations, and which would bear certain relations towards Him. And further, GOD willed that creation should take, at the least, three forms. The first; in objects purely spiritual, or chiefly so. The second; in objects purely corporeal, or chiefly so. The third; in objects partly spiritual and partly corporeal—though this does not exhaust their constitution—which combined both elements. In other words, GOD willed the creation, (1) of Angelic Intelligences; (2) of what theologians call the Creature, all that is neither angelic nor human, the world, Cosmos; (3) of the crown and summit of creative power, the completion and perfection of creative wisdom, in GOD'S own Image, in the Image of the GOD-MAN of the eternal counsels and divine decrees—Man.

V.

Of these three forms of creation, we will confine our attention, on the present occasion, to the effort of creative power and wisdom which falls short of the highest—if we may be allowed to compare them—to the creation of Cosmos, the world, the creature. In this inquiry three principal points may be considered: Firstly; Who was the doer of creation? Secondly; How was creation done? Thirdly; What was done in creation?

I. Who was the doer of creation? The answer from a Christian and a Catholic must be: The great First Cause; a Personal DEITY; GOD.

A Personal GOD. It is of the greatest importance, at the present time especially, that we hold to this primary article of the Christian faith. Apart from physical science or philosophic subtleties in regard to GOD; apart from the false humility of knowing nothing and being powerless to learn anything of GOD; apart from the vanity of developing from one's cultivated consciousness a new definition of GOD, or the puerility of taking a mere humanitarian view of Him, it is the object of infidels to destroy our faith in a Personal DEITY. To place abstract Law in the stead of GOD; to place Nature and her forces in the stead of GOD, and to affirm that there is no GOD; to adopt the pagan idea of GOD being "the enduring power, not ourselves, which makes for righteousness," and to deny that man has a knowledge of Him Who is Righteousness—all these theories result in the denial of a Personal GOD: some of them end in a denial of the personality of man. Of late, indeed, the supporters of these and other heresies have emerged from the self-made mist in which they enveloped their disbelief, to find themselves notorious, if not popular. They have unmasked their opinions, and have more or less plainly avowed their conviction, in language understanded of the people, that they believe not in GOD but in matter, and not even in man, but in a human machine. Nature and her forces; Law and its results; even an Idea and what we may gather from it, are accepted by average men and women of the day, by men and women of more than average intellect and piety, in the place of a Personal GOD.

We believe, thank GOD for it, the Church believes in a Personal First Cause, GOD. However difficult to realize to oneself, however impossible to explain to another, we believe in a Person; One Who, outside Nature, willed creation; One Whose Will finds expression in Law, and with Whom Law is only the expression of His Will; One Whom it is not only possible to know, but Whom we do know; One Who not only without ourselves makes for righteousness, but Who is Righteousness, and even, when we are in personal union with Him, Whose righteousness becomes ours.

On the other hand, opinions to a large extent fashionable and popular affirm the opposite of these truths, facts, or mysteries. Moral beauty and moral excellence, literary experience, intellectual culture, and æsthetic refinement have taken the place of dogmatic faith. Men and women have in themselves fulfilled the awful prediction of the Prophet, that hearing they shall hear and shall not understand, and that seeing they shall see and shall not perceive. Personal Will is replaced by the unbending necessity of abstract Law; and the laws of Nature are supposed to be the cause, instead of the consequence, of what we know to be the Will of a Personal GOD.

In such cases, it is the wiser course, it is the more charitable part, to place truth and error, the Church's faith and man's opinion, in the plainest and most obvious antagonism, in all their naked incompatibility. Having done so, it may be well to leave the subject further untouched. It is impossible to demonstrate the one, even to ourselves. It is hopeless to attempt to disprove the other, at least to our adversaries. Two thoughts, however, may be mentioned which illustrate, without demonstrating, the Catholic dogma of a Personal GOD, of a personal great First Cause. When mentioned they may be left without remark. They both assume the low ground of probability, as it is suitable. They both suggest what we should believe from what has been revealed, as it is right.

1st. Man, to the largest extent we can conceive—and in spite of recent theories of human automatonism—is a personal agent. We cannot conceive any created being with a personality intenser than we feel and know, or more perfect than we are conscious of in ourselves. And man was made, we believe, in the Image of GOD; in the Image, that is to say, of the GOD-MAN of the future, of the MAN in Whom and by Whom the creature and the Creator became one. Can we then believe—whilst carefully avoiding any assent to the idea of GOD being a magnified, or non-natural man—that the image essentially differs from its model; that the statue entirely differs from its cast; that the architype in principle differs from its type? Can we believe, that a personal being such as we know and feel ourselves to be; a being, as we shall allow, intelligent, reflective, self-conscious, accountable, is the product of abstract Law, and a result of animated Nature? Christianized common sense, as well as enlightened human reason, fail to contemplate such portentous absurdities. If not created by a Personal Will, man was certainly not made by a machine: if not made by GOD, man was certainly not self-evolved from matter.

2nd. Man, in the enjoyment of the personality which he possesses, seeks to give expression to such personality by means of language. Naturally and instinctively and without prompting, he finds such expression in the words, I am. The simplest at once, and deepest of words. A child could say no less: a philosopher could say no more: I am. But this formula, by grammatical licence with which we are familiar in Scriptural expressions in regard to the DEITY, is the Name by which the Great GOD has been pleased to reveal Himself from the very first. The assertion, I AM, is indicative to man of the eternal, ever-present, infinite, almighty, all-knowing Personality, Whom we term GOD. Man instinctively adopts the form of words by which GOD would teach us to call Himself. And in the Image of GOD, man was made. The inference is too obvious to be insisted upon. GOD teaches us intuitively to say of ourselves what He has revealed to us, as the truth, of His own Personality. We are assured that the mysterious Name, I AM, denotes a Divine Personality in the One, Living and True GOD.

II. How was creation done? GOD the eternal, infinite, incomprehensible First Cause, the Personal I AM being the doer of creation, what—we may inquire—was His almighty mode of action? How was creation done? Revelation is distinct and exact in its reply: GOD spake, and it was done.

This is only a Scriptural way of stating one of the initial truths of creation, that with GOD to will and to do are identical. It must be so with a personal First Cause Who is almighty. The self-producing, all-powerful Will of GOD is the efficient cause of all things. With GOD, the power originating and the act produced are coincident with the will conceived. His attributes cannot be divided from His operations; nor can His essence be divided from either. He wills:

and what GOD essentially wills, through the attributes of such will, by the operation of such will, becomes. GOD spake, and it was done.

This is true whatever theory of creation may be adopted —so long as creation by a Divine Personality is distinctly admitted—whether it be immediate or mediate, absolute or conditioned. In any case, either actually or potentially, to will and to do are identical with GOD. GOD spake, and it was done.

Compare GOD'S method of creation with human work in two main particulars, and the differentia will appear in marked contrast.

1st. Observe; the one only thing which man can do, at all comparable in effect to creation on the part of GOD, is the production of force, resulting in motion. But force and consequent motion are only indirectly the result of man's will: they do not form the direct effect. Some intermediate agency of necessity exists between origin and issue, between the cause and the consequence. Man, the created, cannot work apart from such appliance of means to end. But the great First Cause of creation dispenses with such intermediate agency. With GOD to will and to work, or to will and to accomplish, are identical. GOD spake, and it was done.

2nd. Observe; even if man's work be comparable with the creation by GOD, another point of difference exists. Take the labour of the discoverer, the inventor, the philosopher, the chemist. At the most, each one in his several sphere of work, mental or bodily, produces fresh combinations or analyses of chemical simples or compounds; evolves new theories from acknowledged physical or metaphysical data; applies ingenious or useful adaptations of mechanical ways and means; conceives and elaborates different results from different causes, tending towards a given end. Between the action of both lies one essential distinction. Man labours upon substance made ready to his hand: he works with created matter. GOD works from that which is increate: He labours upon that which His own Almighty hand has made. In creation, out of nothing something came. The personal great First Cause created all things out of nothing. His will and His work were one. His work was the accomplishment of His will. GOD spake, and it was done.

III. What was done in creation? It would be a question more easy to answer—what was not done in creation, either absolutely or potentially, either in germ or in perfection, either with or without the power of reproduction or development? In creation, out of nothing all things came.

A few efforts of GOD'S creative power, common indeed, but commonplace only to the thoughtless, which may be seen in earth, or sea, or sky, are sufficient for our consideration.

Consider the siderial system; sun-rise, noon-day brightness, sunset glow; moon-light effects, or the starry heavens at night, or the milky way; cloud and mist and dew; storm and tempest; thunder, lightning, or rain. Again: consider the natives of the deep from whale to minnow, shell-fish or scaleless, the coral insect and sea anemone, fish snake-like or plumed or multipede—those abnormal creatures, half animal, half vegetable, half creeping, half flying. Or: consider the inhabitants of the earth, quadrupeds, bipeds, reptiles and insect life; or, its products, the vegetable and mineral kingdoms, rocks once instinct with life, and plants with almost the power of sensation; or, its natural, chemical, or scientific forces, fire, and gas, and steam, and electricity.

These elements of creative power, in their result, may be considered in two ways, alone and in union.

Consider them apart, individually. Think of their number and countless variety. Note their uniformity and infinite differences. Observe the prodigality, almost the recklessness in reproduction, of Nature; and withal, its severe and divine utilitarianism. And mark the order and regularity of the law of GOD'S will in creation; and that, in spite of apparent anomaly, and sometimes of obvious exception.

Consider these elements together, in combination. Take any region of GOD'S earth, whose leading features or prevailing characteristics can be indicated rather than described, in a few words. Take the ice-fields of the poles; the luxuriant vegetation, or the prolific animal and countless insect life of the East and West; the sandy plains and trackless deserts of north Africa or central Asia; the flood-like rivers, primæval forests, and giant mountain peaks of tropical or sub-tropical regions. Take the fauna or flora of any given country; or the products beneath its surface and on its coasts; or its industrial resources, its natural advantages, its climate and temperature, its geological structure or superficial configuration. Or, to speak of home: take the mixture of wood and water, of hill and dale, of cloud and sunshine, of flower and verdant grass, which constitute the incomparable beauty of English landscape scenery.

Consider these facts in, these results of, GOD'S creative power; and remembering the former questions and their answers, Who was the Creator? and How was creation effected? take them as an inadequate reply to the last inquiry proposed—What was done in creation?

VI.

The subject-matter of our meditation now claims our closer and more direct attention: GOD the Creator of man in relation to sin.

In regard to the material creation, we have attempted to answer three elementary questions which may be recalled by the interrogatives: Who, How, and What These questions naturally suggest inquiries into relations which exist between the author, the manner, the results of creation, respectively, and sin.

Existing circumstances prevent our dealing with all three

relations. Into the deeper mysteries, higher truths, and more intimate facts connected with sin in the abstract and its details in human life, there is no occasion to enter. What sin is, in relation to GOD and man ; why it is sinful in the creature, and its mode of affecting the Creator ; how human sin is compatible with a personal First Cause Who is both All-powerful and All-good; in what manner creation ministers to, is an excuse for, or may be made the instrument of, man's sin; and the cause, result, punishment, or cure of committed sin—these points we will not consider. We may well be content to accept the teaching of the Church, or of devout reason, on these and kindred topics in regard to sin : that man's free agency co-exists with GOD'S almighty Will ; that sin is sinful because by it man fails to fulfil the object of GOD'S creation ; that no created thing can make man sin, or is an excuse for man's fall ; that sin once committed is an objective reality in the soul of man, independent of all subjective impressions which may be formed of it, a reality which can only be dealt with by GOD'S own power, either mediately or directly exercised.

Accepting then these elementary propositions, let us turn to the thought of sin in general, as bearing upon the relations which exist between GOD the Creator and created man; and by sin, let us agree to understand conscious, wilful, deliberate opposition from a created being, who is accountable for the gift of free-will, to the Will of his Maker.

As a rule to which there is no exception, the creature, Cosmos, created matter, together with angelic intelligences and human beings, have this law impressed upon them, capacity to fulfil the object of their creation, power to do the Will of GOD. As a rule with one exception, creation, human, angelic and material, does fulfil its object, does exercise its power—to do the Will of GOD : of course, at the present time, apart from the origin of evil and the fall of the Angels. But, to confine our attention to man and matter ; all GOD'S handiwork in the world, with one exception, loyally fulfils His almighty Will. It is nothing worth to urge in extenuation, that the exception alone is capable to offer opposition to His Will; for such power, whilst it confers additional privilege, is burdened with corresponding responsibility.

In any case, however, the exception to the general rule of creation is not found in matter. It is confined to man.

Take the commonest examples, which are equally conclusive with the least common. Does not the sun rise and set with daily regularity; or, does not the moon perform her monthly course; or, does not GOD'S ocean ebb and flow with wonted order: and what is such order and course and regularity but the fulfilment of GOD'S Will in the object of creation? Do not the seasons, Summer, Autumn, Winter, Spring, keep to their divinely prescribed order: and what is such allotted sequence but the fulfilment of GOD'S Will in the object of creation? Do not the birds and insects build their nests, the beasts and fish increase and multiply, trees and herbs bring forth fruit after their kind, and all creation, animate or sensitive, take the means assigned to each for protection, rest, enjoyment and support of life: and what is the following of a natural instinct, but the fulfilment of GOD'S Will in the object of creation?

Take, again, another class of phenomena. Have not certain minerals and plants properties poisonous or harmful to human life? Have not certain others properties which benefit and sustain human life? And was it ever known, under the like conditions of the bodily frame, that these properties were changed from injurious to beneficial, or from nourishing to poisonous? Cannot the chemist, by the union of certain gases in certain proportions, to speak popularly, cause the presence of atmospheric air; or by the withdrawal of one gas from union with another, cause common water to become absent? In either case was it ever known, under the same conditions, that like results failed to follow? And what is this, in both cases, but the fulfilment of the Will of GOD in the object of creation?

Hence, in chemicals, minerals, plants, the sea, and heavenly bodies, we perceive the Law of GOD, the expression of the Will of the personal great First Cause, fulfilled with the same scrupulous fidelity that we observe in the case of the animal creation, of birds and fish, of beasts of the field, and of insect life.

There is one and only one exception to this otherwise universal law of created things. Man forms that single exception. Man is the one and only work of GOD'S almighty hand, created with the definite object of fulfilling His Will, and possessed also of the power to fulfil His Will—man alone fails in the object of his creation, fails to fulfil GOD'S Will, fails by reason of sin.

How can this truth be brought home to the human heart, through the instrumentality of created nature? Perhaps somewhat in the following manner.

Make choice of any one of the creatures of GOD before named and exercise upon it intelligent and devout meditation. For instance: Stand in spirit upon the shore of some boundless ocean. Carefully examine this creature of GOD under various aspects, from many points of view. And then bear witness to its conformity to the Will of its Creator; how it entirely fulfils the object of its creation. For example—

Contemplate its extent, which is unknown; its capacity, which is incalculable; its depth, which is unfathomable; its waves and drops which are countless: speaking, in each case, without scientific exactitude. Contemplate its ceaseless ebb and flow, orderly and regular, uniform even in its want of order and regularity; or, its constant agitation, like the wicked, never at rest; or, its angry billows when roused by the stormy wind and tempest; or, its sullen, heavy, rolling swell, suggestive of further mischief, when the storm has ceased; or, its transparent mirror-like surface in a dead calm. Contemplate its undiminished bulk, though always evaporating; its stationary limits, though constantly augmented; its permanent saltness, though perpetually diluted by rain and river water.

Contemplate, again, its loyal and faithful adherence to the object of its creation and to the Will of its GOD—in its properties, in its bounds, in its capacity, in its stillness, in its action, in these few details, with regard to itself. Contemplate its powers, active or passive, in regard to its fellow-creature, man: either motionless, at GOD'S word, its drops would drown him, its depth would cover him, its weight would crush him, its saltness would poison him: or in motion, at GOD'S word, its waves would wash him away, engulf him, suffocate him, dash him in pieces, almost annihilate him.

Contemplate, as if in the immediate presence of GOD the Creator, and in the actual presence of this creature of GOD, the question of sin. Compare this effort of divine power and its results, with the highest act of creation, and the way in which man fulfils the object of his existence. This inanimate, non-sensitive, incorporeal, soul-less creature of GOD; a creature which yet bears the impress of some of its Maker's attributes, in its everlastingness, immensity and power, in its immutability and vastness; this creature, in endless different ways, perfectly fulfils the object of its marvellous creation, absolutely performs the Will of the Great GOD Who made it. Man, on the other hand, with an organization physical and mental which this creature of GOD lacks; with powers and gifts and qualities incomparably greater than this creature possesses; with bodily frame of unequalled perfection, with mental force of untold capacity, with intelligence comparable to the Angel-host, and with a spirit in communion with the GODHEAD—man, I say, fails to fulfil the divine object of his creation, fails to perform the pure Will of the GOD Who made him. This one creature of GOD, the boundless ocean, is a constant witness to and protest against the sin of man; is an immutable example of fulfilling the object of its creation, in contrast with man who fails to fulfil such object; is an instance of absolute conformity to the intention of its Maker, in opposition to the action of man, who willingly, consciously, deliberately, goes counter to the Will of GOD, by deliberately, consciously, and willingly committing an act of sin.

Any other familiar object in GOD'S book of Nature would be suggestive of the like train of thought. For instance: a ceaselessly flowing river; the everlasting snow; the starry heaven on a dark night; a storm at sea, or in the plain when seen from a mountain top; the instinct and habits of animals, or their organic construction; the results of chemical experiment; marvels disclosed by the telescope or microscope; a common wild flower, a leaf, or a blade of grass.

Ordinary objects, and their history, which can be realized by ordinary minds, are sufficient to bring before the conscience of man, man's sin in the abstract and in relation to GOD the Creator. The fact of their existence, and by existence the fulfilment of the object of their creation; the results of their existence, and by such results the performance of the Will of GOD, is enough to produce this thought in the soul of man: Why do these creatures of GOD perform His holy and pure Will implicitly, and not I? Why do I form the one, solitary exception to GOD'S creation which loyally and faithfully obeys His divine and universal law? Is it reasonable that the creature which has received so much less from His almighty hand should return so much more? Is it meet and right that man, who has received so much more, infinitely more, should return so much less, infinitely less? How can I, in the presence of and surrounded by an obedient, faithful and loyal creation, fail to fulfil the object of my creation? How can I venture to place my human will out of harmony with, and even in opposition to, His Almighty Will Divine? How can I, who know the blessed gain of conformity, and who know the unutterable loss of disobedience—how can I do this great wickedness and sin against GOD?

ADDRESS THREE.
GOD THE REDEEMER OF MAN.

IN meditating upon GOD the Creator, in relation to the sin of man, we have been led to think of one great truth of the Christian Religion. We have been taught to hold the doctrine of the Personality of the Great First Cause, that GOD, the Eternal FATHER, is a Divine Person. In meditating upon GOD the Redeemer, in relation to the sin of man, we shall be led to consider another great truth of the Christian Religion, namely, the Divinity of our Blessed LORD. The Church teaches her children that JESUS is GOD.

This elemental truth, that JESUS is GOD, is almost axiomatic in the Catholic Faith. It meets us, either practically or dogmatically, on many occasions in theological inquiry: and wherever and whenever it may be met with, the truth must be accepted by all faithful Christians. Consider this truth briefly from both points of view.

1st. It is dogmatically true, that JESUS is GOD. S. John the Divine assures us that in the beginning, in the ages of ages, before time was; when GOD was one, sole and alone, abiding in solitude, silence, and repose, the Self-originated, existent, subsisting; then, the Logos, the Divine Word, the Wisdom of GOD of the Elder Covenant, the JESUS of the New Dispensation, was, was with GOD, was GOD.

This dogma, held from the very first to be fundamental, is held and has been held, according to the Vincentian formula, at all Catholic times, in all Christian places, by all faithful people. A chain of evidence exists, binding the present with the past, that the Catholic Church has ever believed this cardinal doctrine, on the Person of GOD the Saviour. The Nicene Symbol which, by our present office, all recite before they receive the Holy Communion, defines it: GOD of GOD, Light of Light, Very GOD of Very GOD. The Creed of S. Athanasius expands and develops it: The right faith is, that we believe and confess that our LORD JESUS CHRIST, the SON of GOD, is GOD; GOD of the substance of the FATHER; GOD, Perfect GOD; One, One altogether GOD. Holy Scripture testifies to it, and has placed on record in what consisted from the first the teaching of the Church. To Catholics it is only needful to recall a few isolated passages, to remind them of the truth. Take the language of S. Paul to the Colossians, that CHRIST is, "the Image of the Invisible GOD": or, his words to the Hebrews, that the SON of GOD was the express "Image of His Person": or, his statement to the Philippians, that JESUS was "in the Form of GOD." Take the words of the Divine Master Himself, when He was pleased to proclaim His Own GODHEAD: "I and My FATHER are One," He said to the Jews; "I AM," He affirmed, using the Incommunicable Name of DEITY, when adjured by the High Priest; "I am in the FATHER and the FATHER in Me," and "He that hath seen Me hath seen the FATHER," He declared to the inquiring Philip—I AM, Whom mortal man hath not seen, nor can see and live, the Fount of GODHEAD, the One, Very, Living, and True GOD.

2nd. It is practically true, that JESUS is GOD. It is a theological necessity, when we affirm CHRIST to be the Saviour of the world, that we likewise presuppose JESUS to be GOD.

In the Christian economy, in relations in which the Creator and the creature come into contact, the divine element, from the nature of things, must precede the human. Take, as one instance amongst many of this law, the mystery in which the elements divine and human more intimately mingle than in any other theological fact, with the exception, perhaps, of the Incarnation of GOD. I mean the mystery of the Holy Eucharist. The Bread and Wine must become the Body and Blood of GOD, before the Sacrifice can be offered: the sacred Offering of the Holy Body and the Precious Blood of CHRIST must be made a Sacrifice before it can become a Sacrament. It must become GOD and be offered to GOD, before It can be accepted for man or bestowed upon man. Nor is it otherwise in regard to the redemption of the human race. The Second Person of the Holy TRINITY, incarnated for man, must be GOD before He can become the Saviour of the world. This will be more clearly seen, when we meditate on the mystery of the Incarnation. Let it suffice now to assent to the truth, practically not less than dogmatically assured, that the Man, JESUS of Nazareth, our Redeemer, both was and is GOD.

II.

The Divinity of CHRIST is a truth specially to be enforced at this day. Of the fulness of Catholic teaching, this doctrine is widely held to be out of date, a mere relic of the past. It is examined and criticised, assented to or rejected from without, as an interesting historical speculation, descended from a former age, but apart from any intimate connection with the present. It is not treated in any degree with the respect due from fallible man to a divine revelation. Efforts are constantly made to extol the Man, JESUS, at the expense of GOD, CHRIST our Divine Master; to elevate the Manhood, and to lower the GODHEAD; to make much of the human nature, by obscuring that which is the divine; even to patronize the Son of Mary, whilst venturing to ignore the SON of GOD.

Amongst nominal Christians, perhaps the most offensive form which such heretical teaching assumes, is one that, with a somewhat pretentious idea of restoring popular veneration for the Bible by means of essay-writing, seeks to restore it after eliminating from GOD's Holy Word much that displeases popular prejudice, or offends popular ignorance. This, to a large extent, is effected by simple means—by the easy method of asserting a self-constituted right to judge Scripture as men judge any other book; and of acting upon such right, by weighing the evidence for or against its contents, with a modern critical standard. The like treatment is adopted towards both the actions and the words of our Divine Master; in either case with little felicity, from a Christian standpoint. Internal evidence, on the words only of CHRIST, estimated by the inner consciousness of the reader, produces strange results. The theory of a germ of historical truth, more or less concurrent with fact, developed by an incapable but presumably honest editor of a later date, who clumsily added to, or transposed, or annotated the recorded words at his disposal with the best moral intentions, which however, practically ended in literary forgery—such a theory is hardly compatible with the fact that the Historical CHRIST of the Gospel was GOD. Nor is the theory more easily accommodated to the fact by allowing the undoubted truth which underlies the opinion, not very reverently expressed, that "JESUS was over the head of all His reporters." Those who accept such a theory, which no doubt includes an element of truth—and on such grounds is the more dangerous as enunciating a half-truth—not unnaturally decline to believe in the absolute Divinity of our Blessed LORD.

This theory may be allowed to be the offspring of a talented and cultured intellect. But, however cleverly worked out, so far as it is destructive of opinions more anti-Christian than itself; and however brilliant and playful in style and often original in thought it may be, this theory displays no depth and little learning on its constructive side, and is disfigured by the profoundest egotism and self-complacency. Moreover, it is as faulty in criticism as it is false to Christianity. As an intellectual exercise, it is impossible, from the text only of Holy Scripture and the positive evidence alone at our command, to divide the Historical CHRIST from the GOD of theology. Criticism has its office in religion; but it has, too, its bounds:

and tradition determines the one and regulates the other. To descend to the level of disbelief, in the domain above indicated, it may be, as it has well been said, that much the CHRIST uttered, or is reported to have said in the Gospel narrative, would have been simply unbecoming had JESUS been only what modern criticism affirms, a devout and well-meaning Enthusiast; would have been utterly unworthy had JESUS not been what the Church has ever declared Him to be, the Very, Living, and True GOD. Apart from Catholic tradition, handed down by Divine protection, the only external source of knowledge whence a picture of the Man, JESUS CHRIST, can be drawn is the four-fold Gospel narrative. The more complete the portrait, the more perfect and larger must be the acceptance of the inspired history, or biographical record. But the same documents which indicate the Manhood, declare the GODHEAD of CHRIST: and it is not easy with any respect for criticism, it is impossible for sound judgment, to draw the line between the acceptance of the one and rejection of the other. Of course, the sceptic, or liberal in religion frees himself from all outward bondage. He is ruled solely by his inner consciousness. But, for Catholics, it is at once un-critical and un-Christian to judge by our inward feelings of the external realities of our holy Faith; or to decide upon the credibility of various statements of fact, or records of speech contained in the account which we believed to be inspired. And even an advanced rationalist might with benefit remember the qualification with which his asserted right to judge Holy Scripture was once made. "I take up this Work" said a deep thinker, "with the purpose to read it for the first time as I should read any other work—as far at least as I can or dare: for I neither can nor dare throw off a strong and awful prepossession in its favour."

Not to those without, however, is the DEITY of our LORD GOD as important, as to those within the fold of CHRIST'S Church. To us it is a matter of life and death—essential to our belief. A doctrine of the Church, the "Communicatio idiomatum," helps us to realize this stupendous truth, that JESUS is GOD. To the communication, or inter-communion, of properties in the Divine Personality, we must hold unflinchingly, both dogmatically and practically. The union of the two Natures, in one Person of the CHRIST is so perfect, that properties of either Nature in the concrete may be rightfully affirmed of both. This truth may, of course, be applied in opposite directions, to the DEITY of the CHRIST as well as to the Manhood of JESUS. It may not be needful to enforce this dogma of the perfect Humanity of CHRIST in regard to His GODHEAD ; but it is not needless to insist on the truth of His DEITY, in all that affects His earthly and human life. As one doctrinal result of this truth, we believe, not only in general terms, that the Historical CHRIST is the GOD of theology ; but definitely, that each act and word, each thought, desire, and feeling of the Man JESUS was the thought, desire, and feeling, was the act and word of GOD, the Second Person of the Holy TRINITY.

This truth is admitted in theory. But in practice a widespread inconsistency appears. Popular Sabellianism denies to Mary the title and honour of the Mother of GOD : and half-hearted Catholics withhold the veneration and devotion due to her, as the logical result of such relationship towards her Divine SON. Popular Protestantism denies to the sacred Species on the Altar the title and honour of the Body and Blood of GOD : and half-hearted Catholics withhold the adoration and worship which is due to GOD'S Majesty whenever He may be revealed and under whatever form He may be present. Short of actual heresy, many fall into a train of thought and habit of speech, or into a mental position that seeks to escape the inevitable by inaction, which practically leads thither. Some, who allow that CHRIST became Incarnate, shrink from the thought of GOD as a helpless Babe ; or decline to say of Him, that GOD died upon the Cross. Many who believe in the Catholic doctrine of the Eucharist, deny that GOD has delegated His power to man in the Sacrament of Absolution. And few, comparatively, are consistent and bold enough to avow their belief in the efficacy of human works, satisfaction for sin, or the doctrine of merit, in union with and not severed from the sacramental life of GOD in man.

We must accustom ourselves to contemplate the Divine Master as GOD on earth once, as GOD in His Church now: now, supernaturally, in the Holy Sacraments, once, according to nature, in the flesh. These two aspects must not be divided, if we would accept in anything approaching to entirety the Catholic Faith. Rather, they should be worked out into details which it is impossible to enter upon here, in either aspect of His holy life. For instance: we should accustom ourselves to think of Him as GOD in each event of His sacred career; in every act He undertook; in all the deeds done to Him; in the words He spake, or were spoken to Him or of Him; in the very thoughts that He willed to entertain. In all these cases, the thought or the word of JESUS, was the thought or the word of GOD; the act of or the deed done to JESUS, was the act of or the deed done to GOD.

It is not otherwise in the life above nature which He is pleased to dwell in His Church on earth. We should accustom ourselves to think of our Divine Master as GOD in every Sacramental outpouring of His grace. We should witness no child made Christian, no youth confirmed with sevenfold gifts, no Sacrifice offered or Eucharist given, no absolution pronounced over a penitent sinner, no marriage vows blessed and made indissoluble, no character conferred in Holy Order, no soul prepared for its last flight—without seeing in each Sacrament of the Church an extension of the Incarnation and the infusion of the Sacred Humanity of JESUS amongst His members; without perceiving in the results to individual souls the will and the work of GOD, in the name and by the power of GOD.

In fine, JESUS is GOD in the sacramental system of His Church; and GOD Incarnate on Mary's knee or Joseph's arm.

JESUS is GOD at the font and the altar, in Confirmation and in Confession; as well as GOD in the cottage, at the carpenter's bench, in the temple, by the sea-shore, in the fisherman's boat, on the mountain-side in prayer. JESUS is GOD at the marriage feast, and in the sending forth of ministers, whether in the Jewish or the Christian Church. JESUS is GOD at the death-bed of His saints and servants; GOD, whilst Himself kneeling beneath the olive-trees, standing before Pilate, mocked and scourged in the Judgment Hall, led along the Via Dolorosa, fastened with cruel nails to the fatal Cross, laid in a tomb wherein never yet had man been laid—Very and Eternal GOD, Who made us, Who was sacrificed for us, Who will judge us at the last Great Day.

III.

Another point, not less important than the Divinity of JESUS, leads us nearer to the subject-matter of our Meditation—GOD the Redeemer of man in relation to Sin. It is this: Not only was every act and word and thought of our Divine Master the thought, the word, or the act of GOD; but all that He did, all that He said, and all that He thought, was done, was spoken, was conceived as the Saviour of the world.

Observe: the union of the Creator with the creature was in no sense caused by the sin of man. Yet, the Incarnation once determined, determined before all ages; and GOD, in the nature of man, having willed to atone to Divine Justice for man's sin: then, it may be reverently imagined, in devout meditation, that the whole earthly life of the GOD-MAN was devoted to the end in view; that not only the whole life, but each portion of it, bore reference to the redemption of mankind; that each thought, every word, and all the actions of JESUS had their origin in a special intention for the salvatorial work by the Sacred Humanity. The earthly life of JESUS, of course, is one portion only of the mystery of the Incarnation in reference to the element of time, and viewed as a continuous act, in the past, the present, and the future. But of its three-fold division—in which we may contemplate its anticipation, its fulfilment, its consequences—the mortal life of our LORD stands midway between His life of glory before and His life of glory after His humiliation respectively. To this period, namely, from the Conception to the Passion, we may confine our considerations on the salvatorial life of the Redeemer of mankind.

Some would restrict the salvatorial work of the CHRIST to the Passion of JESUS, or even, under an extreme pressure of argument, to the last act of that sacred drama—His Crucifixion. Such a partial view of the divine mystery is at once unworthy and cramped. The work of redemption extends on either side of the awful centre of it, both in the past and in the future. Not only the last days, but every day; not only the last minutes, but all the years of that sacred life were salvatorial in character. Each moment given to the work of redemption, specially when instituting means of extending the Incarnation already done, and of applying the Sacrifice not yet fulfilled, bears such a character. Much more, the intercessorial and sacramental life now, whether in heaven or on earth, which is forgotten by some and denied by some, is salvatorial. Every action of our Divine LORD'S earthly life, together with the intention with which it was performed, anticipated its mediatorial function. The like may also be affirmed of each word and all the thoughts of CHRIST. But more than this is true. CHRIST still ever pleads His Passion-merits; He still ever vivifies His Sacramental gifts. He does so, as being GOD. He does so, as being the Saviour of mankind.

One further thought in this part of the question deserves careful consideration. The fact that GOD is the Redeemer of man, and the relation which this fact bears to human sin, find their practical outlet only in the solution of the most momentous of all moral problems—How to live well, so as to be prepared for a good and a holy death? As human beings, men and women living in the world, we want something more definite than abstract propositions, and consequent relations, to guide us and upon which to lean, through life to death. We want a model; a practical model; a living and accountable model; a model which we not only may, but must follow. Such a model exists. It is to be found in the great Pattern and Representative Man, Whose life on earth as GOD is at once the expression of the fact that He is the Saviour of the world, and the explanation of the connection between His salvatorial work and human sin.

How are we to imitate so perfect an example, that our life may be a preparation for death, and that death may be the beginning of our true life? I answer, in two ways—First: by believing, with the entire powers of our soul, all that flows from the double truth that the Child of Mary, perfect Man, was also Perfect GOD. The Catholic faith is only truly held when men are content to believe in, and after they believe in to worship, the Divine Model. Secondly: by seeking, with the whole effort of our will, to become one with this Divine Model. Catholic practice is only faithfully fulfilled when we are content to follow, though infinitely far off, the footsteps of His most holy life; when we are content to do all which is implied in the effort to model our imperfect lives after the imitation of CHRIST. To a Catholic these two elements of imitation are but one: for the Model cannot be perfect if it be not Divine; and if the Model be Divine, we are bound to the completest form of worship, its entire imitation. We may therefore confine our thoughts to the outward expression of the inward truth, that the life of the Pattern and Representative Man was the life of GOD upon earth; and we must strive after its imitation in the three-fold form in which it is presented to us in the Gospel narrative. In the imitation of the earthly life of JESUS, we must follow His Life of Obedience, His Life of Labour, and His Life of Self-sacrifice. These three sources of imitation rise from the like number of divisions in our LORD'S life; and they represent also three of the main marks or notes in the life of man who seeks perfection. The possession of the Divine Model will enable us to test, from time to time, our imitation of it ; and the contemplation of the perfect pattern, in the like conditions of our own life, will tend to stimulate our energies when they are tempted to flag, and to encourage our devotion which is sincere and persevering. These three divisions in the sacred life of JESUS may be considered one by one in order.

IV.

Of the many marvels which surround the sacred life of JESUS, perhaps none involve more divine paradoxes than are contained in the Life of Obedience—the Creator being obedient to the will of the creature ; the All-wise and Powerful being obedient to the un-wise and weak ; the Sinless obedient to the sinful ; in a word, GOD obedient, directly or indirectly, to man. The Life of Obedience extended from the Conception to the twelfth year of the Divine Boyhood. Nazareth, Bethlehem, Egypt, Nazareth again, all and each speak of obedience either to GOD or man. For instance—

Firstly: the Incarnation in the cottage-home of Nazareth declares the obedience of the Everlasting SON to the eternal counsels of GOD the FATHER, before the foundation of the world ; obedience to the mind and will of the Infinite, by which the Creator and the creature were to become one ; obedience to the absolute foreknowledge of the DEITY, Who saw in the ages of ages the fall of man, and was pleased before time was to predestinate man's recovery ; obedience to the tender mercy of GOD, Who would not leave mankind without a Divine Model, in order to enable man, prevented by grace, to work out his own salvation with fear and trembling.

Secondly: the Nativity in the manger-cradle at Bethlehem next preaches in our ears obedience to the powers that be, in regard to earthly nationality, government, law, and taxing.

There was no vague and general obedience to political order or regulation; it was definite and exact, within its proper limits, even to a foreign and conquering power. So far as GOD'S holy law was not invaded by man, the obedience of CHRIST, not only in birth, but through life, even unto death, was decided and perfect. The Divine Master did not refuse to pay the tribute money to the usurping Cæsar. He did not decline to reply to the interrogation of the sinful High Priest when adjured to answer, or, as we should say, placed upon His sacred oath, in a trial of life and death. And this is the more noteworthy, because the imperial government was heathen not Jewish, and the home government was not pure but most corrupt.

Thirdly: Pagan Egypt testifies to the obedience of the Perfect Man to the inspiration of GOD; and suggests that in whatever way the divine warning may reach the soul—by unwritten tradition, a printed book, words spoken, the promptings of conscience, the actions of friends or enemies, dreams, or our Guardian Angel—the supernatural prompting be not neglected. The Holy Infant left His native land, fled to an idolatrous country, returned to His own home—all, equally, at the word of inspiration. Observe here the mode of inspiration. Some of us hold the doctrine of Guardian Angels to be slightly superstitious; and neglect altogether the warnings of dreams. Yet, the Child JESUS was obedient to a heavenly dream. He fled from Nazareth and returned from Egypt, both at the instance of a heavenly messenger. Even if dreams never practically affect our life, does our Guardian Angel never interfere, by suggestions, promptings, outward events, or inward movings? Does GOD'S inspiration never reach our soul by unlikely, or unusual, or unexpected means; or even by the ordinary warnings of conscience? But if it be so—do we respond to the inspiration; do we obey it with the obedience of the Divine Child of Bethlehem?

Fourthly: Nazareth, again, in its sweet home-life, teaches us obedience in the subjection of the Infant JESUS to His

F

Ever-Virgin Mother and aged Foster-father. And who were they to whom He was subject? Mary, whom all generations call Blessed; the one, only peerless woman, spotless from sin; in whom the greatest of all miracles was accomplished, when the Prophet's words were fulfilled, that a Woman should compass a Man, and GOD was born of Mary. Nor was He obedient only to Mary; but also to Joseph. Do we think enough of him, that venerable man, in relation if not to our Lady, at least to our LORD? What should we consider our dignity and honour to be, if counted worthy, like that great Saint, to stand in the place of Spouse to the Virgin Mother of GOD, and of Foster-father to the Infant CHRIST; to be allowed the privilege of protecting the one, and to perform the awful part of teaching the other? What high pre-eminence is here? Let us never forget this, in thinking of S. Joseph. Let us not forget, apart from all details, that to him, as well as to Mary, for twelve long years of childhood, was subjected in obedience, as a Divine Model for us men and for our salvation, the Eternal SON of GOD.

How does this fourfold aspect of the Life of Obedience affect us, in regard to sin? As the life of the Pattern and Representative Man, in all probability it affects us nearly. As the Life of GOD upon earth, in which every action was, by the intention with which it was performed, salvatorial in character, it certainly affects us intimately. The obedience we have considered, as a note of our Divine Master's earthly life, was the obedience of childhood. But obedience does not with us end in childhood. It did not end there with Him. Obedience, different in form and manner from that of childhood, but obedience still, is often, more often than not, lifelong. It is lifelong from at least one of three causes—social, domestic, religious. We may be placed by GOD in a position of earthly dependence; or, we may place ourselves under authority in the world; or, we may enter the religious life, or into spiritual relations, which involve direction on the one hand and submission on the other. In each case, the obedience of the Divine Child may be an example and encouragement to us in our dealings with sin.

What may be supposed to be our Blessed LORD'S measure of obedience, and its kind to GOD and man, to Holy Mary and the Saintly Joseph? What was the obedience which the Infant GOD paid in His Incarnation, His Nativity, His Flight, and His Home Life? What were the characteristics of Nazareth, of Bethlehem, of Egypt, of Nazareth again? The answer is short. The obedience was perfect and complete. Yes: certainly; for the obedience was the obedience, not only of Man, but of GOD. But what were the features of this perfect and complete obedience? It had three main features, if we may reverently say so. It was prompt, cheerful, unquestioning. Can we say the same of our obedience, in our religious, domestic, or social life?

In order to answer this question, it is only needful to suggest three short considerations for our own examination of conscience. 1. The obedience which is not prompt, but dilatory, was not the obedience which the Holy Child paid to the Virgin Mother and Foster-father of GOD. 2. The obedience which is not cheerfully rendered, but grudgingly and sulkily, was not the obedience paid to Mary in the domestic and family arrangements of His early youth. 3. The obedience which is yielded only after questioning and arguing, was not the obedience given to Joseph in the carpenter's shop by the SON of GOD. And remember this—the less comparable to Mary and Joseph are those whom we are called to obey, by reason of human infirmity, the more comparable is our obedience to that of JESUS. And the more we cultivate in our obedience promptness, cheerfulness, and a spirit which is unquestioning, the greater, in theological language, is our merit.

Such were some of the more marked features in the Life of Obedience of the Child of Mary. Of all of them we must ever remember that they were performed with a special intention for the salvatorial work, for the fulfilment of which, under existing conditions, GOD was pleased to become Man.

V.

CHRIST'S Life of Labour extended from His twelfth year to His thirtieth, a period of eighteen years. It began with the words: "Wist ye not that I must be about My FATHER'S business?"

These words form a remarkable gloss upon our Divine Master's life of labour. As the world holds, these eighteen years extended over the very time in which He was not about His FATHER'S business. That began, in the world's opinion, when the Life of Labour was over, and the Ministry had been entered. This fact teaches an important lesson to us. It is one which is specially needed in this existence of haste, agitation, excitement, and want of repose, even in good works. Our FATHER'S business does not mainly or exclusively consist of active philanthropy, or practical benevolence, as such. The Divine Child, at the legal feast, in GOD'S House, in the midst of the Doctors, both hearing them and asking them questions, in fact being catechized, was about His FATHER'S business. The holy Jewish Lad, Youth, and Man (in all reverence be it spoken) was, during His life of labour, subject unto Mary and Joseph; shared with His Mother the household cares of the sacred home at Nazareth; performed His accustomed religious duties as an Israelite indeed; learnt His Foster-father's mechanical trade, and practised it in the sweat of His brow, to obtain the necessaries for the family support; and lived the ordinary life of an ordinary village carpenter until His thirtieth year. And in all these aspects of life, the Saviour of the World was about His FATHER'S business.

"Wist ye not." Mysterious words are these; but they are true. They teach a lesson to at least four different classes of persons amongst ourselves. 1. They are a lesson to the young, before the beginning of active life, in preparation for the ceaseless fight with the world, the flesh, and the devil which is in prospect—a lesson to take all available means of preparation for the conflict, and not to be anxious to begin before the time appointed. 2. They are a lesson to the aged, as our mortal life draws to a close; when the fight is nearly over, and we have to give way to younger and stronger, if not abler men; when we have to live on the recollection of the past, rather than on the anticipation of the future; and when we are fain content to be ministered unto rather than to minister—a lesson to rest and be thankful, if we have in any measure been faithful to our trust; and to gather up the fragments which remain of our allotted span of life, that nothing be lost. 3. They are a lesson to the sick, disabled, invalided, or those whom GOD is pleased to withdraw for a time from the conflict, or even permanently; to those forced to view plans begun which have been left unfulfilled, or completed by another, or developed as we wished or wished not, spoiled or perfected as the case may be—a lesson of conformity to GOD'S blessed Will and of faithful acceptance of it, however opposed to our dearest wishes. 4. They are a lesson to those who periodically give up themselves more exclusively to the affairs of their soul and the concerns of the next life; who enter a yearly Retreat, or keep Advent and Lent duly, or observe other religious exercises with devotion; who retire from the fight, in order to return to it refreshed and strengthened, conquering and to conquer—a lesson of patience with self in times of inactivity; of patience with others when they oppose or misinterpret such relaxation; of patience with GOD, Who may not see fit to furnish us, at once and immediately, with all that we may desire or think needful.

But, in spite of these lessons, how often do the young complain of their time of preparation for active life; how little do the aged bear with equanimity their time of incapacity; how much do the sick dislike the feeling of being a burden to others; and how impatient is the world with us, even if we are not impatient with ourselves and GOD, for the need or the privilege of seasons of retirement for deeper spiritual exercises. In all these cases, the teaching of the Divine Child is the same: "Wist ye not that I must be about My FATHER'S business?"

If a lesson of inaction, however, for due and sufficient cause, may be learnt, still more may a lesson of active work, from the Life of Labour of eighteen years. Of them, indeed, little is recorded, but much may be conceived from a devout and chastened imagination. Take the ordinary features in the life of the Divine Carpenter, Perfect GOD and perfect Man. He rises early, and late takes rest, and toils the livelong day. He helps to support His Saintly Mother and aged Foster-father; and then, after S. Joseph's death, alone supports the widowed Virgin. He is employed in the hard work of a common mechanic, in a trade dignified for ever by such divine and sacred association. Heat and cold, at various seasons of the year, alike oppress Him. His fare must be poor; His clothing, scant; His pallet, ill-covered and hard. He has to bear heavy burdens and use great exertion; to feel fatigue by day and weariness by night. Few can be His pleasures outside His duty: and sorrow, pain, sickness, death, are not kept from His lowly hearth. Such is no exaggerated picture of our Divine Master's life of labour for eighteen long years. Let us picture it to ourselves, and see how much, or how little, it accords with our easier, our more self-pleasing, our less exacting life.

What was the main characteristic of this Life of Labour? Perfection—will be the answer. Yes: it was perfect. Perfect —because the Divine Artificer was both GOD and Man. But what may have been the features of this perfection? We may venture to say that they were three-fold. The labour of CHRIST'S Childhood, Youth, and early Manhood, in all its details, was punctual in point of time, persevering in manner of doing, and honest in the intention in which it was done. In order to compare our labour with that of the Divine Model, it may be sufficient to ask three simple questions, and to allow them to be answered in the silence of the heart. Can we say the like, or anything comparable to it, in regard to our work for GOD and the soul in our spiritual existence, or for man in our worldly condition, in social, domestic, or religious life? First: Is the work we do, either for GOD or our neighbour, done at the right time? not hurriedly? not delayed? neither before, nor after its proper moment? This is the first essential in good work. Secondly: Is our work, for ourself or others, done with perseverance? not distractedly, nor fitfully? now and again, inconstantly? not carelessly and indifferently? without mind and heart being in it? This is hardly of less moment than the first requisite. Thirdly: Is it done honestly? in the best possible way, under the circumstances in which we are placed? and to the best of our finite power, as being sinners and not saints? If not; if not done with punctuality, with perseverance, with honesty, our work is not done after the example of our Divine Model; our life is not comparable with the Life of Labour of the Pattern and Representative Man.

Had the Life of Labour of JESUS lacked these three elements of perfection—punctuality, perseverance, and honesty—it had not been, as we believe that it was, under the influence of a divine intention, in each act of these eventful years of the life of the Redeemer of man; it had not been, as we know that it was, in character salvatorial.

VI.

The divine Life of Self-sacrifice of JESUS CHRIST lasted for three years.

No need is there to dwell on the closing scenes of the Passion of JESUS to learn His divine Life of Self-sacrifice. Short of that awful completion, each episode in the three years' ministry of GOD and Man was a distinct act, and was intended by the Author of it to be a distinct act, performed for us men and for our salvation. Indeed the Life of Obedience and the Life of Labour, as well as the Life of Self-sacrifice, possess severally their own special value and place in the Atonement of our Divine Master. As learning to act, as doing little or nothing, as surceasing to act is equivalent to doing GOD'S blessed Will punctually, perseveringly, and honestly in positive work; so self-sacrifice in the ministerial life of CHRIST is of equal moment for our salvation with the several acts in the sacred Passion of JESUS. This truth is too much lost sight of, in our estimate of the Redemption of mankind. We think, not too much, but too exclusively, of the mysteries of Calvary; not at all, or far too little, of the three years' Life of Self-sacrifice. Hence, we obtain but a partial view of that divine life on earth. Our redemption had lacked perfection, had one act of that three years' life been wanting. Thank GOD it was not wanting. The Self-sacrifice of the Pattern Man, Who is our Divine Model, again, was complete and perfect.

The Life of Self-sacrifice follows, in the supernatural order, directly from the Life of Labour, as the Life of Labour follows from the Life of Obedience. We are members of a body corporate, yet we are one. Sacrifice of will is implied in Christian obedience; and sacrifice of action is implied in Christianized labour. But a Catholic does more, in any life to which he may be called, freely and willingly, than he is bound to do of obligation. And this, because the Master's Life is our model. After a Life of Obedience of twelve years, and a Life of Labour of eighteen, comes the Life of Self-sacrifice of three; not of compulsion, but of free will, voluntarily. One single drop of the Precious Blood, sings S. Thomas Aquinas in his beautiful hymn, *Adoro Te devote*, could ransom all the world from all its guilt. But our Blessed LORD was pleased to shed It all. One single day of Self-sacrifice would have been sufficient to satisfy Divine Justice for the sins of the whole world. But He was pleased to pass a Life of Self-sacrifice of three full years' duration. In these conditions may be found the explanation of the truth, that the ministerial Life of Self-sacrifice was in character, also, salvatorial.

Consider a few points in the three years' life of the Divine Master, GOD and Man, each one of which, equally with the facts of Calvary, bore their part in the sacrifice for us men and for our salvation. Consider the Teacher of righteousness, His career just begun, after forty days of physical discipline and mental anguish, carried into the solitary wilderness to be tempted. GOD Incarnate was personally tempted by Satan, as none other was ever tempted; in the very presence of evil, in a manner we cannot realize; even ministered to by created Angels, as we may be ministered to, if we ask—as we are ministered to, though we ask it not.

Consider, again, a side of the Life of Self-sacrifice of GOD, different to many which we are wont to associate with the redemption of man—the social gatherings of His earthly career, at one of which He performed His first miracle; the marriage and other feasts which He attended, to an extent that made the World, public opinion of the day, compare the more obvious asceticism of the Forerunner with the supposed unmortified habits of the LORD and Master. Or, the acts of corporal and spiritual mercy which He performed, in the abodes of rich and poor; by the road side; as He journeyed; in the chamber of death; at the open grave. Or, the life of ceaseless teaching and preaching to the multitudes in public; to His disciples in private; in the field, by the way, from a boat, on the sea-shore; to one timid man by night; to one lone woman in the daytime, as He sat thus by Jacob's well.

Consider, again, other incidental evidences in the same Self-sacrificing Life, over and above His ceaseless wandering and not having where to lay His sacred head—being hungry, weary, disappointed, destitute, persecuted, angry, lamenting, sympathetic, loving—evidences of nearly every human passion, and of many of the pains, hopes, feelings, and desires of the natural life of a Perfect Man.

VII.

The Life of Obedience, of Labour, and of Self-sacrifice, if we omit from consideration the Passion-life of JESUS, exhaust the divisions into which His earthly career may be separated, and the sources of imitation from which we may seek to follow the example of our Divine Model. But there was another life of CHRIST, which He was pleased to live and from which we may gain wisdom, although we can only follow it in figure ; and it was an existence above nature. This was the Life of Glory ; His life after the Resurrection. After an Infancy of twelve years, an Adolescence and Manhood of eighteen years, a public Ministry of three years, there was a Life of Glory of forty days. Perhaps more was effected in the Redemptorial Life of CHRIST, for us men and for our salvation, in the glorified life above nature of forty days, than in the three-and-thirty years of the ordinary, earthly career of the Child at Nazareth, of the Youth in the carpenter's shop, of the Lord and Master of twelve disciples. But in any case, the glorified life of the great forty days must not be entirely neglected, in any estimate we may form for our imitation of the Pattern and Representative Man.

The thirty-three years' work of JESUS, GOD and Man, related chiefly to the present. His forty days' life was concerned, almost exclusively, with the future. The Glorified JESUS during this mysterious sojourning superhuman amongst men, reduced to practice the system which He had previously established in theory. Now, divine means were adopted, both to extend the fact, and also to apply the results of the Incarnation to the salvation of the human race, upon principles formerly asserted. This change from theory to practice was typified by the change which passed over the Manhood of CHRIST. It was perfected ; and as such it became subject to new conditions. According to the Apostle S. Paul, it became subject to incorruptibility, to glory, to power, and to spirituality—four new conditions; and according to the Fathers, to other three, impassibility, clarity, and agility.

In the Scriptural account of the great forty days, it is less difficult than in the years of His mortal career to view the GODHEAD of the CHRIST in the Life of JESUS; to see in His acts and His words, both speech and action for the salvation of the world. What may have been His salvatorial work, it may be asked, during this time of existence above nature? Translated from the narrative form, in which it is recorded by Inspiration, into the language of theology, the work of the Glorified JESUS was the foundation of the Catholic Church; the organization of that Divine Society which should cause the events of the tiny land of Palestine to become of universal import.

"He spake," we read, "of things concerning the Kingdom of GOD." Amongst other things, perhaps, nay, certainly, we may believe that He spake of these: the principles and foundation of His Kingdom, in a right belief based upon true authority; the government and ordering of His Kingdom, by an ordained priesthood; the rights and customs of His Kingdom, by Canon Law; its worship and sacrifice, in Catholic ceremonial; its discipline, in morals; the mode of dispensing its gifts and privileges, by the seven holy Sacraments of the Church. Nor were these all the things of which He spake. Provision had to be made for a history of the past, for decisions at the present, for teaching in the future. Holy Scripture and tradition, the decrees of councils and creeds, moral theology and casuistry—these words suggest many topics, which cannot be discussed, but which are all connected with man's salvation by GOD, in the superhuman work of the great forty days.

Our Divine Master's Life of Glory is fairly comparable to the sacramental life of grace in man. In this connection our seven-fold sacramental life may be profitably reviewed in relation to GOD, to GOD'S image, to the creature of GOD, and to the soul. Time will allow of two points only being here considered with brevity. Take these two cardinal points, and with them let us test our lives by the Divine Model set before us—Communion and Confession.

1st. Of Holy Communion. As a priest meditating with Catholics, I will venture to ask three elementary questions: 1. Do we receive the Divine Gift as often as we might and have the opportunity, of course under spiritual guidance? and do we make a habit of worshipping GOD daily in the sacrifice of His own appointing, and not rather take some easier form of daily divine service—easier, in regard either to time, or strength, or mental exertion? 2. Do we make due preparation for, and offer worthy thanksgiving after, the reception of holy mysteries; by the previous use of confession, if we are conscious of sin, and by afterwards acting faithfully up to the gift given in communion? 3. Do we come to the Altar in the highest state, bodily and mental; with a recollected spirit, and a frame free from the reception of food—not, observe, fasting out of penitence, but abstaining from reverence? There is no surer method to gain more privileges in the way of celebrations than to use those which we possess frequently, nay, ceaselessly; to use them worthily, before, at, and after reception; to use them in the manner in which the Church has always commanded them to be employed.

2nd. Of the Sacrament of Confession. High privileges presuppose deep responsibilities. Frequent penitence ought always to go hand-in-hand with oft reception. If we are frequent communicants, are we in the habitual use of confession—habitual, which by no means necessarily implies a frequent approach to the sacrament? Again, as a priest meditating with Catholics, I will venture to ask two elementary questions: 1. Do we prepare ourselves for an ordinary confession as we hope to prepare ourselves for our last? Or, do we feel the need of confession less than we once felt it; and seek it less often, less carefully, less penitently, less fervently? Or, do we confess the same sins over and over again, and repeat them after absolution, and take no sufficient steps to conquer them? And, 2. Are we tempted, being out of heart with want of success and wearied of fruitless striving, to give up confession; to give it up, not in theory, but in practice; to give it up as a sacrament, needful in itself, needful for many, for us once, for some always; but not needful for us, not needful for us now? Are we tempted to listen to popular and infidel objections against confession; to ignorant and un-Christian arguments; or even to misguided and pious sophisms—that the sacrament causes us to lean on another, makes us morbid, makes us self-conscious, prevents self-reliance, enfeebles and enervates the conscience, and places a human being between ourselves and our GOD?

In either case, compare our sacramental life with the Life of Glory of GOD our Saviour, in regard to the sin of man. Observe the latter by its results in the history of GOD'S Church on earth, of which the great forty days' preparation was only the precursor. Consider the former as we know, in our inmost conscience, that it exists; and should any marked discrepancy appear, let us determine to make our sacramental life more conformable to the Life Divine.

VIII.

The practical lessons of the Life of Glory, and their application to our own existence are too extended and involved to be dwelt on here. But, in regard to the other divisions in the earthly career, according to nature, of our Divine Master we may meditate. It may be assumed that, more or less faithfully, we do act up to our Model in our life of obedience. We remember the lessons of Nazareth, of Bethlehem, of Egypt, and of Nazareth again. We are obedient to the counsels of GOD; to the powers that be, ordained of GOD; to the direct inspiration of GOD, by spiritual agency; to the indirect inspiration of GOD, by human agency. And our obedience in religious, domestic, or social life is prompt, cheerful, unquestioning. It may be assumed also, that we act up to our Model in our life of labour. We do not forget the Life of Labour of our Divine Master: whether by action or inaction, we seek to imitate it either as youth or aged, both in sickness and in health ; and our labour in the state of life to which it has pleased GOD to call us has been marked, after our feeble efforts, by punctuality in point of time, by perseverance in manner of doing, and by the purity of intention with which our work has been done. All this, and more than all this, may be allowed. But over, and above, and beyond these another life has to be spent.

The Life of Obedience and the Life of Labour, in the case of our Blessed LORD, only led to, and were only fulfilled in the Life of Self-sacrifice. What does conscience reply to our inquiries under this last division of our mortal life, if indeed our life of obedience and labour has led us, after His imitation, to a life of self-sacrifice? Can we conscientiously say that, not indeed in the spirit of our Divine Model, but after our own weak power and feeble will, we have done, as we allow that we ought to have done, more, in any life to which we may be called, freely and willingly, than, as Catholics, we are bound to do of obligation? Have we attempted to do this in the spirit of self-sacrifice, with consistency, generosity, enthusiasm?

Take two common-place points in the outward life, either of which may well represent the index of the new life; the disposition of our time and the employment of our money. A religious Jew, under the elder Covenant, gave to JEHOVAH one-seventh part of his time and one-tenth part of his money. This was given as a matter of course, which involved no especial merit, and at the least. A devout Christian holds this law to be the *minimum* of dedication of self and substance to GOD'S Majesty and GOD'S representative, under the New Dispensation—not the *maximum*. He who has received all from GOD, even the will and the power to return to Him a proportionate part of His benefactions, gives a tithe of money in charity to GOD'S Church or GOD'S poor, and worships daily, actually or in intention, before GOD'S holy Altar. It is not otherwise in this division of his higher life, than a Christian finds it to be in his mundane life of obedience and labour. He is bound to obedience to others, and to labour for himself. But over and above the claims of duty to GOD and of charity to man, he voluntarily does that which he is not forced to do of obligation. Such is the life of self-sacrifice to a pious Catholic.

On both these forms of self-sacrifice in daily life a few words may be said.

1. The Altar-worship of GOD is not only the highest form, and the only really effective form of sacrifice, but it is the sole manner of worship of the Creator by the creature ordained of GOD. As the Paternoster is the LORD'S own prayer, and as the Psalter may be called the LORD'S own prayer-book, so is the Sacrifice of the Altar GOD'S own office of divine worship. As such, it contains, or may be made to contain, every element of Christian devotion, prayer for self, intercession for others, adoration of GOD; hymns and lections; worship, thanksgiving, and praise. Little need is there to disparage other forms of divine worship. Still less need is there to exalt the Hours of Prayer at the expense of the Holy Eucharist, or to prefer what is undoubtedly of human origin to that which is of divine obligation. It may not be given to all, though it is given to many, to abide there, where the holy Oblation and pure Offering are made daily: yet the number of daily Eucharists is, thank GOD, increasing yearly. But, it is given to all, in health and strength, to join in intention daily, by an act of spiritual communion, with the sacrificial offering of some given Church, which each one may know of or know. It is a duty, as well as a privilege, to join in such spiritual offering. It may be effected by the use of a psalm, a hymn, a Gospel-lection, certain acts of devotion, and an Eucharistic prayer: and that day may be accounted a wasted day for grace, in the life of self-sacrifice, in which no effort has been made, however feebly, after Spiritual Communion.

2. It is a noteworthy fact, in the account given in the Gospel of our Divine LORD'S Judgment, at the last great day, that He condemned the wicked for having failed to perform towards His members upon earth the works of corporal mercy —the lowest in the scale of charity. In these days, by reason of the organization of society and division of labour, it is not easy, nor indeed is it possible, for every one literally to fulfil the Evangelical precepts, to feed the hungry, to clothe the naked, to visit the prisoner, and to nurse the sick, as ordinary rules of life. But there is no question, in all cases where the power of personal compliance is impossible, that the Gospel-law may be kept in spirit and by deputy. If persons cannot give their time—cannot, that is, in fact, not in choice—they can give their money; and time is money in the present day. None are too poor to give something, however little; and those who can afford to give but little of their substance, may be able to give, in proportion, more of their labour, of their thought, and of their time.

In relation even to the lowest form of charity, acts of corporal mercy, there are institutions for almost every form of human distress, suffering, and sin. And in connection with any one or more of these institutions, the life of self-sacrifice may, to a large extent, even if on a low level of spirituality, be led. If you can give only of your substance, in money, in the spirit of self-sacrifice, it is good. If you can also give personal attendance, in the same spirit, it is better. If you can give both time and money, it is best of all. It would be inconvenient to individualize any one object of charity, or any class of subjects. In regard to them, I am anxious that the more wealthy should do something beyond their present action in the way of helping their poorer brethren with the substance which GOD has lent, not given, to them; that the less wealthy should give more of their time and influence, of which they are equally the stewards only, if not of their money; that the poorer should seek to help one another and encourage one another, in ways in which the more wealthy are powerless to do, in acts of charity and in works of love. And I shall consider this Retreat to have failed in its effects on the souls of those who have joined in it, to the same extent as it fails to induce all, whatever may be their worldly lot, to do some one definite thing, known only to themselves, their Angel and their GOD, more than, over and above that which they are now doing, and beyond their present standard of good works for GOD, GOD'S Church, GOD'S poor, in the spirit of the Life of Self-sacrifice of our LORD and Saviour JESUS CHRIST.

IX.

Thus have we seen that three characteristics of the Divine Life, which began at Nazareth and ended with the Passion, are Obedience, Labour, Self-sacrifice. If we believe in such a life being a Representative and Pattern Life, we must believe that such obedience, such labour, such self-sacrifice are for us, one by one individually, a pattern to be imitated and an example to be followed. By thus personally, and so far as we are able, acting up to these three characteristics, we may best realize to ourselves one aspect of sin in relation to the Second Person of the Holy TRINITY, the negative side, by its avoidance; and we only can fulfil in practice its positive precepts by striving to act up to the spirit of the motto we have before spoken of, that "Life is the preparation for Death."

Have we thus imitated our Divine Model? I will assume that, more or less faithfully, we have acted up to the imitation of CHRIST in our life of obedience; and that we have duly fulfilled our appointed life of labour. But besides and beyond labour and obedience, it may fairly be asked: Have we adopted, voluntarily and deliberately, the life of self-sacrifice? I do not mean only or chiefly in things of Religion, but in those of the World; in things amongst which the larger portion of our life is passed; in things comparable in our earthly pilgrimage to those instances which we have

G

considered in GOD'S Life of Self-sacrifice on earth, the life which He was pleased to live for three full years.

Ask yourself, Brother or Sister in CHRIST, before we conclude this present Retreat. Ask, and get an answer from your soul. Ask, and be sure that the answer is in conformity with the thoughts, the feelings, the resolves, the determinations which this Retreat, however feebly, may awaken in your soul. What have I done in the past, what may I do in the present, what will I do in the future, please GOD, beyond the claims of obedience and beyond the law of labour, for GOD; GOD'S image, man; GOD'S creature, my own soul—for GOD'S sake? Having done in the past all that is of obligation, shall I follow in the future the pattern of the Divine Model and Representative Man, in the spirit of self-sacrifice? Or shall I, GOD forgive me, act in the present, as if the life of self-sacrifice, which to some is an attraction and to some is a necessity, were to me but a counsel of perfection, which is not meant for such as me?

Our obedience, indeed, with every accidental and personal advantage, may not be, cannot be, as perfect as that of the twelve years' Life of Obedience of the Divine Infant at Nazareth, at Bethlehem, in Egypt, at Nazareth again. But it may be, it must be, at least marked, after our imperfect capacity, by the three cardinal features which the Holy Child's exhibited. It may be, it must be, prompt, cheerful, unquestioning. Our labour, indeed, may not be as perfect as that of the eighteen years of the Life of Labour of the Divine Carpenter at Nazareth. But it must, at least, to be in any extent an imitation, be marked with the features of CHRIST'S human Labour. It must be punctual, persevering, honest. Our self-sacrifice, man's self-sacrifice, will be, more or less, through life, imperfect; for selfishness is a vice never wholly eradicated from human nature, and seldom entirely conquered or held in check. Yet, at an infinite distance, we may humbly hope to imitate the Divine Sufferer in His three years' Life of Self-sacrifice, absolute and supreme. We may not only do much, if not all that is required by the law of obedience and labour; but we may do something, if not much, that is expected from us by the law of self-sacrifice. We may have the will, and, with the will, the power given to us to obey, voluntarily, the law of self-sacrifice, because, and in so far as, we have obeyed the obligations of the law of obedience and of labour. And whilst we have thus faithfully acted during our mortal pilgrimage, in firm belief in the one motto, that "Life is the preparation for Death"; we shall be blessed in our latter end, by realizing the truth of the other motto, that "Death is the beginning of our true Life."

ADDRESS FOUR.

GOD THE SANCTIFIER OF MAN.

THE Third Divine Person of the Holy TRINITY—it is a fact to be accounted for—fails to occupy the position which He ought to occupy, in the thoughts, the feelings, the interests, the aspirations, and even in the prayers, of Catholics. Yet we, Catholics, live under that dispensation in which the Divine Third Person is at once and successively the preventing Influence, the continuing Force, the perfecting Agency and Fulfilment—the dispensation of the SPIRIT of GOD. The HOLY GHOST has now been given by the Eternal FATHER, because JESUS is now glorified. The COMFORTER has now been sent by CHRIST, because JESUS would not leave His Church and Spouse widowed and comfortless.

The Third Divine Person of the Holy TRINITY fails to occupy the position He should in the thoughts, interests, and prayers of Catholics. Yet is He the LORD and Giver of Life; Who proceedeth from the FATHER and the SON; Who with the FATHER and the SON together is worshipped and glorified; and Who spake by the Prophets. Yet, it may be added, is He the Originator and Inspirer, the Vivifier and Sanctifier of the Church's Sacramental system. For without Him, and apart from His divine co-operation, there is no regenerating Influence; without Him, there are no seven-fold codfirmatory Gifts; without Him, there is no sacred and supersubstantial Presence; without Him, there is no absolving Power; without Him, there is no grace of Holy Order; without Him, there is no holy Matrimony; without Him, there is no strength-giving Viaticum for the dread passage of the valley of the shadow of death. There are none of the seven

Sacraments of the Church of CHRIST, apart from the Divine SPIRIT of CHRIST.

In meditating upon GOD the Creator, one great truth which we hold to with the tenacity of faith, in the presence of a fashionable and semi-scientific scepticism, is the Personality of the great First Cause. We believe, with all the powers of our inmost being, in a Personal GOD, the Maker of all things visible and invisible. In meditating on GOD the Saviour, one great truth which we hold to, almost with the energy of despair, in the presence of a less fashionable, but more widespread infidelity, is the Divinity of the Historical JESUS of Christianity. We believe, with all our mind and soul, that JESUS is GOD. But a disbelieving world, whether fashionable or not, though certainly un-scientific, includes both elements of want of faith. And a disbelieving world compels us to insist on the Catholic dogma, that the HOLY GHOST the Sanctifier, in Himself combines both truths. He is GOD equally with our Divine Master. He is a Person equally with the Eternal FATHER. The Blessed PARACLETE is a Personal GOD, with essence, presence, power; with operations and attributes; with majesty, glory, and mode of existence. In short, we, Catholics, in this materialistic age, believe in the Divinity and in the Personality of the HOLY GHOST the COMFORTER.

·II.

In contemplating the Divine Personality of the Holy SPIRIT, three facts in regard to man and his relation to GOD, must always be remembered: three truths in regard to GOD and His relation to Himself, must never be forgotten.

1st. In regard to man. We must remember that the HOLY GHOST, as a Personal Deity, is, firstly, Eternal and Self-existent; and that we are subject to time, and are the work of Another's hand. Secondly: that the HOLY GHOST is Infinite and Incomprehensible; and that we are finite in ourselves, and that without ourselves, we are limited by bounds and bounded by space. Thirdly: that He is Omnipotent and Omniscient; and that we can do nothing, in purpose, course, or completion, without Him, and that we know nothing outside ourselves, untaught by Him. Three salient differences are these, between the Originating SPIRIT and the work of His inspiration which we must remember.

2nd. In regard to GOD. We must never forget that the HOLY GHOST, as a Divine Personality, is, firstly, not a creature, a created being (as the Arians and other intellectual ancients taught); but Himself the Creator SPIRIT. Secondly: that He is not an energy, an influence only, or a mere manifestation of the GODHEAD (as Simon Magus fondly thought, a gift of GOD that could be purchased with money); but the Personal source and Divine fulfilment of all good in Himself and of all grace in us. Thirdly: that He is not the agent, minister, or servant of, or in any way inferior to, if we may dare to use the language of some, the FATHER and the SON (as Macedonius held, and other less intelligent moderns hold); but Consubstantial, Co-eternal, Co-equal with both the First and Second Persons of the Holy TRINITY.

Let us strive to keep in mind these six points; three positive and three negative, in relation to man and GOD respectively, in all our musings on the Blessed PARACLETE.

But more than this must be held of faith. Several further points have ever been believed in the Church of GOD. For instance, to speak only of questions beyond the range of controversy to Catholics: 1. the eternal Origin and Procession of the HOLY GHOST, that it is Divine and Personal; 2. the Personal honour paid and dignity allowed to Him, that it is Divine; 3. His name and style and title, which are Divine and Personal; 4. that Divine worship is required by and paid to Him, as a Personal GOD; 5. His properties and work, which are described with both Divine and Personal characteristics.

We will shortly consider some of these points. Take His eternal Origin. Did not the HOLY GHOST proceed from the

FATHER and the SON, everlastingly, themselves with Him being Uncreated Persons? Take His divine Dignity. Does not S. Paul call Him LORD? The LORD is that SPIRIT—a term entirely inappropriate, if we may so say, to an influence or to an agent. Take His incommunicable Name. Was not Ananias punished with sudden death for having lied in His name—a punishment, we may reverently say, out of proportion to falsity to a name which is not that of a Personal GOD.

Again, take His worship. Is not the Creed distinct when it affirms that He is to be worshipped; and can divine worship be paid to anything short of, or can it be paid to anything less than, the Uncreated Essence? Or, take His work. Does not almost every attribute and operation of the Eternal FATHER, and the Everlasting SON, belong of necessity and right to GOD the HOLY GHOST: almost, I say, Paternity and Filiation excepted? Thus: Omniscience, Omnipotence, Omnipresence are predicated of the Third Divine Person. Inspiration, of course, is affirmed of Him. The creative Power in origination, and the superintending Power of miracles, are declared of Him. Teaching and the Ministry, as delegated powers, are referred back to His authority; as well as the operations and gifts of Grace. And also, these facts in the supernatural life have their origin in His Divine will, and their consummation in His Personal presence — regeneration, absolution, justification, sanctification, as well as the final mystery in the human career, the resurrection from the dead.

These are points in the personal and divine prerogatives of the HOLY GHOST which proceed from Him, either directly from the fount of GODHEAD, or indirectly through the doctrine of circumcession.

III.

Belief in the HOLY GHOST, as held by Christendom, is to be sought in the authorized Creeds of the Church. There are extant three authoritative statements of the faith of the Church on this point, contained in as many Creeds—the first concise, the next developed, the last logically exhaustive, respectively. Of these three formulæ, the outcome of different epochs of the Church, this may be observed: that the more faithful the age, the briefer was the form of belief; and the less childlike the age, the longer became the form. The more sceptical became the world, the more was it needful for the Church to pronounce dogmatically on points once accepted by implication, but now questioned in detail; and hence, it became essential for her to define, to explain, to distinguish, to enlarge, to limit.

This is one penalty which divine truth pays to heresy. Yet is it a willing tax for a loving soul to pay. The temper of mind is narrow and confined which rejoices in the necessity of believing the *minimum* of the faith; which is pained, or indignant, or irritated by the possibility of being called to higher and deeper insight into the mysteries of GOD. The true Catholic temper can never learn too much of divine revelation: it ever thirsts for more and yet more of the faith. And how much the faith has gained from the denials and disclaimers of infidelity we see, first, by the development of the Nicene beyond the Apostles' Creed, and then, by the expansion, both logical and poetic at once, of that of S. Athanasius beyond the form of the fathers of Nicæa.

What does our holy Mother Church call on us to accept, in the threefold belief of the Creeds, in relation to GOD the HOLY GHOST? We will strive to realize this.

I. The simple archaic form of belief, the germ and norm of more elaborate definitions of faith (under whatever form the Apostolic Creed first existed, or under whatever name), with grand, severe and masculine simplicity declares—I believe in the HOLY GHOST. As she had avowed of GOD the FATHER I believe in GOD; as she had asserted of GOD the SON, I believe in JESUS CHRIST; so, the Church was content to say of the Third Person of the GODHEAD, I believe in the HOLY GHOST.

II. Faith was contented with such transparent, unconditioned simplicity: but not so was disbelief. As the faith became less pure, as the minds which received it became more complex in requirement, so were amplification, specification, qualification and detail demanded from theology. And the divine science proved herself equal to the strain placed upon her powers. The Nicene fathers, or rather those of Constantinople, next offer their quota of faith in the Third Divine Person to the Creed of Christendom. They declare: I believe in the HOLY GHOST; the LORD and Giver of Life; Who proceedeth from the FATHER and the SON; Who, with the FATHER and the SON together, is worshipped and glorified; Who spake by the Prophets.

Observe the development from the simple statement of belief which sufficed for apostolic times and men. Of that same Personal GOD, Whom two words, or one composite term, once sufficiently described, it is now predicated, 1st, that He is the LORD GOD; 2nd, that He is the Giver of Life to created things; 3rd and 4th, that He proceedeth, by Divine Inspiration, from the FATHER and the SON; 5th, that He is to be worshipped of all men; 6th, and to be glorified of the faithful; and 7th and 8th, that He has been pleased to reveal Himself, and by what instrumentality—that He spake, and spake by the Prophets. How greatly must GOD'S awful truth have become corrupted, ere it were needful thus to develop the archaic germ, "I believe." At least eight distinct heresies, and probably much more involved unfaithfulness, had developed around a single Person of the GODHEAD, in three centuries of the Church's life. But, for our consolation in modern days, it may be noted, that such heretical development occurred in times which are considered by the students of history to be the purest age of Christianity. They certainly developed in the undivided Church when, if ever, the Church possessed a living voice. They were as certainly condemned in one section of the symbol of Nicæa.

III. Faith, again, was contented with this first development upon the transparent simplicity of the earlier Creed: not so, again, was disbelief. To repeat, in the words of a master, what was before said: the Nicene Creed simply confessed the Unity of the HOLY GHOST with the FATHER and the SON, as the LORD, or Sovereign SPIRIT, because heretics considered Him to be but a minister of GOD; and the supreme Giver of Life, because heretics considered Him to be but the instrument of our reception. But even the development of Nicæa was insufficient. Farther expansion was demanded in the defence of faith, with logical exhaustiveness and theological precision of terminology and detail. Hence, the Athanasian formula of faith contains, at least, six new and positive declarations on the Divinity and Personality of the HOLY GHOST, mostly of a composite character, and apart from those that are negative. They are as follows—

1. The Creed enunciates the religious fact, that there is Another Person of the HOLY GHOST; Another, from the First and Second Persons; Him Whom Scripture terms the PARACLETE, the COMFORTER.

2. Of this Other Person, in relation to the Eternal FATHER and the Consubstantial SON, the GODHEAD is declared to be all one; the Glory, equal; the Majesty, co-eternal.

3. Such as the FATHER is, the Creed announces, such is the SON, and such is the HOLY GHOST: such—a generic term, all the more including and exhaustive from its very vagueness. But the return to definite and scientific statement is prompt and decided: for

4. To the HOLY GHOST are attributed three attributes, which necessarily involve His equality with the First and Second of the Divine Persons. He is believed, in the faith of the Church, to be Uncreate, Incomprehensible, Eternal.

5. Three titles are in the next place given by the Creed, under which the Third Person is to be worshipped and glorified; namely, Almighty, GOD, and LORD.

6. Lastly, the Creed pronounces on the mode of His exist-

ence, in reference to the Holy TRINITY, and on His relationship to each several Person of the same; that the HOLY GHOST is neither made out of nothing, like the universe; nor created from something, as the human race; nor begotten, as was the Archetypal Man, GOD'S Only SON; but proceeding, like only unto His own Divine Majesty.

This is the Catholic Faith, on the Divine Personality, and the Personal Divinity of the HOLY GHOST the COMFORTER, from the clauses of the Athanasian symbol, which, to use the language of the Creed, except a man believe faithfully he cannot be saved.

More, however, may be held, if not of obligation, yet of devotion. For this optional addition to the faith, we turn from the Creeds to those who formulated them; from the sacred Scriptures to the holy Fathers of the Church. From their works, learned men have culled these descriptive titles of the Blessed PARACLETE, which either contain deep truths, or are suggestive of them. They affirm that the Holy SPIRIT is the Love of the Eternal FATHER, and of the Only-begotten SON, which unites Them in the incomprehensible mystery of the TRINITY; that He is the Will of the DEITY and GODHEAD; that He is the Bond of Union between the Co-equal Three; the Kiss of Peace between the FATHER and the SON; a sweet Savour of, and the Ointment poured forth by, the First and Second Persons; the sacred Breath in the divine nostrils of GOD; the Gift, the Seal, the Finger of the Almighty; the infallible Director of souls, and the Ambassador from GOD to man; and the Summum Bonum, in none other than Whom can be found rest and peace and light and love and joy and bliss, both here and hereafter.

IV.

Why has so much time been spent upon the Divinity and Personality of GOD the HOLY GHOST? The answer may be promptly made. For a distinct and practical purpose.

Without consciousness of the fact, many persons at the present day possess an inadequate, if not imperfect belief in the Divinity of the Third Person of the Holy TRINITY. Without affirming it in spoken terms, or even without allowing it mentally, some persons disregard, if not neglect the Personality of the same Divine COMFORTER. Many know little of, some care little for, the Blessed PARACLETE.

There is more than a single reason for this want of consideration and want of belief. It may be well to attempt to analyze some of the causes.

1. By the order of GOD, and in the nature of things, the Incarnate SON bears a more intimate relation and has closer connections with the human race, than either the Un-begotten FATHER, or the Proceeding SPIRIT. Equally Divine and Personal with both, yet our LORD, made Man for us, actually has and still more in sentiment seems to have, a greater personal and divine interest in us than the other two Persons. The fact of creation and the results of sanctification do not involve such close relations as His inestimable Love, in the redemption of souls, man by man, and all that flows therefrom. Hence, the Creating FATHER and the Sanctifying SPIRIT appear to have, even if they have not in reality, less intimate relations towards mankind than our Divine Master. And if this be in any degree true of the First Person, it may be more emphatically pronounced of the Third. Moreover, it is certain, to pass from a divine standpoint to a human, that for our LORD, Who was born and suffered for us, Who lived and died for us, and Who ceaselessly intercedes for us, man himself possesses an interest, a sympathy and a love which do not equally, nor so keenly, nor so powerfully, extend beyond the Divine LORD. One cause is enough for such an human attraction to GOD made MAN. JESUS CHRIST, in the most Holy Eucharist gives us Himself, in His GODHEAD as well as in His Manhood.

2. There is another reason, which in part depends upon the former reason, to explain the neglect with which the Holy

SPIRIT is treated by many amongst us. So much less has been revealed by GOD, either directly by inspiration or mediately through tradition, of the Third Person, than of the Second, or even of the First. The fourfold Gospel is mainly concerned with the life of CHRIST: and though much may be gathered from the Epistles on the essence and operations of the HOLY GHOST, much more, indeed, than at first sight appears, yet such revelation is indirect in character rather than plainly to the point. Nor is it otherwise, in the case of Catholic tradition, whether more or less in solution or precipitated into the form of Creeds. This is noteworthy, inasmuch as we live, as has been before said, under the dispensation of the SPIRIT.

Yet, it is not the less true, that, comparatively speaking, tradition as well as revelation preserves a mysterious silence in regard to the position and work of the COMFORTER in the domain of grace. It only needs a passing allusion to such topics as the mode and manner of the eternal Procession, the limits and scope of Inspiration in Holy Writ, the force of Invocation in the consecration of the Holy Eucharist, the means whereby the benefit of the blessed Sacraments are applied to the soul of man, and the actual results of Prayers for the dead, topics on which the whole Church has not yet pronounced, in order to justify the present assertion. Hence, when inspiration and tradition take the lead, it not unnaturally happens that human thought, and even chastened imagination, follow in the wake, and devote themselves to the sacred birth, career, and passion of CHRIST. The Church and her theologians have ever cared to speak, and write, and sing, and meditate on the sweet Name of JESUS, more often and more fully and more lovingly than on the supreme Fount of GODHEAD, or on Him in Whose eternal Procession both she and they assert their unfeigned belief. And what is true of the Second Person is true likewise, to a less extent, of the First Person of the Holy TRINITY.

3. But there is one more reason which may be assigned for this spiritual, if not supernatural anomaly. It is this. The public worship of the HOLY GHOST, as a Divine Person, as a matter of fact of which no explanation is offered, is limited to a narrow sphere in the Church of the Incarnate. Barely an octave to a single festival, once a year, is dedicated by the Church to the Holy SPIRIT: and fewer prayers and offices are publicly said or offered in His honour or to His greater glory, than of either the other two Persons. Half the Christian year, from Advent to Trinity, with the above exception, is allotted to the Church's Spouse by the Bride herself. Seven days only are appointed for keeping the festival of Whitsun-tide, and for the special worship of the PARACLETE. The feast is then engulfed in the mystery of the Holy TRINITY. And whilst nearly all prayer is wont to end with an appeal to the merits of the Divine Master; and whilst the daily Sacrifice is continually offered to the Heavenly FATHER; few devotions, or collects, or hymns, or prayers are specifically said or sung—with the exception of times of Missions, Retreats, and Novenas—to the Person of the COMFORTER. With the cause of this apparent anomaly we are not now concerned. It is enough to observe the fact; and to admit that it affords a certain amount of reason for what has been termed the devotional and theological neglect of the PARACLETE at the hands of the faithful.

V.

The last reason may be taken as a test, whether or not we are personally and individually open to criticism in this matter; whether or not our faith is inadequate, or imperfect, in the HOLY GHOST; whether we disregard or neglect Him; whether we know little of Him and care even less—the test of worship. We may allow every weight to the divine instinct of the Catholic Church, in her traditional allotment of worship to the several Persons of the GODHEAD. We must remember the amount of revelation which has been vouchsafed of GOD on the work and operations of the Third Person of the Holy TRINITY. And then we shall be in a position to enquire what may be our practice in this matter?

For instance: we pray daily, many times a day, to our FATHER Which is in Heaven. We join, or ought to join, in offering to Him daily, actually or spiritually, the Sacrifice of the Altar. Daily do we use prayers and collects, addressed personally to Him, enumerating His attributes, invoking His mercy, deprecating His wrath, enhancing His glory, beseeching the exercise of His operations. We pray also daily, and many times a day to our SAVIOUR Who, for our sake, came down from Heaven. As a rule, all Christian prayer, in virtue of His words, ends with His Name. The Litany in the Prayer-Book is specially, and the *Te Deum* is mainly, addressed to Him. The prayer of S. Ignatius, *Anima Christi*, " Soul of CHRIST, sanctify me," is a favourite form of devotion to the Sacred Humanity of JESUS, specially in times of retreat. Many litanies and other prayers are used, both in church and at home, in His honour. And hymns, as the old heathen said, are sung to CHRIST as GOD, almost endless in number. Such, perhaps, is an index to the devotional attitude towards the FATHER and the SON of an average Catholic.

But now, let us regard his attitude devotionally towards the Blessed SPIRIT. How often does such an one, let us enquire, unless he be specially taught to this end, actually pray, recite a prayer, to the HOLY GHOST? How often does he join in offering the Holy Sacrifice, with a special intention to His glory, or in memory of His work, or to secure His co-operation? How often does he muse on His attributes, seek His mercy, fear His anger, beg His favours, think of His work, or sing hymns in His honour—in a day, in a week, in a month, in a year? Unless some unusual event occur, it may be safely affirmed of a Catholic of the ordinary type, that he does so seldom or not at all. Such neglect is barely excusable, in ignorance. In spite of knowledge, the neglect is highly culpable.

Not to speak of this topic further than in the matter of direct devotion, there exist many pious devotions, holy prayers, and hymns full of beauty to the COMFORTER, for the use and edification of the faithful. Even in the public offices of the Church such may be found. The Prayer-Book contains two which may be, and ought to be, used of all persons, often if not constantly. First; *Veni Creator*, " Come HOLY GHOST, our souls inspire," which is at once a hymn and a prayer, and with which meditations in a retreat are usually begun. Secondly; the prayer in the Confirmation Office, in most rhythmical prose, which runs thus : " Almighty and Everliving GOD, Who hast vouchsafed to regenerate us Thy servants by Water and the HOLY GHOST; and hast given unto us forgiveness of all our sins; strengthen us, we beseech Thee, O LORD, with the HOLY GHOST the COMFORTER, and daily increase in us Thy manifold gifts of grace, the Spirit of Wisdom and Understanding, the Spirit of Counsel and Ghostly strength, the Spirit of Knowledge and true Godliness; and fill us, O LORD, with the Spirit of Thy holy Fear, now and for ever. Amen." Of the first, nothing need be said. Of the last, it may be observed, that the prayer in the Office is made by the Bishop on behalf of the candidates for the seven-fold Gifts in the Sacrament of the Imposition of Hands. But a slight grammatical change of person from the third to the first, as has been made above, will enable the worshipper to use the prayer for himself and for his own needs.

Let me ask all whom I may reach by these words, as one practical result of these meditations, to use both hymn and prayer daily. The effort will never be repented, and good will inevitably ensue. A Church could be named which publicly invokes the HOLY GHOST daily in sacred song. Large spiritual blessings are known to flow from that Church.

Many private persons are wont to do the like. Some make a habit of falling to sleep repeating the words of a short Litany of the Divine SPIRIT. Remember, the Creed says, that the HOLY GHOST is worshipped. In such a case, the assertion is equivalent to a command.

VI.

In regard to the subject matter of our meditation, the HOLY GHOST in relation to the sin of man, it may be said that there are at least four ways in which the Third Person of the TRINITY is to be worshipped by faithful Catholics In man's ceaseless warfare with the Evil One, the HOLY GHOST is, 1. our Inspirer; 2. our Patron and Benefactor; 3. our Defender; 4. our Guide. Under each character He is to be worshipped by man. We will take these characters in order.

I. The SPIRIT of our LORD GOD is the Inspirer of every member of His Church. The attribute of Inspiration is perhaps the first in order of time, if not the chiefest in importance of the four which have been specified. For we shall fail to make proper use of His benefactions, it were almost useless to be protected by Him, He would be powerless to direct us, unless in each case the soul consents to be previously infused with the Inspiring SPIRIT. In this relation, it is essential that good thoughts, holy wishes, pure intentions, high aspirations, be conveyed into our hearts. In a state of sin, whether habitual or accidental, whether mortal or venial, we need in different degrees such dispositions to be placed there. With the process by which this may be effected, we are not now concerned; but only with the fact. And as a fact, we are very far gone indeed from original righteousness, even after our baptism; and we are so far gone, that self-inspiration is impossible. Hence, if we need inspiration, inspiration must come to us from without. Where may such inspiration be found, save in the Divine Personality of GOD the HOLY GHOST? As the Inspirer of mankind, He is to be worshipped of the faithful—hopefully in making request for grace, and gratefully when the grace requested has been given.

This position is so evident to us that it were wiser to consider any objections which may arise to another, in order that we may be prepared with an answer to him that asketh us, with meekness and fear. And objections may be taken in two ways, from opposite points of view—from one of GOD'S prerogatives, and from one of man's highest privileges. These objections turn upon the term Inspiration, and what the term is thought to import for private Christians; and upon the interference with man's free-will, which the exercise of inspiration even by man's Maker is supposed to involve. We will consider the least important, but more difficult objection to be answered, first; and the more momentous, but less difficult objection to be answered, afterwards.

1. Inspiration, it is urged, with some plausibility, trenches on one of man's highest and most valuable of gifts, the gift of free-will. This is the objection plainly stated. An emphatic negative in reply must be given. It does not, in reality, trench upon this grant of GOD to the creature of His hand. The Gospel is a religion of freedom and of liberty; a religion of liberty to do right, and of freedom to do well. It is also a religion of power—potential and actual; with possibility of doing well, and capacity for doing right. Such power, presupposes liberty and freedom. For in Christianity there is no compulsion. There is one thing which Almighty GOD has been pleased to make impossible to Himself—the salvation of man without man's willingness. Apart from free-will we can be redeemed—yes. Apart from free-will we can be sanctified—no. We cannot be finally saved without, and much less against, our own consent.

Outside the Gospel there is also freedom and liberty: liberty to do ill, freedom to do wrong. But, beyond the pale of Christianity, such liberty and freedom is, in truth, compulsion. Apart from divine grace, we cannot of ourselves exercise the power of doing good. Paradoxical as it may sound, GOD'S slave is really free: there is no true servitude in grace. But he who takes sin for a servant, is truly a slave to his own servant: sin's freed-man is in bondage to Satan. Yet, man's free-will may overcome his power for good, his liberty and freedom to do right. This we observe daily Even when inspired, we may and do successfully resist the leadings of Inspiration. But uninspired of GOD, man is powerless to do right. An evil tree cannot bring forth good fruit. There is, therefore, no valid objection in the supposed infringement of man's free-will by the Inspiration of GOD.

2. A second objection lurks in the term Inspiration, and in what is implied by the term. Inspiration, again, it is urged, is an act of the Supreme DEITY which is exercised in definite and special ways only. It is exercised by an agent, or by means, duly authorized and authenticated. It may be exercised in a corporate body organized by GOD; or by a human agent chosen of GOD; or through the written Word of GOD. But in any case the term is applied under specific conditions: it is not used indiscriminately to all private Christians: and what the term imports is not to be claimed by all. Such is the objection.

The true answer to this objection is to be found, again, in returning a direct negation. We are not bound to confine the blessing of Inspiration, to take a crucial instance, to the supernatural faculty by which GOD'S Will is made known to us, past, present, and future, absolutely and truthfully, in the pages of the Holy Bible. Of that blessed volume we are justly jealous. But itself teaches us that we are all priests before GOD to this extent, that we are inspired to know His will, as well as inspired to do it. Neither need the word and the thing be confined to the thought, the feeling, the aspiration, the suggestion within the heart of man. GOD'S hand is not shortened. He can save by many or by few. In many ways outside man's heart may GOD speak to His creature.

A book, a conversation, a newspaper article, a sermon or meditation, the criticism of enemies or the severer judgment of friends, Nature herself, the conduct even of the wicked and much more the actions of the good—these may be taken as inspirations from the HOLY GHOST to us, may have been intended by GOD to be indirect revelations to us of His most holy Will. The divine Scriptures and accidental circumstances both come to us through the Will of GOD, be it direct or permissive; may both be equally inspirations of GOD the HOLY GHOST, the same in kind, though different in degree.

These objections are insufficient to make us doubt of the inspiration of the faithful by GOD the HOLY GHOST.

II. Inspiration, however, is not enough in the Christian warfare against sin, even the Inspiration of the HOLY GHOST which respects the free-will of man. It is not enough, unless the same Blessed SPIRIT is pleased to be also our Patron and Benefactor in His seven-fold gifts of grace: and as such He is to be worshipped of the faithful.

Consider the value of both efforts of grace and their mutual interdependence. Inspiration is a spiritual faculty or power, a spiritual energy, force, or principle of action. In popular terms, it is the will to do good. Without Inspiration the seed will not grow in man's inner life. But it is not the life, and still less is it the seed. The life of the soul is GOD Himself. The seed must be implanted by GOD Himself; and a second effort of grace, by GOD the Benefactor, will furnish the material to be vivified by the first. Free-will must of course correspond and co-operate with the gift: but the gift itself is God-given—by the HOLY GHOST. Capacity for good predisposes the soul towards holiness: or at the most makes the soul harmless. But in the great harvest of the Last Day it is for the fruit of Judgment that we look, thirty-fold, sixty-fold, an hundred-fold. And such increase comes from the hand of man's divine Patron.

Take a parallel case to this spiritual fact in daily life—the intellect. The human mind possesses the faculty of vital force, the principle and will to do great things for human thought. But of what value, either to others or to its possessor, would it be if, with power or energy sufficient, it could only be affirmed of such a mind that it is not furnished with intellectual gifts, that it is not conversant with philosophy, history, science, music, art, or language? So also in the moral agent. A being with capacity and power to gain the highest levels of sanctity, of whom it may be only said that he is not proud, self-willed, slothful, impure, bad-tempered, or untrue, of what moral worth is such a character? Negatively, nothing disgraceful has been said; but positively, nothing that is noble has been affirmed. Hence, inspiration is not all, in the warfare against evil and for good. We must be active religionists, not passive agents of inactivity, or at the most receptive agents of potential holiness. The HOLY GHOST must be our Patron and Benefactor to sow the seed of His seven-fold gifts: and He is to be worshipped, in one of many ways, by the active use of the divine graces which He inspires us to employ.

III. As inspiration alone is not enough in our warfare against sin: so, in our efforts after practical holiness of life, benefaction is not enough. In this world of actual wickedness we require defence and protection. Hence, the HOLY GHOST is our Defender. He not only gives capacity for holiness, and imparts positive virtue; but He is pleased to supply both, with means of defence. Protection is of equal value, perhaps, with inspiration and beneficence. At certain stages of the inner life, it is even more important. But in any case there is inter-dependence between inspiration, benefaction, and defence: and equally with man's duty under the exercise of the former attributes, is GOD, the Defender and Protector of man, to be worshipped.

The various ways in which our Inspirer and Benefactor is

also our Defender, are incalculable. Still we may strive to recall a few, though perhaps not the most prominent in the life of each one individually. Take a few cases in relation only to sin. In our disposition towards temptation, He is our Defender, lest we fall into temptation. In the hour of temptation from sin, He is our Defender, lest we fall into sin. In the very act of sin, oftentimes He defends us from plunging deeper into wickedness. In our first feeble efforts after repentance, He generally defends us lest we be discouraged. In the sad trial of discouragement even, He defends us from the blackness of despair. In perseverance, He still more defends us, lest by a sudden revulsion of feeling not unknown, we cast to the winds our resolutions and in the end ourselves become cast away. In all these cases, the Blessed PARACLETE is our Defender: and as such, as the protector of our spiritual life from the font to the altar, and from our first Confession to our last Viaticum-reception, the HOLY GHOST is to be worshipped in perseverance to the end, in temptation, in penitence, in discouragement, even in sin, and much more in holiness of life.

IV. Once more. In addition to being in due order the Inspirer, Benefactor and Defender of the elect, the HOLY GHOST stands towards His spiritual creation by whom He is worshipped in the position of Personal Adviser and Divine Guide. This office of the COMFORTER is momentous, specially to those who, living in the world, are anxious, with His help, to live as little as may be of or for the world. Here, I would rather be content to indicate instances in which He may be our Guide, than desirous to discover reasons for His course of action, or the modes of it. Take, then, a few cases in the mixed relations of life, in which religion and society, if they do not clash, more or less harmonize.

Take certain temptations of modern life. Never mind what they may be. You know the special temptations of your life; your confessor knows them; your Guardian Angel knows them; GOD knows them. Whatever they may be, the questions arise: When should we flee from them; to what extent should we accept them; when should we utterly repudiate them; and, is it ever lawful to make a compromise with them? Our Divine and Personal Guide will help us to decide. Take certain questions of morals, and hard or intricate cases of casuistry. Here too you are yourself conscious of such instances; your confessor, your Angel, and GOD are likewise conscious of them. The questions arise: How far, or how little ought we to conform our inflexible standard of morals to the graduated scale and fluctuating system of conventional morality? At what point ought we to resist? Under what conditions should we silently, not hesitatingly, ignore; under what, should we openly and boldly denounce, the falsehoods of society, the detraction of the world, licensed immorality, thinly disguised impurity in word, and fraud and dishonesty not at all concealed in act, but rather blazoned and gilded with the tinsel of success? Again, our Divine Adviser and Personal Guide will teach us how to decide.

So, again, as to questions of certain duties of life: When, under certain conditions, we ought to do; not to do; to intermit or postpone; to undertake and fulfil; to act secretly or avowedly? And, as to the pleasures of life, as they are called, of course as to such as are sinless in themselves: What to enjoy or decline; what to accept with reserve, or to repulse under any condition; what to use for one's own relaxation, or for the satisfaction of others? So, too, of sorrow or sickness: How far is it lawful to be self-indulgent, or to refrain from indulgence, under either condition; when to fight against, or to yield to, the demands of both? Lastly, of society, not the least difficult of all the problems to solve: How much or how far we may enter into its vortex, without danger of being engulfed; what forms we may employ, without being compromised; whom we may know or associate with, or with whom we cannot be acquainted without danger, or at least, loss of consistency? In all these cases, the Third Person of the Holy TRINITY, Whom we are bound to worship, will be not only the Inspirer, Benefactor, Defender of His children; but also, if they will permit Him, He will be their infallible Adviser, and their Divine and Personal Guide.

VII.

We have thus meditated upon the work and office of GOD the HOLY GHOST, in the spiritual life, under the four-fold aspect of the inspirations of GOD, of the benefactions of GOD, of His personal defence, and of His divine guidance. The last matter for consideration is more intimate to ourselves. It is this. In regard to our own individual sin, how do these four operations of the Third Person of the Holy TRINITY affect us, in our inmost life? We will examine our consciences on these four operations in order.

1st. Let us employ self-searching in relation to the manifold inspirations of the Divine and Personal SPIRIT of GOD. How do we stand in the presence of sin here? Without being careful to define an inspiration of GOD exactly, it is impossible that we can have arrived at our present position in the domain of grace, and not have been subjected to almost numberless indications, direct or indirect, of GOD'S pleasure in the course of our action, or of GOD'S will in the possibility of our acting. Such we may take to be inspirations. Have we resisted such inspirations? Have we resisted them knowingly, willingly, consciously, deliberately? Think, for a moment, before any response be mentally made. Has any good thought, wish, or aspiration, for self or towards another, presented to the soul from without or conceived from within—both being from the great Inspirer of the faithful—been willingly and consciously put aside, not encouraged, allowed to die a natural death, or stifled in its birth? Can we respond with a clear conscience to this enquiry—that, without good cause, there has not? Has any design or plan for GOD'S glory, the good of souls, our own good, our neighbour's benefit, presented to the soul from without, or conceived from within, been knowingly or deliberately abandoned, or neglected for a time, or postponed to a more convenient season? Can we answer, as we look GOD in the face—that, without sufficient reason, there has not?

Or, again, to employ self-vivisection in cases of mixed character, in which we did not altogether or at first cast aside GOD'S suggestion; or, in which we did not eventually abandon it without a struggle; or, in which we played with it, fast and loose, dallied with it, as with something we were free to take or to leave—let us further cross-question the witness that always will speak the truth if it be allowed, the divine conscience of humanity. Has anything in our life and in consequence of an inspiration, been begun from a high motive, been modified by a low motive, been not completed from a bad motive? Anything, I mean, which would change the course of our life; which would affect the life of another; which would influence ourself inwardly; which would tell upon others outwardly? And, once more, has such been considered again and again; thought of and not thought of; encouraged now, and now suppressed; and finally resisted and rejected? But whatever the motive, whatever the effect, whatever the result—yet, still, it was an inspiration from GOD: and being an inspiration from GOD, how was it treated?

Of course, I speak of a genuine inspiration; not of a daydream, nor of a phantasy; not of castle-building, nor self-seeking imagining: and of such only need these enquiries be made. But, in the case conceived, a Retreat is a fitting time to ascertain the facts; to learn the cause and note the result; and to decide, as in the presence of GOD the HOLY GHOST, to what extent the past fault may be remediable; how it may be atoned for and repented of in the present; and how it may be avoided in the future.

2nd. Let us exercise self-examination in regard to still more numerous benefactions of the Personal and Divine COMFORTER. Our presence here to-day, our existence on earth now, our assured measure of health and strength, the blessings we enjoy and the law of compensation which governs the withholding of those which we lack—these are indications absolutely numberless, that we are beneficiaries of GOD the HOLY GHOST. Such being some of His benefactions, in what position do we, as recipients of His infinite goodness, stand in regard to sin? Our soul may be compared to a sheet of pure white paper, duly prepared by inspiration to receive the impress of divine type, in the benefactions of the Blessed PARACLETE. Of my own soul, not less than of yours, do I speak. Has your soul been placed in this position? Has it been impressed by the lavish, prodigal generosity of the great Master-printer? Can you read printed on your soul characters of grace, syllables of grace, words and sentences of grace, pages and volumes of grace? If so; all has been impressed by GOD the Benefactor. If so; what may be the result of all? Think, again, for a moment. Take only the seven-fold gifts that we daily pray for to Him, and be self-judged; take these elementary but most needful graces, and be either acquitted by self, or self-condemned—spiritual wisdom and understanding, spiritual counsel and ghostly-strength, spiritual knowledge and true godliness, and the spirit of GOD'S most holy fear.

One of the seven divine and personal gifts of the COMFORTER will probably be sufficient by which to try yourselves. Suppose the spirit of ghostly-strength be made the touchstone for your conscience. Has this virtue been impressed upon your soul by GOD your Benefactor? What is the result? You have been placed in temptation in which this virtue has had full scope for spiritual action. It matters not at all, in what special temptation you may have been placed. It matters everything, in what manner you have employed the special means placed at your disposal for resisting the temptation. How did you use the gift of the Third Person of the Holy TRINITY? How did you use your ghostly-strength to overcome the assault of your ghostly foe? Did you feel the instinct to withstand the temptation? Were you given the will and intention not to fall, but to conquer? Had you power and might, if only you called them forth, to remain passive, steadfast, unharmed, if not unattacked? The power, the will, the instinct, were all God-bestowed of GOD the Benefactor. All, all came from the ghostly-strength of the PARACLETE. And how did you respond? Did you co-operate with grace and succeed; or did you co-operate not and fail? Is it not painfully true, that though sometimes you were brave and constant, yet that more often you were fickle and cowardly? You either neglected the instinct, or tampered with the will, or ignored the power, or perhaps did all these in turn; and you fell. You gave way before the attack; you succumbed to the sin. Never mind under what definite and special temptation you fell. It was from your besetting fault, which your GOD, and your Angel, and your confessor, and your conscience know. The temptation mastered you, in the stead of your mastering the temptation, because you did despite unto the spirit of the Divine COMFORTER'S Ghostly-strength.

Again, a Retreat is a fitting time to ascertain the facts of this failure in the spiritual life; to learn both its cause and effect; and to decide, under the influence of the ghostly-strength which still remains within you, how the failure may be remedied, how it may be repented and how it may not be repeated, respectively in the past, the present and the future.

3rd. The protection of a Personal and Divine Defender affords us another means of probing our individual sin, in regard to the third operation on our souls of the HOLY GHOST. What position do we assume in the presence of sin? Our self-searching may take the following form in this case.

We may have assented, on the whole, to the divine inspirations; we may have accepted, with proper dispositions, the greater part of the divine benefactions; but yet, we may have presumptuously interfered with the personal defence wherewith He has been graciously pleased to surround us. Can we plead guilty to this charge? Let us examine into our lives.

The larger proportion of those who hear me have been placed, by the blessing of GOD, in that position in the world, in society, or in circumstances, in which they are to a great extent shielded, if not positively free from all, or almost every form of gross, vulgar, or deadly sin. The sixth, seventh and eighth of GOD'S Commandments, and many of the Deadly Sins, are, to us, and in their primary sense, almost if not altogether unknown in their breach. So far as this may be the case with any one of us, we ought to thank GOD heartily for so great a mercy. But our gratitude must be tempered with other considerations. The case is not exhausted against our souls, even though we be not tempted to theft, adultery, or murder, or to covetousness and gluttony, and hence fall not. The same Personal Providence which has, as a fact, defended us from the commission of these heinous sins, would equally defend us also from the commission of sins not gross, not vulgar, not deadly. Indeed, He does so defend us, if only we have been prepared to co-operate with His protection. But, the question is, have we been thus prepared, and are we thus prepared? Have we accepted such divine protection, and do we practically act up to it? Think again for a moment before we make answer. Without entering into the minutiæ of detail, can we charge ourselves at least with self-will, in the case of little infidelities, small laxities, insignificant liberties, infinitesimal remissnesses in our spiritual life. Remember that such evidences of imperfect conformity to the Will of GOD, are serious in proportion to the amount of grace in spite of which and against which they are committed; and do not forget that they tend to blunt the edge of human susceptibilities, that they positively remove the bloom from the fruit of divine satisfaction.

Are we then absolutely guiltless in this respect, with regard, for instance, to perfect charity, frank truthfulness, self-surrender which has conquered sloth, sweetness of temper notwithstanding natural irritability, profound humility, angelic chastity in thought, word, and deed? Or do we admit into our lives such evidences of want of faithfulness to the divine protection of a Particular Providence? Do we assent to them, allow them, encourage them? Do we defend them, apologize for them, or even boast of their commission as infidelities only, as only little or venial sins? In any case, a Retreat affords an opportunity for self-knowledge on this point; for penitence, if we have fallen; for amendment, if we are truly penitent.

4th. The infallible guidance of a Divine and Personal Adviser may be suggestive to our minds of some deep searchings of conscience, in regard to sin. What may be our relations towards the Consubstantial and Co-eternal SPIRIT under this, the final head of our meditation? It may be assumed that the work and operation of the Third Person has, to a certain extent, taken root downwards and borne fruit upwards in our inner life: that, on the whole, we have been faithful to His inspirations, thankful for His mercies, strong in the power of His defence: that, in a general way, we acknowledge Him as the supreme Director of our life. Moreover, we may have escaped from actual compliance with some special unfaithfulness; we may have to a large degree conquered our besetting fault; we may have not only accepted, but, to the best of our power, fulfilled the object of our existence. In consequence, our spiritual life has become comparatively peaceful within and calm without.

A time comes, however, when a change is imminent. The actual cause need not be imagined. But the change comes;

and with the change comes a trial, a temptation. This temptation becomes an epoch in our supernatural career. A question of morals arises: a choice has to be made between duties, not really conflicting, but which seem to conflict. We are harassed by some trivial infidelity: we are threatened by the recurrence of past temptation, which unhappily led to past wickedness. The particular change there is no need to indicate. Let each name to himself his own experience. But it meets us: and the question for us is, how do we meet it? We are tempted, let us suppose, by "the occasion of sin," as the phrase is understood. We are tempted by the time, place, or person; in thought, word, or deed; through an occupation, pleasure, or even duty: tempted as we have been before tried, the same in kind or different in degree, the like in degree or different in kind: tempted in the occasion of sin. The kind or degree is immaterial. It may be a severe temptation to a deadly sin. It may be a light temptation only to a venial sin. But, from one point of view, the more insignificant the temptation the more dangerous it becomes.

How do we act? Do we act under the Divine and Personal Direction of our true Guide; or do we follow our own leading? GOD the great Director of souls points, through an enlightened and sensitive conscience, to a means of escape. We will not pause to particularize it. A word from others, a thought self-originated, a passage in a book, a glance from one we love or respect, outside example, principles we cannot forget—these, simply or combined, indicate the line of action commended to our conscience by our Heavenly Guide. And we decline the guidance. Believing in our own power and strength; trusting to the insignificance and weakness of the temptation; presuming on the efficacy of GOD'S grace apart from, and not in harmony with human co-operation; relying on our own feeble, prejudiced, short-sighted, judgment in spiritual matters—we fall. We fall deservedly. We fall perhaps deeply, certainly out of all proportion to the actual temptation. We fall, it may be, out of grace, and into hardness, deadness, presumption, impenitence. And why? Because we would not permit ourselves, in spiritual matters, to be advised by the Divine Guide and Spiritual Director of souls, GOD the HOLY GHOST.

For the last time it may be repeated, a Retreat is a convenient opportunity in which to remember the experience of the past in the present; to prepare in the light of the present for the future; and to allow the past to be the guardian of the future by the present use, for the conquest of our sin, of contrition, confession, and satisfaction.

Second Day of Retreat.

MAN THE IMAGE OF GOD IN RELATION TO SIN.

ADDRESS FIVE.

MAN CREATED BY GOD.

THE only true and Christian method of meditation upon first principles of the faith with regard to such cardinal questions as the great First Cause, the Image of GOD, and GOD in union with Man, is, as we have seen, to begin with GOD and to end with man. In the last three meditations we have dwelt upon the Three Persons of the Blessed TRINITY in relation to sin. In the next three we will consider the like number of the primary conditions of the creature of GOD made in His image and after His likeness; bought by His Precious Blood; inspired by His Sanctification. We will consider them in the like relation, namely, in relation to man's sin.

In passing from the meditation of the First Cause to the work of Almighty Will and Power, the same elemental truths meet us again repeatedly. But they meet us from different points of view—from those that are human, instead of from those that are divine. GOD being the Creator, Saviour, Sanctifier of man, we have, therefore, in the next place to dwell upon Man, the Image of GOD, made by GOD, bought by GOD, made again by GOD—in relation to sin; upon Man created, redeemed, re-created by the Sovereign, Saviour, Spirit.

II.

This three-fold division of the subject almost exhausts the more intimate relations between the great First Cause and the Image of the Invisible. They involve a composite consideration of two main points only. For the only two factors of meditation which of necessity must be considered in estimating the primary dogmas of faith are, GOD and the soul alone. All meditation may be resolved, or resolves itself, into this simple formula: in the universe two beings alone exist, GOD and myself. Let such be the tenour of our thoughts now.

This position is true, in spite of a third indisputable factor, and in spite of consequences which inevitably flow from it. The third factor of a perfect meditation is one which bears certain relations to both the other factors, to GOD and to one's self. Theologically, it is termed the "creature." Everything made of GOD which is not man is the creature: every human being who is other than self, is the creature. The consequence which follows from this admission is two-fold. We are powerless, as a matter of fact, to ignore our relations to either form of the creature of GOD. The external world absolutely forces itself upon our attention: and whether we will it or not, we are our brother's keeper, and in some manner or degree he asserts his natural claim to influence our lives, engage our thoughts, and augment our cares. But in meditation we are freer than in fact. In meditation, GOD and the soul alone are necessarily essential to consideration: our self and our Maker alone. Nothing outside GOD, FATHER, SON and HOLY SPIRIT, on one side. Nothing beyond one's self, past, present, or future; one's origin, position, destiny, on the other side. Such are the only essentials of true and Christian meditation.

GOD and the soul alone, is a soul-subduing, God-inspiring thought: the creature face to face with the Creator; the result with the Cause which produced it. Under any circumstances, to be alone with GOD is at once subduing and inspiring, fearful to the lower nature, hopeful and loving to the higher nature of man. For instance: sitting alone, reading or writing, in the early hours of morning, whilst others sleep; walking alone in the dead of night in the silent streets, or watching alone the live-long night beside the death-bed of one well-loved; wandering alone for pleasure in a mountainous or in a deserted country, far from human intercourse or human habitation; standing alone when travelling on the deck of a vessel, with a sail-less horizon; or kneeling alone abroad, in some vast church, before the Altar of the Blessed Sacrament—all these instances of actual or sensational loneliness are suggestive that we may be the only created being in the world, the only being in the Creator's sight. And in proportion as they are thus suggestive, they become soul-subduing and God-inspiring. But what these instances suggest, is: GOD and the soul alone are. GOD and the soul are alone in the universe.

In all, or nearly all of the chief concerns of life, whether spiritual or temporal, this truth is unquestionable, that GOD and the soul are alone in the world. In all, or nearly all the main relations of human existence, GOD works for man, on man, with man, alone, and one by one. Take the less spiritual relations, yet not the wholly temporal, as instances. As a rule, we are born alone—with occasionally abnormal exceptions. To a wide extent, at a later period of life, even in the busiest career or in the largest family, of many of us at certain seasons, and of all of us sometimes, it may be said that we live alone—alone in much that relates to feeling, imagination, recollection, desire, or dread. As a rule, with the exception of accident, martyrdom, or war, we are called upon to die alone: in some religious orders, the members, carefully tended to almost the last, are deliberately left, crucifix in hand, to die absolutely apart from human intercourse. Alone, with no exception whatever, on the flight of the soul and for particular judgment at the moment of death, we shall be personally judged and shall be either reassured by a foretaste of bliss, or appalled by the anticipation of woe. And, although in external company with countless others, yet one by one we shall be sentenced to an everlasting condition, to an estate lasting for ever, at the last Judgment-day. Whilst, to those for whom it is prepared, the union of the creature with the Creator, before the great White Throne, will certainly be effected, not in the aggregate, but individually, one by one.

Take the more spiritual relations, from which, however, temporal accidents cannot be wholly excluded, and into some of which they avowedly enter. Between these limits of the soul's career, birth and doom, origin from nothing and incorporation with the GODHEAD, the same law holds good. We are not less alone than formerly. We are not otherwise treated than singly by our Creator, Redeemer, Sanctifier. In all the more intimate spiritual relations between GOD and the soul, we are acted upon, as well as act, one by one. Two apparent exceptions may be made to this general statement. Man worships GOD through the medium of the Church, it is true, in numbers and as a corporate body : and as a corporate action such human worship is accepted by GOD. But our worship, as to its intention and execution, whether in its higher form of sacrifice, or its lower form of praise, thanksgiving, or prayer, is weighed individually, and is blessed or rejected accordingly as each act is offered, one by one. In one sacrament, also, it is true that the presence of another is presupposed and essential—when two members of CHRIST become sacramentally one. Yet, even here, the assent and consent of both members alike is required individually, one by one, before the alliance is ratified and made indissoluble by the blessing of the Church. But, otherwise, each Sacrament of the Church is received by, and all the spiritual workings of the HOLY SPIRIT are effected upon, mankind, not as a race of beings, but as the individuals of a race. Their benefits are conferred personally, man by man. One by one, and alone, must they be accounted for.

For instance : Baptism is administered alone, and thus are we made what we were not before, a member of CHRIST, the child of GOD, and an inheritor, by covenant not by mercy only, of the kingdom of heaven. Alone do we receive the imposition of the Bishop's hand in the sacrament of Confirmation and the outpouring of the SPIRIT'S seven-fold gifts. After a true, humble and hearty individual confession of sin to a Priest, we are absolved by GOD singly. Singly, also, are we blessed by reception of the consecrated Gifts at GOD'S Altar. So are the Priesthood set apart for their high and dangerous office of being made the servants of the servants of the Good LORD. And so, too, are we given the last blessed sacraments here on earth, it may be in holy Anointing, it must at least be in the Holy Viaticum for the passage of the valley of the shadow of death. In all cases and in each case, the sacraments of the Church are conferred by GOD to the soul, alone. In short, both GOD and His Church deal with us, as we are fain to treat ourselves, our children, our friends, our penitents not in the gross, but individually. Hence, it is not un-meet to hold, in systematic meditation upon primary truths, that in each case two points of view have to be considered, though much flows from them, the divine and human; that two beings alone are existent in the world, though much is connected with them, GOD and the soul of man. A Retreat is no unfit time to meditate on the soul and its GOD alone.

This three-fold division of the subject, the Image of GOD in relation to sin—Man made, bought, and made again, I may repeat, nearly exhausts or includes all the more important relations between GOD and the soul on the side of sin. It represents three great primal positions in which the creature can stand in the presence of the Creator. Firstly: the state of nature, prior to the state of grace: when sin is negative more than positive; when it consists in the absence rather than the presence of something, and is not actual but original; when, if the equilibrium of the forces of good and ill is not perfect, yet the forces of evil are at least undeveloped and the forces of good are certainly not implanted. Secondly: under the dispensation of holiness, after partaking of the Divine Personality: when grace is decidedly in the ascendant; when it is actually easier to do good than to do harm; when the equilibrium cannot be called perfect, because the preponderance is obviously on the side of uprightness; when man has only to will in order to be saved. Thirdly: the bondage of sin, when man wills not to be saved and is consequently lost—lost perhaps for ever: when he has fallen from grace into sin; when he has fallen below nature, far below the negative position of lacking somewhat, beyond original sinfulness, into actual, positive, deadly revolt against GOD; when Satan has decidedly the upper hand, and the equilibrium of forces is for the time shattered, and can only be restored with difficulty, even if at all. This three-fold division of the subject it is helpful to bear in mind.

III.

In meditating on GOD the Creator in relation to sin, we were led to see how, before time had any existence, GOD was. He was: Three in One and One in Three; Self-originated, Self-existent and Self-subsisting; Self-contained, sufficient, absorbed. He was: a pure, free Spirit; an uncompounded Essence; dwelling in absolute silence and repose; one and alone. As such, GOD was Good, Wise, Just, True; GOD was beautiful, powerful, merciful and loving. But, being one and alone, notwithstanding the incomprehensible mystery of the Trinity in Unity, there was none to whom He could exhibit His wisdom or truth; none before whom He could display His beauty and power; none with whom He could be at once just and merciful. But a change ensued in the counsels of the changeless One. GOD was pleased to increase His own accidental glory. He was pleased to surround Himself with objects and things which He could love, and which would fulfil His blessed will; with beings and persons to whom He could be good, and who would adore and honour His infinite and endless perfection. In brief, He willed creation. GOD spake, and it was done : He commanded, and it was created. He surrounded Himself in three ways. And of these three forms of creation, the crown and summit of creative power was the last. The last factor in Almighty conception was a created being, in part angelic, in part cosmical, in part of a third nature ; a being created, not developed ; created in the Image of GOD, in the Image of the GOD-MAN of the future ; a being which we call Man.

In meditating on the Image of GOD in relation to sin, we shall be led to look at the same truth from another point of view, from the human instead of the Divine. The result of GOD'S creation, in regard to the existence of man, is contained in the words which man alone can pronounce, I am: or in other two words of like import, man's personality. I myself ; I, not another ; I, the same as I was created, the same as I exist, the same as I shall die ; I, undeveloped out of, indegenerate from anything else worse or better, the stronger survivor of no less perfect or weaker being, the natural selection of no tentative or unsuccessful effort of partial origination ; I, the absolute creation of Almighty Will and Power, with all my defects and shortcomings, with all my analogies and relations to other portions of the universe, with all my dependence upon and connection with the lower types of creation, yet created as GOD willed that I should be made, and created with the organism which man perceives that I possess —I am. I, who had no present being, entity, or existence ; no past history, memory, or life ; no future career in prospect of gain to hope, of loss to fear, of design to plan or perfect— I am. One who, by the will and pleasure of the great First Cause can now say, I have been, I am, I shall be. One who now knows that he had a past to which he can revert, who realizes that he has a present which he can enjoy, who believes that he shall have a future for which he can prepare. One who knows that he is a temporal creation out of increated matter, directly or indirectly; who believes that he has an eternal character impressed upon a thing of time; who is conscious, with all the faculties of his mind, that he once had a beginning; who is powerless to conceive—I speak advisedly, so long as such faculties are un-impaired—that he shall ever have an end.

Nor is this all. The result of GOD'S creation of man is not confined to two words, however all-containing—I am. Man was created a sensitive, reflective, self-conscious, accountable being—who knows that he is such. Man was created a being possessed of unity, personality, individuality, identity—who realizes such creation. He was created endowed with understanding, memory, will; sometimes with genius or talent, always with capacity for acquiring knowledge and power of applying it; moreover and especially, with an intuitive sense of right and wrong, and a conscience more or less attuned to accept the one and to reject the other. He was created a being so constituted as to feel both pleasure and enjoyment, gifts which excite no remark; as well as grief and pain, which are more marvellous though not inexplicable, when we reflect on the absolute goodness of his Creator: a being capable of doing good to others and receptive of harm from others: a being who can rejoice in health and strength, but who bears about with him the elements and seeds of disease, decay and death. He was created, lastly, actually enriched with five senses, in the order of nature; potentially endowed with seven spiritual gifts of the HOLY GHOST; and predestined, here and hereafter, of GOD'S love and mercy, to be made an individual partaker of the Divine Nature, and to become incorporated into a personal and transcendental union with the GODHEAD.

Such was GOD'S creation of man; partly material, partly spiritual, partly psychical. The image of GOD was created with a body, or physical organization allied to, but distinct from, the animal world, perhaps in every way its superior;

with a spirit comparable to, even if distinguishable from Angelic Intelligences, lower once but higher in the end, higher even now than they, by reason, at the least, of the price paid for man's ransom; with a soul, an emanation from the Divine Essence, capable of seeing GOD and living, and destined to return to the fount of GODHEAD conjoined to the Creator, incorporated with the Redeemer, and inspired by the Sanctifier. The union of body, spirit, soul in man, alone of GOD'S creation can be self-described by the words, I am. The union alone possesses the singular and incommunicable attributes of man's personality.

Here it may be well to pause, in order to make a diversion. The word "creation" has been used to indicate the origination of man, first, because it is the true term, and next, because any other term is misleading and conveys a wrong, if not a false impression. On this wide topic it is at once difficult and dangerous to speak briefly. But the danger may be risked, if the difficulty can be surmounted. It cannot be affirmed too broadly or uncompromisingly, that any theory of the imagination of man which is based upon the principle of development, as opposed to that of creation; or any theory which searches for man's beginning in a germ or a norm, common to himself and less highly organized forms of creation, is at once actually unphilosophic and radically anti-Christian. But, on the present occasion there is no need to employ forcible language upon this question. It is sufficient to observe that the new theories, it may almost be said the cant terms, touching the "struggle for existence," the "survival of the fittest" and "natural selection," however undeniable, as a fact apart from any conclusion from it, when applied to the development of species in the lower creation, or even to the varied forms of the human species, are theories only, and are not demonstrated problems, when applied to the order of created beings which we call man. The theory of man's development from a less perfect organization is simply not proved. One evidence of this is enough. The creative hiatus which exists between the most degraded type of savage man, and the nearest approach to humanity in animal existence, is incalculable : and not only no discovery has been made, but no traces which on any reasonable hypothesis could lead to a discovery have been made, of a partially developed being, half human and half brutish, to fill the gap which avowedly exists between a complete man and a complete beast. The boldest flights of scientific imagination in our new teachers has failed to supply this hiatus. Until a proof of man's development from the brute creation be offered for the consideration of Christians, we may fairly accept the very sound premise of anti-Christian professors, and apply it against themselves. We may decline to assent to any theoretic position which is not clearly founded upon scientific evidence, which is not capable of positive proof.

Another consideration is not without its value, however much of self-assertion, from the circumstances of the case, is forced to enter into the statement. From one point of view there is much that is worthy of true admiration, and deserving of imitation at our hands, in the lives and researches of modern scientific men, truly so called. The devotion to the cause which they have at heart, the perseverance which they bring to their self-appointed task, the simplicity and patience with which they study the work of GOD'S hands, even if they do not always acknowledge His will—these and other traits demand and should receive our sincerest respect and honour. But other qualities which appear almost necessarily to be associated with scientific enquiry, and still more with amateur dallying with science, when not held in check by the sanctions of Revelation, cannot be disguised and must not be overlooked. It is enough to state these qualities without producing instances in support, which would be out of place.

First ; their dogmatism, whether or not the result of pride, is unbounded. The dogmatism of science is incomparably fiercer than that of theology, and is proportionately inexcusable, inasmuch as it is the product of variable opinion, not of assured faith.

In the second place; their opinions are formed on evidence far from conclusive, and on generalizations far too rapidly and hastily formed. Hence, there is little or nothing trustworthy in their conclusions as such; of which we, non-scientific observers, are conscious from the instability with which they are held, and the levity with which they are abandoned. The conclusions of to-day have certainly upset the results of yesterday; and the results of to-morrow will probably condemn the conclusions of to-day. But both are delivered with an air of infallibility: and if the professors may be credited with humility in owning their mistakes, they cannot claim the inspiration of sobered wisdom which prevents them from speedily and dogmatically reiterating fresh error.

But, in the third peculiarity is contained the most fatal obstacle to our acceptance of the unsupported dicta of transitional science. It consists in the absence, to an appreciable extent amongst many, if not all, of these new teachers of the world, of the logical faculty. Whilst the clergy are beyond question and comparison the inferiors of scientific men in the study of Nature and her laws, they may with some reason affirm themselves to be at least acquainted with the laws of thought. It is impossible to read the treatises of those who aim at leading scientific conjecture at the present day, without perceiving the grave failing here noted. The dogmatism and rash generalization of scientific men are as nothing to their want of logical precision. Specious assumption takes the place of solid argument: a high probability, which falls short of actual demonstration, is accepted in the stead of evidence: and the surmises, more or less acute, from the earlier pages of the same author, or from a prior volume of a kindred writer, are built upon as a sure foundation of positive proof. This failure in argumentative power is observable alike in purely scientific works, and in essays of a semi-historical and political character which are based upon them. In any case, the absence of the logical method, in regard to the creation of the human race, which is the point before us, is a fatal objection to the permanent value of such scientific enquiries. It effects, however, more for the Catholic. It altogether relieves him from the necessity of harbouring doubts in his old traditional faith : and in the presence of neological theories, however intelligent and attractive, it enables and even obliges him to pronounce, with whatever qualifications on the question at issue, the just verdict of " not proven."

IV.

Another thought in relation to the Image of GOD may well be proposed for consideration. The perfection, crown, and completion of GOD'S creative power was man. This proposition is undeniably true, in the abstract. But we must be on our guard that it be not narrowed nor limited in our acceptance of it. We must take no mere human and temporal view of such creation, of such image. Past and present are ever present with the Creator of all things. Hence, we lose much of the force of this thought when we confine it only to the present. It acquires its fulness only when we learn to hold three points : 1. that man, the centre and summit of creation, was created in the image of GOD, because from all eternity GOD was pleased to will the fulfilment of creation by the increase of His accidental glory ; 2. that such increase of glory was accomplished by the union of the creature with the Creator, under the form of man ; 3. that such form of man, willed from eternity, was the express Image of the FATHER, the GOD-MAN of both past and future, the Son of Mary of the present, CHRIST JESUS our LORD.

This extended view of the relation of man to creation, modifies some difficulties and removes others which beset the question. We may now, without hesitation or fear of any undue exaltation of the human race, its past career, its future destiny, affirm not only that man is the perfection and summit of creation, but also that for man's sake the mystery of creation was perfected. No language can be too decided for this assertion when we believe that, fore-ordained from all eternity, in the Incarnated GOD-MAN and not alone in the created image of GOD, was the fulfilment of creative power realized. Accepting this revelation, we can believe nothing short of the truth, that all creation was effected for Man's sake alone; all had reference to Man alone; all culminated in Man alone; all had meaning, value, power from Man alone— the Uncreated GOD in the form of Man. Accepting this, we may allow that, apart from the Archetypal Man in Whose Image created man was made, the human race possesses only a secondary, reflected and minor interest in creation. As a human being, indeed, he is the highest, most perfect, and chiefest of GOD'S works; but of himself and apart from his fore-ordained career and destiny, he is one only of many of the creatures of GOD, above the lower types of organization, though lower in the cosmic scale than the Angelic Intelligences. It is only because man was made in the Image of GOD, in the form present from all ages to the counsels of the Holy TRINITY, that he is supreme. Once admit that he was made in the Image through which the glory of the Unchangeable Majesty was augmented; once allow that the union of the Creator and the creature was predestined in the form of humanity, and man becomes the central point of creation around which everything revolves; and creation is seen to have been designed, effected, perfected for man's sake.

Keeping in mind this truth, that in the eternal counsels of the TRINITY the Son of Mary was the Archetypal Man not less than in time He was pleased to become the Representative and Pattern Man, creation presents itself from a fresh point of view. Not only was material creation in all its parts and as a complete whole emphatically declared to be good; but for the object of its existence, for the purpose for which it was made, for the end to which it was destined, it is and must be good. The greater glory of GOD cannot be increased, even accidentally, by aught that is not absolutely good: and such increase was to be effected by the union of the Creator with the work of His own Almighty hands. Let us then observe how and in what manner material creation contributed to this end; how and in what manner it were possible that GOD in the form of Man fulfilled the object of creation, fore-ordained before the foundation of the world.

The explanation can only be given in general terms in this place. But careful thought will show a development from the lowest forms of creation to the highest, not less scientifically and far more logically exact than the development theories of our new teachers. This development also can be accepted by theologians: indeed it is one explanation, though I would not say the only explanation, which satisfies all the conditions of truth. By its light we perceive, in the outward and physical manifestations of GOD'S power in action, that man is indebted, for his material existence, to each effort in succession of the Divine Will, lower in the scale of nature than himself. Of course, spiritual and psychical elements were superadded: but, for what man is indebted to matter, there was a true development, and yet, man was created in the predestined Image. From many evidences of this law which is stamped upon man, take four points: 1. man's earthly origination and end; 2. man's continuity and support in life; 3. human protection; 4. human enjoyment. In all these cases we may observe the law of development which rendered possible the union of the creature with the Creator; we may see how, in regard to man the created medium of such union, all the creatures of GOD, in use or abuse, produce or tend to produce the temptation to sin.

First: take man's earthly origin and end; what we came from, what we return to. However the mystery of our creation may be explained, it is clear that man was not created out of nothing: he was made from pre-created matter. This at once is a long step in the path of development. There is no need to refer chemically to the constitution of our bodies at the first. Suffice it to say that in the further development attending the close of our earthly career, our bodies will be reduced, if not to the elements of nature, almost to elemental substances, by the fresh action of created matter. Nor is the law of development less clear if we advance from the origin of the race to the first beginning of any member of it; from the earthly end of any member to our own dissolution. Development is the same in either case; and the requirements of nature for the increase of the human family, not less than the nearly inevitable surroundings of an average death-bed—are alike suggestive of the possibilities of sin even in one destined to increase the glory of GOD by ultimate union with his Creator.

Second: consider man's continuity and support in life. How is the body which was made from the material creation, sustained by the material creation? I answer, to a large extent, if not entirely, by these elements of human life: by gas under the forms of air and water, by light, by the earth and its mineral productions, by the flour of wheat and other vegetable life, and by flesh meat of animal existence. Of these, on the chemical combinations of gas, and on light, the larger part of creation which minister to man's support depend. Of the remainder, there is a clear law of development underlying their office and work in the life of man. Each ingredient in his composite existence plays its systematized part. The mineral products of earth are essential to the life of grass: the grass of the field is needful for prolonging the life of animals: and the animal creation helps to sustain the life of man. Hence, from inorganic matter, through the various forms of organism, up to the higher organization of animal existence, everything in material creation tends to the continuity of the earthly existence of man: man, whose form GOD took in the Person of CHRIST in time: man, himself created, eternally in the divine decrees, in the Image of GOD. How the question of sin enters into the relations between man and the material means of his sustenance and continuity is less obvious, at first sight, than the same question considered under the next heading. Still, there exist relations between man and the animal world, between man and the inanimate though organic world, even between man and inorganic creation, in the use and abuse of GOD'S gifts, into which questions of sinfulness and sinlessness cannot but be allowed to enter.

Third : reflect on man's protection in life. Having traced his many-sided sustenance through brute beasts to the vegetable kingdom ; through vegetables to earth and its mineral products, and even to gas and light—how does the material creation minister to the protection of man's life ? how does the question of sin affect such protection ? Reflect on the raiment he wears, the houses he lives in, the fire that warms him, his means both of defence and offence, the luxuries and refinements of life, artificial objects of utility or necessity, natural objects which tend to improve health or check disease —what are all these, and many other various adjuncts to the protection of the life of man, but products of material creation, animate or inanimate, in endless forms and under countless combinations ? What are all these, but steps in the law of development from the lowest to the highest forms of matter, all of which lead directly to the protection of man's every-day life, all of which tended indirectly to the Divine Life which one day was to appear? What are all these, in their employment or neglect ; in the use to which we place them or the abuse to which we subject them ; in the thoughts which they inspire or the longings which they create ; in the time we devote to their acquisition or the money we squander on their possession ; in the duties we postpone in their search or the opportunities for good we neglect when they are secured—what are these elements in the protection of man's life, but sources of temptation to sin to many souls, the cause of falling to some, and a possible means of purification, self-conquest and union with GOD to all, in the relations between sin and the human family?

Fourth: think of man's enjoyment. Here, once more, the law of development is apparent, though perhaps in a less potent form than in the two previous cases, because, and only because human enjoyment is less momentous than human protection, support, or origination. Still, if man's sensual gratification produces any effect upon his life, to a similar extent an effect has been produced upon the Life Divine which sprung from it in time, although from which it was designed in eternity. Such pleasures and enjoyments, however, in their use or abuse, intensify much more closely than before the relations of the image of GOD with sin. But, in both aspects, whether in regard to human wickedness or to the mystery of human development, the causes and issues of man's gratification in life are, as a fact which is beyond controversy, due to material creation. Think of them, so far as possible, abstractedly, in the strict meaning of the term sensual, and apart from man's mental powers. Think of them without importing into the question any details of such enjoyment in the present; without complicating the consideration with reference to the understanding which once grasped the enjoyment, the memory which dwells on its results, the will which must decide upon its acceptance. Think of them only as those that enter into man's being through the avenue of the senses, the five gateways of knowledge as they have been termed, the five portals of temptation as we may estimate them—the sounds we hear, the perfumes we smell, the flavours we taste, the sights we see, the sensations we feel. In each case, the gratification which ensued to the human frame, through the medium of the senses, was due to, was caused by, the influence of material creation; and hence, such enjoyment bears some relation, good or bad, to the question of sin.

V.

A further thought in relation to man and his creation may be dwelt upon. The crown and summit of GOD'S creative power is a being composed of a three-fold combination. It is needless to specify these integral parts. They are easily named: but it is not always easy, sometimes it is hard, to distinguish between them in their results, even if their differences of nature be distinct.

1st. The outward manifestation of the human race, the Body of man, was created by a personal great First Cause in the image of the GOD-MAN. Hence, even in his bodily relations, man may be considered to be a miracle of creative power—on this ground, as a being in which it were so much as possible for the Creator of all things to assume the form and characteristics of the creature; as the impersonation of a race of which it were possible that GOD should become one, when the WORD was made FLESH, and CHRIST was born of Mary. In meditating on the outer form of man, the earthly and perishable body which yet has had impressed upon it the elements of eternity, there is no need to think of our origin—what we came from; nor yet to recall our mode of existence—how we live and move and have our being; nor yet, again, to speculate on our latter end—whither we are tending and where we shall go. It is enough to consider what we are, what man is, as expressed in the formula, I am. Two points out of many may be considered.

(i.) We may think of the combination of opposites, almost the union of antagonisms, which dwell together, and even pervade the same human frame, to a large extent all human frames—the body of man. For instance: A man has ability to perform one function common to the human family; he is incapable to perform another, to the like extent common. The same person is blessed with health in one organ of the body; he is also, perhaps, blessed with sickness in another. Feebleness in the childhood of the race, beyond the helplessness of the young of any other animal, may be contrasted with strength in his manhood, which, directly or indirectly, is beyond the strength of all other. Inferior to the lower creation in the number of his requirements to sustain the vital forces at the highest state of efficiency; he is superior to the animal world in the faculty of obtaining them, and of making the best use of them when secured. Or, to pass from the evidences of life to its principle: man possesses power to transmit life to others, and to take away life, whether his own or another's; he is powerless to convey it to himself, or even to prolong beyond its predestined span of being his own short-lived existence. In sickness, he has capacity for taking poison which will be productive of benefit; in health, he receives food which may tend to his bodily injury. At all times his tenacity of life is great: and yet, how little is needed to quench the vital spark—a draught of air, a false step, an insignificant accident in a non-vital part, a shock to the nervous system, a little more or a little less of the ordinary appliances of existence, and the bowl is broken or the thread is snapped: and yet, again, how do weak women fight against incurable disease, how do strong men collapse under a slight attack. In all cases, our mortal life is begun only to draw to an end: we are born only to begin to die.

(ii.) We may think of the adaptations of means to the end, which are exhibited in each member of the human body. For instance—the eye; with its power to convey impressions of visible things to man's inner consciousness, their position, form, colour in themselves, their proportion or size, similitude or difference, distance or nearness in regard to oneself or to other things—a power which we do not fully realize until there is danger that it be lost or lessened. The ear; with its power to convey sound to the inner consciousness of man—a power, again, the value of which we cannot always realize until it be withdrawn—the simple sounds of nature, grand or low; the sweet sounds of music, alone or in harmony; the potent sounds of the human voice divine, soft or clear;

a power so marvellously ordered as to reject or modify sounds that would disturb or injure, whilst accepting, almost inviting, those that insure safety or cause pleasure. The heart; with its power to collect and disperse and collect again for reiterated dispersion the source of life, by regular pulsation, through arteries and endless veins—so long as life lasts, a type of perpetual motion. The hand; with its almost infinite power of varied motion, on which a volume, not might be, but has been written to indicate the divine handiwork upon human matter of an Almighty Creator.

All these adaptations of means to end, all these combinations of opposites in the body of man, the creative work of a personal First Cause, not in themselves, but in relation to the attitude which man takes towards them, and the manner in which he employs them in order to fulfil or neglect the object of his creation—all have a bearing on the question of man's sin.

2nd. The inner part of the composite being of man, his Spirit, was created by a personal great First Cause in the image of the GOD-MAN. If this be true of the outward casket which enshrines the gem, much more is it true of that which is enshrined, man's immortal spirit. We will confine our thoughts to three elements of one integral portion of man's spirit, the powers of his mind—the understanding, the memory, the will.

(i.) The Will is well called a power of the mind. What motive power in nature exists, which is comparable to a determined, resolute, inflexible, positive mental decision of man—I will? Short of performing a physical impossibility, nothing seems to be beyond its capacity for doing or suffering. The only power comparable to it, in the opposite direction, is the power of negation—I will not: none can make a man do that which he wills not to do. But consider the power of the affirmative statement. Not of the lips but of the spirit—I will. It spite of active opposition or passive discouragement; in spite of deficiency of means or resources in myself; in spite of want of sympathy or want of help from others—I will. Not now, perhaps, but some day; not to-day, but next year; not next year, but before I die—I will. Even if I conquer not time, which patience subdues; if I overcome not persons, whom tact and perseverance may win; if I secure not opportunities, which in general unexpectedly offer themselves; even, hardest battle of all, if I subdue not myself who eventually must be vanquished; yet —I will. I will get place and position; I will obtain learning and knowledge; I will increase money and lay a foundation for fame; I will grasp power and exert influence; I will "buy the truth" and "get wisdom"; even, if I take the proper means, I will secure true happiness and peace of mind both here and hereafter. Is anything beyond the power of man's will of which to possess himself, whether in this world or the next?

(ii.) The Memory of man may best be realized when we compare the almost exhaustless store of an intelligent educated, cultivated, thoughtful man with the un-burdened, un-tenanted mind of an infant: when we reflect on all that a child must not only learn but remember, must not only remember but digest and assimilate to its mental powers, before the infant mind can be developed into that of a full-grown adult. Reflect on a few points only in the mental composition of an average English gentleman, not by birth only, but by culture and refinement. Reflect on the languages, dead and living, which some men acquire; the science and art which they investigate and study; the history and politics which they can recall, argue upon, and act up to; the business matters and money-market transactions in which they labour or speculate; the persons they know and the characters they are forced to read; the future they have to provide for, whilst they must not neglect their present work in life—these, not to speak of the truths of Religion, are all, more or less, stored in, these all influence the memory of a single human being. He has to remember them, or to act upon them, or to let them minister to his life, or to make his life influence them; and even if he be forgetful and allow some to escape his memory, he has, by an effort of the mind, to recall them. Moreover, by a mental process which it is difficult to explain, but which every one practically adopts, there are certain details of knowledge, facts, or events that are either unconsciously not remembered, or are deliberately placed aside and forgotten.

(iii.) The intellectual part of man, as distinct from his memory and will, is termed the Understanding, It includes, amongst others, the inventive, philosophic, imaginative, logical, and imitative powers of the mind. The understanding can compass the principles and expression of art, be it architecture, sculpture, painting, or music; can master the elements and trace the results of science, be it geology, chemistry, astronomy, or mathematics; can follow the outline of the laws of thought and fathom some of its philosophic depths; can learn the details and apply the practice of the trades of the artisan, or mechanic, or other labourer; can reproduce the words and actions of others, and conceive, with more or less approach to the truth, how persons have thought, spoken, and acted under known circumstances, how they would act, speak, and think under imagined or possible circumstances.

These powers of the mind, the understanding, memory, and will, the work of a divine and personal First Cause in the creation of the human race, are some of the integral parts of the composite and many-sided spirit of man. It needs only a glance at the manner in which man applies or ignores his power, even more superficial than has been taken at the powers themselves, to assure us that these three elements enter deeply and widely, whether by the guilt of omission or of commission, into the question of man's sin.

3rd. The innermost and most central portion of man's being, the Soul, was created in the image of a Personal . GOD. This fact, if there be degrees in certitude, is far truer of the soul than either of the spirit or the body of man. Both the body and spirit of man, be their wonders never so great, pale before the marvels of his soul. Here we stand upon the margin, if again there be degrees of ignorance, of a more absolute unknown than in the two former cases. Here it were better, wiser, more reasonable, more humble to ask certain questions, and to allow GOD to answer them to each inquirer in the silence of his own most hidden being. Consider its source: whence comes the soul of man to man; how came it and by what means; when did it come and by what agency—to you, to me, to all? Consider its composition: of what elements does the soul consist, or does it consist of any integral parts; is it a pure indivisible essence, or is it composite in character, part divine and part human? Consider its existing condition: what evidence can be produced for the existence of the soul; how does it live; how does it act; what are the results of its action on itself, on others, on GOD? Consider its future destiny: whither goes the soul; how does the soul go; why does it go; to whom does it go; to what does it go—from this life to the next, from time to eternity? If these questions, Brother or Sister in CHRIST, should prove insufficient for devout meditation, consider this further inquiry: have I a soul, and how am I assured that I have one?

The soul of man, of which such all-momentous questions may be asked, is perhaps less the creative work of a divine and personal First Cause, than an emanation from the essence of the Almighty; and may be described, again perhaps, not so much as a positive creation in the image of the GOD-MAN, as a scintillation from the Light of Light and as an effluence from the source of DEITY temporarily severed indeed from its sacred origin now, but destined to be re-united to the GODHEAD for endless ages hereafter. But here we tread on unknown ground; and our steps must be wary. Yet may it be hazarded, that more intimately, far more intimately than either the body or the spirit of man, is the soul affected by the question of sin—more intimately, if not in the cause of sin, at least in its results; more intimately in the next life, if not in the present.

VI.

In meditating upon GOD the great First Cause in relation to the sin of man, we were led to consider sin in the abstract. As we meditate upon the like truths from a different standpoint, from a human rather than from a divine, and consider man, made in the image of GOD, in relation to sin, it may be wise to adhere to the same principle. We will consider man's sin, therefore, apart from its moral character, whether in regard to its cause or consequence. We have seen also, though it be difficult to frame a definition of sin, yet, that sin is capable of being identified with some of its results which bear a physical aspect. In this light we will endeavour to obtain an estimate of sin in the abstract, by comparing certain acknowledged effects in nature with the hypothetical results of sin.

The results I would ask you to meditate upon are threefold. In each case, sin must be considered as an objective reality; outside and apart from self; independent of and distinct from all we think about it, feel about it, believe about it; without reference to our caring or not caring that we have sinned, to our being afraid or fearless of having sinned, to our instinct that somehow and somewhere our sin will find us out and will have to be accounted for. In each case, sin must be considered as an act in the moral world; and as such, and so far as it is possible, it must be compared to an act in the physical world. These three results bring us face to face with three main characteristics in an act of sin committed by man, whether it be a deed done, a word spoken, or a thought deliberately encouraged. We will take them in order.

I. The first characteristic of sin in man made in the image

of a Personal GOD is this: an act once done, is done for ever. It is a law of nature, that a force once generated, continues intact until another force diminishes or checks its effects. A common-place instance of the result of this law in motion, may be seen in a rolling ball. A ball once set in motion will roll for ever, if gravitation and friction be counteracted, if obstacles be removed from its path, and if it comes into contact with nothing external to itself. Another instance may be given, of permanence in an act done. Drive a nail into a wall. So long as the wall and the nail remain under the same conditions, positively and relatively, so long will the nail remain fixed in the wall. Not otherwise is it with man's action in the moral world: not otherwise is it with sin.

For example—to take the simplest cases of this law, as equally apposite with the most involved—if you strike a person in anger, a blow is given. It is something done: it is done for ever. No after action can undo the blow, can make as though it had not been done. You may be sorry. The other may be forgiving. Both may forget. GOD may absolve. Anything done by either human being falls short of causing the deed to be undone, of causing it not to have been done. No earthly power can do this—not even the mighty Power of GOD. The guilt of the act may be pardoned: but even absolution does not undo that which once has been done. It is a case of the nail in the wall. Again: if you set a story rolling along the path of life—be it true or false, bad or good, kind or scandalous—the story goes on rolling, perhaps for ever, certainly for ever so far as the speaker's power is concerned. Once past your lips, it is something done, done for ever. It is worse than the material ball once set in motion, which the longer it travels the further it recedes. It is worse: because, so far from friction and gravitation tending to stop it, so far from obstacles standing in its way on which it may impinge, the impetus of the story is increased and the path of its career is cleared by the repetition or invention, by the exaggeration or suppression of others. You may indeed be sorry—if the story be false, or if, even though true, it be told with a bad motive. Your victim may forget it. It may be forgotten by both: and GOD may have pardoned it. Anything may be done but one: it cannot be re-called; it cannot be unsaid. It goes on, does the story, be it denied or substantiated, be it explained or explained away, further and further from you indeed in this life; it goes on expanding in ever widening concentric circles, wave after wave, on the ocean of time until, far from receding from you in the next life, it will break at your feet on the shores of eternity.

II. The second characteristic of sin in man made in the image of a Personal GOD is this: an act once done, the doer of it loses all control over the action. Some of the features of this characteristic appear also in the lineaments of the first. But some, also, are new. The examples of the ball and the nail are again apposite here. After the ball has left the hand, its course cannot be changed by the hand which impelled it. After the hammer has smitten the nail, the inclination of the nail cannot be altered by the action which determined its course. Not otherwise is it with the deed done, or the word spoken. Once done, once uttered, the actor loses all control over his action. The blow may have caused some serious physical result to a delicate organ, or its effect may have been unnoticed. The story may have effectually blighted a person's character, or it may have fallen harmless, saving only to the person who gave it utterance. In both cases alike, the actor has lost power over the work of his hand or the fruit of his lips. You may try to stop it, and seek to prevent some of its results. You may attempt to turn it, and hope to counteract some of its effects. You may, indeed, succeed, to an extent, in mitigating the evil, and even in bringing good out of bad. But, in controlling your action once done—no. A stone cast into the sea. A bird let out of a cage. The wild animal escaped from the snare. One liquid mixed with another. These are faint images of a blow struck or a word spoken. All control over either, once having been done, whether by the actor or speaker, is gone, gone for ever.

III. The third characteristic of sin in man made in the image of a Personal GOD alone remains to be considered. It may be thus formulated: an act once done, can only be counteracted by a power superior to itself. And the term "counteracted" is used in a wide sense in this formula. Some of the features in this characteristic, once more, appear also in the lineaments of the first two: but some also, again, are new. In this case, too, the analogy of physical creation will help us to understand the laws of the moral world in the action of sin. A small effort may produce motion, which the same effort, or a power many times multiplied, is unable to restrain. Witness the locks of a canal, or the flood-gates of a tidal stream, which perhaps a child might open, but which many men could not close against a full rush of water. If the resisting or opposing power be only equal to, not to say less than, the energizing force which it essays to counteract the impetus of the body in motion will carry it through such opposition or resistance. Witness the course of an express train, and any insufficient power to withstand it. So in the moral world. Man has almost infinite power to create force and motion in the sphere in question: he is infinitely powerless to counteract it, when once action has been taken. It is thus with the word spoken and the blow given. Neither can be counteracted by the human agent who originated them. For their undoing, morally but not physically, the word and the blow require the infinite power of the Almighty Creator of all things, the personal great First Cause.

In the discussion of these three characteristics of an act of sin, our consideration of them has been restricted to a deed done and a word uttered. This limitation has been advisedly made. With the time at our disposal, it had been impossible to discuss the more intricate question of the bearing of these characteristics on a thought deliberately encouraged. Moreover, the last division of sin does not stand so clearly upon the same ground as the two earlier divisions. That all three occupy the same position from a moral stand-point, we are assured on the authority of our Divine Master, in terms which admit of no qualification, and with a distinctness which prevents our mistaking them. But, from a physical point of view, it may be admitted, the analogy lacks completeness, at least with our present highly imperfect knowledge of the cause and effect of mental action upon our corporate being.

But, although the influences of these characteristics upon encouraged sinful thought have not been treated vocally, there is no sufficient reason why they should not be considered in silent meditation, each in the solitude of his own meditation. Indeed, knowing as we do know, the power and strength and reality of sinful thought which is deliberately encouraged in our soul, even though it find not consummation in act or speech, there is much need of our undertaking such a meditation for ourselves. It is not improbable, nay, it is more than likely, that the meditation on the sins of thought wilfully entertained, which we make for ourselves, will be far more profitable to our souls than those on the sins of word and deed, which another has made for us. And this probability will be increased if we are content to adhere to the lines above indicated, and we meditate on sins of thought under the same three-fold heading of sins of action, namely, that an act once done, is done for ever; that an act once done, the doer loses all control over it; and that an act once done, can only be counteracted by a power superior to itself.

ADDRESS SIX.

MAN PURCHASED BY GOD.

WHEN, in the infinite wisdom and eternal counsels of the Most Holy TRINITY, it was predetermined that GOD'S accidental glory should be increased by the act of creation, then, in the perfect and absolute foreknowledge of the Creator, all that ensued from such determination was seen as definitely, point by point, as if it had already occurred. The mystery of the Incarnation of the Second Person of the TRINITY formed a portion of the results of the act of creation.

In future addresses certain truths in relation to the Incarnation of GOD will be considered, of which one may be mentioned, and only mentioned, now: the union of the creature with the Creator was predetermined apart from, and independent of, the sin of man. In no sense was sin, or its atonement, the primal cause of that marvel of all marvels. But, though the sin of man was not the primal cause of the Incarnation, yet, in some sense and to a certain extent is influenced the accidents of that mystery, viewed in connection with man—namely, the time of its accomplishment, the manner in which it was carried out, the surroundings amongst which it was enacted, the effects which flowed from its fulfilment. And more than this may be admitted, without suffering man in any degree to trench upon the prerogatives of GOD. In the plenitude of the permissive Will, sin was allowed by GOD to exercise an influence on the death of CHRIST, and its results. Indeed, it must be reverently held in relation to man's purchase by GOD, that the sin of man, for its atonement, demanded the death of GOD.

The single word "Incarnation" mentally opens out a wide prospect for devout thought. It even necessitates some allusion of a dogmatic character—not, however, as regards Catholics in retreat for their own soul's sake, but rather for their intellectual support when, after retreat and against their will, they are forced to hear the doctrine of the Church questioned; and still more against their will, when they are forced into argument in its defence. One thought of a controversial kind will be sufficient for us to entertain here. It is this: the inconsistency of that mental position which, whilst in terms it acknowledges the Divinity of our Blessed LORD, yet disallows the dogma which is correlative to it— that His sacred death was the actual price paid for man's sin.

Apart from reference to the teaching of Catholic tradition on this point, there exists a fatal objection to the affirmative side of this negation—namely, that CHRIST died for something short of sin. The assertion is at issue with the truth which in words is accepted—namely, that JESUS was GOD. At the least, there is a logical inconsistency in a failure to receive both truths. For, if we believe in the absolute and perfect Divinity of the Historical CHRIST of the Gospel, if we believe that JESUS was Very, Living and True GOD, there is in the nature of things a want of consistency between the hypothetic cause and consequence of the Incarnation, in the opinion which admits that for any result short of the redemption of the human race CHRIST was pleased to die. It is, to man's power of reason, utterly inconceivable that so stupendous an event should have occurred in the universe merely to produce a moral effect however great, or to supply man with a moral example however perfect—inconceivable, of course, without the sanction of Revelation. Revelation alone could persuade mankind that the Creator of all things took upon Him the nature of man, and endured such a life as He endured, and suffered such a death as He suffered, in order to teach the human race the elements of morality. The consequence is infinitely out of proportion to the cause: there is no earthly example with which to compare it. If CHRIST'S life and CHRIST'S death were efficacious only to give men a model of humility, of patience, of gentleness, of purity, of truthfulness, of self-abnegation, of love—it is not too much to say, with all reverence, that His devoted life, and His awful death were works of supererogation. The like results might have been secured by means infinitely less momentous and infinitely less costly.

But more than this truth forces itself on the religious consciousness of man. If this superhuman career produced no results beyond the evidence of a spotless example, it is impossible to believe in the Divinity of the perfect Man. We may indeed accept the moral teaching of His sacred and sinless life; but apart from the GODHEAD of CHRIST in union with the Manhood, it is difficult to see what ethical teaching may be deduced from the Gospel narrative of His sacrificial death. No. Let us be as consistent in our acceptance, as others are in their denial, of GOD'S truth. Let us either frankly believe in the Divinity of CHRIST and the Atonement for man's sin; or admit that a denial of the price paid for sin necessarily involves a rejection of His Divinity. To accept the Deity of CHRIST and not to accept the Atonement, is logically indefensible. When, however, we loyally hold to both revealed dogmas, then and not before we may make our own the words of the Collect for the Second Sunday after Easter, and pray unto Almighty GOD, Who has given His Only SON to be both a sacrifice for sin and also an ensample of godly life, to give us grace to receive that His inestimable benefit, and also to endeavour ourselves to follow the blessed steps of His most holy life.

II.

The Incarnation and Death of GOD, the sin of man and man's purchase, stand in mutually intimate relations. In such relationship four points may be considered which will to an extent exhaust the question of purchase. They are as follows: 1. the Person by Whom the offer of sale was made, in man's purchase from sin; 2. the Person willing to accept the offer of sale, and to pay the price required for man's purchase from sin; 3. the Object offered for purchase; and 4. the Terms on which the purchase was made. In other words, we may take these forms on which to meditate: by Whom, Who, What, How much? in relation to sin.

We will take these questions in order.

I. The Person Who consented to the purchase of man, by Whom, indeed, such purchase was in any wise made possible. This was none other than GOD Himself, the great personal. First Cause of all things; the Self-originated, existent, subsisting; the Eternal, Omniscient, Omnipotent; the Ever-present, Everliving I AM; the Everlasting FATHER of the Co-equal SON; the One, Very and True GOD. Such is the Person by Whom the purchase of the creature from the effects of his own sin has been accepted in the divine decrees in the ages of ages; by Whose consent it was accomplished in the course of time past; by Whose co-operation it is fulfilled now, and will be fulfilled individually in His Church unto the consummation of all things.

On the attributes and operations of the Almighty FATHER, in relation to the sin of man, we have already meditated. But there is one further line of thought, that has more than a single branch and bears especial reference to the purchase of man, which is deserving of careful consideration. Of the many attributes of the great personal First Cause, perhaps none is expressive of so many other attributes, none is connected with or involves so many more, none offers so large and incalculable a contrast to the creatures of His Almighty hand, as that of Infinity. Moreover, it is noteworthy that the larger part of the attributes of the DEITY which are not covered by the noun substantive with the same import, may be expressed or emphasized by the use of its adverb, "infinitely." Apart from the profane speculation which, in plain terms, would personate GOD as man, only infinitized, this attribute presents a difference between the Creator and the creature which nothing can diminish or overcome. In all the qualities of man reflected or derived from the Divine Being, infinity is an element which cannot be obscured. In all the relations of the GODHEAD which exist without reference to the human race, infinity is an element which cannot be ignored. Infinity is essentially an attribute of the DEITY, as finality is essentially a characteristic of mankind—a changeless characteristic of man, in regard to any approach towards the infinite, in spite of the element of eternity in the life to come which has been supernaturally conveyed to a thing of time. From a divine point of view, this element of infinity must be held to be stamped upon all that primarily affects the question of man's purchase by GOD. How may this be stated in order to commend itself to our consciousness? Perhaps, by considering the question by the light of a typical example.

We have seen that the Person by Whom the offer of purchase was made is infinite in His attributes and operations. We shall see that the Person Who accepted the offer of purchase is infinite; and that the price which was paid for the purchase is infinite in character. Can we forbear to believe that infinity also is impressed upon the cause that required the price to be paid, the offer to be accepted, and the offer to be made of man's purchase from sin—which cause is known as the guilt of sin? If we fail to assent to the position that infinity characterizes the guilt of human sin, we are reduced to the alternative that an infinite price was paid for an object that is finite; that One could give and One could receive that which is infinite, on behalf of that which lacked infinity. No: the sacrifice of the Eternal SON to the Everlasting FATHER for the sin of the world was not made for anything which failed in the characteristic of infinity. The guilt of sin is infinite, however hard it may be to predicate and prove such a characteristic of aught that is human. Finality alone adheres to the finite agent who sins.

This position may be defended on several grounds. One is sufficient for our present purpose—one which lays no weight on the infinite greatness of Him against Whom sin is committed, on the infinite littleness of him who commits the sin, on the power possessed by the creature of counteracting the object of the Creator in the work of His hands, or on the results of sin if carried to their legitimate conclusions. It cannot be doubted that infinity attaches to his sin, if only for this reason, that finite man was unable to atone to the Infinite; his sin demanded, his sin obtained, an atonement which was infinite. Expiation which fell short of infinity was not, could not be, accepted; could not be, was not so much as, offered. Expiation on the part of the creature was as impossible as that on the part of the Angelic intelligences; was equally impossible with expiation on the part of the sinner himself. Hence, it is not unreasonable to affirm that the sin of man against GOD—not in regard to itself, nor in regard to its results, but in relation only to its atonement—bears in GOD'S sight the impress of infinity.

This conclusion leads us to another thought of momentous importance, in the question of man's purchase from sin. If the sin of finite man be stamped with the impress of infinity, what can be said of the punishment due to that which so clearly bears such features? This alone can be said: that the punishment due to, the punishment which will be required for, the guilt of sin is infinite. And infinite punishment to man who is finite in his creation, though endowed with prospective immortality; to man who in his creation is capable of infinite pain as to extension, though incapable of it as to intensity—is punishment without end, everlasting, lasting for ever. This is one aspect only of a mysterious, awful, and most painful subject. It is not the truest aspect. It is not one which is open to the fewest objections. It is not the easiest explained to any inquirer. It is not the fittest to

L

urge upon disbelievers. But it is true and certain and beyond controversy in itself. And it is a view of truth which is not unsuitable in a Retreat, to the subject under discussion, and for the consideration of faithful Christians.

Perhaps the explanation of the doctrine of everlasting punishment which is least offensive in the eyes of a world professedly Christian, which is equally suitable for a Retreat, and is more conformable to the teaching of the Sacramental system of the Church, may be stated thus: that one who consciously dies in a state of wilfully mortal sin, dies outside the state of grace; and it is only to one within such a state of grace, and during life, that worthy repentance for deadly, wilful sin can be made. It is wise to formulate the case broadly and without qualifications, in order to perceive the principles involved. Special or anomalous cases need not detain us. The case supposed is the case of a baptized Christian, living under the sanctions of a covenanted dispensation. Such an one is conscious of the effect of sin; namely, that wilfully sinning, he fails to fulfil the object of his creation. He is assured and knows that, in the present life only consists the period of his probation; in the present life only he enjoys the mysterious power of being able to withstand the will of his Creator; in the present life only he can secure the blessed privilege of restoration to his covenanted position, even when he has wilfully failed in the object of his creation—of course, upon specified terms. The covenanted mode of pardon for sin, in a Christian, during this life, is pledged by GOD only to grace conveyed through the Sacraments of the Church. Indeed, grace is needed to predispose us to desire grace, as the Collect teaches us in the words: Prevent us, O LORD, in all our doings.

Of course, in estimating the case supposed, we do not presume to place limits on GOD'S mercy: we are content to abide by the limits which GOD Himself has imposed. And these limits are two-fold: they are, absolutely and to all men, confined to this life; and they are, by covenanted mercy, restricted to the Sacramental system of the Church. Grace is only attainable through the Sacraments, not apart from them, not without a desire for their reception, not without a desire inspired by GOD. Grace is only attainable in this life, not in the next life, not in the intermediate state, not at the moment of death. But by grace alone, in GOD'S Church, and by methods which need not be here described, can sinners become reconciled to an offended GOD: by grace alone can they escape the eternal punishment due to sin. Hence, sinners who are so unhappy, and it may be added are so criminal, as to die outside a state of grace, and in a state of mortal and wilful sin, are simply powerless to repent thereafter—powerless, beyond all other reasons, on two grounds, 1. because they are cut off from GOD'S preventive grace to feel contrition for sin, and 2. because they are beyond the power of Sacramental grace to bring such contrition to perfection in the fruits of penance. The result, however awful, must be spoken: the retributive punishment due to such guilty souls is infinite.

It is not without cause that this very painful subject has been here touched upon. Serious heresy has, of late, been broached upon the doctrine of everlasting punishment; and those who ought to have been defenders of the truth, whether clergy or laity, have, in certain instances, either directly abetted or indirectly supported the heresy, in sermons, books, and pamphlets, letters to newspapers, or reviews. Of this form of disbelief, as of some others, it has been well remarked, by one who has written learnedly in defence of the incriminated dogma, that it is seldom found as an isolated item of heresy in a man's unbelief: and the justice of this statement has been observed in the attacks upon the doctrine that have recently been made. In relation to the question of our meditation, it is almost impossible for those who deliberately harbour a doubt on the eternal loss of souls, to be possessed by a true realization of the nature and result of man's sin. This ensues from a repetition of the error before condemned, in principle—namely, the estimate of sin from a human stand-point, in the stead of one that is divine.

It may be natural, if not excusable, for one who looks at sin on its human side only ; who recognizes how the world, even its less worldly portion, looks upon sin ; who believes that, in comparison with the All-pure and in His sight, there exists but little difference between the greatest sinner and the greatest saint ; who, if he consider sin in the light of GOD'S attributes, views it in the aspect of His infinite Mercy rather than of His absolute Justice—it may be natural for such an one to entertain a doubt, whether or not the punishment of the guilt of sin can be everlasting. But our holy Religion is revealed and above nature. And when we estimate sin on its superhuman side, in regard to GOD Who suffers instead of man who causes Him to suffer ; when we remember, at the least and apart from all other considerations, the divine atonement made to the Infinite Himself by the Everlasting SON ; when we remember that the sacred Blood of JESUS CHRIST was shed as payment for the least sin, and realize all that is contained in these words—then, it is natural too on our side, and it needs no apology from us, to believe in the continuous stream of Catholic tradition which teaches, that the punishment due to man's sin is everlasting ; and that such punishment, if not remitted in this life, will, as a revealed fact, last for ever.

One caution only need be added to what has been said on this topic for thought. The Catholic doctrine of Purgatory, or by whatever term the Intermediate State, and the condition of the soul therein, may be described, in no wise touches, or indeed can be forced into contact with, the doctrine of the Eternity of Punishment. The teaching of the Church on the Intermediate State is the greatest possible comfort to those who know their own unworthiness under the highest state of grace to which man can attain. It is also an inexpressible relief to be able to think of a state of purification for those of whom at their deaths we, without any breach of charity, may be doubtful in regard to grace. But the one dogma cannot be utilized by those who deny the other. A condition of nearer and still nearer approach to such perfection, that we may be able to see GOD and live, is prepared only for those who pass into it, by GOD'S mercy, in His divine favour. The true doctrine of Purgatory affects those alone who die in a state of grace. The heresy of Universalism is applied to those who die in a state of unforgiven sin. These two positions are irreconcilable.

II. The Person Who was willing to pay the price required for man's purchase from sin. This was none other than the SON of GOD; Consubstantial, Co-eternal, Co-equal with the FATHER; Very and Eternal GOD. It was none other than the Divine Being Whose GODHEAD we hold; the Logos, the Word, the Wisdom of GOD; Who in the beginning was, was with GOD, was GOD—GOD blessed for ever. Amen. It was none other than He, MAN and GOD, Whose every act, every word, every thought, was the thought and word and action of GOD: Whose every act and word and thought was performed, uttered, conceived as the Saviour of the World: Whose whole life was a life of redemption, purchase, atonement, in regard to man—in a word, salvatorial: Whose life was salvatorial, not only, not chiefly, not exclusively in the sacred Passion, though for purposes of devout contemplation pre-eminently there; but in each phase and in every detail of it: Whose life, whether of obedience, or of labour, or of self-sacrifice, or of glory, was, through the intention with which He was pleased to live, a sacrificial offering for the sin of man, and in this way too was salvatorial.

Such was the Person willing and able—able, powerful first; then willing, wishful, desirous with intense desire—to fulfil the terms of purchase in regard to sin. And on some aspects of the human life and superhuman attributes of this Divine Person, we have already meditated. But, perhaps, the last point above mentioned may not have been realized with sufficient clearness; namely, the Salvatorial Life of CHRIST. Let us endeavour, then, to make this characteristic of His sacred life more distinct to our own consciousness.

The view or opinion, for it cannot be admitted to be more definite, that would confine the Salvatorial Life of CHRIST within the boundary of His Passion-woes, is as limited and confined as the opinion or view, that the Incarnation itself was a divine device to counteract the sin of man. Both perhaps arise from taking man in the stead of GOD as the initial and central point in theology. It more nearly approaches an article of faith to hold that, in the sacred life, every act and word and thought of JESUS possessed its sacrificial character and had a salvatorial value. Such an estimate is allowed, by many persons, to have force in a devotional aspect, and even as a poetical licence in religious verse; but in no sense is it allowed by them in CHRIST'S life before or after His Passion, and it is often restricted to the culminating point of the Passion itself, to the act of crucifixion. But, if such an estimate be true, it is true of the life of CHRIST as a whole, as well as in every part, whether before, at, or after the Passion of GOD. Indeed, we should do well to consider the Passion itself, not as a distinct portion of the sacred life—for where does the Passion begin, and where does it end?—but rather, as an element in, as an integral part of, His earthly career; separable, of course, in meditation from all that went before, and from all that followed, but separable only in thought. This method of viewing the life of our Blessed LORD will enable us to perceive three marked stages in the divine drama of the Incarnation, in relation to man's sin. The three acts are these: 1. before the Annunciation to Mary in the ages of ages; 2. during the three-and-thirty years of the Infancy, Ministry, Death, and Resurrection of CHRIST on earth; 3. after His Ascension into heaven, and His Session on the Right Hand of Power.

In the first of these divisions, the Eternal WORD was

Saviour by anticipation, to speak as man speaks, in will, not in deed; or, to speak more exactly, He was Saviour in the eternal counsels of the divine decrees. In the second division, JESUS was the Saviour actually in thought, word, and deed, the Mediator in a life of sacrifice. In the third, CHRIST is the Saviour retrospectively as well as in the present, and prospectively as well as in relation to the past, the Intercessor on the great White Throne. The salvatorial life by anticipation developed into the sacrificial phase; and the sacrificial phase was perfected in the intercessorial. Indeed, from one point of view, and in relation to time, the sacrificial life was the only one to which we can point as having had both beginning and end. The anticipation was pre-ordained from all eternity: the perfected life will have no end until the consummation of all things. Inspired history tells us of the one: faith and reason combine to assure us of the other—that the intercession will be ceaseless, that the sacrifice of the Cross will be re-newed continually in heaven, so long as the unbloody offering of it shall be repeated here on earth.

The salvatorial element in the Incarnation of GOD includes three distinct phases. All the three epochs, if we may so speak of that which is really indivisible, have their several sacrificial value: 1. as that of the Lamb slain before the foundation of the world; 2. in the actual offering of the sacrifice itself on the Cross of Calvary; 3. by the perpetual re-presentation, in union with the unbloody offering on earth, of the offering in heaven.

Of the first epoch—the Lamb slain—it is not easy to speak; nor indeed, is it necessary—though types and figures of the Old Testament help us to realize the anticipated sacrifice. But, inasmuch as the future is ever-present with the past to the Eternal, the results of the Incarnation in relation to man's sin were equally real to the mind of GOD in their salvatorial aspect prospectively, as if their salvatorial character had been set forth in time before the world, Angels, men, and devils, upon the Hill of Calvary.

Of the last epoch—the perpetual re-presentation—it may be reverently asked: Why did our Blessed LORD ascend to the Right Hand of GOD with all the marks of the Passion imprinted on His glorified Body, if He had been pleased to abandon His salvatorial character when He left the widowed Church on earth? Why did He bear on high to the Throne of GOD the wounds of the nails and the cruel spear on His sacred hands and feet and side? Why were not obliterated the effects left by the agony, the smiting and buffeting, the crown of thorns, the three-fold fall, the scourge with knotted thong? Why did He ascend glorified indeed, but still the Man of Sorrows in His outward appearance, such as His disciples and the holy women recognized and worshipped? Why were these things recorded and handed down to us, if not, amongst other and deeper reasons, to assure us that the evidence of the Passion-act in the salvatorial life of JESUS are pleaded continually by our great High Priest in heaven?

Nor of the actual offering on the Cross is it otherwise, if we may consider its culminating point as typical of the entire sacrificial life of CHRIST. The salvatorial element is here clearly seen by all men. But all men do not clearly see that the truth which they admit of the closing scene of that life may be affirmed also of all its scenes; they do not see that what they affirm of the Passion itself as a whole, is true also of each element in the Passion. It is not, however, with the Passion as a whole that the devout disciple is alone concerned. It is not with its fearful yet blessed events in the aggregate only that Holy Church deals in her commemorative offices. Each and every portion is commemorated by her, and each scene and every act must be individualized by us, as an integral part of the salvatorial life of the divine Sufferer. Each act which He performed and every deed done to Him; each time He opened His sacred lips and the words which fell from them, and every word which others spake to Him; each scene in the Passion and every actor there; the place, the time, the manner, the circumstance—all and everything have a sacrificial value in regard to the sin of man: all and everything played their part in the salvatorial life of Him Who was willing and desirous to pay; Who was able and powerful to pay; ay, and Who, thank GOD, did actually pay, the price required for the redemption of the human race.

III. The Object offered for purchase. This was none other than Man—you and I; collectively and individually; as a race, and as units of the race. Man—you and I; as if none other had been created, as if none other had sinned. Man, with all his sins upon his head, the representative of the world, with the world's sin for all time past and all time to come to be atoned; you and I, as types of mankind, with all our sins upon our head, as if none other had to be atoned. Man was the object of purchase; Man, of whose creation we have thought in the last meditation, of whose sanctification we shall think in the next, whose redemption we are considering now—Man, who for purposes of thought stands alone in creation with GOD. Man, again, whose personality, identity, individuality, is expressed in the words, I am. Man, endowed as we have seen with memory, understanding and will; who is, moreover, an intelligent, reflective, accountable, self-conscious being, composed of spirit and soul and body— Man was the object purchased.

Such was the object offered for purchase, the object actually purchased from sin, Satan, death, and hell. Such was one result of the sin of man atoned by the Blood of GOD.

On the object of purchase we have, perhaps, sufficiently meditated before. But there is one point in connexion with the divine price paid for human guilt, which has not been considered and demands some attention. This point has two aspects, one turned towards GOD, one turned towards man. From it we perceive the infinite compassion of GOD and the infinite ingratitude of man. It may be stated thus: as man in reality exists in the world alone with GOD; so, with no figure of speech, the price of man's purchase, the Precious Blood-shedding, was offered, was accepted for his individual sin, alone. This is a truth which it is hard to realize; but it is a truth. How this is to be explained by reason, may not be easy to perceive; but it is capable of explanation to faith. If the Precious Blood be not shed for your sin and for my sin, shed as if none other had to be atoned; then, your sin and mine, and each act of your sin and mine, in thought, word, and deed, of commission and omission, deadly and venial, are un-atoned, and we are yet in our sins. If the Blood of CHRIST has not taken away the sin of each individual sinner, then the overpowering thought absorbs us, that GOD and the soul are not alone in creation; that another reality exists; that the blessed duality has given place to a trinity of existence which cannot be called holy; that sin has still to be reckoned as an element which stands between the creature and the Creator; and that GOD, and the soul, and sin, form the triad with which both theology and humanity are concerned.

It were needless to insist upon this proposition, which is almost self-evident to faith, were it not that here too heresy has been rife. It is a popular opinion, that the purchase of man was made as the purchase of a race only, and that his sin was atoned in the aggregate alone. CHRIST'S Blood, it is said, was shed for the sins of the world; not for your sins and my sins individually, but only for yours and mine in the gross. This view of the Atonement can claim indeed the virtue of simplicity; but it is imperfect from not being exhaustive. It is grand in outline; but it is wanting in detail. Tested by the touchstone of the Christian Religion, personality, it fails to bring home to the individual sinner the consciousness of personal guilt for individual sin. Indeed, the theory possesses no means of personally applying the benefit of the purchase-price to the sinner purchased. How could it possess the means, when it deals, not with particular sins, but only with sin in general? Why should it exercise the means, even if it be possessed of them, when hypothetically it affirms that the world's sin has been atoned by the world's Redeemer, and systematically denies that individual sin has been purchased by individual redemption? These questions are not easily answered.

But it is easy to perceive why no effort has been made to answer these questions by those who hold to the theory. Once be persuaded of the guilt of sin in the gross only, and not of sin in detail; once be deceived by the opinion that the atonement of such guilt was made for the universe alone, and not man by man, and the sense of the guilt of sin in the individual is lost in the feeling—or rather, in the absence of feeling—for the guilt of a whole world. Even if it were possible for finite man to realize the guilt of the world, its weight would affect him but little, simply from his inability to bear it. But finite man can realize, after his ability, the weight of his own individual sin; and when the weight of personal guilt is realized, it is felt to be unbearable. We are therefore happy in being able to place such burden upon One, Who is both willing and powerful to bear it. We are thankful to believe, not only that the world's guilt, but our own personal and individual guilt, has been atoned; not only that the sins of an universe, but the sins of each unit of it, have been purchased, at the price of the Precious Blood.

This is the only true view, the only opinion which approaches to the Catholic faith on the side of the question of man's purchase. It is the only explanation of the mystery which honestly accommodates itself to the further mystery of the Sacramental system of the Church, and the application of the purchase-price of sin to the object offered for purchase—man. Hence, we may be assured that, whether in the Upper Chamber, when our Divine LORD was troubled, or in the garden, when He was in agony; whether during the live-long night of insult, or the morning hours of torture; whether before the council of His countrymen, or at the tribunal of the conquering heathen power; whether along the Way of Sorrows, or whilst hanging hour by hour upon the Tree of

Shame—indeed, we are assured, that at some time, in the depths of His infinite omniscience, and from the boundless fount of His compassion, He foresaw; and that foreseeing, He anticipated; and that anticipating, He offered in sacrifice for each individual sin of each individual sinner in the universe. If He did not; if He overlooked or omitted any sin of any sinner; if there be a sin in our own individual soul which He neither foresaw nor offered for in sacrifice, mark the result: that sin of that soul was then unatoned, is yet unatoned, will still be unatoned at the Judgment Day. From such fearful oblivion, we may heartily pray: Good LORD, deliver us.

IV. The Terms on which the purchase was made. They were none other than the sacred Blood of GOD, His own most Precious Blood, infinite in power, infinite in value, infinite in efficacy—shed for the sin of man. It was shed by GOD for man. It was shed for man to GOD.

GOD'S Blood-shedding for man. Little, or nothing, can be added to these few plain words, or to convey to our soul the awful and blessed truth, as a reality and a fact. Much indeed may be added in explanation and defence of the Catholic doctrine of the Atonement, much also in the way of illustration and comment. But, in this place, we may take for granted the dogma itself as taught by the Church, and be content to show the manner of the precious Blood-shedding and some things which flow from it, for devout meditation, in relation to the terms on which was made man's purchase from sin.

There were five principal sheddings of the most precious Blood of CHRIST in His sacred Passion. Before we recall them one by one, we will endeavour to picture the Passion of our LORD as a whole, in some of its more touching features. Let us meditate upon it, remembering that it is GOD'S Passion for the sin of man on which we meditate, that it includes and expresses the terms on which man's purchase was made by GOD. And let us not forget that we shall meditate in the presence of GOD: that GOD and the soul are alone in creation : that each point in the Passion may be the price, that one or more points in the Passion must be the price paid to Eternal Justice by Infinite Love, for your individual and personal sin and for mine.

III.

Go mentally over the Passion of CHRIST, and forget not that such was the purchase-price for the sin of man. Come with me to the Upper Chamber, prepared by the careful hands of Faith and Love, the Apostles S. Peter and S. John. Enter into the spirit of the words of JESUS : " With desire have I desired to eat this Passover with you before I suffer "; and see in these words a prophetic anticipation in thought and will of the sacred Passion. Watch the Divine Master washing His disciples' feet; and observe the particularity of the account—even to the laying aside of the ordinary vesture, the girding with one that was not usual, the pouring of clean water, the wiping of the feet when cleansed. Listen to the warning of betrayal, to the same disciples, from the lips of One of Whom it was truly said : " Never man spake like this Man " ; and mark how little was the warning observed, in its indirect teaching at the least, in the strife which immediately arose as to which of His twelve Apostles should be greatest. Listen to the warning of denial, from One Who as GOD knew what was in man ; and mark how, and in what temper, and with what professions of loyalty to His cause, Peter, the Apostle indeed but not yet the Saint, took the warning of his LORD.

Call to mind the details of the religious feast of the Last Supper—the closing ceremonial, in one sense, of the Jewish dispensation by the Same GOD Who had instituted it—the eating together of the Paschal lamb, and the dividing between themselves the love-cup. Dwell upon the details of the religious feast of the First Communion—the opening rite, in one sense, of the Christian dispensation by the Same LORD Who commanded it to be perpetuated in remembrance of Himself

—details which have more or less guided the Church in her re-newal of the like feast under changed conditions from that night to this day: details, in which the faithful can at the least recognize the Priest and the Victim; the unleavened bread and mixed cup; the lights; perhaps typical of incense, the bitter herbs; certainly the offering of the Sacrifice and administration of the Sacrament, by mysterious anticipation; the sacred words of institution; the preliminary self-searching for the confession of sin, which S. Paul enjoins; and reception fasting from earthly nourishment, which is world-wide in its obligation.

Such was one of the primary elements in the system pre-ordained by GOD, by which the results of the purchase-price for the sin of man could be applied to each individual soul for whom that price was paid.

Call to mind again, CHRIST'S last discourse, the last long conference between the Divine Master and His Apostles, contained in four entire chapters of the Gospel according to S. John, and the words we love to dwell upon which they contain: His consolation of His disciples; the many mansions in His FATHER'S house; the peace which He leaves, not as the world giveth; the love wherewith He loved His own; the new Commandment which He gives; the promise of the COMFORTER, to abide for ever with us; the warning of persecution for His sake; the great Intercession; the last marvellous prayer; and the final hymn.

Such was the remote anticipation, in word and to His Apostles, of the actual purchase of man by GOD from the guilt of sin.

Call to mind, once more, the divine action which followed immediately upon the divine words spoken. Upon these acts of CHRIST, also, we love to dwell. They went out, from the world, into the mount of Olives. They enter into a garden, the garden of the Church, Gethsemane. Here ensues, one fulfilment of the prophetic anticipation of the Passion, in the practical realization of the Agony—the Agony of GOD.

Jesus divides Himself from the Eight; divides Himself from the Three. He is alone by Himself; He is alone with God. His disciples are asleep. He is engaged in prayer. He, upon His knees on the damp, cold earth beneath the olive-trees, in the cold, bright light of the Paschal moon, is engaged in prayer. What may be the prayer? "If it be possible, let this cup pass from Me." Thank God, Brother or Sister in Christ, that it were not possible—not possible in conformity with the eternal counsels of the divine decrees—for had it been possible, where at the last Great Day would the ungodly and the sinner appear? Who may He be Who utters the prayer? It is the Eternal, Living, and True God. Thank God, Brother or Sister in Christ, that it were so: for now we have the possibility of salvation, even though with difficulty we scarcely be saved in the day of the Lord Jesus. Meantime, whilst He is sore amazed and very heavy and exceeding sorrowful unto death; nay, whilst His sweat was as it were great drops of blood falling down to the ground, His disciples slept. They slept, not once, not twice, but thrice. And then came the kiss of treachery.

Such was the proximate anticipation, in act and deed, of the actual purchase of man by God from the guilt of sin.

Behold God, Who is Supra-local, Eternal, and Infinite, surrounded by man, finite and confined by time and space. Behold men and soldiers, with swords and staves, sent to capture Him Whom twelve legions of Angels burned to liberate. Behold lanterns and torches provided, in order to discover, in the silver rays of the Paschal moon, the Light of the world; and cords and bands to secure Him Who hath the keys of heaven and hell. Behold Him led away by the creatures of His own Almighty hands, Who is the Judge of quick and dead. Behold; and forget not that such was part of the Passion-price of sin.

Behold Him led, as the Lamb of God, before Annas, Caiaphas, Pilate, and Herod; and realize all He suffered at each stage of His condemnation. Consider the examinations which He underwent, by night and by day; private and public; before His own countrymen, before strangers; in the court of the chief priests, at the bar of foreign conquerors. Consider some details of these examinations; and forget not, again, that such formed another portion of the purchase of man's sin. Consider the false-witness levelled at Him Who is absolute Truth; the charge of blasphemy made against Him Who is the Divine Word and Wisdom of GOD; the challenge to prophesy offered to Him by Whom alone holy men of old prophetically spake; the sentence of death pronounced against Him Who holds in His hands the final issue, both of eternal life and of everlasting death.

Again: Think of another class of Passion-woes, which came to Him from the malice of enemies—the physical pains of His sufferings. The cruelty and torture; the spitting and smiting; the buffeting and scourging—all were inflicted upon a frame weakened by fasting, fatigued by exertion, worn by want of sleep, injured by ill-treatment—for He was perfect Man. Think of another class, which came to Him from the thoughtlessness, carelessness, selfishness of friends—the mental sorrows of His agony. He was deserted by His disciples—they all forsook Him and fled. He was thrice denied by one. He was betrayed by one. He was followed by two—by one from afar; first one and then the other—two only at most, entered the palace of the High Priest to see the end; and at the end, He was supported by one alone out of the Eleven. Think of His mental as well as His bodily anguish—for He was perfect Man.

But He was also Perfect GOD. With this truth in view, call to mind the closing scenes of the Passion of the GOD-MAN. Call to mind the delivery of the Divine Prisoner from one tribunal to another; the change in the charge from blasphemy to that of sedition; the vacillations of Pilate; his questionings and arguings, with the people, with their Victim; his declarations of the innocence of our Blessed LORD, and his ineffectual attempt to pacify the populace; the washing of his hands, and the final condemnation to the death of the Cross. Call to mind the purple robe of kingly power; the white garment of one bereft of sense; the cruel crown of thorn; the bulrush and mock sceptre of real power; the bended knee and false worship to the True DEITY; and the *Ecce Homo*—Behold the Man, though He was also GOD.

The last, sad journey had now to be made, along the *Via Dolorosa*. It was not long; though much happened on the road. Though painful and full of woe, the Way of Sorrows was not unmingled with some alleviations to its bitterness. These must not be overlooked. For, if He were at first cross-laden, yet He was at length relieved by one coming out of the country; if He endured a three-fold fall, yet the blessed Veronica and the band of holy women wept for Him; if the people had cried "Crucify," yet a great company bewailed and lamented Him; if all His disciples forsook Him and fled, yet a little company of faithful friends were gathered around the Cross. Around the Cross? Yes. For Calvary is now reached. The transverse beam of the fatal Tree is now fixed. The Divine Sufferer is now extended on it. Each hand is nailed separately. Both feet are transfixed. The Cross with its Divine Burden is raised aloft, and planted in its allotted place.

Lastly, behold JESUS, GOD and MAN, exposed between heaven and earth; a spectacle to the world, to Angels, devils, men; the accepted Sacrifice for the sin of man. Listen to the seven Last Words from the Cross—that chair of the Divine Teacher. Witness the earthquake—that testimony of Nature to Nature's GOD. See the soldier with his spear, and what resulted—the mingled sacramental stream of Blood and Water from the riven Side. Join with the heathen Centurion, O Christian Men and Women, and say: Truly, this was the SON of GOD. And remember, that on such terms was our purchase made; such was the price which was paid by JESUS CHRIST for your sins and for mine.

M

IV.

There were five principal sheddings of the Precious Blood in the Passion of JESUS. The first took place in the Garden of Gethsemane. The next was caused by the sharp points of the crown of thorns. The third flowed at the Pillar of Scourging. The fourth fell drop by drop from the wounds of the cruel nails. The last came from out the Side of CHRIST, dead upon the Cross. We will consider these in order.

1st. In the Garden of Gethsemane took place the earliest shedding of the Precious Blood, which was to be poured in a full stream upon the Hill of Calvary. Alone amongst the deserted olive trees, in the cold dews of a moon-light night in spring, surrounded by the damp luxuriance of eastern vegetation, on His knees, nay, after the custom of His nation, prostrate, with His face upon the earth, the divine Sweat of the Son of Man was as it were great drops of Blood falling down upon the ground, enriching with marvellous fertility the garden—may we not add, the Garden of the Church. This was the voluntary, and if we may venture so to say, the gratuitous shedding of the Precious Blood, in anticipation of those other sheddings which, not less voluntarily offered, were essential to the sacrifice for the sin of man. The Church individualizes this sacred shedding, and teaches us to pray, "By Thine Agony and Bloody Sweat, Good LORD deliver us." Behold, in such shedding, the first divine instalment of the purchase-price of sin.

2nd. On the sharp points of thorn which formed His earthly crown is to be found the second Blood-shedding in the Passion of CHRIST. These points were so severe, tradition suggests to devout meditation, that a gauntlet had to be worn for the protection of the hand that wove it; so severe, that a wooden lever was required to force the twisted thorn upon the head that was doomed to wear it. Placed on His sacred head in mock token of most kingly sovereignty, forced on His sacred brow to produce the acutest pain, we may venerate the crown of thorn and worship the Precious Blood thereon as the second out-pouring, not by anticipation but in reality, in the sacrificial offering of JESUS for the sin of the whole world.

3rd. At the Pillar of Scourging flowed yet more freely than either from the crown of thorn or in the bloody sweat, the Life-blood of the SON of GOD, for the sin of man. Faint from long-continued fasting, exhausted by want of sleep, wearied by judicial examination oft repeated in public and in private, defiled with shameful acts, insulted with shameful words, alone in the midst of heartless enemies and deserted by still more heartless friends—the CHRIST of GOD stands bound at the Pillar of the Scourge. There He receives, with knotted thong, upon His virgin back and side and breast, again tradition tells us, the felon's doom of forty stripes save one. Such was the third instalment, at once voluntary and essential, in the divine purchase of the human race.

4th. By the wounds of the cruel nails in the sacred hands and feet of JESUS, was the fourth Blood-shedding caused. Through skin and flesh, through bones and muscles, through sinew and tendon, of those hands which were so often raised to bless, of those feet which went about doing good, were forced, the iron nails of executioners harder than the nails they smote. On these three nails, transfixed in the most sensitive parts of the human frame, for three long hours, was suspended the weight of that tortured body which was born of Mary. The Precious Blood that fell drop by drop from those four wounds formed the last instalment of the actual purchase-price of sin willingly offered, in life, by the Saviour of mankind.

5th. From out the Side of CHRIST flowed forth, in mystic mingling, the final shedding of the sacred stream. Behold, in this last shedding, a divine work of pure supererogation. It was voluntary still, but it was not essential. All the Precious Blood that was required by Divine Justice to be shed, had already been outpoured by Divine Love. The consummation of the sacrifice for sin was retrospective; and the full payment of the purchase-price of man, good measure, pressed down and running over, was paid at the demand of the Gentile world, by the thrust of the soldier's spear. The side of CHRIST, typical of His own divine Bride and her treatment by the world, pierced by the spear now powerless to be cruel, gave forth a common tide of Blood and Water—fit emblems in their two-fold form of two great Sacraments of the Church, fit emblem in their two-fold mixture of the mingled cup of one.

Such were the five principal Blood-sheddings in the Passion of our Divine Master—during the Agony in the Garden, by the points of the crown of thorn, at the Pillar of Scourging, from the wounds of the three nails, with the spear-thrust of the Roman soldier. The precious Blood was thus shed for your sin and for mine. Such, in part, were the terms on which was purchased from infinite Justice by tenderest Love the soul of man who had fallen into sin. This purchase-price from Satan and everlasting death was paid by JESUS CHRIST for your soul and for mine.

One thought is common to all considerations on the details of the Passion of our Blessed LORD. We have dwelt on the lavish prodigality and yet, the divine utilitarianism of the GOD of Nature, in the mysteries of creation. May we not say the same of Grace, in the redemption of man by GOD, that the like characteristics are apparent? Can we not perceive a severe utilitarianism as one result of supreme prodigality; and a divine jealousy that grace, superabundantly bestowed by GOD, should be proportionately utilized by man? One drop of the Precious Blood sufficed to cleanse all the world from all its guilt. And yet it pleased the Good LORD to shed it all. It was shed, as we have followed the course of the Passion step by step, once by anticipation, in the Bloody Sweat; thrice in actual reality and voluntarily, drop by drop; once again, in retrospect and as consummating a perfected action, in the full tide of mingled elements. In each of the Blood-sheddings in the Passion of our Divine LORD which have been enumerated, and which when combined form a brief history of the Precious Blood, may be traced a two-fold characteristic. We have perceived one of the two elements in the foregoing account. It fertilized the soil of the olive garden. It dyed the spines of the thorny crown. It saturated the leather of the knotted thong. It stained and encrusted the surface of the iron nails. It crimsoned the Gentile spear, and flooded the rock-floor of Calvary. It—the Blood of GOD. Was ever witnessed such profuse prodigality? And yet, withal, may we not perceive also a mystic, if no other form of divine utilitarianism? Mystic, I say; for, without trenching upon the subject matter of a future meditation, and without saying more than sufficient to supply a train of thought for future consideration, are there not five blessed Sacraments at least, in which we may utilize, or may hope to utilize these sacred out-pourings of the Precious Blood? If no other form, I say, of divine utilitarianism; for may we not reverently suppose, without pressing too closely upon the analogy between the type and anti-type, that the five sacred Blood-sheddings may be the special atonement for the sins of man, through the five senses of his mortal frame?

V.

The five Sacraments of the Church of CHRIST, available to all faithful persons, were instituted of GOD, as remedies for the sin of man.

The mystic relations of these five Sacraments towards the five principal sheddings of the Precious Blood of CHRIST are not obscure. For instance:

1. The voluntary anticipation of the Passion of JESUS in the Garden of Gethsemane may fitly be compared to, or according to our temper of thought, may fitly be contrasted with, our own involuntary reception of the initiatory rite of our holy Religion as infants, in the Sacrament of Baptism.

Both pre-suppose a succession of future events. Both derive their full value, whether in regard to sinfulness or saintliness, only from the future actual succession of such events, in the Life of GOD or in the life of man.

2. The crown of thorn, which together with the purple robe, the bulrush, the bended knee, and the *Ecce Homo* more truly declared than His enemies could realize, the empire and sovereignty of the Son of Man; and yet again, in an opposite direction, the fulfilment of His own prophetic words, that His Kingdom was not of this world, may represent in figure the completion and fulfilment of the baptismal covenant, by the crowning of the neophite in the Sacrament of Confirmation with the seven-fold gifts of GOD the HOLY GHOST.

3. The fulfilled or perfected Christian is in figure strengthened and refreshed by the weakness and exhaustion of the Man of Sorrows at the Pillar of the Scourge. Can any type of strength and sustenance be more complete than the flour of wheat and the juice of the grape? Can any natural reality be less conducive to the actual support of man than a single drop of Wine and a Wafer-bread of transparent thinness. And yet, we are assured that the Paten and the Chalice contain and convey the super-substantial Food of Angels for the service of man; and in more than a single sense, the Body broken and the Blood outpoured by the cruel lash of yet more cruel men, is a figure of the Sacrament of the most Holy Eucharist.

4. The wounds in the sacred hands and feet of JESUS are not so much a type of the Sacrament of Penance, so far, at least as the cause of both may be considered—as identical with it. Both are the result of sin. The first gave divine satisfaction to GOD for the sin of man. The second applies such divine satisfaction from GOD to the soul of man. It is not too much to say that either apart from the other were, in the divine economy of man's redemption, useless. The wounds in the hands and feet had been without avail, were it impossible to apply their merit to man's necessity. The appli-

cation of a form of reconciliation were sacrilegious, had not a divine satisfaction that was also human been made, which inspired such form with reality, power, and life.

5. As the initiatory rite of Baptism, in a sense, anticipates all future sacraments, so does Unction, in a sense, consummate all past sacramental gifts and graces, in the last offices of the Church for the soul of man. As such, it is no unworthy antitype of the divine work of supererogation, in the retrospective shedding of the Precious Blood from the side of CHRIST. The preparation of man for the passage of the valley of the shadow of death, is aptly typified—be it in comparison or contrast—by the sacramental stream of Blood and Water, which flowed from the riven side of JESUS after He had been pleased, for man's sake, to taste of the bitterness of death.

The five natural senses of the mortal body, common to all the children of men, may be considered, in relation to our present subject, as five portals to the soul by which the sin of man may enter.

Of these five portals, it is surely not too great a tax upon a reverent belief in the divine utilitarianism of GOD'S dealings with His intelligent and accountable creation to hold this: that the precious Blood-sheddings in the Passion of JESUS made an atonement for the sins for which they are respectively responsible. It may not be edifying to make the attempt, it might not be successful if the attempt were made, to allot specifically to each sacred effusion a divine satisfaction for the sin of each several human sense. Yet, may it be held, without irreverence and without specification, that the Precious Blood which was shed in the garden, beneath the crown of thorn, under the infliction of the scourge, by the iron nails, and from out the sacred side, did as a fact atone for the sin of the human race through the medium of the sense of hearing and smelling, of touch and taste and sight.

In most of the forms for the examination of conscience with which I am acquainted, self-searching is made to turn upon breaches of the Ten Commandments; or, upon our falls into the Seven Deadly Sins; or, on the three main sources of sin, in relation to GOD, our neighbour, and ourself—in each case, in the way of omission or of commission. In no form are the five senses, and their use or abuse, systematically made the subject-matter of self-examination—at least, in none that has been published of late years. But, in a valuable little Manual of devotion, published abroad for the benefit of our Roman Catholic brethren in times of persecution about two centuries ago, such a form may be found. The book is entitled, "The daily Exercise of devout Rosarists, in order to live happily and to die holily." It contains a brief system for the examination of conscience on each of the five senses—the sense of touch, of taste, of sight, of smell, and of sound.

It is impossible in this place to offer even an abstract of the questions that have been made and asked with the object of soul-searching, on the results which these five avenues import in relation to sin. But, some effort may be made briefly to indicate how and in what manner the senses may become subservient indirectly to man's salvation; how and in what way they may become co-adjutors, with GOD Himself and with regard to sin, in man's purchase. This, perhaps, may best be done by considering, not the sins into which we may have unhappily fallen, by yielding to the dictates of our bodily senses; but the sins over which we have had power graciously given us to avoid, or the sins which by GOD'S grace we ought to have conquered, and still hope to conquer, by their systematic mortification.

Although the point has been already discussed, yet, a few preliminary words are needed before we directly entertain any questions on this topic.

The Christian Faith being, as we are well aware, a religion of liberty, those who are in a state of grace are in possession of moral power to do right and to merit reward. We have no right to do wrong, even if willing to accept the awful consequences of so doing. Nay, we have not really the liberty of a choice in our actions, between wrong and right. We have no choice for these, amongst other reasons of more moment: because we are beforehand pledged to hold to the one, pledged to avoid the other—before, that is, we can either mentally or physically exercise the power of choice by free-will. The liberty that we possess gives us the power which those under the bondage of sin cannot enjoy and do not exercise. It is the liberty of fulfilling the object of our creation. It is the liberty to perform GOD'S holy Will. It is the liberty of being fellow-workers with GOD in our purchase from sin; and to work out our own salvation with fear and trembling. How can we best employ this true Gospel liberty? I reply—not by always making use of GOD'S gifts to the full extent of their lawful enjoyment; but by making use of them, sometimes and on some occasions, to a point which falls short of their full legitimate use. In other words, by accepting the principle of religious mortification. We may deny ourselves gratifications which are positively lawful, and offer up the self-denial as a sacrifice of our natural will to GOD. This self-denial will produce a double effect. It will obtain for us, in union with the Person of JESUS CHRIST, a certain amount of merit in proportion to the intention and extent of the mortification. And it will secure for us, as moral and accountable agents, an increase of strength in our super-human will, and of consequent power against gratifications which are not positively lawful. There is no surer method of being pleasing to GOD, than to deny ourselves in things harmless for His sake. There is no surer way to obtain spiritual force against things harmful, than voluntarily to abstain from those that are avowedly legitimate. And these results follow from the use of mortification of our bodily senses.

These thoughts may prepare us to consider the following questions with patience, even if they come before us in a new light religiously. They will refer, it may be repeated for the sake of clearness, not to sins into which we may have fallen by temptation, but to sins which we may avoid by the use of systematic mortification. Take, then, the five senses of the human body interrogatively, and in view of the five principal Blood-sheddings in the Passion of CHRIST; and consider with me:—

1st. How have we been wont to mortify the sense of sight, with a view of being made well-pleasing to GOD, and of seconding the purchase of our souls, by the Agony in the Garden? Do we ever, as an act of self-denial, abstain from reading that in books or magazines, in novels or newspapers, which does not tend to the soul's edification? If we are not accustomed thus to deny ourselves, we fail to use our Gospel liberty to the full extent to which GOD intended us to use it.

2nd. Has it been our habit to mortify the sense of taste, and thus to gain merit and to co-operate with GOD in our purchase from sin, by the shedding of the Precious Blood beneath the Crown of Thorn? Do we as a rule, of course with many exceptions, abstain from what we may lawfully enjoy, in the quantity of our food, in the quality of our food, and in the time of taking our food? If we are not in the habit of thus mortifying our sense of taste, at the least at certain times and seasons, we fail again in the use of the liberty wherewith CHRIST has made us free.

3rd. Do we seek from time to time, even if not continuously, to mortify our sense of touch, in order to increase our power of self-restraint, and to augment by never so little the purchase-price for sin, paid though it were in full at the Pillar of the Scourge? Specially, do we mortify ourselves in this self-seeking age, in matters which more or less closely, but not exclusively, are affected by the sense of touch: for instance, in our dress, in the furniture of our houses, in our carriages, for the sake of personal adornment, luxurious surroundings, or the pride of possession? If not, if we do not thus accept, even in small matters of sense, the principle of mortification, we fail a third time to fulfil the law to which we are pledged, the royal law of liberty.

4th. Are we sometimes careful to mortify the sense of smell, and thus to work with GOD for man's purchase, as well as to obtain a victory over self, by the shedding drop by drop of the Precious Blood from the Wounds of the three-fold Nails? Specially, if called upon to minister to poverty, in squalor, misery, disease, or death, do we accept as an integral portion of such a call, all the inseparable circumstances which are attendant upon poverty; and which, whilst the rich are pained only by a passing glimpse of, the poor are forced to abide with through life, from birth to death? If not, if we accept not the opportunities of voluntary mortification which these cases afford us, we fail in yet another instance of choosing the higher and nobler part in the exercise of our liberty, and of proving ourselves to be, not the freed men of Satan cursed with actual bondage, but the slaves of CHRIST blessed with true freedom.

5th. Can we honestly say that, as a rule, we are accustomed to mortifiy the sense of hearing with the positive intention of self-sacrifice; and thus, in a sense, with the result of completing the sacrifice for the sin of man, in corporate union with Him from Whose sacred side in death flowed forth a mingled tide of Blood and Water? Can we truly affirm such to be the case, if we voluntarily listen to, or encourage any of the various forms of sin against charity in the case of our neighbour, detraction, false witness, unkind judgment, or one of the worst forms of scandal, religious gossip? If this cannot be affirmed, we fail for the last time, and to the extent of our neglect of mortification, in establishing our claim to a personal union with the SPIRIT of CHRIST in the purchase of man; for where the SPIRIT of the LORD is, there is liberty, and in the exercise of Christian liberty in regard to mortification we have failed.

In the little book which has been named, a supplementary examination of conscience is given—not on a sense, but on a faculty. To the above five questions on the sins of omission in relation to the senses, may profitably be added for all of us one more inquiry, on sins of commission, in sins of the tongue. Have we ever willingly done despite, by the use of the God-given power of speech, to the five Blood-sheddings in the Passion of our Divine LORD? Have we, in relation to, and even when engaged in mortifying, our sense of sight, or taste, or smell, or touch, or sound, willingly, deliberately and consciously, against GOD, against our neighbour, or against ourself, gratified sinfully our faculty of speech?

ADDRESS SEVEN.

MAN INSPIRED BY GOD.

PERHAPS the mode of explaining man's relation to his sanctification by GOD, which is at once the simplest to the minds of any, and which is open to the fewest objections from all who accept the principle of inspiration, is this—to affirm of the seven-fold Sacramental system of the Church, that it imparts supernatural gifts and qualities, which are not otherwise certainly obtainable and cannot be otherwise assuredly obtained by the recipient.

All the Sacraments of the Gospel possess this characteristic. But Holy Baptism is exceptional in design and in results, as well as in form, from the remaining six. It differs in kind and degree from the others. It stands sole and alone in its unapproachable importance. For, the other divine Sacraments presuppose its reception. They cannot be administered apart from or independently of it. It shares with the most Holy Eucharist only the dignity of being generally needful, of being needful for salvation to all men. But it surpasses the Eucharist in the simplicity of its essentials, and in the universality of its agents. It is not only the initiatory rite of our holy Religion, but it places us in a new estate, under fresh conditions, with different relations towards both GOD and man. In brief, it surrounds the natural man with an atmosphere of spirituality. On the basis of Baptism is built a sacramental edifice of five stages, for the sanctification of ordinary Catholics living in the world—from the last platform of which the soul takes its mysterious flight, by GOD'S mercy, heavenward.

More than this it is not necessary to state, in order to remind Catholics living in the world of the work and office of

GOD the HOLY GHOST in man's sanctification. Over and above admittance into the fellowship of the faithful, we are supplied in Holy Baptism with grace—that supernatural adjunct, God-given to Adam, in the power of which and by virtue of which he was made pleasing to GOD. Beyond all the gifts of nature was given by GOD to Adam, the capacity to please his Creator. The supernatural addition was bestowed apart from, and complementary to, the act of creation. It was bestowed then upon Adam, as it has since been given to Adam's offspring, individually, and not only as the head of a race. It was a free, spontaneous gift of GOD'S goodness—a gift which the recipient was equally free either to accept or to decline. The question would be interesting, though hardly edifying, to speculate upon the results which would have ensued had Adam retained this supernatural, and super-added gift. But, as a fact, he lost it. The grace returned to Him Who had been pleased to make the offer of it, as well as actually to bestow it. And deprived as he was of grace, the question is not less interesting to us fellow-sufferers with our first parent, though not in this matter likewise guilty with him, and becomes far more important, to consider the results which have as a fact ensued from what is theologically termed, Adam's fall.

The results are at least two-fold; and affect both himself and us. The result to Adam, in relation to his descendants, is obvious. That which he, as a created human being, had forfeited, he was powerless to transmit to his children. A man cannot leave to posterity what he himself has lost, or has been deprived of—be such possession in the order of nature or in the order of grace. The result to us in relation to our ancestor is not less clear. We have been born into the world lacking something which was the possession of our first parent. The children of the natural man could not inherit the capacity to become pleasing to GOD which their father had only acquired supernaturally, and had, in the exercise of his own free-will, voluntarily and deliberately surrendered. How they may, individually and one by one, regain that which their forefather had lost, is the subject-matter of the present meditation. But the capacity to please GOD now becomes ours in virtue and by the power of union, not with an individual member, but with the personal head of a race. Thus, the terms of the divine compact with man are entirely changed. That which was bestowed upon the first Adam of free-will, is given to us of right. That which was the inheritance of his children, subject to conditions which he alone could fulfil or break, is transmitted to us trammelled with no conditions but those for which we personally are responsible. And this change ensues from the change in the relationship between GOD and man. Our rights and the unconditioned terms of our inheritance arise from our connection with the Second Adam. As the Head of a new race, He is pleased to confer on His descendants both the right and the power to inherit their true patrimony. We have only to place ourselves in the proper relations towards our super-human progenitor, in order to secure all and more than all that we lost in consequence of our descent from our natural ancestor. In union with the Man, CHRIST JESUS our LORD, we have capacity to please GOD: we are pleasing to Him. Such capacity is acquired, in various degrees and for different ends, through the instrumentality of the seven-fold Sacramental system of the Church. It is acquired by man through the inspiration of GOD the HOLY GHOST.

It is the teaching of the Church, that every human being born into the world is furnished by his Maker with grace sufficient to lead him to eternal life. To think otherwise, were to do despite unto some of the principal of GOD'S essential attributes. But, beyond the range of this universal law, that salvation is within the grasp of all, there are many degrees of sanctification and personal holiness of life to which, as distinct from the general law, our attention may on the present occasion be restricted.

Of course, between the first Adam and the Second Adam individual members of the human family—both without and within the boundaries of the favoured people—were more or less enabled to become pleasing to GOD, had more or less power bestowed upon them to fulfil the object of their creation, to do His blessed Will. But such capacity was exceptional; it was not normal. Such power was given not by covenant, but of free bounty. The primal head of the created race, fresh from the Creator's hand, deprived his offspring in the future of the power and capacity of doing good. It was reserved for the Divine Head of the new creation to bestow, beyond the possibility of failure, and assured by covenanted mercy, to His spiritual children, also in the future, what their natural forefather had forfeited and cast away. And mark the result. So far from its now being an exceptional event that man can please GOD; so far from its now being of GOD'S free bounty that man has capacity and power to fulfil the object of his creation—with filial boldness we may venture to claim, as of right, to be placed in this supernatural attitude. We may claim to be accepted as sons, in our thoughts, words and actions, well-pleasing unto our Heavenly Father. We do claim this position, by reason of our oneness with, and by our incorporation into, the Person of the Eternal SON. We claim it in virtue of CHRIST'S Sacrifice, and through the instrumentality of the blessed Sacraments of the Church.

Such power is the power of GOD the HOLY GHOST in man's inspiration; and such are, in brief, the results of man's capacity when sanctified by the same Blessed SPIRIT.

II.

Sin in regard to man's sanctification by the HOLY GHOST may be viewed in two aspects. It may be considered, first, theoretically, in relation to the essence of GOD'S inspiration, and as to certain principles upon which the HOLY GHOST is pleased to grant sanctification. It may be considered, secondly, from a practical point of view, in relation to the accidents of man being inspired, and as to some of the results which flow from man's corporate and individual sanctification.

To-day we will confine our attention to questions of principle, rather than to matters of practice.

As a question of principle, the sanctification of man by the Holy SPIRIT of GOD is, or is equivalent to, spiritual re-creation. For what is sanctification, and in what does it consist? It may take at least two forms. Sanctification is the act of making holy that which lacks holiness, even though it cannot be said that the object of sanctification is actually unholy or positively wicked. In this case, the work of the HOLY GHOST is concerned with man in his natural, uncovenanted estate, a child of Adam indeed, but not yet the child of GOD. Sanctification, again, is the act of imparting additional holiness to that which has already been made holy; or, it is the act of restoring holiness which once given has been either forfeited by sin, or has been lost by carelessness, or has lain dormant from causes beyond the control of the object of sanctification; or, it is the act of infusing holiness of a fresh kind or of a larger degree to those who have benefited by former infusions, and have acted up to grace conferred. In this case, the work of the HOLY GHOST is concerned with man in his state above nature, as a child of GOD, in the lower, the average, and the highest stages respectively of covenanted inspiration. But in either instance, actually, and to an extent in all the divisions of the latter case, sanctification is, or is equivalent to, the re-creation of the human object by the Fount or Source of all Holiness. The result in all cases is union, more or less complete and perfect, between the Creator and the creature: a union begun in time which can only be consummated in eternity: a union by which man, now and since the Incarnation of GOD, under a covenanted dispensation by which GOD has been pleased to bind Himself—man made by the Everlasting FATHER, and purchased by the Eternal SON, is made pleasing to GOD and capable to fulfil the object of both creation and redemption, by the inspiration of the Co-equal PARACLETE, through the Sacramental system of the Church.

N

Theologically speaking, of course, man, the creature of GOD, is and can be made again, man is and can be re-created but once, once only—namely, in the initiatory rite of Holy Baptism. But each several sacrament is possessed of its own special grace and efficacy for the soul of man, to that extent that re-creation may with propriety, or at least by accommodation, be predicated of it. To this topic of thought, which is certainly suitable for times of retreat, we will now turn our attention.

In a certain sense, if not with theological precision, it may be affirmed of each Sacrament of the Church, that it makes again its recipients. Take the five sacraments which all are more or less common to all faithful persons living in the world; namely, Baptism, Confirmation, Confession, Communion, Viaticum.

Take them in order: 1. Without doubt the Sacrament of Baptism makes again its recipients; makes them again wholly, in body, soul, spirit. It places each of the three component parts of perfect manhood in a new relation to GOD. The body becomes a temple of the HOLY GHOST. The spirit is united to the sacred Humanity of JESUS. The soul, as the intermediatary between both, may without a want of reverence be esteemed to be the dwelling-place and field of divine labour of Both the Divine Persons in the union of GOD the FATHER. 2. There is, perhaps, less certainty in speaking of the sacrament which, as a rule to which there may be, and sometimes are exceptions, comes next after Baptism in order of time, as effecting in the object of it a re-creation. Confirmation, by giving vitality to the grace of Holy Baptism; by sowing seed in the heart duly prepared by grace; by adding seven distinct supernatural gifts to an infused principle of grace; and by supplementing and completing the spiritual powers of grace to the standard of a perfect manhood—Confirmation may be said to make us again.

3. There is less uncertainty in speaking of the action on faithful souls of the Sacrament of Penance. Whether it pre-

cedes or follows either confirmation or communion, in both cases it may be almost said spiritually to re-create the penitent. Its operations are manifold. Does the grace received in baptism lie dormant? Confession revives it. Has the grace received in confirmation been lost? Confession replaces it. Do the seven Deadly Sins, or any one or more of them, need to be uprooted? Or, is there necessity for rekindling the flame of any or of all the seven Gifts of the SPIRIT? In both cases, Confession is the sacrament of spiritual restoration. Hence, in its three-fold division of contrition, confession and satisfaction, Penance may be said to re-create those who submit to it. 4. The most Holy Eucharist re-creates us in a different way. Having been sanctified, fulfilled and renewed, this sacrament raises us to a different level of spirituality. It almost places us in a new atmosphere of sanctity. The simplest words in such a case express the deepest truths. But, for the child of wrath, for the candidate for the seven-fold gifts, for the penitent sinner to be made one with CHRIST, and for CHRIST to become one with him, is a mystery so great, that the change which ensues may fairly be termed a re-creation. Incorporation into the sacred and sinless Humanity of JESUS, at His own altar, makes us again.

5. And not to speak of the other two sacraments which do not touch all and may not touch any, the Last Sacraments of the Church, the sacred Viaticum, by giving us supersubstantial Food for our last journey; and if so be, by anointing us, as the Apostle S. James commands, with the SPIRIT'S power; and certainly, by assuring us of our plenary forgiveness, after our final ordinary or life-long confession of sin—the sacred Viaticum at the hour of death makes us again, and sends us once more and for the last time re-created by divine grace into the presence of our Maker, of our Judge, of our Sanctifier.

Each of these five forms of divine sanctification employs a different supernatural agency for the re-creation of man. We are made again through their instrumentality either positively or negatively, whether by direct or indirect modes of inspiration, by the Holy SPIRIT of GOD. These five methods of inspiration may be recalled severally in a few words. Holy Baptism may be described as the primary act of positive spiritual beneficence to the soul of man, from his Creator and after his birth. Confirmation in youth may not be unfitly compared to an act of infused vitality, affecting the entire spiritual system. Penance is the sacrament which in manhood supplies either a negative and indirect defence against sin, or provides for an effort of restorative and re-creative grace. The most Holy Eucharist is simply the divine incorporation of man, be he youth or aged, the union in this life of the Creator with the creature. And the Last Sacraments of the Church, in the decline of life, or at its close, will prove themselves to be a strengthening and supporting Viaticum for the dread passage of the valley of the shadow of death. Such are the five notes of sacramental sanctification in the Church of CHRIST.

III.

Sanctification is the divine and personal work of GOD the Inspirer in the soul of man. In the divine decrees and eternal counsels of the Holy TRINITY in relation, firstly, to the union of the Creator with the creature; secondly, to the obstacles furnished by the latter which hinder such union; thirdly, to the means adopted by the former in order to consummate such union—in regard severally to sin—man's re-creation and sanctification, his being made again and being made holy, occupy an important position. Made by the creative power of GOD the FATHER, purchased by the mediatorial power of GOD the Saviour, we are made again and made holy, in fulfilment of the divine Will for the union of GOD with man, by the sanctifying power of GOD the Inspirer.

Of this Divine and Personal Deity, we have seen in a former meditation:

1st. That the HOLY GHOST is not only the LORD and Giver of Life, as the Creed affirms ; but also, that He is the Benefactor, the Vivifyer, the Restorer, the Incorporator and the Strengthener in the five blessed Sacraments of the Church —all of which, as a rule, apply to all faithful Christians living in the world.

2nd. That the Blessed Paraclete is a Personal GOD with divine essence, with divine attributes and operations, with divine majesty and glory; and that almost every attribute and operation which may be affirmed of the First and Second Persons of the TRINITY—Paternity and Filiation excepted— may be predicated and are declared of the Third.

3rd. That of the Holy SPIRIT three facts in relation to man must always be remembered—He is Self-existent, and Infinite, and Omniscient ; and that three truths must never be forgotten—He is not a creature nor a created being, He is not an influence nor a manifestation, He is not an agent nor a minister.

4th. That the HOLY GHOST the COMFORTER is Divine and Personal in His origin, in His name, in His dignity, in His worship, in His work.

5th. That, over and above the dogmatic language of the Creeds, the Fathers authorize us to employ more familiar and even endearing titles towards this Divine Person. They assure us that He is the Love, the Will, the Kiss of Peace of the Holy TRINITY ; the Gift, the Seal, the Finger of GOD ; the Director of souls, the Ambassador from GOD, and the Summum Bonum to man.

6th. Lastly, that the Holy SPIRIT, in man's ceaseless warfare with the Evil One, is in an especial manner our Inspirer, our Patron, our Defender and Protector, our Adviser and our Guide.

These facts and truths form the basis of all that I shall attempt to place before you in the following meditation. They have been repeated, not only because of their intrinsic importance, and because they are apt to be forgotten in speaking of the HOLY GHOST, but also because, as was before observed, the Third Divine Person of the TRINITY fails to occupy the position which He ought to fill in the thoughts, in the interests and even in the prayers of Catholics.

Bearing in mind these truths and facts in their relation to the five modes of re-creation which affect the case of ordinary persons living in the world, we must advance to another point. We must bear in mind that, whilst they all form an integral portion of the work of one and the self-same SPIRIT, dividing to every man severally as he may need; yet, that the mode of such work is not one but manifold, it is varied and not uniform. The five stages in the Church's Sacramental system all more or less distinctly bear the marks of at the least four definite characteristics. The Holy SPIRIT is pleased to work for the inspiration of man who is the victim of sin, and through the channels of His own appointment, in the four ways following: 1st, by human agency; 2nd, by material substances; 3rd, by ceremonial form; 4th, by the virtue of His own divine power. In other words, admitting the presence of the Divine Person of GOD the HOLY GHOST in the Sacraments of His own appointment for the relief of sin-sick souls, the end proposed by the use of these means of grace is attained, and the sanctification of the sinner is effected, by the concurrent influence of these three distinct causes—ceremonial usage, material elements, human personality. These are three marks or notes in the spiritual life, in man's supernatural existence, which, with hatred not unmixed with fear, the world abhors; but which we as Catholics, with respect not unmixed with love, heartily accept. It is not unsuitable, when more or less severed from the world in retreat, that we should avail ourselves of the opportunity of discussing these several notes and marks in the higher life, with calmness and without distraction, in order to decide if the world be right in its dislike, or if we are wrong in our reverence. We will dwell on these points in their order.

IV.

In the first place: in regard to man's sanctification by GOD, the HOLY GHOST is pleased to work for the sinner's re-creation through the medium of human agency. This is a point of much importance to be realized by our own soul; and when realized by ourselves, to be enforced on others. For the world affirms, that GOD dispenses with created personality in matters of grace; that He acts directly and immediately on the soul; that He neither seeks nor employs the agency of man. And what the world affirms is re-echoed by many who would feel injured at being included in such an exhaustive term. Those who admit the doctrine of the Incarnation of GOD and believe in the Atonement, and even those who to an extent believe in the doctrine of grace and receive that of the sacraments, join with the latitudinarian, the sceptic, the materialist, and declare (in terms however inconsistent on the lips of some) that they decline to allow man to stand between their soul and their GOD. This is the true explanation of the popular, and even (in a sense) of the devout and religious antagonism to the principle of Sacerdotalism which now obtains so widely. The natural man, be he wholly rationalistic, or wholly sectarian, is impatient of and denies both the right and the power of human agency in the things of GOD.

Like all heresy, this opinion is based upon truth. Were it not based upon truth, the devouter and more faithful minds who so eagerly cling to the principle would be at once shocked by its avowal, and would cease to entertain it. But, it is based upon the most certain of truths; though the truth is exaggerated in one direction, is shattered in another, is distorted in a third, until the phantasm, the torso, or the anomaly becomes but a half-truth which is wholly false. It is one of the most assured of divine truths, that no created thing, and especially no creature of GOD entrusted with the gift of free-will, and all that flows for good or bad from this responsibility, has either power or right, in the true sense of the terms, to stand between man and GOD.

Least of all does the Catholic Faith commit itself to a denial of this truth: least of all, I say, for to an extent those who follow or bind themselves to the teaching of a human person, or of a human system, or of a printed book (in all reverence for the Holy Volume itself, be it said), or even of an authority in the past in opposition to the living voice of GOD'S Church—practically deny this axiomatic truth. But the Church does not hold, we do not teach that man does stand, or that man can stand—not even the ordained priest, the servant of his Master's servants—between his fellow-sinner and the GOD of both. Had the world, and those who inconsistently accept the world's argument, spoken potentially in the place of speaking absolutely, the world and the Church had been found in unwonted agreement. That the Eternal, the Infinite, the Omniscient, that the All-good, All-just and Almighty, needs not human aid in His divine work of re-creating souls, the Church in common with the world admits. That the Creator is pleased not to employ such co-operative agency in the work of salvation, the Church emphatically denies in spite of the world. Whilst she condemns the proposition, that it is so much as possible for man to stand in the place of GOD; she declares the principle, that in man's sanctification the HOLY GHOST is pleased to work through the instrumentality of human agency.

Here, at the outset of this inquiry, we are forced to make two distinctions.

In relation (1) to ourselves, we propose to discuss these deep questions of human agency, material substance and ritual order, in connection with the sacraments, as Christians, not as rationalists or semi-infidels; as Catholics under the privilege of being in covenant with GOD, not as those who on any ground reject His covenant; as within, not as without the Church of CHRIST. This will ensure our not being led away by any system of human invention, however apparently complete and perfect; our not being led astray by any teacher, however really able and learned—at issue, in either case with Catholic tradition. When we have discovered the teaching of the Church, we shall probably the more easily adhere to it.

And this prepares us to receive the second qualification of the broad principle that we are considering: and which may be described (2) in these terms: GOD is not tied to, bound by, or confined within the limits of His own divine appointment. This is true both in conjunction with and apart from the covenant of grace. It is true also beyond the range of grace —in the domain of nature. In neither case is GOD limited to that expression of His Will which, in either instance, we call Law. In both cases, GOD may, GOD sometimes does, reach the same end, or the like end, by different means—actually without the use of sacraments in grace, and so far as man can perceive, without the intervention of law in nature. An earthquake, a famine, a peaceful migration, a conquest, some human invention or addition to the stock of human knowledge, some calamity and the decay of material civilization—these and other causes may produce abnormal results in a country, or a people, or amongst individuals which would otherwise have been accomplished by the orderly fulfilment of the ordinary laws of nature, of human society, or of man as an unit of his race.

Nor is it otherwise with grace. It need not be hazarded that the very highest forms of sanctity are acquired without the use of the sacraments, or outside the Church of CHRIST. It may almost be asserted that they are not. But it can be confidently affirmed, that a high position in the supernatural life may be and has been attained by those who, in GOD'S providence, have been denied or severed from the means of grace. Of course, such sanctity is acquired of GOD'S free mercy, uncovenantedly. But, as a fact, it is given. Hence, both in grace and in nature, the Author of Law, in either expression of His divine Will, is pleased to act from time to time independently of the order which He has nevertheless been pleased to establish.

We need not trace the analogy further in the action of nature; but, it is important to remember the result which ensued in a work of grace, when the divine gift had been abnormally bestowed, in an instance which has been expressly handed down to us through tradition by GOD Himself. I allude to the case of Cornelius, described in the tenth chapter of the Acts of the Apostles. The story of Cornelius proves to us the value of sacraments, even in the case of those who have been re-created by GOD independently of sacraments. S. Peter commanded those to be baptized who had already as he said, "received the HOLY GHOST as well as" the Saint himself. If baptism were thus administered after the uncovenanted reception of the Divine COMFORTER, how much more essential must not the sacrament be to those who have not been made partakers of His sacred presence. And of the sacrament of baptism it is unquestionably true, that it is one of the instances in which GOD is pleased to work for man's sanctification through human agency: it cannot be had without such agency. Whilst, then, GOD is not limited by or confined to His own means of conveying grace; yet, He is pledged to bestow grace, the Church assures us, through the medium of the sacraments. Such bestowal by GOD indisputably proceeds through human agency.

Can any analogy be found, outside revelation, outside grace, in the realm of nature, or in the accidents, or even in the essentials of a common manhood, which may reasonably support the principle of human agency being an accessory in the sanctification of man by GOD? Let us consider this question with care.

Take the case of human life, of ordinary men and women living in the world. What relations of life are, or on any definite theory could be carried out, apart from the personal agency of others? Can one be named—in the natural, or in the domestic, or in the social, or in the political-life of man? Consider them and reply. Take the lowest form of natural instincts. Can we eat or drink—save in the lowest stages of savage life, if even we be content with the grass of the field and water from the brook—can we eat or drink, apart from human agency? No: it is impossible. Ascend a stage higher in the scale of life. Can we be clothed and sheltered, however humbly and insufficiently; can we enjoy the innocent pleasures of home-life, the tender relations of married-life, the softening and subduing responsibilities of family-life; can we be taught or amused, or even be self-instructed or paradoxical as it may sound, be self-absorbed—apart from the agency, direct or indirect, of our fellow-man? No: it is beyond our finite and dependent powers, in our domestic and social arrangements. Ascend to a wider platform in the scale of existence, to the political-life. Can we stay at home in peace, or go abroad in safety; can we be defended if attacked in time of war, be righted if wronged in time of peace, be governed at all times; can we follow our own devices, plans and aims, so long as they do not interfere with the equally lawful occupation of others—apart from instrumentality of our fellow-men? No: political-life returns the like answer to the other estates of man's corporate existence.

These cases do not exhaust our inquiries. Do we escape from human dependence in childhood? Are not the phrases, self-help, self-taught or self-raised men, or even self-governed people, figures of speech which conceal one element at the least of truth? Is it possible to be nursed when ill, or buried when dead; or can we be so much as brought into the world —apart, in each case, from the medium of our fellow-men? No: it cannot be. Personal existence itself, and every relation of man's natural life, from birth to death, is and must be dependent upon human agency.

What then can be done in this life apart from others? Apparently, the world can do but three things: the first is to generate thought; the second is to employ force for the production of motion; the third is to cease to exist as man. It requires no human agency to exercise our mind; none to lift one's arm; none to give up the ghost. We, Catholics, can do a fourth. We can think, move, die, and also adore: we can adore the personal great First Cause, the Sovereign, Saviour, Spirit—apart from human agency: adore the TRINITY by faith; by prayer; by praise and thanksgiving; by worship and sacrifice. But the world can exercise only three functions of life, the work of the brain, the work of the hands, and the final work of ceasing to work. For, though human agency is needed in order that we may be born, and being born to live; no power of man is required to give existence to thought, to cause the action of mind on matter, to restore the spirit to GOD Who gave it. Indeed, more than this is true, in an opposite direction: no human agency can curb the thought of man—it is his own: none can force the will—it is free: none can prevent man from yielding up the ghost—it is in GOD'S hands. But, beyond this three-fold limit, of self-consciousness, free-will and death, there is no natural relation of life in which man is not dependent upon his fellow-man. Human life is the aggregate and sum of human agencies.

The question now arises which demands an answer. If this analogy be true; if in every other relation of our life human agency is essential to human existence; if in political-life, in social-life, in domestic-life, in the natural-life the influence of others is indispensable—why should we exclude from this otherwise universal law the chiefest, nearest and most momentous of all relations, the religious-life? Why should we accept three simple, elemental, world-wide cases —thinking, acting, dying—and deny a fourth which is an exception only to those without the Church, and which is allowed by all to be involved and complicated—religion? It is not easy to return an answer which will bear the test of reason. It is impossible to supply a reason which will bear the test of faith. The analogy between the natural man and the supernatural man is complete and perfect. The same law holds good in regard to both. Nature and Faith are at one. GOD is pleased—in ways which we shall hereafter be led to consider—to work for man's sanctification, through the sacraments of the Church, by human agency.

Nor is this principle held only by the Church. Every form of religion, which in any degree is in possession of an organized system of faith or worship, believes and acts up to a belief in human agency as an element of influence in the soul of man. The false religions of antiquity; the false religions in the East of to-day; the true religion of the elder dispensation, both before and after the Christian era; the parodies on Christianity found in the far West, as well as on this side of the Atlantic of late years; imitations of the Catholic religion at home and abroad; the great Protestant bodies severed from the true faith on the Continent and their representative offshoots and imitators in England; the very dissidents from the truths which we believe, who are still within the communion of the Church—all concur in a practical assent, and for the most part agree in a theoretic adhesion, to the principle of human agency in the work of divine sanctification.

Indeed, it is not easy to determine at what point in the teaching of heresy or schism this initial truth is denied. Those within the Church who speak evil of sacerdotalism, accept the ministerial functions of an authorized clergy— which is distinctly a form of human agency. Those who reject the principle of a ministry ordained by an external and superior authority, avail themselves of the individual powers of preaching, teaching and personal intercourse from self-elected pastors or from pastors chosen by the flock—which is not less clearly another form of human agency. And those, be they within or without the Church, who neglect most consistently all personal influence in religion, which comes to them on authority, and who rest most exclusively upon private judgment, self-realization of doctrine, and independence of form and ceremony: even these cannot wholly escape from the principle of human agency, which follows their steps from end to end of their crude theory, through the unfelt but real and potent force of tradition.

In order to show the truth of this position, it is not needful to insist upon the fact that in a Christian country few adults have failed to be influenced in childhood by the inculpated principle, or can entirely free themselves in after life from the results which have inevitably ensued. It is sufficient to show of these theorists, that their nominally self-evolved form of religion is instinct with human agency. The system which they have adopted, not being of divine origin, must be of human development. The teachers of such system in any case, whether true teachers or false, introduce in their own persons the same fatal objection in regard to humanity. And the very fountain-head of their system, their acknowledged source of belief and practice (however much it may be in reality at issue with both), itself is possessed of a decidedly human element. The Holy Bible, although it not only contains but is GOD'S inspired Word, yet in its origination, in its preservation, in its transcription, in its translation, and in its explanation by those who ignore tradition and authority, contains a large infusion of the non-supernatural. And what is true of the foundation is still more true of the structure which is built upon it, and is most of all true of the builders engaged upon the labour. In view of the use to which they apply the Word of GOD written, the work from base to summit is essentially human: in other words, the work is one of human agency alone. The main differences between the teaching of the Church and of those who dissent from her teaching on this point are three-fold: 1. that the Church acknowledges the principle of human agency, through the medium of the sacraments, whilst others seek to eliminate such principle; 2. that the Church consistently employs in action the principle of human agency, whilst others unsuccessfully attempt to ignore it; and above all, 3. that the Church possesses power and authority to vivify the principle of human agency, and to make it a vehicle of imparting divine grace, whilst others do not pretend to convey grace through such agency, and would be impotent to transmit grace should they venture to make the attempt.

Our topic for thought, we may remember, is Man inspired by GOD, in relation to sin. How does this topic bear upon the question of human agency? Human personality, as the first element in GOD'S divine method of man's sanctification, may take two forms in our minds. Individual agency may be either, 1. undervalued, or held in little estimation; or 2. over-estimated, or valued beyond its legitimate importance. It may be decried, or it may be exaggerated. Both extremes are faulty. Both are almost, if not altogether, fatal to spirituality. The first tends to dependence alone on one, who of any person with whom we are intimately acquainted is certainly the least trustworthy—I mean one's self, as known to himself, to his confessor, to his Angel, to his GOD. The second tends to the ignoring beyond due limits of one, who in all cases of conscience ought not to be ignored, and as a fact cannot really be ignored—I mean, again, one's self, blessed with the gift, and burdened with the responsibility of free-will, for the employment of which we shall be judged at the Last Day. It is doubtful whether of these two forms of treating individual agency is the worse—the under-valuation or the over-estimation of man's co-operation with GOD. Both are radically bad. The one places self, absolutely; the other places man, so far as it is possible to place man—in the stead of GOD.

In this perplexing matter of avoiding two opposite faults in the spiritual life, the golden mean is to be sought. The golden mean of according due influence to human agency, without making self the supreme arbiter in all cases of difference; or, of yielding due submission to human authority without losing all claim to self-responsibility, is one of the most difficult of moral problems to solve. It is not easy to make a definition of it which will stand the test of criticism.

It is not easy to conceive, mentally, an explanation which will accommodate itself to practice. But practically, the theory is found to be soluble, in the case of humble minded persons who are likewise faithful. The golden mean can be and is practised. But of the two unwise extremes, a Catholic temper of mind is perhaps more tempted to the latter than to the former. The Protestant spirit, as a fact, fails in the first more than in the last. We, Brothers or Sisters in CHRIST, must be on our guard against both. We must seek to abandon our individuality rather than insist on it with over-eagerness. We must bow to due authority, whilst not effacing from the moral problem our self-accountability.

Apart from popular misconception in the use of terms, and in spite of its being a self-evident proposition—conscience was given to us by GOD to employ, not to suppress. As a corrollary to this, "direction" in the Church of GOD is intended, amongst other results, to perfect the gift. One great end of spiritual direction is to give healthy powers to man's conscience for its edification and use: in order to inform and indoctrinate, to stimulate and strengthen, to enlighten and to educate. These powers of the conscience will enable it 1. to guide the soul aright in some particular point in question, and 2. to supply the soul with a principle by which it may exercise a right judgment in all things. This is the true end of direction. As such it is of untold value, being one form of human agency, in union with the Sacramental system of the Church, towards man's sanctification by the HOLY GHOST.

With these truths in our mind, let us question our conscience on both the extremes which have been named.

I. Let us examine in the first place, the temptation which is wont to assail the more Catholic temperament—the overestimation of human agency in the soul's conflict. Have we ever exaggerated this means of sanctification? Have we given too much weight to it in theory, and relied upon it over much in practice? Have we bowed before man's co-operation in principle, or lived upon man's judgment in a particular or individual expression of such principle? Have we, in short, too eagerly sought priestly advice, or counsel, or decision; and have we followed it blindly, and in a self-satisfied spirit, or without the exercise of Christianized reason? If so, to what results in our inner life and our outward relations has such exaggeration led? Has this over-estimation of spiritual authority produced in our soul, a conscience weakened, enervated, undecided, vacillating, changeful? Or, towards others, absorption and insularity, want of sympathy and a feeling of supposed superiority? Or, towards the object of the exaggerated sentiment, fear, childish dependency, or even subserviency, on the one hand; or undue attraction or familiarity on the other? Or, in relation to GOD, a too little realization of His direct office and work in the soul, in spite of, nay, by means of the delegated powers and operation of human agency?

II. Let us examine, in the second place, the fault into which the more Protestant-minded conscience is certain to fall—the under-valuation of human agency in the sanctification of the soul. Have we ever depreciated this means of inspiration mediately offered by GOD the HOLY GHOST? Have we not only neglected this means of ascertaining the divine Will; but prevented others from using it—by advice, command, or example? Have we not only thought lightly of this agency; but spoken harshly, bitterly, contemptuously, sarcastically, even untruly of it? Have we not only failed to avail ourself of human agency, when the option was lawful; but also failed to obey its directions, counsels, or suggestions when, really, there was no option, and the obligation lay on the other side? Have we not only been self-persuaded into failing to see that GOD could employ human instruments for a superhuman purpose; but have ventured to deny that He ever does; and thus, consciously or unconsciously, have deceived others into the like delusion? And has such antagonism with divine principles led to worse results? Has it led, in self, to deadness, hardness, self-assertion, self-sufficiency? Or, towards others, to criticism or condemnation, to distrust or detraction? Or, towards our priest to want of reality, unreal agreement, causeless antagonism, or severance, which is not only uncalled for but harmful? Or, in regard to GOD, to isolation, self-dependence, absence of living faith, tepidity in divine love?

These questions may be considered to be typical rather than exhaustive. They may beneficially be answered before the close of the present Retreat.

V.

Next: in relation to man's sanctification by GOD, the HOLY GHOST works for the sinner's re-creation, not only by human agency, but also by the means of material substance. This is a still harder truth for the world to accept. It is bad enough to be dependent in spiritual matters, as the world cannot escape from dependency upon human agents, on man, feeble and fallible as he is. But, to be the slave of matter, whose master man prides himself in being; and to be forced to allow that matter can influence and affect man's spirit, when man's prepossessions lead him in the opposite direction —this insult to the dignity of manhood is even worse. The world bluntly denies all spiritual obligation to material substances. It declines to argue the point. Nor, on its own principles, is the world in error. In this materialistic age, when the *minimum* of belief attracts the *maximum* of believers, when nothing which may be colourably denied is believed upon authority, when little is believed save on the evidence of the five natural senses of the human body, or which can be proved by demonstrable or mathematical evidence—it is a bitter draught to be forced to take, without any palliative qualification, that material substances are channels of spiritual powers. And yet, Christians who simply accept the creeds of the Church, without necessarily assenting to any dogma which flows from the creeds, are pledged to this position.

In considering the question of human agency in the divine

work for souls, we took the world's view of worldly things. We eliminated religion; and argued apart from it. In considering the question of material substances, we will argue in accord with the teaching of the Church: we will take a religious view of a religious subject. Observe: we appeal to the simplest form of Christian belief which all can understand; which none can, strictly speaking, be Catholic without accepting. We do not appeal to Holy Scripture, nor to the decrees of councils, nor to the works of the Fathers, nor to the pages of history, nor to the teaching of tradition. These authorities may all be read in two ways; and some of them require learning and leisure to be read at all. But, to our children we teach the creeds. We use the creeds in our daily private devotions. The creeds are plain, decided, unambiguous—if any form of human language which is employed to convey thought and not to conceal it, can be so described. And one of three creeds, which are received of all faithful men, is distinctly committed to the principle we are considering. The Nicene creed affirms: I believe in one baptism for the remission of sins.

Observe, again: the Nicene creed is of universal obligation, of world-wide acceptance. No Catholic with ourselves, as we have seen, receives the Holy Eucharist, without first reciting its clauses in their integrity. Holy Church thinks fit to recite it daily. And the Nicene creed binds all who say it to this principle: that sin is forgiven in, with, and by the means of Christian ordinances, that is, the reception of the sacraments of the Church. I believe in one baptism: the creed declares. For what end? To what purpose? Is it to gain admittance to the Christian family; to secure membership in the Church of CHRIST; to be re-created the child of GOD; to be made an inheritor of the kingdom of Heaven? No; it is not—not primarily, not chiefly, not only. First and foremost, though other effects follow in due course, it is for the forgiveness of sin. I believe in one baptism for the remission of sins.

These simple words cover the whole position, in principle. For what is the principle for which we contend? The sanctification of man by material substances. What is the principle which is here involved? That for the remission of sins we are baptized. And what do the simple words of the creed import? What is remission but a spiritual result? What is baptism, as to its outward form, but a material substance? Baptism is performed: a few drops of pure water are used; a few short words are spoken; the action and language are contemporaneous, and the intention of the officiant to do what the Church enjoins is assumed—and remission of sins follows; the remission of original sin in the case of an infant; the remission of actual sin in the case of an adult. Is it wrong therefore to affirm that, in this instance and in the mind of the Church, a spiritual result ensues from the employment of a material substance?

A Catholic, then, finds himself placed in this dilemma—if indeed he can take a view antagonistic to that of the creed's teaching. If he admits the sceptical principle, that material substances, vivified by the HOLY GHOST, are powerless to convey spiritual influences, he denies the creed. If he accepts the creed of Christendom, that remission of sins ensues from Holy Baptism, that is, from the concurrence of water, words and intention, he condemns the sceptical principle. And the like dilemma meets all who question the action of the same law in other sacraments of the Church. For the law which obtains in the case of the initial rite of our holy Faith, obtains also, directly, in the chiefest of the sacraments, the most Holy Eucharist, and in the Last Sacraments, as well as indirectly in the remaining four, Confirmation, Penance, Ordination and Marriage. Flour of wheat and water, and the juice of the grape and water, and the creature of oil, these are distinctly material substances which, under certain conditions, convey spiritual results. And although, of material substances, the like truth cannot be affirmed in regard to the remaining sacraments; yet, the like truth can be affirmed of a combination of two or more of the media through which the Holy SPIRIT is pleased to work for man's sanctification, namely, human agency, material substance and ceremonial form. To the principle which underlies all these cases, the Catholic is pledged in virtue of his adhesion to the article of the Nicene creed which declares: I believe in one baptism for the remission of sins.

Our topic for thought, again, having this for its subject-matter, Man inspired by GOD in relation to sin—how does this topic bear upon the question of material substance? How do material substances, in GOD'S system for man's sanctification, tend to help or to hinder the results which have been attached to them by Him?

In attempting to answer this inquiry, it may be wise to answer it in the spirit, rather than in the letter. It is not easy to see how the material substances of the sacraments can bear any direct reference to the sin of man. But, if we turn to the principle which governs the use of material substances in the Church of GOD; and if we consider the application of this principle to the sacramentals of religion, the end which we have in view will be attained—namely, to give a practical issue to the lessons which have gone before. And the governing principle is this: the employment of outward clothing as a vehicle for conveying inward grace. It will not be difficult to see how such exterior circumstances can be charged, in the sanctification of man, with temptation to sin.

It would be affectation to suppose that we, personally, are tempted to undervalue the influence of material substances, in the sense in which the words are here used. Our temptation would rather lie in the opposite direction, to over-estimate them. And in dealing with such temptation, it is an obvious remark, that a danger always exists for a pendulum which has been unduly strained in one direction, to rebound unduly in another. Re-action and action are morally, as well as physically proportionate. If, at some time of our spiritual career, we have been at one with the world on this question, it is probable that we may feel more than the Church requires now. Nor is there any need to over-value mere material agencies in themselves, in order to fall into danger. It is enough if we give undue prominence to the outward expression of divine truth. For example, to take an extreme case: If we, personally, be unable to give to GOD the worship due to Him, by reason of the outward form in which it is offered to His Majesty; if our prayers be less collected, more indevout, more distracted, less fervent when debarred from, than when in the enjoyment of divine worship of a Catholic type—then we are guilty of giving undue weight to accidental circumstances; we over-value, in the sense in which we use the words, the importance of material substances.

Perhaps GOD sends us this trial to test our faith. He permits us to suffer from a partial, or occasional, or even from a more permanent deprivation of divine worship of the highest type. It matters not what may be the cause of such deprivation, whether it comes from the exercise of power of those in authority, or from fickleness and want of stability in those under authority, or from our own change of circumstance, abode, or otherwise. In any case the loss is inflicted upon us, without our fault, and against our will. Of course, the loss I speak of is a loss in detail, not in principle; or a loss æsthetic, not sacramental: for we cannot compare shadow with substance, or the Hours of Prayer with the Sacrifice of the Altar. But, in the accidentals of divine service of any kind, if we yield to the trial, we fail in one of the highest of earthly duties —detachment from the influence of external things. And in such a trial, GOD often tests our reality, perseverance, and love. This is not said in order to disparage what is known as "high ritual." GOD forbid. It is said to suggest resignation, if not contentment, to those who love it, as I love it, as they ought to love it, when in GOD'S permissive Will devout persons are temporarily deprived of it. Judge yourselves in this matter. Are you, as a fact, less fervent and devout; are you perceptibly to yourself, to your Angel, and to your GOD, more distracted and unrecollected, whilst worshipping at a meagre and even at a slovenly form of divine service, than when assisting at a function which is ceremonially lavish and exact? If so—ought you so to be, in view of the true value of material agencies in relation to man's sanctification?

These inquiries have been broadly stated in order that they may enclose a wide number of cases. They may with profit be made minute and definite during the present Retreat.

VI.

Lastly: in relation to man's sanctification by GOD, the HOLY GHOST works for the sinner's re-creation, not only by human agencies, not only by material substances, but also by the means of ceremonial form. This is the hardest truth of all for the world to accept. Man's personality may be yielded by the world as an agency of inspiration by GOD—for was not our Divine Master MAN, as well as GOD? Material substances even may be tolerated as means of imparting divine grace after some fashion—for, to the world, are not the Sacred Elements, Bread and Wine? But that ritual form and outward ceremony should be capable to co-operate, or as a fact do co-operate for man's sanctification—no. In no sense, and with no qualification, will the world accept this position. It utterly rejects the idea as superstitious.

Why? Mark the reason. Because of unbelief: because the world denies the truth, reality, and efficacy of that which ritual form and outward ceremony at once express and convey, in the blessed sacraments of the Church. This, the third way in which GOD is pleased to work for man's re-creation, becomes the test of our acceptance of the two earlier methods. It is useless to assent to man's agency, and to consent to the use of material substances, if we fail to acknowledge the value of ceremonial form. It is useless, as failing to acknowledge a divine system of grace in its entirety; and hence, as causing its imperfection. Because we believe that sacramental forms and ceremonies are sacramental and grace-conferring before they are, in being, and after they cease to be forms and ceremonies—therefore we believe them to play their assigned part in the mystery of man's inspiration by GOD. And it is because the world denies the efficacy, the reality, and the truth of the blessed sacraments, that it denies, therefore, the power of that which both conveys and expresses them. The world, in support of its disbelief, appeals to the rites of the Jewish religion. What is a sufficient answer to this appeal? That the elder dispensation was a religion of form and ceremony, apart from and without divine grace; but, that the newer dispensation is a religion of form and ceremony, in addition to and together with divine grace. The former was typical, and foreshadowed the gift of GOD; the latter is a reality, and conveys it. Between the two lies the essential difference, in mathematical language, of *minus* grace and *plus* grace. In fact, no religion exists without a recognized ceremonial form, however rudimentary or degenerate: none is devoid of outward expression of belief or duty. Our holy Faith is the only religion which gives to ritual form and ceremony their sacramental reality and truth. The world denies this. It consistently denies that ceremonial form affects the sanctification of man by GOD the HOLY GHOST. But we, thank GOD, are otherwise and oppositely pledged.

On this division of the subject it is not needful to dwell at length. The principle which is advocated under the head of ceremonial order has been fully discussed under the sections which have gone before. Indeed, ritual form is at once the outcome and the expression both of human agency and of material substance combined. If the position at which we aim has been secured in either of the previous divisions of the argument, and still more if it has been secured in both, we may assume its truthfulness in the present and last division; and we may pass on at once to what flows from the principle in practice.

Our topic for thought, once more, being this, Man inspired by GOD in relation to sin, we may enquire—how is this topic connected with the question of ceremonial form? How does ritual order, which has the sanction of CHRIST'S Church and which is instinct with life, in the work of sanctification by the HOLY GHOST, afford any temptation to man to sin?

These relations may perhaps be conveniently dealt with here, as in the last section, in the spirit rather than in the letter. We considered the question of sin in relation to material agencies, from the standpoint of their actual deprivation. We will consider the question of ritual order from that of its spiritual enjoyment—with brevity and by the help of the following searching inquiries: 1. Do we use every form and ceremony, under which sacramental grace is veiled, with the reverence, devotion and care we should use if brought into direct contact with GOD'S grace, that is, with GOD Himself apart from ritual order? 2. Do we employ the lesser details of ritual order with the like care that we bestow upon the greater, or do we devote to the less common ceremonies the same exactness that we bestow upon the more popular—forgetful of the fact that both are used in the worship of GOD, and that if any authorized form is neglected, it is our part to seek after its restoration? 3. Do we strive intelligently to understand, and to be able to give a reasonable answer for the ceremonial forms which we use in order to obtain GOD'S grace; being persuaded that a reasonable intelligence does not detract from the spirit of devotion, but rather enhances it?

Again: 4. Do we take exception, without cause or reason, to certain developments of ceremonial form which are based upon Catholic authority, and hence are our lawful inheritance, even although they may lack the authority of continuous usage in our own communion of late years? 5. Do we oppose the re-introduction of given forms of ritual order which may tend to perfect our mutilated office, or may give unity and completeness, dignity and grace, devotion and beauty to our own *minimum* of rite and ceremony? 6. Do we fail to encourage the development of authorized and customary ceremonial for any reason short of the highest, or for any reason in which personal predilection, in ourselves or others, and the unworthy fear of consequences, which are in GOD'S hand, play their part? 7. Do we co-operate—to the utmost of our power, whether by argument, or by advice, or by sympathy, with our means, our personal labour, and our moral support—with those who are attacked and harassed either through the nominally regular forms of legal procedure, or the irresponsible tribunals of social life—both of which result in the persecution, mild in form but bitter in feeling, of the age in which we live?

These suggestions for self-examination are samples only of those which may be brought home to the soul, by introspection and retrospection, in the course of the present Retreat.

VII.

The HOLY GHOST is pleased to work for man's sanctification, through the Sacramental system of the Church, not only by human agency, not only by material substance, not only by ceremonial form, but also, by His own divine power. All without this, all apart from this, were useless, empty, vain. Ceremonial form, even divinely instituted, when severed, if such be possible, from divine inspiration, would be vain. Material substance, even divinely sanctioned, when denied the divine fulfilment, would be vain. Human agency, even divinely ordained, when withdrawn from divine co-operation, would be vain. All and each were vain, if detached from the authority and influence, from the office and work of GOD'S Holy SPIRIT in the re-creation of man. Water in Baptism, Episcopal hands in Confirmation and Holy Orders, Bread and Wine in the most Holy Eucharist, the Church's blessing in Marriage, Oil in Unction—together with the priestly action and the ritual order which He employs—would be worse than useless, would be more than empty, if not inspired by the divine power and presence of GOD the COMFORTER.

But, in the Church of the PARACLETE, under the inspiration of the SPIRIT, nothing is empty, nothing is useless, nothing is vain. For there is found the indwelling of the HOLY GHOST, Who makes living and true and real all that He is pleased to touch, and everything by which He is pleased to work. He it is Who preserves the use of human agencies from degenerating into tyranny on the one hand, into servitude on the other, into idolatry on both sides. He it is Who prevents the employment of earthly, created and material substances from lapsing into refined materialism. He it is Who transforms the lifeless letter, the outward form of ceremonial observances into divine and life-giving sacraments. Having, directly or mediately, inspired ritual order; having bestowed upon matter capacity and power to minister to the spirit, and to convey that which is spiritual; having set aside more or less completely from earthly things, the personal and individual agency of a priestly caste—He, the Third Person of the Holy TRINITY, performs His divine part in the contract which Himself has made with man, He fulfils the divine conditions which Himself has imposed upon man. He gives divine power to human words spoken and human acts done; to common water outpoured, to common bread broken, and wine mingled, to the two-fold imposition of a Bishop's hands, to the priestly union of two members of CHRIST into one, and to the creature of oil administered—divine power, that the dead letter becomes a living word, and that the human, material, ceremonial ordinance becomes a spiritual, life-giving sacrament. By His power, outer forms are made inward realities; matter becomes the channel of divine grace; humanity produces superhuman results. Such exercise of divine power ensues in virtue of the Sacramental system of the Church—from the direct promise and even the command of GOD, and from GOD'S covenant with man—a covenant and a promise beyond which GOD is not bound, but within which GOD has been pleased to pledge Himself, to impart grace to man.

Third Day of Retreat.

GOD IN UNION WITH MAN IN RELATION TO SIN.

ADDRESS EIGHT.

THE INCARNATION OF GOD.

WE have considered two out of the three subjects of the present Retreat. We have considered, 1. GOD, the great personal First Cause, in relation to sin; and, 2. Man, created in the image of GOD, in relation to sin. We have now to consider, 3. the Personal GOD in union with created Man, in relation to sin.

On the first day of Retreat, we dwelt upon GOD the Creator, the Saviour, the Sanctifier. On the second day we dwelt upon Man—made, bought, inspired. To-day we will dwell upon the Incarnation of GOD, the Sacrifice of the Cross, the Sacraments of the Church—all three in relation to the same profound mystery, sin. In other words, we shall meditate upon the Love of GOD, as exhibited in the divinely-instituted means of counteracting the effect, of expiating the guilt, and of restoring the loss, which has ensued from human sin.

There are three points of observation from whence GOD'S Love, as exhibited in the union of the Creator with the creature, may be estimated. The subject may be viewed, 1. in the ages of ages; before the existence of time, past, present, or future; as conceived in the divine decrees and eternal counsels of the Infinite and Unchangeable. It may be estimated, 2. in the past; as adopted in time, whether remote or proximate, when present and future exert their influence, when cause and effect have in consequence to be considered. It may be treated, 3. in the present, contemporaneously, as regards to-day; when, having been conceived in eternity and adopted in time, the divine scheme of union is applied to the soul of man in relation to sin. As life presents itself, these three phases can only be separated in thought; they are indivisible in reality. Expiation applied to the soul of man to-day cannot be divided from the adoption of the principle established in the spiritual world yesterday. The adoption of the principle of union yesterday cannot be divided from the conception of the divine decrees from all eternity.

As the points of observation, whence GOD'S Love is exhibited in the union of the Creator with the creature, are threefold, so it may be considered with more or less of reference to the Three Persons of the Holy TRINITY respectively in each case. Of course, by the doctrine of circumcession, in all three estimates of the mystery divine and human, all Three Persons of the GODHEAD are severally involved. But, in the sacred economy, and in the relation which the Persons of the Holy TRINITY stand towards man, we may reverently meditate, more or less exclusively, on the attributes and operations of each several Person in each separate case. For example: The union of the Creator with the creature, as affecting the means of expiation—which were conceived in the eternal counsels, before time was, brings before the mind the Person and functions in regard to man of GOD the FATHER. The same union, as influencing the means of expiation which have been adopted in time past, remote or proximate, brings before the mind the Person and functions of GOD the SON, the Word and Wisdom of GOD. The same union, as regulating the means of expiation, which are extended and applied in the present, brings before the mind the Person and functions of GOD the HOLY GHOST, the Comforter. In no case, however, must we be so absorbed in the attributes or operations, in the office and work of any one Person of the GODHEAD, and of His sacred functions in relation to human sin, as to be forgetful, even for the moment, of the other two divine Persons.

Hence, GOD'S Love, in the union of the Creator and the creature, is to be considered under three distinct heads. 1. The Incarnation of GOD, more especially in relation to GOD the FATHER. 2. The Sacrifice of the Cross, more especially in relation to GOD the SON. 3. The Sacraments of the Church, more especially in relation to GOD the HOLY GHOST. The first point will lead us to think more of the Mind and Will of GOD essentially, and as revealed in eternity, than in either the present or the past. The next point will reveal to us more of the Divine Attributes sacrificially, and as exhibited in time past, than in eternity. The last point will teach us more of the Divine Operations sacramentally, and as working in the present, than in the past or in the ages of ages.

Of course, the time at our disposal is insufficient for more than a superficial review of some of the salient points in these vast and absorbing theological topics. It will be wise, therefore, to make choice of a few divisions in each subject, and to treat them with the fulness which circumstances permit. Of the three questions to be discussed, the Incarnation of GOD, in relation to the Eternal FATHER, demands our consideration on the present occasion.

II.

"It is necessary to everlasting salvation," says the venerable symbol of S. Athanasius, that we "believe rightly the Incarnation of our LORD JESUS CHRIST: for the right faith is, that we believe and confess that our LORD JESUS CHRIST, the SON of GOD, is GOD and MAN."

Not one word, observe, do these clauses contain on the object, cause, or reason of the union of the Creator and the creature. The creed simply enunciates a matter of fact, gives expression to a dogmatic belief, pronounces a theological statement. It declares that on the acceptance of the fact, and on the confession of the dogma, hangs our eternal destiny. It declares, with many qualifications and many conditions in relation to the nature and person, to the essence, attributes, and operations of our Divine Master, that CHRIST our LORD is GOD and MAN. Nor, observe again, is any reason or object assigned for the union of the creature with the Creator, throughout this symbol of faith—least of all is human guilt assigned as the cause of the mystery of the Incarnation. Indeed, later on in the creed it is expressly stated that, for our salvation, the Incarnated GOD was pleased to suffer for us. But the Passion of JESUS is not the same with His Incarnation. It is not identical with the Incarnation, even when the latter had been accomplished in time. It is very distinct from the Incarnation, which was everlastingly decreed in the eternal counsels of GOD in the ages of ages. In theology, not less than in other exact sciences—for theology is both a science and is exact in its definitions and demonstrations—we must be careful of confusing, to any extent, cause and consequence.

It is true, the Nicene creed affirms that "for us men, and for our salvation," JESUS CHRIST "came down from heaven:" and also, later on in the same division, it declares that He "was crucified also for us, suffered, and was buried." But it is worthy of careful notice that the article which enunciates the dogma of the Incarnation stands between these two clauses : and of the Incarnation itself, and as apart from its direct consequences, or from what flowed from it indirectly, the creed certainly does not assert that it was a divine invention for the remedy of man's sin. In other words, the most universally used of all the creeds pronounces on the union of the Creator and the creature, essentially, and as conceived in the mind of God and decreed from all eternity : not on the Incarnation as adopted in the past, nor as extended in the present; not on that phase of the mystery which permitted the Passion, sacrificially ; not on that phase which necessitated its extension, practically, in the Sacramental system of the Church.

These truths are important in meditating on the Incarnation of GOD. In the permissive Will of GOD and when contemplating the expiation of man's sin, then, we may admit that the Incarnation became an element in the divine scheme of redemption, became an instrument in GOD's hands which He was pleased to employ for man's sake. But the Incarnation, abstractedly, was wholly independent of man's sin. It was no divine device, pure and simple, for man's salvation. We may admit also, in the fullest manner, that man's salvation and man's sin produced their effects on the accidents of the Incarnation—on the accidents of the age in which it was accomplished, of the locality in which it was fulfilled, of the sacred person by whom it was accepted, of the earthly surroundings by which it was accompanied. But, as the essential cause—no. In any case, it is an inadequate view to take; in some cases, it is an unworthy one.

Here, in the question of the Incarnation, as in many theological matters, the principle upon which and the temper in which one approaches Catholic doctrine is of more moment as a test of orthodoxy, than the precise statement of dogma which is made. Persons imbued with Christian belief may be allowed a latitude of expression which must be denied to those who are not so imbued. This is an equally valid position, whether or not the Church has or has not definitely pronounced upon the question. It applies, though in different ways and in different degrees, to the ante-Nicene Fathers and to post-Augustinian writers. What might lawfully be written on the Divinity of our LORD by the former, may not, without qualification, be affirmed now. What might lawfully be said on the question of the free-will of man by the latter, may not, without being supplemented, be declared now. The doctrine of the Holy TRINITY, as an actual belief, was inferentially presupposed in the one case. The doctrine of divine grace, as a sacramental reality, was practically presupposed in the other. Our individual use of the language in both cases, whilst denying their principles or ignoring their practice, would cause us to be un-orthodox, and even heretical.

Nor is it otherwise with the dogma of the Incarnation.

Tempered with a belief in co-ordinate truths of the Catholic faith, it is comparatively indifferent which of the rival theories of the Incarnation be received. Severed from such full belief, it is of almost vital importance which theory be adopted. In conjunction with Catholic tradition, the theory accepted by the Protestant is defensible. Apart from tradition, and when made the central point of popular Protestantism, the theory, that the Incarnation was designed to counteract the sin of man, is not only dogmatically indefensible, but is full of danger to the person who holds the opinion, and is a low and debased theological idea in itself. To conceive of the Incarnation—the greatest, deepest, most stupendous mystery ever offered to the faith of man—simply as a divine scheme to countervail human wickedness, may this ever be far from the belief of Catholics!

On so momentous and awful a topic of thought, the human mind fails to grasp the whole truth. Human speech fails to convey even so much of truth as may be grasped intellectually. But, in profound adoration and in the presence of ineffable mystery, we can but believe, we can hardly affirm more than this: that, the Incarnation of the DEITY was conceived in the eternal Mind, was accomplished in the divine Will, was extended in the absolute Foreknowledge of GOD, in order to increase the glory of the Infinite and Unchangeable, by the union of the creature with the Creator: the glory —of course, accidental; the union—of course, in the nature of man. If this be allowed, namely, that the Incarnation is something deeper, higher, wider, less superficial, more mysterious, more unfathomable than a divine antidote for human sin or man's wickedness; then, it may be admitted, I repeat, that as to the accidents of the Incarnation, as to its circumstances and manner, as to the co-operation of time, place and person in its fulfilment, development, and application, it pleased GOD that human guilt should influence, in most matters which fall short of the primary cause, the union of the creature and the Creator. And in this restricted sense, as one element of the mystery of GOD made MAN, it may be profitable to meditate upon this side of truth.

III.

The divine Incarnation, from the point of view which we propose to take of the mystery, namely, as affecting or as affected by the expiation of human sin, has now to be considered. It has to be considered as eternally existing in the divine mind of the Blessed TRINITY, rather than as consummated on behalf of the whole race of man by the Sacrifice of the Cross in time past, or as extended to each individual member of the race in the Sacraments of the Church now. As such it may be treated as the first act of a sacred drama, which was commenced in eternity before time was begun, which will be concluded in eternity after time has been ended, —in the absolute union of the future, not in the partial union of the present, of the creature with the Creator.

The union of the creature and the Creator, in the predestined form in which such union was to be effected; the union of human nature, body, soul, and spirit, with the Divine Nature, Three in One and One in Three, involves three distinct considerations. These considerations affect either the Persons of the Holy TRINITY severally engaged in the work of expiation, or the means, direct or mediate, which such Persons were pleased to take towards the same result. Each divine Person entered into a new relationship. The attributes and operations of all the divine Persons were concentrated upon a common end. Hence, the Incarnation of the DEITY may be viewed, 1. in regard to GOD the FATHER, when the mystery was conceived in the eternal mind of the GODHEAD; in regard to GOD the SON, when its fulfilment was undertaken by the Divine WORD; 3. in regard to GOD the SPIRIT, when it became accomplished by the operation of the HOLY GHOST in the person of the Blessed Mary. We will take these three divisions of the topic in their order.

I. Of the Incarnation, in regard to the GOD the FATHER.

In the ages of ages, of which we have spoken, when GOD was one and alone; the Self-originated, existent, subsisting; dwelling in silence and repose—GOD willed. In the eternal counsels and divine foreknowledge, what GOD was pleased to will, was, became; what GOD was pleased to will, became present to His Majesty whether in its beginning or end, whether as to its cause or result. In the ages of ages, GOD willed and creation was. In the course of time, GOD spake and it was done. Creation, however, was only a portion of the will of GOD in action—perhaps the least part. As such, creation was not conceived as an end, but rather as the means to an end evolved from the eternal mind of GOD. The end in view was the increase of GOD'S accidental glory by the union of the creature with the Creator. Towards this end creation was the first stage. The Incarnation could not have been fulfilled by the Second Person, it could not have been extended by the Third Person, had it not been conceived in the mind of the First Person of the Holy TRINITY.

Creation is a wide term. ¡We have seen some things which are included within its bounds. We have seen that it may be viewed in three well-defined divisions: spiritual creation; material creation; and creation which combines both. The last, creation in part spiritual and in part material, embraces each form of created things, and combines features from all of them. Hence, it may be taken as the representative of GOD'S effort of creative power, as the initial act of the union of the creature and the Creator: in one word of the Incarnation. Of course, that effort which combined both matter and spirit and super-added grace, was Man. And as man is the representative of creation, so also has he been made by GOD its perfection, summit, glory, crown. The union, therefore, of GOD with man involves not only union with the representative of creation, but also union with the highest development of created spirit, union with the lowest development of created matter, and union with all intermediate and commingled developments. It pleased GOD in willing that the Creator and the creature should become one, to will also that such oneness with the GODHEAD should be made in the person of man.

This was the first stage in the Incarnation. In the eternal counsels it was decreed—with absolute foreknowledge of man's power of free-will to be given him by GOD; with perfect consciousness of man's use of free-will to thwart GOD'S Will; with predestinated means of influencing the one and of counteracting the other—that the union of the Creator with the creature should be accomplished in the person of man. This divine decree, in the ages of ages, we may reverently ascribe to the Will of the Everlasting FATHER.

II. Of the Incarnation, in regard to GOD the SON.

In the revelation of GOD to man on the doctrine of the Holy TRINITY, not only has there been revealed a distinction in the divine personality, but also a difference in the divine operations—perhaps also a difference in the divine attributes. In any case, special characteristics in relation to man are affirmed of each several divine Person of the DEITY. Thus, to speak only in general terms and in regard to human sin: the FATHER is revealed as the source and fount of creation and as bestowing upon mankind the God-like gift, equally fulfilled with blessing and danger, of free-will; the SON is revealed as the cause, if not the author, of man's redemption, in virtue of which the consequences of GOD'S gift of free-will misused have been counteracted; the SPIRIT is revealed as the restorer of grace and holiness, and of consequent power to please GOD, which had been forfeited by the misuse of GOD'S gift and had been repurchased for man by the offering of the Precious Blood. These characteristics seem to point to that Person of the GODHEAD Who should take action, so to speak, in the next place, to fulfil the eternal counsels of the TRINITY for the union of the Creator with the creature in the person of man. That divine Person, it need not be said, was the Everlasting SON, the Historical CHRIST of the Gospel, the Child of Blessed Mary.

Apart from the teaching of revelation, it is not too much to say that the uninspired intellect of man would have been powerless, not only to conceive the doctrine of the Incarnation as we hold to the truth; but also, if through vague tradition it had possessed an indistinct idea of the doctrine, would have been powerless to imagine the means and agency by which this stupendous fact in the universe was accomplished. Man alone could not have positively stated, even had he acquired a knowledge of the Three in One and One in Three, by which divine Person the mystery of the Incarnation was fulfilled. But, realizing as we have been taught the transcendental relationships which exist between the Co-eternal and Co-equal THREE; and knowing as we know the Person of the Holy TRINITY Who actually undertook the next stage in man's redemption from sin—we can perceive the reason of that which otherwise we could not conceive, namely, why the Everlasting SON, rather than the Eternal FATHER or the Consubstantial HOLY GHOST, should elect to take upon Himself the office of the Redeemer of Mankind. From the analogy of the constitution of man, who was made in the image of GOD, we are enabled with bold humility to argue thus.

Of all the modes of indicating the will of man, and hence, of giving expression to that which most closely represents man—the word of man is the most intimate, definite, and exact. This mode deserves such a description far more truly than any act or expression of man; although, of course, the act and the look, as well as the word of man may be expressive of the very opposite of that which constitutes the agent, or the actor, or the speaker respectively. The word of man, so far as outward expression can represent inward personality, is man—is man to such an extent, that the daily life of each individual of the human race, whether ordinary or extraordinary; not less than the whole fabric of society at large, whether family, social, political, or national, is built upon this assumption. Man's word, of course again, truthfully given, is the outcome of man's self. It is the man. It is the man, so far as any organism outside man himself can arrive at an estimate of him, of his mind and his will, of his power and capacity, of his desire and wish, of his past history, and his future intention. We cannot get nearer to the individuality of our neighbour than by securing his word. His appearance may belie him. His actions may be capable of two interpretations. But in his word—truthfully spoken—we may trust.

Hence, we venture to argue, upon the basis of revelation, from the image of GOD to Him in Whose image he was made; from man to GOD. We get nearest to the Personality of GOD when we can claim His Divine WORD. His Divine WORD is—not only expresses, or represents, but is—GOD; is the Omnipotent, Omniscient, Omnipresent; is the All-true, the All-holy, the Ever-merciful, the Ever-loving; is the One, Very, Living and True GOD. Holy Scripture teaches this when it terms the WORD the express Image of the Person of the Eternal, Infinite and Incomprehensible; when it assures us that in the beginning was the WORD, that the WORD was with GOD, that the WORD was GOD. So far, therefore, as man's finite reason can perceive, it was meet and right that the WORD or Logos, the WORD or Wisdom of the FATHER, the WORD and Sender of the SPIRIT from the FATHER, should be pleased to effect the union of GOD with man. It was meet and right that the WORD of GOD should accomplish the eternal counsels and divine decrees of the Holy TRINITY, by effecting that union of the creature and the Creator which we call the Incarnation.

III. Of the Incarnation, in regard to GOD the SPIRIT.

Remember that two stages in the argument have been gained: 1. that the Creator and the creature should be united in the person of man; 2. that such union should be effected by the instrumentality of the Divine WORD. In other terms, the end to be attained is seen to have been pre-ordained; and the Agent Who will effect the end is seen to have been self-elected. What remains to be determined is the means by which this divine Agent may accomplish such predestinated end. Here, again, it would have been impossible for the uninspired intellect of man to have antecedently determined by which Person of the Holy TRINITY the means should be taken to insure the end in view. But the action of the Third Person, inspiration has revealed to us, now comes into play. GOD the HOLY GHOST will be seen to supply the means by which the Agent may attain the predestinated end. He will fulfil in time the divine scheme which had been conceived before the foundation of the world. He will accomplish that work which in GOD'S Will was essential to the restoration of fallen man from the power of sin. The Incarnation of GOD the WORD, to the greater glory of GOD the FATHER, was consummated by the special instrumentality of GOD the Blessed PARACLETE.

How was that to be done on earth which had been decreed in heaven? Two divine problems had to be solved: 1. How GOD the SON could become man without ceasing to be GOD; and 2. How GOD the All-pure could take the nature of sinful man and yet remain pure. In stating the answers to these problems, we must remember, again, that man's uninstructed reason were powerless to conceive them; and further, that even when inspired to perceive the truth, his reason has capacity only to accept and not to master the teachings of faith. Both problems were solved by different attributes or operations of the Third Person of the TRINITY. The self-dedication of a humble Jewish Maiden, under the inspiration of the HOLY GHOST, overcame the first difficulty. The Overshadowing by the HOLY GHOST of an Immaculate Virgin overcame the second. The WORD took Flesh from the pure blood of a sinless daughter of Eve; and remained what He was before, the Eternal, Living, and True GOD. By the Virgin-birth of the Virgin-born, the All-pure took the nature of sinful man; and yet, in the person of spotless Mary, was untouched by the defilement of sin. In other words, and in terms which we must fully accept though we may not fully grasp, GOD became MAN, being born of Blessed Mary, and having been conceived by the HOLY GHOST.

IV.

Such is the Incarnation of GOD, in relation, 1. to the supernatural means which were adopted for its fulfilment in time; 2. to the Agent, personal and divine, Who was pleased before time was to undertake it, and in the course of time to accomplish it; 3. to the Almighty Mind and Will which, in the eternal counsels, conceived the mystery and decreed its realization.

The divine Incarnation thus taxed each several Person of the Holy TRINITY for its completion, conjointly and separately, by the exercise of various if not different attributes and operations of the GODHEAD. As such, it is the most stupendous of all theological facts; it is the most soul-subduing of all supernatural mysteries; it is the most incredible of all divine miracles; it is the most unfathomable dogma to the human intellect. It is the one dogma to be accepted of faith—simply and alone. It is the one dogma which reason, or sense, or experience, or history, or experiment, or imagination, utterly and entirely fails to explain. Man is powerless to account for the heavenly paradox, to harmonize the earthly contradiction. Believe that; and there is nothing which we cannot believe. Believe that; and there is nothing which we ought not to believe, which we can fail to believe on the like evidence. Believe that; believe that from the ages of ages the Incarnation was predetermined in the divine decrees; that the WORD of GOD in Himself united the Creator with the creature; that GOD was manifest in the Flesh of a spotless Virgin—and nothing which we are called upon to believe, on the like authority, can consistently be disbelieved. And the authority on which we, Catholics, believe the Incarnation of GOD, is the authority of the Church.

These words reveal a boundless field of inquiry on the outskirts alone of which we can allow ourselves to enter. The question of authority is one on which, as a rule, persons are averse from entering, on two grounds: 1. It is a question of almost overpowering difficulty in itself, from a theoretical point of view. 2. It is one which leads to endless difficulties, when we pass from theory to practice. And both these grounds of aversion are intensified to those who are pledged to the Anglican position in the Church of CHRIST. To the Liberal in religion they are comparatively easy of solution. To our Roman Catholic brethren they offer no sensible obstacle. To ourselves, it cannot be denied, nay, it is keenly felt, that they present grave issues either for acceptance or for rejection.

On the question of the influence of authority in matters of faith, it may be broadly stated, however paradoxical it may sound, that it is of more importance why a man believes than what he believes. In other terms, the authority on which he accepts any portion of the Christian Religion is of greater moment than the portion of the Christian Religion which he accepts. It is not the articles of the creed which a man believes, but the reason of his belief in the articles which is all-essential. And why? Because the principle of belief is more important than the truths which are believed. In faith, the foundation is everything; the superstructure is nothing, or next to nothing worth, in comparison. It were better to hold a single article of faith on authority, than the whole creed upon the basis of private opinion—why, we will endeavour to see further on. It may suffice now to point to an infallible judgment which plainly teaches this principle.

When our Divine Master was pleased to offer a test of faith to His as yet uninspired disciples, what form did it take, and on what principle was the decision made? The test, avowedly, was belief in the GODHEAD of CHRIST, however far short of the entire truth that doctrine could at that time be realized by the Twelve. The form which the test took was a question: "Whom do men say that I, the Son of Man, am?"

The principle on which the decision was made, undoubtedly was the principle of authority. The answers of the other disciples were not only wrong in themselves; but the opinions on which the answers were given were based on a false foundation—private opinion. The answer of Peter was not only the right answer; but it was the only reply which was founded upon authority—the authority of GOD. Hence, were uttered those marvellous words of CHRIST which elevated the faithful disciple to the rank of chief in the Apostolic College: "Blessed art thou, Simon Bar-jona." And why, we may pause reverently to inquire? Not because the test had been taken, and Peter had not been found wanting. Not because the form of his answer corresponded to divine fact. But, because the principle upon which the answer of Peter had been returned was the true principle, the only true principle of belief, the principle of authority—upon the authority of GOD. "Blessed art thou," says our Divine LORD: "for flesh and blood hath not revealed it unto thee, but My FATHER Which is in heaven." The doctrine of the Incarnation was held by Peter (who was not yet the Saint), not on the grounds of public opinion, of prophecy, or of history, cognizable by human reason—for thus may we interpret John the Baptist, Elias, or one of the Prophets, to quote the replies of the other disciples; not on the grounds of private opinion—for CHRIST'S reply distinctly disposes of this supposition: but on the only authority by which the Apostle could be influenced, at that date more or less unconsciously, the authority of GOD Himself. We may, indeed, marvel at the reward which awaited this deference to authority; and may even permit ourselves to think that it was incommensurate with the amount of faith displayed. But GOD judgeth not as man judges. The foundation of the Church upon the Rock of Peter, in whatever manner CHRIST'S words and promise may be interpreted, was the immediate result of Peter's acceptance of the Incarnation on the authority of GOD. And it is worthy of remark, that the note of authority has ever been a decided characteristic of the Church of Peter from the very first.

The question of authority in matters of faith may be discussed either on abstract grounds, or from a practical standpoint. Perhaps the practical argument in its favour is more suited to times of retreat. Perhaps, too, the remark above made—"that it were better to hold a single article of faith on authority, than the whole creed upon the basis of private opinion"—may make a good point of departure for its consideration. And the article of faith which at the present time is before our minds is the Incarnation of GOD in relation to the sin of man.

There are two grounds, it need hardly be said, upon which we may yield assent to the dogma of the Incarnation—private judgment, and the authority of the Church. These opposite principles of belief, though stated in a few words, cover a large area of differentia in each case. There are almost endless ways in which ordinary men and women living in the world can exercise private judgment, or can submit to authority respectively, on the doctrine of the Incarnation. For instance, a man may be led to hold the doctrine after long years of study, after deep consideration, after many earnest arguments with others, after much anxious thought with himself, after constant prayer to GOD for light to see the truth. His intellect, his memory, his imagination, his logical faculties, his prepossessions or antipathies, his prejudices or aversions, his mental gifts, his acquired powers, his will—all play their part in his acceptance of the truth. Nor are these, again, the only influences which bear upon his final adhesion. Circumstances of birth, family connections, social relationship, political position, the influence of friends, even his state of health, these are a few of the outside causes which, practically, are found to influence a man's decision, unconsciously perhaps, but with more or less of direct agency, on behalf of private opinion.

Nor are the influences less manifold which weigh with a

man in the scale of authority. The reception of truth upon the basis of authority reaches the believer, in GOD'S providence, in ways that are simply countless. It may come to him from his father's knee, or on his mother's lap. It may reach him through the teaching of some religious-minded nurse; or, later in life, of some pious master; or again, later on, through the acknowledged Catechism or formularies of the Church. It may strike him in a sermon, from a book of devotion, in conference with those who walk in the house of GOD as friends, during the quiet of silent meditation, even after a heated discussion with a theological opponent. Or, it may force itself upon his conscience from the creeds, from the works of the fathers and doctors of the Church, from her acknowledged theologians, or from the devotions of Christendom, its holy Scriptures, and its many liturgies. In each case the amount of authority varies; but in all it is practically identical. The man believes upon evidence not of his own estimating; upon a principle not of his own making; and upon grounds which he is powerless either to augment, or diminish, or in any way to alter. He believes on an authority external to himself, on the authority of the Church.

How do these two systems of belief vary? How do they vary to such an extent that it may be fairly affirmed, that it were better to hold one point of faith on authority, than the whole circle of belief on private judgment? I answer—on three grounds: 1. Because religious truth which comes to us from without, demands an acceptance which is external in its assurance. Objective faith cannot be made subservient to subjective impressions. This is evident from the nature of things. It were superfluous, if private judgment be the tribunal of objective truth, to have instituted an infallible and supernatural society for its dispersion amongst men. If private judgment be the court of final appeal in matters of doctrine, the office of the Church as a teaching body is gone. 2. Because, as a rule, and for the vast majority of mankind, it is simply impossible for any given man to arrive at a reasonable judgment upon so obscure, involved, endless, transcendental a question as the Incarnation of GOD. Life is not long enough, life is not free enough, even were the mental powers, and acquirements sufficient, and were the energy, perseverance and zeal possessed for such an overpowering enquiry. 3. Because, even if the will, the capacity, and the result be allowed, it is self-evident that a doctrine which a man has persuaded himself into at one time, he is capable to persuade himself out of at another. Nothing is so proverbially capricious as the human mind; and on such an all-important matter as religion, of a religious-minded person it is not too much to say, that any decision at which he may have arrived on the grounds of private opinion must always be surrounded by an atmosphere of doubt. Except in the case of persons with more than an average share of self-valuation, and these are far from having the child-like temper of a Christian inquirer, every one must, at some time or other, in life or in death, experience a want of certitude, if not a positive doubt, in his own individual judgment.

For these three reasons, on which meditation will supply far more material for thought than can be expressed in words, the above assertion may be justified. From the nature of things, an objective creed cannot be allowed to be tested by subjective belief. It is impossible for any single person to exhaust the dogma of the Incarnation, and to arrive at a rational conclusion thereupon by the exercise of his own powers alone. And the human mind is so constituted that theological certitude, based on private opinion, can never be permanently assured to any given individual soul. Hence, it may be affirmed, that it were better to hold to a single doctrine upon authority than many dogmas upon private judgment. The Church is the supernatural teacher of truth to man. Divine truth is in no wise comparable to a mathematical problem. Though it be an exact science, in its definitions and terminology, in its premises, arguments and conclusions, in its decisions and judgments—the dogmas of theology are not capable of mathematical proof. They are provable only by the demonstration of faith upon the basis of authority. With this realization of truth, and with this belief in a teaching voice, the conclusion seems inevitable, that the Church is the only trustworthy authority which is incapable of change in matters of faith.

Further questions on the legitimate use of private opinion in matters of faith, and on the expression of the living voice of the Church as an authority to which we must submit, are suitable topics for thought in times of retreat; but they are too wide for present discussion. That private judgment possesses a legitimate use in questions of doctrine, appears to be inevitable. Otherwise, how can they submit to the Church who have been, in GOD'S providence, born and bred external to the fold of CHRIST? But how it is to be exercised, when it may be employed, where it must be ignored?—these are not always easy questions to be answered. Again, the living voice of a teaching Church appears to be an absolute necessity in the case of one who accepts objective truth on the basis of authority. But where, in our own case as members of the Anglican communion, that living voice resides; how ·that teaching power is exercised; when its voice may be heard; and how we are practically guided into all truth by its direction?—these, again, are questions which are extremely difficult to answer. That replies may be given, and are given to them on both sides, by learned men, cannot be doubted. But it is wise, it is expedient even for the unlearned to entertain such questions; indeed, it is impossible to avoid their inquiries, living as we live midway between the sanctions of unbridled licence in liberty of thought, and the claims of unlimited and infallible authority in matters of faith. Their consideration will help us to decide, how far liberty of thought is compatible with deference to divine authority; to what extent we must resist the one; to what extent we are in possession of the other.

V.

The Incarnation of GOD, accepted on the authority of the Church, is an important dogma to be insisted upon at the present day. It is important, if not for ourselves who believe the doctrine in our relation to GOD, at least for ourselves in our relation to those who deny it. It is important, also, to all who accept the doctrine, and on whatever grounds they accept it, in relation to those doctrines which flow from it. In the case of those who deny the Incarnation of GOD, it is well to present for their consideration a faith which is consistent, self-contained and exhaustive. In the case of those who accept the Incarnation, it is necessary to urge upon them its logical conclusions. The former may some day be won over to the faith. The latter must be persuaded to accept not only the truth, but the whole truth, on the authority on which they accept a portion of it. This persuasion is more necessary than, perhaps, is commonly imagined. It is needed by two classes of persons: 1. by those who have been educated outside the Church, and have in later life been led, by the mercy of GOD, to accept the doctrine in question; and 2. by those, born within the fold of CHRIST, who have emancipated themselves from more or less of Protestant tradition to hold the Catholic faith. The first class are tempted to think that the Incarnation is the only dogma of faith which separated their past from their present position. The last are hard to convince that they are bound to believe other doctrines on the like authority to that on which they receive this. Both classes have to be shown that the Incarnation is the foundation, not the summit of a Christian's belief; that other articles of belief which logically flow from it must be accepted as legitimate results of holding the Incarnation. Both have to be taught that the believer in the Incarnation, accepted or not by private judgment, does not occupy a position which enables him to survey the field of revelation and to receive what further points he may be pleased to select; but rather, that he occupies the place of the unlearned, and that from the foundation of the Incarnation of GOD, he has to be instructed in other truths equally assured, upon evidence which is identically the same—the authority of the Church of GOD.

The point to be mastered is this—If we believe in the Incarnation, we cannot consistently deny other doctrines which reach us on the same authority. If we do not deny the Incarnation, we are bound to believe other doctrines which the Church also teaches. This position will be the more conclusive, to some minds, if it can be shown, as it can be shown, that these further doctrines of the Church are the legitimate, logical and necessary developments from the central and initial dogma, of the union of the Creator with the creature.

Take, for the moment, three doctrines only, which we firmly believe on the teaching of the Church, but which were denied by faithless Jews of old and are denied, equally and almost in the same terms, by faithless Christians of the present day, namely, Baptism, Communion and Confession.

Baptism, Communion and Confession. In each case we have, whether for our guidance or our warning, three points for consideration: 1. our Divine Master's own teaching by word, or by action, or by both combined, to which to point; 2. the witness, authority and discipline of the Church, to which to defer in explanation and fulfilment of her LORD'S works and words; and 3. the objections and cavillings, the doubts and denials of the Jews eighteen-hundred years ago, whose language is still actually repeated by nominal Christians eighteen-hundred years after.

In this consideration two points must be remembered. The first is this: In the light in which we view the mystery, the Incarnation of GOD was fulfilled on behalf of a human creation; of man, as a race of intelligent beings honoured with the gift of free-will; of man, in the abstract. In order to apply the benefits of the Incarnation to man in the concrete, to the human race individually, some means or some method of application must be found or made. Selfishly speaking, or speaking in regard to immortal souls, the union of the Creator with the creature had been incomplete or imperfect were there no means of availing one's self of the blessings of the union, man by man. But a method was devised by the Holy SPIRIT of GOD by which such blessings might be secured individually; namely, in the Sacramental system of the Church. And in this system of application are three amongst other channels of reception, or extensions of the Incarnation as they have been called—three of the sacraments above named, Baptism, Communion and Confession.

The second point to be remembered is—that in morals, the following principle is axiomatic : If a man desires anything, he desires the means by which he attains it. This axiom becomes a law when applied personally in questions of doctrine. If you believe anything, you believe not only that from which it is a necessary conclusion, as well as that which is a legitimate and logical deduction from it, but that also which is required for its fulfilment. If you believe in the union of the creature and the Creator, you believe in all that leads to and secures the personal fulfilment of the Incarnation to the human race, man by man. The Incarnation, as a divine fact in eternity, necessarily requires some means of development in time, for the benefit of agents possessed of free-will. Three of such essential developments—essential, that is, in the divine foreknowledge and permissive Will of GOD—are the sacraments above named, Baptism, Communion and Confession. And in them, as taught by the Church, we believe.

Let us take the three sacraments in order.

I. The Nicene Creed teaches us to believe in "One Baptism for the remission of sins." We need not stop to inquire, though we are able to explain, the exact relation which the sacrament of Baptism holds to the doctrine of the Incarnation. It is enough to say, that the Incarnation, as the expression of the divine Will for uniting the creature and the Creator, man

by man, were incomplete in regard to the individual man—
you and I—without such an extension : its full benefits are
secured only, in one direction, after such extension has been
made and in virtue of it. This extension of the Incarnation
was declared by the Incarnate Himself, in the days of His
ministry, to Nicodemus. Yet, do we believe in the teaching
of the Church on this point? Do we believe that a certain
result of the Incarnation does not and cannot flow from it to
individual souls, apart from Baptism? If we so believe, let us
further inquire why we thus yield our assent? Is it for any
reason which falls short of the only true one—because the
Church pledges herself to this belief? If we believe not, we
fail to believe one article of the faith, which we are bound
consistently to believe, from the assent we have given to the
dogma of the Incarnation. If we believe not, we practically
adopt the language of the timid and doubtful follower,
though he afterwards became faithful and true, who came to
JESUS by night and argued: "How can a man be born
again, when he is old?"

II. The Catechism of the Church teaches us that, in the
Holy Communion, the Body and Blood of our Divine LORD
are verily and indeed taken and received—taken, observe, as
well as received ; that is, the sacred Species is the Body and
Blood of CHRIST when "It is accepted," and before "It is
consumed." We need not stop to inquire, again, though we
are able to explain, the exact relation which the sacrament
of the Eucharist holds to the doctrine of the Incarnation. It
is sufficient to affirm, that the Incarnation, as the fulfilment of
the eternal decrees for the increase of the greater glory of
GOD, in the person of each several and individual member of
the human race—you and I again—had been imperfect without such a second extension : its complete benefits are
secured only, in another direction, after such extension has
been made and as a result of it. This further extension of the
Incarnation was declared by Him Who revealed Himself to

His own countrymen, and on an eventful occasion in His earthly ministry, as the Bread which came down from Heaven. Yet, do we believe in the teaching of the Church on this point? Do we believe that a certain other result of the Incarnation does not and cannot flow from it, to the soul of man, apart from Communion? If we believe this truth, let us further inquire, what is the reason of our acceptance of it? Is it on any grounds which lack the true theory of belief— namely, that the Church offers such belief for our assent? If we believe not this answer in the Catechism, we reject another article of the faith, which we are bound in consistency to believe, from our acceptance of the truth that the WORD was made Flesh and has tabernacled amongst men. If we believe it not, we make our own the language of the faithless disciples of CHRIST, who, it must be remembered, thereupon forsook the Divine Master, when they had sceptically asked : " How can this Man give us His Flesh to eat?"

III. The Ordination Service teaches us that to the priesthood has been entrusted, by the SPIRIT of GOD, power to remit or to retain sin—to forgive, or not to forgive, the sin of man. We need not stop to inquire, once more, though we are able to explain, the exact relation which the sacrament of Penance holds to the doctrine of the Incarnation. It is only needful to show that the Incarnation, as the foreordained result of the divine purpose that the creature should become one with the Creator, in the person of each individual of the human race—you and I amongst others— would have been wanting in perfection without such a third extension : its entire benefits are secured only, in a third direction, after such further extension has been made and in consequence of it. This third extension of the Incarnation was declared by CHRIST Himself, both in act when He, as the Son of Man, forgave the sinner, and in word when He said to the Apostles, that as He was sent by the FATHER, even so did He send them—to absolve and to withhold the benefits of absolution. Yet, do we believe the teaching of the Church on this point? Do we believe that a certain third result of the Incarnation does not and cannot flow from it to each individual soul apart from Confession? If we are led to believe in this dogma, let us further inquire the cause of our giving assent to it? Is it for any cause which will not bear the test of Christian certitude—a certitude which relies on the competency of the authority which claims it, namely, that of the Church. If we believe not in this God-given power to the Priesthood in ordination, we deny a third article of the faith, which we are bound logically to believe, in virtue of our assent to the truth that GOD was made MAN in the Person of JESUS CHRIST. If we believe it not, we deliberately adopt the language of the infidel Jews of old—adopt it against infinitely more grace and more light and more evidence than they—who allowed themselves to return this answer to the Eternal, the Infinite and the Almighty: "Who can forgive sins, but GOD alone?"

We, thank GOD, have been taught to believe, and do believe in the Incarnation of GOD, in regard to the sin of man, individual man, you and I. We, thank GOD, believe this dogma on the authority of the Church. On the same infallible authority, the teaching voice of the HOLY GHOST, we also believe in the three-fold, amongst other, extensions which are not less logically than religiously demanded for the complete fulfilment of the mystery of the Incarnation. We believe in Baptism, Communion and Confession. We believe in the remission of original guilt in the laver of regeneration; in the objective reality of CHRIST'S presence on the Altar; in the pardon of actual sin by the absolving power of the priesthood. And we believe these Catholic verities which flow from the Incarnation of GOD, because the same authority that teaches the one which is infinitely more hard to believe, teaches also the others which are infinitely less hard to believe.

The argument adopted in regard to the three extensions of the Incarnation which have been discussed, is, of course, true in relation also to the remaining four extensions. On the denial of these developments nothing more need be said. But it may be added, that it was not without a purpose that the three extensions above treated were selected from the whole number of seven; nor was it undesignedly that inquiry was made on the grounds on which we accept them. There is, it may be feared, some reason for supposing that the grounds of our belief, as Catholics, are not always the most stable. A few words on this topic may not be misplaced.

In the providence of GOD, these three selected extensions of the Incarnation are the three which, of late years, have been called to bear the brunt of popular opposition; and which, consequently, have been more warmly defended than other sacramental extensions, by their supporters. From one point of view, we may trace the permissive Will of GOD, in the order in which Protestant enmity has been displayed upon Catholic verities, during the successive attacks which have been made on our position. From another point of view, we may perceive the more direct agency of the HOLY GHOST leading the Catholic Revival to pronounce in the face of Protestant misbelief, the successive truths behind which we are entrenched. But, from a third point of view, it would appear to be a question with many of us, whether or not such pronouncement or such defence has not been made more upon private opinion than upon the authority of the Church. And this question is brought before the mind of an observer of the course of the Revival from the evidence of several facts. First: the order in which these truths have been offered for acceptance is one that, though to an extent logical in itself, was not systematically adopted, but forced upon its adherents by haphazard and from without. Secondly: the verities which have been announced in the adopted order, have been defended and enforced, as if each one in turn contained within itself the essence of Christianity, and that everything, dogmatic or practical, beyond its bounds, was of secondary importance, even if it were of obligation to be held or to be practised. Thirdly: because, as a rule, the class of minds which has been led to grasp these several truths, and the defenders of, and it may be said, the confessors for, them, have been prone to complain, each one in turn, of the developments of their own principles at the hands of their successors in the fight for dogmatic and practical faith.

Into these three points, I have no intention to enter here. But I desire to draw our thoughts to their consideration, either in silent meditation or in solitary self-examination. If we shall discover that we have been tempted to ignore the revealed proportion of faith, or to choose our own order of receiving divine truth : if we have cause to think that in our reception of, and still more in our teaching or witnessing for, dogma or discipline, point by point, we are absorbing or dispersing the essential features of Christianity : if we cannot conceal from ourselves, and if it be patent to others, that our sympathy and interest are confined to those who have exactly reached our spiritual level, and are withheld from those who have been led to ascend higher in the faith—then, in any one of these cases, and still more in a combination of any two, or of all three cases, it may be fairly assumed that we have been led to accept Catholic truth, or to adopt Catholic usage, not upon the authority of the Church, but by the light of private opinion.

VI.

The principle which underlies the position above assumed towards the Incarnation of GOD, may be carried for our own benefit beyond the instances of Baptism, Communion and Confession. For our own benefit, I say, who accept these developments of the mystery; not for the advantage or instruction of others who reject them. And a Retreat is no unfitting time to dwell on similar and further extensions.

The three cases already quoted are sufficient on which to found a theory, or to state a principle. They are so plain, that they can be denied by few who aspire to hold the Catholic faith as a whole, and not merely in a fragmentary condition.

But, if these cases be true in themselves, they must be true as instances of a law which extends a long way beyond their own limits. Baptism, Communion and Confession are elemental cases, indeed, but they must also be typical and representative. A Retreat is a suitable time to descend below self-evident realities, and to apply the result to the soul's good.

How does the question of the sin of man enter into or depend upon the dogma of the Incarnation, in its legitimate, even if secondary developments, beyond the case of the sacraments which have already been considered? How—not objectively, as an abstract theological proposition, about which there can be no doubt to a believer; but, as a subjective reality, on which there may be endless shades of opinion, and many of them just? as a reality in regard to ourselves, individually, you and I, one by one? as the outcome of the Incarnation, logical and even necessary for its complete fulfilment in the daily life of members of the human race? There are many of such points of doctrine or discipline, too many to be mentioned in this place. Nor, indeed, need any be named. For, we are now considering, for the moment, a question of principle, not a matter of practice. And, as a principle these points present themselves to our faith with the like authority that the Incarnation itself is offered for our acceptance: the like authority—the same in kind, but different in degree.

The question, then, for our solution is this: What may be our mental position towards these points? How have we placed ourselves in relation to them, subordinate as they are to larger and deeper truths, but not superfluous; complementary, indeed, as they must be considered, if not essential to any comprehensive statement of the whole counsel of GOD? What is our actual practice? Or, if we have been lately led to see old truths in a new light, and to adopt points of Christian discipline which we formerly neglected, what may have been our mental attitude or wonted practice? When these subsidiary details of Catholic dogma or Christian discipline, theologically ensuing from the Incarnation of GOD, have been offered for our belief or use, how and in what temper and with what results, Brothers or Sisters in CHRIST, were the offers met by us? Did we once, or do we now—or are we prepared to do the like in the future—accept them loyally, believe in them faithfully, value them heartily, defend them against all gainsayers boldly and intelligently, and make use of them ourselves simply and devoutly? Or, on the other hand, when these points were offered for our acceptance, did we once, and do we now—and are we penitent for our fault in the past—look on them with suspicion, as something extreme; speak of them with disparagement, as open to criticism; warn others against them, as not knowing to what further developments they may lead; reject them, at first sight, inconsiderately and with disdain; or take to them eventually coldly and with distrust, or condescendingly and half-heartedly, or inconstantly for a time and only to give them up?

If we once did this, or anything comparable to this, before we submitted to the claims of the Catholic faith, we are bound, now that we are blessed with more light and knowledge, to make humble acts of reparation for the evil that has been done or said, or for the good that has been left undone or unsaid, through ignorance and unbelief. If we do this, or anything comparable to this now, under the genial warmth and greater fervour of Catholic teaching, we cannot act more wisely than to employ some part of the present Retreat in attempting to master this question. We cannot better employ our time than in seeking to discover, where and how and why we are wrong, and how and in what manner we may amend—for, that such a mental posture towards the teaching of the Church is not that which one should cultivate who strives after a child-like temper in religion, may be fairly assumed.

Here I would prefer to leave to your own consciences to discover the special points to which allusion has been made. It may be helpful, however, even to one soul, that some of them should be mentioned. For the sake of one for whom CHRIST died, those who are conscious of what I have referred to, or are happily unaffected by it, will kindly bear with the recitation of certain points, shortly enumerated. With their recitation I will conclude this address.

Observe, I shall not mention sacraments; at least only one will be named. But there are many points of faith and matters of discipline, comparatively speaking of minor importance, which tend to complete the perfection of the Christian life and which are outside these blessed means of grace: and to some of these I would beg leave to refer. Hence, I venture to ask on your behalf, Brother or Sister in CHRIST:—

1. Have I ever disparaged, or do I still disparage, the sign of the Holy Cross? do I make use of it boldly and openly, as if I were proud of it; or secretly and hurriedly, as if I were ashamed of it? do I fail to employ it myself, or have I ever discouraged its use in others? or, am I wont to use it lightly and without consideration?—a sign used from the first days of the Faith, not only in divine service, but on almost every occasion of daily life.

2. Do I lightly esteem, or actually disregard, the reception of Holy Communion fasting from earthly food? do I avoid receiving at late Celebrations, even fasting, out of regard to the scruples of others? do I adopt the inconsistency of a partial abstinence from food, in order to yield to the prejudices of others?—"fasting," not for sin, but out of reverence; "reception fasting," world-wide in its obligation in both East and West, co-extensive in time and place with Christianity, and in accord with the institution of CHRIST Himself.

3. Have I deliberately, after having been otherwise taught, or carelessly, before being aware of the duty, deprived the holy dead—father, sister, spouse, or friend—of the benefit, such as it may be, of my poor prayers? or, do I justify my neglect by suggesting to myself that I, personally, think such prayers avail not, because I, personally, cannot tell how they avail?—when no extant liturgy of the Church of CHRIST is known to be without prayers for the faithful departed.

4. Am I wont to fail to honour, revere and love the human Mother of the Divine LORD Who died for me? because some in time past—a reason to make Angels weep and Satan smile—have loved, reverenced and honoured, as I, personally, think, over-much the Blessed Mother of GOD.

5. Am I wont to fail to take advantage of the privilege, for it is not suggested as a duty, of simply asking the holy Saints for the benefit of their prayers? or, to be content with the indirect, circuitous and not very faithful plan of praying GOD to move them to pray for me? or, of stifling the conscience by allowing myself to doubt if the Saints indeed hear our prayers or not?—forgetful of, at least, fourteen centuries of precedent, in the public offices of the Church, and the private testimony of all the greater Fathers?

6. Do I permit myself to speak against self-dedication to GOD in vows, in the Religious Life or otherwise? or, against those who are led by GOD to take them?—when myself and all Christians are already pledged to the principle of vows in one, or perhaps in more than a single sacrament.

7. Do I feel indifferent to, or do I fail to pray daily for, one of the greatest needs of the Catholic Church, the corporate Re-union of Christendom? or, do I practically hinder such Re-union, so far as my own soul is concerned, or my influence may extend, by uncharitable and wicked attacks, or by ignorant and destructive criticism on the belief and practice of Western Christendom?—forgetful of the fact that such want of union and its cause hinders the fulfilment of our LORD'S own promise and of His most earnest prayer.

8. What practical steps, whether by prayer to GOD or by urgency with man, have I ever taken in the past, or will I take in the future, for the restoration of the primitive custom of Reservation of the Blessed Sacrament, and of the introduction of the beautiful evening counterpart of the morning sacrificial offering, the Rite of Benediction?—remembering, that of these usages we, Anglicans, alone of the mighty West possess them not.

9. Shall I desire, when my earthly end approaches, to receive, amongst the Last Sacraments of the Church, the simple, touching, and efficacious Sacrament of Unction?—a sacrament plainly enjoined by an Apostle, and to be denied to no faithful man because, whilst not forbidding its use, our own Communion has failed to provide for a form for its due employment.

Brother or Sister in CHRIST, I entreat you to answer these questions to yourself, as in the presence of GOD. If your self-searching unhappily points to sins of omission in regard to these and similar subsidiary extensions of the Incarnation, ask yourself the further question—Why have I thus failed? If your self-searching happily allows to you to affirm that, by GOD'S grace, you have not been found wanting, make one more inquiry—On what authority have I done the little which, by GOD'S mercy, I have done, whether in practice or in belief?

ADDRESS NINE.

THE SACRIFICE OF THE CROSS.

ALTHOUGH the Incarnation of GOD may not be conceived as a divine device to remedy the sin of man, viewed in its primary intention ; yet, it is difficult to assign to the Sacrifice of the Cross, in its fulfilment, a reason apart from human sin. The Death of JESUS CHRIST and the sin of man are intimately, if not inseparably, connected as effect and cause.

Although the Incarnation of GOD was decreed in the eternal counsels and divine decrees of the Holy TRINITY, irrespectively of man's sin, as to its essence—in the intention which pre-ordained it, in the means of its accomplishment, and in the main result which ensued from it ; yet, we have had reason to see that, as to its accidents—in its time, in its place, in its manner, in its surroundings—it was not independent of human sin. The union of the Creator with the creature, by the permissive Will of GOD, became influenced in its secondary results by the failure of the creature to fulfil the object of his creation.

One of the secondary results of the Incarnation of GOD—secondary from a divine stand-point, though all-important from one that is human—was the Sacrifice of the Cross. Hence, whilst we may view the Incarnation in the light of the after Sacrifice, we are at liberty to contemplate the Sacrifice as a later stage, and as a legitimate development of the prior Incarnation. Both theological facts, both divine mysteries are, in short, with relation to the sin of man, two sides of the same eternal truth. They cannot be divided in reality. They can only be separated in thought. On the present occasion, we will consider the Sacrifice of CHRIST on the Cross in regard to human sin—to your sin and to mine—both personally and collectively.

II.

The expiation of sin, on the part of GOD, and on behalf of man, was the result of no simple or self-contained cause. It is difficult for human thought to determine whether or not it were possible for the expiation of sin to be otherwise than involved and complicated. Probably it were not. Probably, in the order of creation, redemption and sanctification, as they were willed by GOD, man's sin could not be forgiven by any single act—for at least two reasons: 1. because of the complex nature of sin, in itself; and 2. because of the complex means which, as a fact, Almighty GOD was pleased to adopt for its expiation.

The first reason will appear sufficient if we reflect on the human origin, cause and consequence of sin; the divine object of man's creation, and how such object was thwarted by human sin; the absolute perfection of man's creation, and the possibility of his sinning as a consequence of such perfection; the actual results of man's sin, and the results which would ensue were it possible to extend them to their legitimate conclusions. The dethronement of GOD and a human usurpation in His place; the employment of an absolutely perfect faculty in a manner to ensure an absolutely evil result; the increase of the greater glory of GOD surrendered in favour of the diminution of His accidental glory; and the decision of man to follow his own will instead of performing the all-holy will of his Maker—these truths alone, in the nature of sin, are sufficient to establish the condition of its complexity.

Nor is the evidence less conclusive on the complexity of the means by which the expiation of sin was effected, directly or mediately. The eternal counsels of the Holy TRINITY, which decreed the union of the creature with the Creator; the decision of the Eternal WORD to fulfil the mystery of the Incarnation; the action of the HOLY GHOST to render such fulfilment possible; the life and death of our Divine Master; the organization of His Church and her application of the Sacrifice of the Cross to the individual needs of man in her Sacramental system—these truths also point to the sufficiency of the second reason. The divine decrees in the ages of ages; the WORD made Flesh; the Annunciation to Mary; the three-and-thirty years' Ministry; the seven-fold Sacraments of the Church—testify to the fact that, whatever may be the characteristics of GOD'S method of man's restoration, simplicity was not one.

To these two reasons may be added a third. So far as human observation of the divine mode of operation, either in the material creation or in empire of grace, justifies the statement of a theory, it would appear that GOD invariably is pleased to adopt the simplest means which are competent to secure the end which He has in view. This law in the operations of GOD is repeated in many of the greatest works of the creature of His Almighty hand. The profoundest discoveries and the inventions which have to the largest extent benefitted the human race, are often the result of the simplest principles or of the plainest truths—as men judge afterwards, by the light of experience. If then it can be added to the truth of the complex nature of sin, and to the fact of the complex means which were adopted for its expiation, this further principle that both in grace and in nature GOD is wont to work directly toward the object of His Will—it may be hazarded, there is a high degree of probability in favour of the position, that it was not possible for the expiation of human sin to be otherwise than involved and complicated.

These thoughts supply an answer to the assertion frequently heard in certain theological circles, of the simplicity of the Gospel scheme of salvation. The simplicity in question, on the lips of those who give utterance to the opinion, is only the result of eliminating from the Catholic system those elements which private judgment decides to be unnecessary or unedifying. There is indeed a simplicity in the system of Holy

Church which the faithful realize, and which comes from a child-like temper in accepting truth upon competent authority. But, these two phases of simplicity are not identical. And, in any case, the sin of man, which of itself, in the permissive Will of GOD, is complex and involved in its nature, was expiated in the past, and is expiated in the present, by means which, through His direct and immediate agency, are the very opposite of simple. Indeed, a system more deeply complicated it is hardly possible to be conceived.

The sin of man—viewed in the past, as well as in the future; viewed in the present, day by day; viewed personally, in regard to your sins and mine—is only partially and imperfectly described by the term "expiated." In the course of expiation, would be the truer and more theological phrase. The expiation of sin forms a continuous act of three stages, in the past, in the present, in the future: or, more exactly, 1. in eternity, 2. in time past, 3. in the present. It expresses a continuous, never-ending idea in its results; a reality beginning before time was, and in its operations ending only when time itself shall come to an end. It has, moreover, a double aspect, towards GOD and towards man. Expiation, as we are now viewing it, is two-fold in its operation; for, although man cannot be saved apart from GOD, it is not less impossible that he can be saved apart from himself. The sacred Blood of JESUS CHRIST cleanses from all sin. Yes: but, we, men and women, in union with the same Divine Master, must work out our own salvation with fear and trembling. For there is one thing which GOD, in His creation of man, is powerless to do— to force men to be saved; to save men in spite of themselves. Man can lose his soul of and by himself alone. He cannot be saved apart from his own personal will and work, apart from his own personal desire and effort.

From this double meaning of the term expiation, it cannot be said that human sin has been washed away, satisfied, atoned by divine agency: but rather, that sin is in course of expiation through the joint action of GOD and man. It is not a matter of mere theological history : it is not simply a question of the Divine Will in the past. It is rather a contemporaneous fact in the earthly career of man. It is something which bears the impress of the eternal Mind that willed expiation, in creation, redemption and sanctification, in the attribute of a never-ending present. It is something which, though originated by GOD, can only be perfected by man ; which, though conceived in outline by the great First Cause, can only be developed in detail, and was intended to be developed in detail, by the work of His Almighty hand.

These thoughts open out a wide field of religious truth—a field on the borders of which Protestant inquiry is content to stand, but the extent of which Catholic theology alone is competent to explore. Of course, in a certain sense, human sin was atoned in the Will of GOD, in the ages of ages, when the Incarnation was decreed. It is atoned in the Justice of GOD, at the present, when the Sacrifice of the Cross is offered. It will be atoned in the Mercy of GOD, in the future, when the Sacraments of the Church shall be administered. Or again, we may consider human sin to be expiated in the counsels and fore-knowledge of GOD, in eternity; in the action and suffering of GOD, in time past, on Calvary ; in the gifts and graces of GOD, in the present, by the seven-fold Sacraments of the SPIRIT. But in both cases it is expiated, or it is in course of expiation by the joint action of GOD'S purpose and intention with man's submission and co-operation.

It is not easy to say which attribute of the GODHEAD, as exhibited in these three phases, most deserves the profound gratitude and the adoring love of the creature. As men created in the image of the GOD-MAN, and in view of the life of the GOD-MAN and all that it involved for the sake of us men and our salvation, the Sacrifice of the Cross, perhaps, most imperatively claims our devotion. To the immediate truth which underlies the term—namely, that GOD died for Man—we frankly yield our absolute assent and our boundless adoration. But, as in the case of many another truth of our holy Religion, not less certain, not less affecting, we cannot, having regard to the due proportion of faith, remain in it alone, hold to it alone, believe it alone. Such a course were not imperfect faith to follow; it were heresy. It is heresy, because it fails to take a complete view of truth, of which the events of Calvary form only an integral part. It is heresy, because it elevates a portion of the faith into the position of the whole; because it gives to a portion the dignity and effect of the whole. Such an opinion is content with the present only, and with that which concerns self chiefly. It is indifferent to divine facts, which disclose or augment the greater glory of GOD in relation to man. It is forgetful of the past, which gives to the present reality; and is doubtful, if not sceptical, of the future, which gives to the present efficacy and power and worth.

Nor are these the only grounds on which it were harmful to exaggerate, in the scheme of man's redemption, the relative importance of the Death of CHRIST—for its intrinsic value it is impossible to overvalue. It is not unusually found that those who assign an undue prominence to the Sacrifice, do not hesitate directly to disparage the Sacraments—which disparagement may be understood on certain theological principles; and even indirectly to depreciate the Incarnation —which depreciation is inexplicable on any theological principles that deserve the name. But, it is equally true that divine truth lies in no extreme, nor in any partial statement. The fact of the expiation of the sin of man by the outpouring of the precious Blood on Calvary is the middle term between two other co-ordinate, co-equal and co-relative dogmas. One of these doctrines was the necessary preparation for, the other is a logical result from, the common dogma which lies between them. Both are of equal importance, of equal necessity, for a consistent whole. The first is of eternity; the second is of time. The one is of time past; the other is of time future. The one was fulfilled by the Incarnation of

GOD; the other is in course of fulfilment in the Sacramental system of the Church. The Sacrifice of the Cross stands midway between them. It comes from the first; it leads to the second. It is equally indispensable to both. Both apart from it, in view of human sin, were valueless.

Hence, there exists in the Church of GOD a logical sequence of dogma in three stages; a sequence which places the Sacrifice of CHRIST as a middle term, whither itself is led, whence itself is developed: 1. the mystery of the Incarnation—the Creator and the creature united in the eternal counsels of the GODHEAD, by the Will of GOD the FATHER; 2. the Sacrifice for sin, on the Cross of Calvary, in the Person of JESUS CHRIST, in time past; 3. the extension of the Incarnation and the application of the sacrifice, by the Inspiration of the HOLY GHOST, in the Sacramental system of the Church, in time present. Do we not well to hold, that the Sacrifice of the Cross and the expiation of the sin of man is no isolated, solitary, or self-contained fact, awful indeed in itself and precious to us, but apart from all else in the economy of revelation, as Protestant theology would teach us? Do we not well to accept the teaching of Christendom, and to believe and to act upon our belief, that the Sacrifice of CHRIST JESUS our LORD is the middle term of a three-fold revelation from GOD to man, in which, in relation to humanity, each several term is dependent upon the other two, and all three terms are essential to the full proportion of divine faith?

III.

It is a world-wide belief is sacrifice for sin. No doubt it forms the residuum of the original promise made to Adam, perpetuated in outline by natural tradition, but worn away in detail in the course of ages. It exists, under some form, in the offering of blood or as a bloodless offering, in the offering of person, will, word or deed—in every religion which is worthy of the name. It exists in vigour, as a present reality; or in decay, as an influence of the past. If it claims not life from tradition, it represents the instinct of mankind, savage or civilized. To us, the doctrine of sacrifice is more than a natural tradition, represents more than the instinct of mankind. To us, it is a divine revelation. And hence, as we learn divine truth from without and do not originate it from our inner consciousness, our belief in the doctrine becomes less vague and misty, more definite and exact. But the same cannot be affirmed of all. There are many who fail to accept the teaching of the Church; and many more who inconsistently hold both to it and to opinions which are either incompatible with the dogma, or go far to obscure or counteract its effects.

Before we consider the Sacrifice of the Cross from the stand-point which has been selected, it may be helpful to some minds if a reply, however brief, be attempted to certain popular objections against the doctrinal aspect of the question. These popular objections usually take three forms. They may be mentioned, answered, and left.

I. We have seen that, if the sin of man against his Maker be not infinite in essence, it is charged, in its relations towards other facts and mysteries in the universe, with the characteristics of infinity. The Sacrifice for human sin, as the Church teaches, was not only infinite in its characteristics, but also in its essence. Almighty GOD is not known to employ a superfluity of power in action in the realm of grace. He is known, so far as the human intellect can judge, not to employ such superfluity in that of nature: for, divine prodigality combined with divine utilitarianism, mark His work in both empires. Hence, nothing short of an infinite satisfaction could avail, if any satisfaction were offered for the sin of the creature: nothing short of an infinite atonement could be made, if any atonement were accepted, by the majesty of the Creator. But the greatness of GOD against Whom sin is committed, and the greatness of sin committed against GOD, equally demanded an infinite satisfaction for the least deadly sin of man: and more than an infinite satisfaction could not be paid, it was impossible to pay, for the greatest. That satisfaction was made in the Person of JESUS CHRIST, on the altar of the Cross of Calvary.

The thoughts which flow from this statement supply an answer to the objection to the doctrine of sacrifice, that the Divine Benevolence apart from the Divine Justice could have been satisfied, might have been satisfied, some dare to conceive, ought to have been satisfied, with something which fell short of infinitude, as the expiation of human sin. We may perceive that this were impossible.

II. The infinite Sacrifice which was both demanded and paid for the sin of man against GOD, was personally both GOD and MAN. He was MAN—and the debt to be satisfied was infinite. He was GOD—and the infinite demand was satisfied. As the Second Adam, as the Representative and Pattern Man, as the personal Head of a new creation, He paid the infinite penalty required for sin—we paid the penalty in Him; guilty human nature paid it in His sinless Manhood. As the Second Person of the Holy TRINITY, as the Eternal SON, as the Judge of all the earth, divine Justice was satisfied with His offering for sin; and His offering being infinite, was accepted—He was accepted on our behalf; perfect human Manhood was accepted on behalf of our sinful nature. Hence, as the Priest and Victim are one in the Holy Eucharist, so in the eternal Sacrifice of which the Sacrament is a daily representation and renewal, He Who offers and He Who accepts the Sacrifice for sin is One; MAN and GOD; as MAN, guilty; and as GOD, guiltless.

The thoughts which flow from this statement, again, supply an answer to the objection to the Innocent suffering for the guilty. The objection stated in other terms resolves itself into an objection against GOD suffering for man, against GOD being made Man, against the union of the Creator with the creature, against the eternal counsels of the Holy TRINITY, against the entire Revelation of GOD to man. If the objection be valid, we must receive Catholic tradition burdened with the objection and in spite of it. If it be not valid, we can receive, unburdened and unquestioned, the Catholic tradition which teaches us, that if CHRIST'S Sacrifice was accepted, we must have been guilty; if the accepted Sacrifice was CHRIST'S, He must have been innocent.

III. Man was made in the image of GOD. From this premiss it may be argued that, in a certain sense and at an infinite distance, man's conception of right and wrong, of justice and injustice, of punishment and pardon, is a faint and imperfect reflex of GOD'S attribute: faint and imperfect, but still a true reflection. But, the inner consciousness of man accepts the principle, that human punishment which precedes pardon has, and ought to have, a retributive side for wrong done by man. So, in an ineffable manner, we may argue, from an earthly point of view, of punishment in the sacrifice for sin which is not human but divine, that it is and ought to be retributive. Cases may be mentioned in which, in human punishment, a corrective element to the guilty does not enter. It is not essential, even for punishment inflicted by man, that it should have such an element. The first duty of civil government, in such a matter, is the protection of the innocent, not the reformation of the vicious. It is, at the least, within the bounds of probability that the human instinct which dictates such a line of action is a reflex from the mind of Him in Whose image man was made.

The thoughts which flow from this statement, once more, supply an answer to the objection that divine punishment cannot be, and ought not to be, vindictive. In a true sense of all the terms employed, and in relation to certain results of the divine Sacrifice for the sin of man, it is and justly is vindictive; and Holy Scripture confirms this judgment of human instinct.

Of course, these answers to popular objections are meant for those who accept the doctrine of sacrifice, but have such objections forced upon them from without, rather than for those who by reason of such objections reject the doctrine. In consequence, they are avowedly superficial: but this is of the less importance, as of the objections to which they aspire to reply, the same remark may be made. The objections also are superficial. Neither are these answers the only replies which may be given. The objections may be also met by making reference to the facts of nature—facts which the objectors to the doctrine of sacrifice equally with its defenders cannot fail to admit. For instance:

1. Retributive justice inevitably follows, and often speedily and obviously follows the breach of the laws of nature; for example, in sanitary matters. It would be difficult to find those who affirm that such a breach of GOD'S law should be followed, at the hands of nature, by corrective punishment; difficult for them to formulate the opinion which they might entertain; still more difficult to find adherents for their opinion when formulated.

2. That the innocent suffer for the guilty in the kingdom of nature is almost a truism to assert. It only falls short of a truism to declare that the same law obtains in almost every department of human life and in nearly all human relations—domestic, family, social, political, national, universal. It is no valid rejoinder to say, that the guilty often, though not always, suffer for their own guilt. The two statements are not contradictory. Rather, they illustrate each other: for both are true. We are members of a corporate body, in nature as well as in grace. If one member suffers, all the members suffer with it, in both cases.

3. The objection that the Divine Benevolence ought to have been satisfied with a sacrifice for sin which fell short of the sacrifice demanded by Divine Justice of necessity fails, if the two former objections do not hold their ground. The objector has an equal right to complain of the inevitable and necessary and irremediable results of nature—that, under certain conditions, fire will burn him, water will drown him,

poison will injure him, hunger will slay him. But a man is not forced to starve himself, nor to poison himself, nor to drown himself, nor to burn himself. Neither is he forced to sin. If he fails in the object of his creation, and if he violates the laws of nature, in both instances alike he must submit to the consequences which inevitably follow by the all-holy Will of GOD.

Viewing the mighty subject in the light of a central action of a complicated system which the sin of man has, in the permissive Will of GOD, necessitated, there are many ways in which the Sacrifice of Calvary may be considered by Christian men and women living in the world. As a rule, in Protestant theology, a simple aspect of the Sacrifice is taken, namely, that of the Death of CHRIST. This, of course, we admit to be an overpowering element. We only deny that it has a sole, or an exclusive, claim upon our attention. We only affirm that it is an element in the divine scheme of salvation, that it is not the whole scheme. To the Death of our Divine Master, we, Catholics, are specially attracted, piously devoted, uncompromisingly committed. To it we bring the best, the noblest, the highest, the purest of man's affections, as a tribute all too poor for its deserts, but as an offering of all that we can bring. To it we devote our memory, understanding and will, in thought and speech, in act and deed, in meditation and contemplation. To it we dedicate the efforts of our imagination, the labour of our intellect, the work of our hands, in art and science, in music and painting and sculpture. In remembrance of the Death of JESUS for our sakes, we stamp fifty-two days in the year—one weekly—with the impress of abstinence and mortification. In memory of the Passion which preceded His Death, we dedicate yearly forty days consecutively to the more exclusive attention of the causes which in ourselves led to it. Nor does the Church fail to recall the sacred fact day by day: for, in her daily offering of sacrificial worship all the year round, she shows forth, at GOD'S Altar, the LORD'S Death until He comes again to earth.

In other forms of devotion, also, the Passion of CHRIST takes a foremost position in the love of the redeemed. Yet, the precious Death is not the only, even if it be the chief element and culminating point in His divine Sacrifice. Other elements and other points can claim important, though, it may be, subordinate positions. Amongst them may be named three which may supply topics for thought in times of retreat : 1. the Sacrifice of His Glory, as GOD ; 2. the Sacrifice of His Life, as MAN ; 3. the Sacrifice of His Will, as the GOD-MAN. As the sacred Life and Death of JESUS was fore-ordained in eternity; as the intention was one and the same with which the details of both were performed, namely, the salvation of man; and as the latter formed only the central point towards which the former ever converged—we may, perhaps, more profitably seek to estimate the Sacrifice of the Cross, in relation to the sin of man in its three-fold division, than in its complete entirety. We will, at the least, make the attempt; and we will meditate on the three above-named elements of CHRIST'S Sacrifice in their respective order.

IV.

I. Of the Sacrifice by JESUS CHRIST of His Glory, as GOD.

It is not easy for us to conceive how, and in what manner and by what means the glory of the source, origin and fount of all honour can be increased. It is more difficult for us to conceive how, and in what manner and by what means such glory can be lessened. Of course, in both cases, not the essential glory but the glory which is capable of change, whether of diminution or of addition ; in both cases, by the act and deed of man, or on behalf or for the sake of man.

As a theological fact which allows of no question, the accidental glory of GOD admits of change, both of increase and of decrease; admits of change, both for man and by man. For instance: if, as the Apostle assures us, our Blessed LORD "emptied Himself of His Glory"; if, as we know, He was pleased to be "made in the likeness of man," we can hardly fail to believe, in some transcendental manner, that for us men and for our salvation, the glory of JESUS CHRIST is capable of diminution. On the other hand, the command of the Apostle that every action of human life even the most ordinary, even the actions which man shares in common with the beasts that perish, be done "to the glory of GOD," proves to us that the glory of JESUS CHRIST is capable of augmentation. Hence, it is an allowable form of words to employ, that our Divine Master was pleased to make a sacrifice of His Glory as GOD.

The question then arises: How was JESUS CHRIST pleased to make a sacrifice of His accidental glory as GOD? The answer is distinct: in many ways, in too many ways to be mentioned here. But one proof is sufficient to establish the point: the Creator, in the Person of the Everlasting SON, became united in the Person of JESUS CHRIST to the creature. And this one proof contains two degrees, at the least, of a sacrificial diminution of His accidental glory. For, not only did GOD become Man, as a fact; but in the manner of His taking Flesh and tabernacling amongst us, He was further pleased to take upon Himself the form of a servant, the form of a slave.

Such, in brief, is the Catholic faith on this question. But, for the purpose of devout meditation, more may be said in the way of expansion. Consider, then, with me what is necessarily involved in this one statement—the union of the Creator with the creature of His Almighty hand. GOD became Man; and as a consequence, almost as a necessary consequence, these events followed:

The Centre of the divine worship of Angels and Archangels, of Principalities and Powers, of Cherubim and Seraphim was not only denied earthly homage, but was held in disesteem by men—"Can any good thing come out of Nazareth? Shall CHRIST come out of Galilee? Is not this the Carpenter's Son? How knoweth this Man letters, having never learned?" The Fount of all dignity, of Whose real honour earthly titles, courtly customs and human ceremonies are but types, was humiliated—He was born in a stable, He lived a life of hardship, He died a death of shame, and He was indebted for a last earthly resting place to another man's tomb. The Cause of all power in heaven and earth, the Omnipotent, the Almighty, was Self-made powerless—He was weak and feeble in the days of His Infancy, being wrapped in swathing-bands without power of motion in hand or foot; He was dependent upon the will and pleasure of others, restrained by powers Self-created, being subject unto Mary and Joseph, in the days of His Youth; He was taken captive, bound with cords, dragged hither and thither, mockingly vested and shamefully unclothed, and led away to be crucified, the Divine Victim of passive endurance, in the days of His Manhood.

Again: The Incomprehensible and Illimitable was confined by the bounds of space. The Eternal and Everlasting was subjected to the course of time. The Wisdom of GOD permitted Himself to lack knowledge, to acquire knowledge, to increase in knowledge, even to withhold from Himself knowledge. The Word of GOD caused Himself to be born, as other infants are born, speechless; and condescended to learn the use of language, as other children learn, at His Blessed Mother's knee.

What are these instances in the life of CHRIST, whether accepted as a necessary outcome of the Incarnation, or endured as a non-essential result of GOD dwelling amongst men, but evidences, in only a few cases, of the sacrifice of His accidental glory, by JESUS CHRIST, as GOD?

But, the evidence for the sacrifice of His glory is not exhausted. Not only in the attributes and operations of GODHEAD, not only in those qualities and parts which in man are comparable to his physical and intellectual nature, not only in the outward events of His career which He passively endured at the will and pleasure of man; but also, more marvellous than all, in His moral qualities as Perfect Man was He pleased to consent to a lessening of His glory. No diminution of accidental glory is so vast, no humiliation is so great, no divine paradox is so inexplicable as this. However true it is that GOD may be affirmed to be the Centre of worship, the Fount of honour, the Cause of power; however true it may be that He is the Illimitable and Everlasting, the very Wisdom and Word of GOD; yet, it is even more true that He presents Himself to our conception as the All-holy, the All-pure, the All-true, as Goodness itself, Righteousness itself, Love itself. Yet, for three-and-thirty years we find Holiness dwelling with wickedness, we find the All-good in the presence of all that is evil. Can any form of sacrifice of glory be more complete than this—the Sinless in contact with the sinful?

Take some examples of this form of sacrifice. At His birth He was the truth-loving cause of Herod's dissimulation, and the innocent cause of the murder of the Innocents. His flight into Egypt placed the divine and exiled Child in a land of false gods, and in the midst of a debased system of idolatry. For thirty years, even under the domestic care of spotless Mary and chaste Joseph, He lived in an atmosphere of sin, which even His pure presence in His own village could not disinfect. For the last three years of His earthly career, in the busier haunts of men; in a capital city with a population of mingled Jew and Gentile; in the crowds who thronged His footsteps, led thither by mixed motives of good and evil; and in more direct dealings with wickedness, He was voluntarily in daily personal contact with human sin. Nor was the Divine Master's contact with the principle of evil confined to a voluntary intercourse, nor to His intercourse only with man. His Ministry opened with the mysterious conflict held with the Prince of Evil, which we call

His Temptation, when He was driven by the SPIRIT into the wilderness. His Ministry closed whilst He was suspended between heaven and earth, a spectacle to Angels, the world and demons, in the midst of two malefactors, on either side one.

CHRIST'S ordinary and ministerial life, however, between His Temptation and His Death supplies many more instances of the sacrifice of glory in contact with sin. For example, to take but a few: Did He associate with His own countrymen in their marriage or other feasts? It was in the company of publicans and sinners, avowed or notorious. Did He exercise His ministry of mercy to the sick and dying? It was exercised, directly and certainly towards the latter, and indirectly and possibly towards the former, as an antidote to wickedness and sin. Did He, again, teach and preach in public? The object of the Beatitudes and Parables was to make men cease to do evil and learn to do good. Or, did He hold conference in private? The object of His midnight argument with the Master of Israel who would not confess Him before men, and His lengthened conversation with the Woman of Samaria who had had five husbands, was in both cases and in different ways to convince the soul of sin. Did He, once more, perform in His own Person the "greater miracles" which He promised that His Apostles should perform? This power, beyond that of cleansing the leper, giving sight to the blind, or raising the dead, was exercised on behalf of those taken captive by Satan, in the toils of sin. It was exercised by the absolution of the hidden sins of the sick of the palsy; and by the non-condemnation, which was equivalent to a forgiveness, of the woman who was openly taken in adultery.

Nor would the evidence in our possession of the extent to which our Divine LORD made a sacrifice of His glory, in His contact with sin, be complete, if we failed to take notice of the action of others in relation to CHRIST. Of His brethren —were they not urgent with Him to take premature action to show Himself to the world, as not believing in Him? Of

His friends—went they not out to lay hold on Him; for they said, He is beside Himself? Of His own town's people —were they not filled with wrath against Him, and did they not lead Him to the brow of the hill, that they might cast Him down headlong? Of the people of Jerusalem—did they not take up stones to cast at Him in the Temple? Of His fellow country-men—were they not offended in Him, when He taught in their synagogue? Of the Gergesenes—did they not beseech Him to depart out of their coasts, after He had cured the possessed of devils?

Nor, again, must we fail to take notice of the actions of other classes of persons, or of types of a class, in relation to CHRIST. For example: 1. Of the Scribes—who said, that He had an unclean spirit. 2. Of the Pharisees—who took counsel that they might destroy Him. 3. Of the people— who wished to make Him a king, against His will. 4. Of Herod—who sought to kill Him, without cause. 5. Of the chief-priests—who accused Him of sedition, contrary to the truth. 6. Of the false witnesses—who laid to His charge things which they could not prove.

Were not all these facts in the life of CHRIST, instances in which the All-holy and the All-pure was brought into contact with impurity and unholiness? Were they not cases in which His accidental glory was tarnished; in which our Divine Master voluntarily offered up the sacrifice of His glory, for our salvation—for remember, He was GOD?

In view of the Sacrifice of His glory as GOD, by JESUS CHRIST, a personal question arises to which we must seek in retreat to find an answer. How, in the relation of sacrifice to human sin, do we follow the imitation of our Divine Master? I will not ask, how we—you and I—voluntarily lessen or limit our own human glory, by the many forms of self-humiliation which the Saints have loved to take. That might be too much to expect. We are not Saints. At the most, we can only hope to attain to a measure of sanctity which falls far short of that. I will not ask, how we—you and I—frankly accept the limitation or the lessening of our human glory, directly from the hands of GOD. We are probably faithful and true to this extent, that if we be persuaded of GOD'S immediate action in our humiliation, in any of the endless ways in which man may be taught his own nothingness, we should not rebel, we should submit. But, it may fairly be asked of a body of Christians who profess to follow the example of the CHRIST, how we bear ourselves, when our position is compromised, or our dignity is lowered, by others? How we, men and women living in the world, who are not Saints, but yet are members of a crucified Head, conform to the sacrifice of our glory at the hands of our fellow-man? How do we accept the sacrifice of our human glory, who are not the centre of worship, nor the fount of dignity, nor the cause of power; our glory, who are neither infinite nor eternal; our glory, who are wise only in our own conceits, and who use words, often if not always, more to conceal than to confess the truth; our glory, who avowedly to ourselves are not all-holy and all-pure, and in the sight of Angels are not full of goodness, are not full of love?

Let us take a single instance and try ourselves by the self-imposed standard. Let us take an average instance, neither high, lest we escape from the test by its want of appositeness; nor low, lest we triumph over it by reason of its want of force. For example: How do we feel, or think, or speak, or act, in any of the common-place events of life if—to use the terms before employed—our glory be diminished, if—to use the language of the world—our self-importance be lessened by some other person being preferred to oneself? It matters not at all what may be our own individual position, or powers, or qualities, or gifts. These accidents only tend to intensify or to moderate our estimate of the result. It matters not whether the other be our equal, our superior, or our subordinate, in age, rank, acquirements, or talents. Such elements only vary the terms of the problem, without affecting its solution. It matters not what may be the subject matter of our spiritual trial. Our self-importance can be lessened in endless ways—and the greater may be our belief in our importance, the more will be the chance of its being lessened by others.

Preference may be shown in our word being doubted, in our motives being questioned, in our actions being misunderstood. We may be condemned and blamed, we may be criticised and censured, we may be ignored and overlooked. Another may be preferred to us; we may be deferred to another. Others succeed where we fail, we being really the superior; we have not an opportunity to succeed, others being allowed a chance denied to us. Our advice is not asked, our counsel is not taken, our acquaintance is not sought, our friendship is not reciprocated, our love is not returned. Nay—our birth, position, influence, intellect, power, wealth, personal appearance are not valued as they ought to be esteemed, are estimated below the same respective gifts of others.

What may be—in sentiment, thought, word, or deed—the result in our own souls of this diminution of our self-importance? What result may ensue as known to GOD and to our Guardian Angel, even if unknown to our confessor and concealed even from ourself? Do we feel angry, envious, or jealous; vexed, ruffled, or saddened? Do we think that of ourself, of our neighbour, or of our GOD, which we should not like, we should not wish, we should not dare to utter? Do we allow ourself to say some word of disparagement, contempt, criticism or condemnation; or prevent ourself from saying some word of kindness, gratulation, or sympathy? Do we permit ourself to act towards that other, or even towards some third person, as may be dictated by the outcome of such word, such thought, or such feeling? If so; if tried by this single test we fail, how can we say that we follow the imitation of the CHRIST, in the sacrifice of His glory as GOD?

V.

II. Of the Sacrifice by JESUS CHRIST of His Life, as MAN.

For a good man, says the Apostle, perhaps some would even dare to die—though scarcely, even for a righteous man. But for a bad man — ? Not even his charity, who made himself all things to all men, that he might by all means save some, could entertain such a thought as that. Not even his charity, who could wish that himself were accursed for his brethren, could reach this level. Yet, for whom did the Good Man, the one and only Good, dare to die—aye, and did die? Emphatically, for the bad; for those who were not good; for the bad before they were made good; for the bad, after they had fallen away, and before they had been restored. The Good Man dared to die, not only for the bad, as the world counts badness, but for those whom GOD declares to be not good. He dared to die, not only for the grossly vicious, the vulgarly wicked, or the openly profane, transgressors against the sixth, seventh and eighth Commandments of GOD; or, in the Deadly Sins of the Church of pride, envy, gluttony or sloth; or, in the works of the flesh as named by the Apostle, idolatry, hatred, wrath, strife, or heresy: but also for those whom GOD sees to be evil, those who lacked the divine fruits of the SPIRIT, love, joy, peace, long-suffering, gentleness, goodness, faith, meekness and temperance. For such as these the Good Man died. And herein, as the Apostle says, GOD commendeth His love towards us, in that, while we were yet sinners, CHRIST died for us. But more than this also is true. He not only gave Himself to death once; but He gave Himself in life for three-and-thirty years. JESUS CHRIST sacrificed His Life, as Man, for human sinfulness.

What is meant by the sacrifice of His life? I answer: The sacrifice of a living, thinking, feeling, moving existence; of an intelligent, reflective, accountable, willing, self-conscious personality; of the earthly career, before birth, in birth,

THE SACRIFICE OF THE CROSS.

through life, to death, even after resurrection, of the GOD-MAN, JESUS CHRIST. The sacrifice of His life means the sacrifice, for us men, of His hidden life in Mary's bosom; of His birth in the manger of the ox, the sheep and the ass; of the twelve years of His sacred infancy; of the eighteen years of honest toil in His youth and early manhood; of the three years of His painful ministry; of the hours of His passion; of the days of His resurrection-life. As a babe, He was borne helpless in His Mother's arms. As a child, He was about His Heavenly FATHER'S business. In His early years, He was subject to His earthly Foster-father. During His public ministry, He devoted Himself to its cares, duties, labours, sorrows. In His passion-hours, He yielded Himself a willing victim in all its scenes. During the great Forty Days, His only work was the development and perfecting of His sacrificial life—all, for our salvation.

How was His life on earth a Life of Sacrifice? I reply, that every stage of it bears a sacrificial character—either in the intention with which it was passed, or in the accidents with which its details were surrounded. In both cases the principle of sacrifice is visible. For example, to take but a few salient points for meditation: Was not His Blessed Mother a lowly maiden, and His reputed Father a humble mechanic? Did He not live in a lowly cottage, work as a carpenter, company with poor fishermen? Did not He renounce every thing and every person when He began His ministry—mother, family, trade, friends, home-life, personal ease and comfort? Did He not fulfil His ministry—not self-pleasing but self-dedicating—on behalf of others, teaching, preaching, healing bodies, saving souls, working miracles? Was He not often-times hungry and thirsty and weary; angry and saddened; homeless and houseless; in danger of life, or of personal safety; a sufferer both from undesired popularity and from undeserved opposition; the victim, at one time of political intrigue, and at another of social depreciation?

Apparently, the entire period of the ministry was one long-continued sacrifice of His life as Man. For, He failed not also, over and above His work for man, in making a sacrifice of Himself to GOD, in His religious duties. As a conscientious Jewish citizen, He did not allow His missionary labours to come into conflict with His more strictly religious duties to GOD. As a representative Man, He is a model for our devotion. We read that He spent whole nights on the bleak mountain-side, and long hours in the enclosed garden, in prayer to GOD. The language of His prayers, at the tomb of Lazarus, on the feast day in Jerusalem, in the Upper Chamber, in Gethsemane, on the Cross, have been preserved for our instruction. He frequented the service of the Synagogue, and even assisted in its ministrations. He presented Himself, whether as child or adult, at the customary times for the Temple worship in Jerusalem. And He did not neglect seasons of retirement, after special times of ministerial labour, for spiritual refreshment and edification, seasons which we term Retreats.

Such—short of a record of His sacred Passion and all its bitter memories—such is a rapid outline of the Life of Sacrifice for human sin, which formed a portion of, and an element in, the Sacrifice of the Cross, by the MAN CHRIST JESUS our LORD.

Is there any thing comparable in our life to the Life of Sacrifice of JESUS? This is another personal question which arises from the above considerations, to which we must seek to find an answer in retreat.

Is there any thing in our life which, by a good-natured stretch of even Apostolic charity can be forced to include the idea of sacrifice in our individual existence? Is our life, as a fact, a life of sacrifice to the greater glory of GOD the FATHER? Is it a sacrifice, in devout reparation for our sins; or, on behalf of the souls of others; or, out of love for JESUS; or, for the sake of His Spouse, the Church—to the glory of

God? In former days, perhaps, there was that about us which might be fairly termed enthusiasm; a reality, a devotion, an intensity, a thoroughness which led us to make a sacrifice of our life to some one special thing, an idea, a sentiment, a belief, a plan, or a person. Did we ever make such a sacrifice, even for a while, to the cultus of the world, of position or wealth, of success or influence, of popularity with others or of happiness (so called) for self? If so, in time past, when we were younger; or, indeed, if not so, yet now, in the present, as we get older, is there any enthusiasm about us, any reality, or devotion, or intensity or thoroughness towards Religion in any possible form? Is there enthusiasm to the extent which, in any sense, makes us sacrifice our life to God, to His Church, to our neighbour, to our own soul? Do we, as a fact, sacrifice it to any one single conception or idea, to any entity or person, to any fact, mystery, or truth in the Catholic Religion?

Or, on the other hand, is not this rather a plain, unbiassed and frank description of self-analysis? That we, of course, bow down in profoundest adoration before the super-human Self-sacrifice of Jesus Christ, for our sakes. That we, in a lesser degree, but still with sincere appreciation, venerate the triumphs of self-sacrifice in the persons of His Saints. That we honestly respect the courage of Martyrs, the constancy of Virgins, the sanctity of Ascetics, the firmness of Confessors. That we love to dwell on the imitation of our Divine Master and His Servants; and care to read of the triumphs of the Saints, both men and women. But—that for ourselves, that for you and I, we as a fact, painful to realize and humiliating to avow, we lead more or less selfish, self-pleasing, self-occupied, self-devoted lives. That we live, indeed, under the nominal restraints of our holy Religion; perhaps, outwardly for Religion; even, it may be, in Religion—yet, fulfilled, absorbed, eaten up with self; with self as beginning, middle and end of our entire life; with self as the motive power, however disguised, of every action; without the spirit of mortification or self-denial; without a spark of that un-earthly enthusiasm which influenced the actions of Saints, and which consumed the will of the Divine Carpenter of Nazareth when He, as Man, sacrificed His life for our salvation.

Of this enthusiasm I will take but one example. Are we prepared, either in ourselves or in others with whom we may be connected, to give up family or friends, position or influence, work for man or work for GOD, or all these combined at a single stroke, rather than accept a religious principle which we, from our souls, believe to be false, rather than deny a religious principle which we, in our conscience, know to be true? Such principles may meet us, do meet us, in times like the present, both in Church and in State, and on the confines of either where the interests of both conflict. I ask therefore, as in the presence of GOD: Are we content to continue in the easier course of self-pleasing, want of definiteness and compromise; or, will we generously follow the call of GOD to a higher and a purer career, even if it be one of self-sacrifice?

VI.

III. Of the Sacrifice by JESUS CHRIST of His Will, as the GOD-MAN.

From the instant of the Incarnation to the moment of His giving up the Ghost—both being voluntary acts—our Divine Master was subject, in His earthly career, to the will of another. In other terms, He was pleased to make a sacrifice of His Will.

Here, the divine paradox in the Sacrifice of the Cross, from the three-fold view which we take of it, becomes the most involved and complicated. The sacrifice of His glory as GOD and the sacrifice of His life as MAN, neither present such difficulties as the sacrifice of His will, as the GOD-MAN, being, as there were two wills in one Person, one human and one divine and both perfect. Yet, the two-fold cause produced but one effect: the double principle of action resulted in one harmonious course. Read the holy Gospel in this light, with the design of tracing the twin principle of a single issue in, the Divine Life on earth. It will afford a wonderful insight into the central words and acts therein preserved. From its study we shall see how in some cases, how in many, the wills human and divine might have been but were not at discord; how in all recorded instances they were, though they need not have been, in harmony. Yet, in nearly each event of life His will, as the GOD-MAN, was sacrificed to another, for us men and for our salvation.

In this examination of the inspired account, the same events meet us in a different guise. It is somewhat similar to the use of a single psalm with a variable antiphon. This fact will relieve us from the necessity of making a minute examination on this occasion of the sacred life, from the present point of view; though it will prove a valuable help towards realizing the Gospel-narrative, if we follow the lines laid down in our private research. We may, however, briefly indicate how and to what extent our Blessed LORD made a sacrifice of His will during His earthly life; and the fact that a double principle resulted in each case in a single course of action will not be allowed to escape devout consideration.

There appear to be three modes in which the Divine Master made a sacrifice of His will, human and super-human.

1. Simply at the dictates of His own personal free-will, when we may reverently suppose that there was no conflict, even in intention, between His human will and His will divine. Although the cases in which this mode prevailed occurred chiefly in the early life of CHRIST, they cannot be exclusively confined to that period. Amongst others may be mentioned these: the Eternal WORD in the bosom of the Blessed Virgin; the newly-born Babe in swathing-bands; the Infant in the manger-cradle; the exiled Fugitive in Egypt; the Youth in the carpenter's shop; the Man in the home-life of Nazareth—in each case there was a sacrifice of His will by JESUS CHRIST, to that of Mary and Joseph.

2. Apart from and in opposition to the absolute will both human and divine, and yet in accordance with the permissive will both of GOD and MAN. This mode may be seen in action in the middle stage of CHRIST'S earthly life. The whole course of the Ministry, when GOD came in contact with man, is tinged with this colouring. For example: Was not JESUS, as the Prophet, disbelieved and doubted: and was not such doubt and disbelief a sacrifice of His will Who was Truth and knew that He spake truth? Was not JESUS, as the Preacher, mocked and scorned, misunderstood and misinterpreted; as the Moralist, accused of sensuality and of indifference to sin; as the Physician, told to heal Himself; as the Wonder-worker, challenged to work miracles, prevented from working miracles, declared to be Beelzebub on account of His miracles, and discredited after He had performed miracles? And was not such antagonism, in other forms, a sacrifice of His will Who was both GOD and MAN? Was not JESUS, as the Master of twelve disciples, betrayed by one, denied by one, doubted by one, forsaken by all? And was not such treatment, again, a sacrifice of the will of the Creator, for the sake of those to whom it was sacrificed, to that of the creature?

3. In conformity with the Will of the Eternal FATHER, after, as we may reverently assume from the inspired record, what in man would amount to a conflict between the higher and lower will, though both were perfect. The Passion of CHRIST from the Upper Chamber to the tomb of Joseph is one long account of this mode of the sacrifice of will. We will recall only two instances of it. First: in the Garden of Gethsemane; in the cold clear light of a Southern moon; from under the shade of the sombre-leafed olive trees; amid the long damp grass, or from the upturned earth at night; from JESUS on His knees, on His face, did this cry go up to heaven, not once, not twice, but thrice, "FATHER, not My Will but Thine be done." Second: on the bitter Tree, at midday; in the parching heat of an Eastern sun; after a night of insult and a day of ignominy; when faint from fasting and

weak from loss of blood; having been bound, scourged, spit upon, mocked; after hanging three weary hours suspended in shame between heaven and earth, JESUS cried with a loud voice, once only and not a second time, "FATHER, into Thy hands I commend My Spirit": and having said thus, He gave up the Ghost.

These three modes of sacrificing His Will, apart from the evidences afforded by the Sacred Passion—namely, in childhood to His parents, in adult age to His enemies, in death to His GOD—present a sharp and striking contrast to our self-pleasing, self-adored, and self-sufficient lives. Are these hard words? Are we self-sufficient and self-absorbed, and self-pleased; in a word, selfish? We do not think that we are. We think that we are not. Let us then try ourselves by the imitation of CHRIST; and thus, in a third way make answer in retreat to yet another personal inquiry.

The three modes in which our Blessed LORD made a sacrifice of His will, being both GOD and MAN, take with us, men and women, a two-fold form; namely, those in which we have, and those in which we have not, the power of choice, in the matter of sacrifice.

1. In cases in which we possess free choice whether to accept or to decline the sacrifice of our will, let us ask ourselves: Have we ever used, and if we have upon occasions used, do we habitually practise, voluntary self-sacrifice? Do we employ self-sacrifice in large matters, if as we say, we are above its use in small things? Do we employ it in little things, if we feel our power unequal to use self-sacrifice in those that are important? Have we or do we sacrifice our will in some one point which affects the course of our life, from a certain event or date forward; or which affects the details of existence, in our daily round of life?

2. In cases in which we are powerless to exercise choice in accepting or declining, or in which we cannot avoid submission to the sacrifice of our will; and yet, in which we may

have the merit of placing our will in accord, or the de-merit of failing to place our will in conformity with the Divine Will, let us inquire: Do we accept the Divine Will, even it may be after a struggle between our higher and lower will, loyally, cheerfully, entirely? Or, do we give it a half-hearted assent, and strive to escape its full consequences, and seek to minimize those results which are the least to our taste? Or, do we give no assent at all, or refuse assent; and though we are powerless to hinder the effect of the Divine Will, yet do we yield sullenly and churlishly, allowing it to pass over us like the winter blast, which is unpleasant indeed, but must be endured?

Details of the sacrifice of our will, in both cases, may be left to our own hearts. Whether in outer circumstances, or inward feelings; whether in relation to others, or as affecting ourselves; whether in health, position, object in life, or pleasures; whether in present plans or future prospects; whether in the employment of time, money, or influence; whether in dedication to GOD or man; whether in work for the Church at GOD'S bidding, or working in some other way at GOD'S call, or ceasing to work when GOD says that our work is done—in all and in each of these cases and in many others, there may be, there must be a sacrifice of our will, either voluntarily or without choice, if we would follow the imitation of our LORD JESUS CHRIST.

ADDRESS TEN.
THE SACRAMENTS OF THE CHURCH.

THE difference between the Catholic Faith and any system of religion which lays claim to dogmatic exactness, is on no question more wide than on the mysterious subject which finds a solution in the Sacraments of Holy Church. This subject, on which we have dwelt in the last two addresses, is the expiation of human sin. We have seen that expiation consists in a continuous course of action. It was conceived in eternity. It was continued in time past. It is being fulfilled and perfected only in the present.

The Catholic belief in the forgiveness of sins is complete in three stages of divine work. These stages may be concisely stated. The terms, Incarnation, Sacrifice, Sacraments, are sufficient to bring them home to the mind. On the other hand, the Protestant system may be even more concisely stated. If truth and simplicity were synonymous, this system would be unequalled. By its theory, the last of the three elements in GOD'S divine plan is ignored; the first is overlooked; and the middle term remains as the one, great, and only cause of the forgiveness of the sin of man. In other words, in the system accepted by one entire half of our fellow-countrymen who are without the pale of the Church, and by about three-fourths of the remainder who are nominally within her bounds, the dogma of the Incarnation is practically depreciated; the use of the Sacraments is, in principle, absolutely swept away; and the Sacrifice of Calvary—or rather, the believer's inner assent to the fact of the divine offering—stands out, supreme, sole, and alone in their scheme of salvation. A grand scheme, doubtless: grand—if true.

As Christians, however, we are bound by, we are bound to,

the system of salvation revealed to His Church by her divine Head. The Protestant system, emphatically, is not such. As Catholics, we are committed to the system traditionally handed down by CHRIST'S Church. Protestants and non-Catholics avowedly, decline to be trammelled by such tradition : they are careful, rather, not to follow tradition ; to follow, indeed, anything in preference to it. And the tradition of the Church binds us to the three-fold division above named —the Incarnation of GOD, the Sacrifice of the Cross, and the Sacramental order of the Church. As Catholics, too, we are more concerned with the teaching of our holy Mother, than of those who submit not to her teaching. Hence, we may well leave those that are without to the judgment of their Master to Whom they are accountable. We may with advantage confine our attention to that marvellous and super-human system, in design comprehensive and in detail all-pervading, which adumbrated by GOD in the divine decrees, and fulfilled for the human race on Calvary, is extended and applied to individual souls in the Seven Sacraments of the Church, by the power of the HOLY GHOST.

II.

In the ages of ages of which we have before thought, when GOD was Self-existent, Omnipotent and Good—for we need not pass beyond these three attributes of Deity—He willed the increase of His accidental glory. Such increase of glory He was pleased to will by the act of creation. In the absolute foreknowledge of GOD—past and future being ever-present with His Majesty—and by the divine decrees, in willing the act of creation, GOD willed all that creation involved and all that resulted from creation. Hence, all the issues of creation, in relation to the completion and summit of creation, man ; the entire history of man, perfected in the gift of free-will ; each result of the use of free-will, in the mystery of human sin ; the necessary consequences of sin, in regard to death ; and the victory over death, by man's restoration—all these points, and infinitely more, were present to the mind of GOD equally with the intention to create, equally with the will to create, equally with the act of creation. Contemporaneously, so to speak of the Eternal, with the will to create—in spite of death, in spite of sin, in spite of free-will—was the will to unite the creature with the Creator. Indeed, to augment the accidental glory of GOD by such union, and irrespective of all secondary issues, was the final cause of creation. Such union was decreed from all eternity, was decreed independently of man's restoration, of human death, of human sin and of man's free-will, in the counsels of GOD in the mystery of the Incarnation, GOD made MAN in the Person of JESUS CHRIST, the GOD-MAN of the future.

This being enforced, as almost of faith, then we may admit, without a shadow of reserve, that man's free-will, sin, death and restoration, made their influence felt in all the subordinate elements of the great central truth. Although the fact, so to say, of the Incarnation was unaffected, yet the surroundings of the fact, namely, the time, the place, the manner, the circumstance, were not unaffected, were indeed greatly influenced. As a part of such disturbing influence—human agency and its action—a sacrifice was needful to expiate the sin of man before GOD; an infinite sacrifice was needful—infinite, because the guilt to be atoned bore the characteristic of infinity. Such infinite atonement for infinite guilt was made by JESUS CHRIST.

Here we perceive two stages in the divine drama in relation to the human race: 1. the Incarnation, to unite manhood to the GODHEAD; 2. the Sacrifice, to atone for man's guilt to GOD'S Justice. Eternity originated the scheme. The past has developed it. In what way may the present fulfil GOD'S will towards man? In what way may individual souls be benefited by the will conceived by GOD the FATHER and by the action taken by GOD the SON? I reply: without presuming to affirm that no other answer may be made, nor other form of words used—in the following manner.

The Incarnation having been decreed by the First Person of the TRINITY, on behalf of the human race in the aggregate; and the Sacrifice having been accomplished by the Second Person, in the abstract; the Third Person of the TRINITY completed the divine work by making that concrete which had been done in the abstract, by causing that to become particular which had been made general. In other words, the HOLY GHOST personally extended the Incarnation of GOD, and personally applied the Sacrifice of the Cross to the individual souls of the human race, by the origination of the Sacramental system of the Church.

The Sacraments of the Church form the crown, perfection and glory of GOD'S spiritual work for man, as man formed the glory, perfection and crown of GOD'S material work in creation. They stand as the culminating point of a series of divine actions, expressive of the eternal will and mind of GOD. The theory of the Incarnation became developed into the Sacrifice: the exercise of free-will and its results demanded the development that GOD'S intention should not be frustrated. From the Sacrifice was evolved the practice of the Sacraments, in order that the divine intention should be fulfilled. Hence, the Sacraments of the Church perform a double function. They are the logical sequence of the Incarnation in theory. They are the necessary development of the Sacrifice in practice. In both cases, they extend and apply the will and purpose of GOD from the human race to the human individual. They individualize the other two efforts of GOD for souls, personally, man by man.

GOD'S eternal will and purpose for the souls which He, in intention had created and redeemed and sanctified, was this. Not only that a race of self-conscious, intelligent, responsible beings should be, in the aggregate, united to the GODHEAD: but that the human race, man by man, should be thereto united. Not only that the sins of the human race, in the abstract, should be expiated by the Precious Blood; but that the sins of the whole world, soul by soul, should thereby be atoned. Such, in brief, was GOD'S blessed will for individual souls. His will, under both conditions, was fulfilled by the instrumentality of the Sacramental system.

Consider the position of the human race, in the gross, had the Sacramental system not been revealed by GOD the HOLY GHOST. Consider our individual position, had the Incarnation not been extended, had the Sacrifice not been applied. There would have been displayed in the sight of the universe a magnificent design on the part of eternal Wisdom, almighty Power, absolute Justice, unconquerable Love. Infinite Wisdom and Power would have conceived and executed the mystery of the Incarnation. Infinite Love and Justice would have offered and accepted the Sacrifice. GOD would have become MAN. GOD would have died for man. Both mighty facts would have been accomplished in the abstract. A creation, in the race of man, would have been united to the Creator. The sins of the creature against the will of the Creator would have been atoned. Both, again, in the abstract. But how could this magnificent design have been made practical? How could the unit of creation, how could the individual of the race, how could the soul of man, one by one, have been affected? How could you and I, personally, eighteen centuries after the Sacrifice had been accepted, and ages of ages after the Incarnation had been conceived—how could you and I have been individually made one with GOD; how could your sins and my sins have been individually forgiven? In short: how could the Incarnation of the GOD-MAN have been extended to you and me individually as units of the race: or, how could the Offering of the Precious Blood have been applied to your sins and to mine, as to those of personal and accountable agents with immortal souls? How could either result have been accomplished, apart from the extension and application obtained by the Sacraments of the Church?

Here we encounter a practical difficulty of portentous moment. Under this overpowering weight, non-dogmatic theology absolutely fails. It collapses. It is content with mere subjective ideas, the creation only of the human intellect: ideas which have not even the credit of theological ingenuity in their invention; which can claim only a partial acquiescence in a fraction of Christendom for a limited period; which rest upon the authority of isolated passages of Holy Scripture to the exclusion of the consensus of the Universal Church; and which, intellectually, create results from causes morally and physically powerless to produce them. These ideas we need not pause even to state. Dogmatic theology, on the other hand, alone solves the otherwise insoluble problem. It solves the problem of eternity in the course of time, by pointing to the Sacraments of the Church, vivified by the divine Personality of GOD the HOLY GHOST. In the purpose and will of GOD, we are bold to affirm, that the Incarnation of the Creator and the Sacrifice of the Redeemer could not have been extended and applied to each member of the human race apart from the seven-fold Sacraments of the Church. Apart from the Sacramental system, the union of the creature with the Creator, man by man, could not have been effected.

Little need is there to search for illustrations of this truth. The commonest facts of daily life are more than sufficient to show the value and import of the last stages of expiation and union, in relation to the earlier stages of Incarnation and Sacrifice—personally and individually. The Sacraments of the Church bear the like comparison to what they are designed to extend and apply, that pipes bear to a cistern of water to a thirsty man, that money bears to a granary of wheat to a hungry man. The holy sacraments are divine channels, which convey the water of life to a thirsty soul. They are the current coin of the heavenly merchant, which purchases the bread of life for a hungry soul. The cistern may be full of water and the supply of bread may not fail: but, unless some means be found to convey nourishment to the fainting man, the flow of water will not quench his sense of thirst, nor will the abundance of bread satisfy his pangs of hunger. Both may have been God-given by divine Beneficence. The human recipient may be in absolute need of both. But, until some intermediatary be established between man's individual want and the divine means of relief, the cause will not in his case produce the consequence, nor will the demand for his support be followed by the supply.

III.

The Sacraments of the Church in relation to the sin of man, both in the course of nature and in the order of grace, take a seven-fold form. Does this statement strike any of us as being doubtful? Brother or Sister in CHRIST, I would ask you to bear with me, until you have heard, as S. Paul said, the defence which I shall make unto you. I shall make it, as the Apostle made his apology, to fellow-countrymen and in the Hebrew tongue—to you and in the Gospel-language of our holy Religion. To most of us, the seven-fold division of the Sacramental system will only appear to be a commonplace in the Faith.

The seven-fold division of the blessed sacraments is a marvel of ingenuity, method and arrangement. Its exhaustiveness and simplicity betray the inspiration which prompted the wisdom of its development, that it was not human but divine. If we take for granted, for the moment, what we shall afterwards show, the relation which they severally bear to the two great initial truths of Christianity and which have been discussed, we shall at once perceive the superhuman instinct by which they were organized. It had been impossible for the uninspired intellect of man to originate and perfect a system which looks so simple from without, and yet is found to be so comprehensive when it is estimated from within. The means of obtaining the heavenly bread, and the channels which convey the water of life to individual souls, are worldwide in their scope. They extend the Incarnation of GOD to every possible need of man in the course of nature. They apply the Sacrifice of the Cross to every possible form of sin in the order of grace. In both cases, by the attributes and operations of GOD the HOLY GHOST.

Familiar as many of us are with the Sacramental system of the Church under some aspects, it is my duty, as you were warned at the outset of the Retreat, to recall to your minds old and well-known truths. Suffer me, then, to repeat once more the old, old story of GOD'S love for man, and how GOD is pleased to work out such love systematically and in practice for man's eternal happiness. In its repetition it is not always easy to know in what sequence to take the sacraments, or in what relation or connection to treat them. But there can be no doubt of the order both of the Initial Rite and of the Last Sacraments of the Church in regard to man's birth and death. There can be no doubt of the relation between other two sacraments, Confession and Communion; nor of the requirement to come holy and clean to the heavenly Feast, on the part of the earthly guest; nor, again, of the relation in order of time between Confirmation and the Holy Eucharist, on the part of the recipient. There can be no doubt of the connection between the sacrament of Holy Orders and, with the exception of Baptism in cases of necessity, all other Sacraments of the Church on the part of the administrator. Nor, once more, are we left without guidance as to the position of Holy Matrimony in the supernatural sequence: for the Church has provided for a Marriage-mass, and the reception of the sacrament of the Eucharist coincident with submission to the sacrament of Matrimony presupposes obedience to the requirements of Baptism, Confirmation, and Confession. The like observation, of course, applies to the reception of the sacrament of Orders: they must have been preceded also by the same three sacraments.

Hence, it cannot be asserted that we are left without a guide as to the mind of the Church on the question of the due order and sequence of the sacraments. Consideration will show the relation in which the five sacraments, in which all the faithful may participate, are meant to be considered.

And with regard to the remaining two mysteries, which are not generally necessary to salvation, and are only necessary for some persons under certain conditions, or for all persons under others, we may perceive that as they ought to be preceded by certain sacraments, so they may be followed by the final earthly mystery of all.

Before we consider the Holy Sacraments one by one, I would venture to remind you of certain dogmatic truths; 1. That we meditate on the Sacramental system of the Church, which was originated and inspired, which was vivified and sanctified by the Third Person of the Blessed TRINITY. 2. That in meditating on the PARACLETE, we meditate on One Who is GOD equally with the FATHER, and a Person equally with the SON—for we believe in the Divinity and Personality of the HOLY GHOST. 3. That in relation to this Divine Personality, we must remember, amongst other facts, these three —He is Self-existent, Infinite, and Omnipotent: we must not forget, amongst other truths, again, three—He is not in any sense a created being; He is not an influence only; He is not a mere minister of the TRINITY. 4. That the Holy SPIRIT is pleased to work, for man's sanctification, through channels of His own appointment in three several ways: firstly, by human agency; secondly, by material substances; thirdly, by ceremonial form—as well as by His own personal and divine power.

These four points we have considered in former addresses. We may take them for granted now; and, in reliance upon their catholicity, we may meditate briefly upon each of the seven divisions of the Church's Sacramental system, by which the Incarnation of the Creator is extended, and the Sacrifice of the Redeemer is applied, by the Third Person of the TRINITY, to the individual souls of men. Without claiming for the arrangement any credit beyond that of convenience, the order in which the sacraments will be treated is as follows:—1. Holy Baptism; 2. Confirmation; 3. the most Holy

T

Eucharist; 4. Penance; 5. Marriage; 6. Holy Orders; 7. the Last Sacraments of the Church. This arrangement, it may be observed, in no wise militates against the old Catholic division, which recognises the two greater and the five lesser sacraments. Such a division has reference only to the dignity of these means of grace, not to the manner and order in which they severally influence the soul of man.

I. Of the Sacrament of Holy Baptism.

As we have previously been led to see, the sacrament of Baptism, in all cases the initiatory rite of our holy Religion, is more easily explained as supplying an absent element in the soul which is thereby made Christian, than as counteracting any present fault. In this view of the opening stage in man's superhuman career, it may be asked: Has man been born in the course of nature, wanting that super-natural principle which Adam had resigned, and which, therefore, he was powerless to bequeath to his descendants? Has he been unprovided with a spiritual gift, over and above the natural qualities, however perfect, which he inherited from the first Adam? Has he need to be made, though all-unconscious of the need, a member of a new race of spiritual beings, a child of the Second Adam, and all that is implied in these theological phrases? Especially, has the recipient of Baptism need, in his spiritual relations, of new and higher principles of action to be implanted within him; of new and more powerful means of action to be placed within his reach; of new and holier results of action to be acquired at his will and pleasure? Has he, once more, been created apart from certain relationships to each several Person of the TRINITY; and is it necessary that he should submit to a new creation in order that he may be enabled to fulfil the object of his first creation, and to increase the accidental glory of GOD, by being made the child of the FATHER, a member of the SON, and an inheritor of the SPIRIT'S gifts in the kingdom of Heaven.

If this be so, then Baptism supplies all that is required. It re-creates the soul of man. It makes him an unit of a new race. It places him in a covenanted relation with GOD. It provides a foundation of grace on which to work. It imparts that supernatural principle upon which the remaining gifts and graces of the SPIRIT may be grafted, and in virtue of which alone they will bear fruit. And it produces these amongst other spiritual results, because it is the first stage in the extension of the Incarnation and in the application of the Sacrifice; it is the first effort of GOD the HOLY GHOST, in relation to human sin, to unite the creature to the Creator and to make him personally partaker of the precious Blood-shedding, as an individual of the race, man by man.

II. Of the Sacrament of Confirmation.

The infant is now placed in a covenanted relation to GOD. He has acquired a right to be pleasing unto GOD. He is possessed of power to please GOD. What may be the next stage upwards, that he may secure the full benefits of the seven-fold system of grace? As a child, he gradually comes to feel the need—or, the want is present even if he feel it not —of further power and greater strength in order to resist the attacks of childish temptation or even the attacks of actual sin. The negative aspect of Baptism now requires an addition of a positive character. The ground has been prepared in which the divine seed has been sown. The seed now requires to be stimulated into life. We will suppose that the divine gift has not been withdrawn; and that the soul's baptismal robe has not been sullied. Grace given in the first sacrament still of right belongs to the neophyte. But it is time that the supernatural principle be quickened and energized into action; that the harvest of the Great Day of thirty, sixty, or an hundred fold be allowed a chance of realization.

If this be so, Confirmation in due course follows upon Baptism. It supplies the want and provides for the need, which childhood demands. It stimulates and vivifies the almost dormant principle previously infused. It is less than a positive and actual gift or grace, on the one side, in that it is complementary to the principle imparted in Baptism. It is more than a negative and supplementary infusion of the SPIRIT'S power, in that it bestows seven distinct gifts and graces of the SPIRIT. It is, in truth, a many-sided sacrament, various in the forms in which it meets different souls, various in the results with which it benefits different souls; but suitable to the position in which it meets the recipient at a period of spiritual life between that of the unconscious infant and that of the matured adult, at a time when the faith, the affections, the sentiments and the will of the child are being developed into those of manhood. As such, it forms the second stage in the extension of CHRIST'S Incarnation and the application of His Sacrifice. It is a positive and direct extension of the union of the creature with the Creator; for it places the recipient one degree nearer to the measure of the stature of the fulness of CHRIST, in the development of the Sacramental system. It is an indirect and negative application of the Sacrifice; for, whilst, on the theory presupposed, the neophyte has not sullied his baptismal garment, and hence requires not sacramental cleansing, yet the seven-fold outpouring of the HOLY GHOST is of itself a preventative against sin, by fulfilling the soul with the presence of divine power.

III. Of the Sacrament of the Most Holy Eucharist.

The child who has become the youth, or better, safer, more Catholic, the child still child-like, desires nearer intercourse, more converse, closer union with his GOD. The supernatural principle has been imparted in one sacrament; it has been strengthened with a seven-fold power in another; it requires to be matured and brought to perfection in a third. The ground has been prepared; the seed has been fertilized: these efforts must produce results. The recipient of grace would become, in a strict sense of the terms, an incorporated member, and not merely an associate of his Crucified LORD and

Master, and of the super-human Society which He founded. The confirmed in grace would be made, in the truest sense, a member of His Body, of His Flesh, and of His Bones. He would dwell in CHRIST, and would have CHRIST to dwell in him. He would be one with CHRIST, and would have CHRIST to be One with him. Need more be said on the Sacrament of Sacraments, which is so dear to the soul of all Catholics; or on its effects on their spiritual life, which are so near to their inmost conscience? I think not.

But, if this be so, the third sacrament of the mystical series, the Sacrament of the Altar, provides both the charter of incorporation and also affects the union itself, of the disciple with the Divine Master. By its reception the child of the FATHER, the inspired of the SPIRIT, becomes one with the Everlasting SON. The infant in the spiritual life who has developed into the youth has become matured in the divine image of the GOD-MAN. The change in this case has been more than one of degree, it has been one of kind. If in Baptism we were re-created in our human form, in Communion we have been incorporated into a form that is divine. If in Confirmation grace was added to our spiritual character and forced upon us from without, in the Eucharist we have been engulphed and only not absorbed in the Fount of all grace. In the other sacraments we receive a measure of grace and assimilate it to our needs: in this sacrament CHRIST receives us and assimilates us body, soul and spirit unto Himself. It is true that outwardly we eat the Flesh and drink the Blood of GOD; but the result which ensues is less that He is pleased to become One with us, than that we become, in some transcendental but most true manner, members of His sacred Body and of His Flesh and of His Bones.

In the case of the Holy Communion the relation between the sacraments on the one hand, and the Incarnation and Sacrifice on the other, is too self-evident to need more than an indication. If we believe, as we do believe, in the presence of CHRIST, really, truly and substantially under the Form of Bread and Wine in the Holy Eucharist, we cannot refuse assent to the position that the greatest of all sacraments is in itself an absolute extension of the Incarnation of our Divine LORD, and a direct application of His Sacrifice of Calvary. "Do this;" offer this Sacrifice; make the un-bloody Offering; renew this day by day, "as oft as ye shall drink It, in remembrance of Me;" renew this Sacrifice of Blood—is the command of CHRIST Himself, for the application of His Sacrifice. "Take, eat; This is My Body"—are the words of CHRIST which prove the extension of His Incarnation. In both cases—personally, to the individual souls of the faithful, man by man.

IV. Of the Sacrament of Penance.

Hitherto we have advanced in an unbroken course from Baptism to Communion. We have been led, through the intermediate and supplementary ceremonial of Confirmation, from the initiatory rite of the Faith to the function which matures and perfects the Christian man. We have followed the lead implicitly and without hesitation. But, to use a homely phrase, we have reckoned without our host. We have watched the career of the godly and upright, but have failed to take account of the influence effected in the life of man, by Satan, by sin and by spiritual death. This omission must now be repaired.

It matters little at what period of the spiritual existence the influence of the fourth sacrament comes into operation on the Christian soul. It may be the child of Baptism; it may be the youth of Confirmation; it may be the adult of Communion—in any case the baptized, or the confirmed, or the communicated, falls into sin, into deadly sin. In spite of the God-like principle infused by the first sacrament; in spite of the seven-fold gifts added by the second; in spite of divine grace communicated in the third—the soul sins wilfully against light and knowledge, against the power and influence of the SPIRIT, and the personal indwelling and presence of our Blessed LORD. For wilful, deadly sin, after baptism—the case alone which we consider—the Sacrament of Penance is the only covenanted mode of forgiveness: for venial sin, it is the best and the devoutest method. Covenanted, I say—because GOD does not bind Himself, although He wills that we shall be bound, to His own laws in the empire of grace, either more or less than in the realm of nature. Only—because man is not at liberty to look beyond the laws of grace, either less or more than outside the laws of nature, whatever course GOD may be pleased to adopt, in order to deal with human sin.

Does the sinner, then, feel the need of Absolution for committed sin; the need of an assured acquittal from the guilt of sin; the need of pardon from one who possesses both power and authority to forgive sin? Does he feel that sin, however he may define it, is in his soul; that sin, however it came thither, dwells in his soul and abides there; that whatever efforts he may make against sin, he is powerless to lessen or remove it thence; that he is only powerful to augment it or to place it there originally? Does he feel, again, that a mere sentiment of sorrow for sin is of itself insufficient to deal with sin in the present: or that amendment in the future, though essential in the divine scheme of pardon, does not of itself, and apart from the sacraments, cannot be and is not expiation for the past? Does he feel, once more, that our forgetfulness of sin does not necessarily imply forgiveness, but rather, only suggests our indifference: and that neglect of sin which we are conscious of having committed does not by any means prove its unimportance in GOD's sight, though it often leads on our part to callousness and impenitence?

If this be so, Penance, the fourth of the Sacraments of the Church, is open to the penitent—in the three-fold form of contrition out of the love of GOD, for having offended GOD; confession of sin to GOD's minister; and satisfaction, whether before or after priestly absolution, for sin committed. The relation which this sacrament bears towards CHRIST'S Incarnation and Sacrifice will be more or less intimate according to the view which we take of these two divine facts and of their connection with the Sacramental system. If we believe that the primary cause of the Incarnation was the sin of man, and that the only result of the Sacrifice was its expiation, the connection between Penance and its supernatural antecedents is absolute. The ordinance which alone completes the divine scheme of pardon must be inseparable from the integral parts of that scheme. Even if we admit that the sin of man was a secondary cause of the Incarnation, and that the Sacrifice fulfilled GOD'S will in that secondary cause, the connection of Penance with the results of such cause only falls short of being absolute. At the least, it is the only means with which we are acquainted for the fulfilment of the divine intention in the earlier expression of GOD'S will. As such, it clearly both extends the Incarnation and applies the Sacrifice to individual souls. For its operation is two-fold: its action is both negative and positive. It not only effects the pardon of sin, but re-imparts the grace which has been lost. It not only effects the forgiveness of the sinner, but re-instates him in the favour of GOD from which he has unhappily fallen. As these results are accomplished man by man, it may be affirmed that the fourth sacrament produces two effects. It directly applies the atonement of the world's sin to the individual of the race; and also, it indirectly fulfils the will of GOD, by re-uniting the creature who has severed himself from the divine union with the Creator—with GOD, Who is pleased again to consent to re-union with man.

The fifth and sixth Sacraments of the Church are not generally necessary to salvation. They are, when viewed abstractedly, essential to no individual of the race. They become essential to some persons only under certain well-defined conditions. Hence, it seems to be needless to dwell at length upon either. Both may be shown, equally with the preceding four sacraments, to bear the like relations to the same two divine facts, though relatively to each other in opposite ways and in different degrees. For, whilst the same two-fold law holds good in the case of Holy Matrimony and Holy Orders, which we have traced in the case of the earlier sacraments: yet, it may be shown that Marriage has a nearer relation to the union of the creature with the Creator, as producing elements for such union; and that Ordination has a closer affinity to the atonement for sin, inasmuch as its effects are pre-supposed in the act of forgiveness. But in either case, the more remote relationships may be perceived. For, in a secondary sense, the sacrament which ensues in the augmentation of the union is a preventative against sin: and indirectly, the sacrament which provides for the pardon of sin ensures in the act of forgiveness the mystery of the sinner's re-union.

However, these two sacraments cannot be overlooked: and this may be said of either of them:

V. An adult still, the child of four sacraments would fain partake the blessings, incur the responsibilities, and risk the dangers of a fifth. Himself, in one relation and in common with his parents, an earthly type of a heavenly Trinity, he would in fresh relationship self-repeat the mundane similitude, as one of a family triad, father, mother, child. Does he, then, feel it to be essential to perfect manhood, and to be advantageous to his spiritual aspirations, that he and another should become one in the LORD? If it be so, Holy Matrimony blesses the union of two with a sacramental oneness which earth cannot really divide, though it seeks to sever; and which heaven only will fully consummate, even if transcendentally, in the union of both with GOD.

VI. Once more, an adult still, the child of Baptism, the

youth of Confirmation, the communicant and the confessed, desires to partake of more blessings, ventures to incur higher responsibilities, and accepts the risk of greater dangers in another sacrament. His heart is fixed upon that which, if rightly conceived and consistently fulfilled, is the nearest approach to a life-long self-dedication of which man is capable. His natural gifts are such as make him wish to be a servant of servants to the faithful. His supernatural sympathies are such as make him wish to minister continually before the LORD and His Church in holy things. Does he, then, believe himself to be called of GOD to take upon him the onerous and ceaseless labour of the Priesthood—not as a profession or employment with certain duties to be performed at given times and seasons: but rather, as one of an order or a caste, whose time is at the command of every one but himself; and whose duties, far from consisting of certain actions more especially required at his hand, are life-long and never-ending? If it be so, Holy Church can supply this want also: and the sacrament of Orders more than fulfils his deepest aspirations, more than exhausts his most devout desires.

VII. Lastly, the child of earth, in the seven ages of man, is now aged. He may, indeed, be young in years; but we will suppose him to be old in grace. In any case, his last hour approaches. He has need, whether the want be realized or not, of strength for the way—the way of the valley of the shadow of death. How may he obtain it?

The sick man, as we suppose, in life has benefited by all the sacraments which his spiritual state demanded. The sacramental strength which he requires is three-fold in its form; and consists in part of a repetition of former receptions, and in part of a reception of another and a fresh means of grace. The Last Sacraments is the title of the final action of the Church on human souls, by which this composite result is attained. It were impossible that, at such a time, a want should be felt by the devout soul, and should not be supplied in the Church's Sacramental system.

It cannot be denied that there exists more mystery in connection with Unction, than with any other of the seven sacraments. This, perhaps, arises from a double cause: 1. the cessation of the miraculous results which originally followed its reception in primitive times—although such results have not been unknown in later days; and 2. the manner in which the Church has been guided to adapt its employment to the requirements of the faithful, in consequence of such cessation. In so complex a system as that of the sacraments, it is only reasonable to expect that some points should be more clear and some should be more obscure. This *a priori* expectation is realized in practice. The rite under consideration appears to be less distinct in its operation than others. And it is, perhaps, this want of plainness in its use that justified the singular account of the sacrament with which we are familiar in the XXXIX Articles—if indeed the words really apply to Unction, which may be open to doubt. The expression, a "corrupt following of the Apostles" appears to be as involved as the use of the sacrament itself. For, if Unction be declared to be a "following of the Apostles," it is not easy to justify the assertion that its use is "corrupt": and if its use be "corrupt," it is difficult to know how it can be a "following of the Apostles." Probably, if the words apply to Unction, the explanation glanced at above supplies a key to the true meaning of the expression: and the Article in question only intends to bind its signataries to the position, that the later development and the earlier employment of the sacrament are not conspicuously in accord. To this, of course, we can offer no objection: and as the Articles confine themselves to a further negative statement in regard to Unction, which is beyond all question true, and leave us free to explain and to employ it, as we are led of GOD, we can but seek light where it may be found, and follow the dictates which may be suggested by an enlightened conscience.

Without presuming to dogmatize on so difficult a topic of thought, it may be offered for consideration that the three-fold combination in the Last Sacraments unite to make the flight of the soul at the moment of death secure, if not facile. It cannot be supposed, however holy may have been his life, that as the end draws near the penitent will fail to desire once more to make a full, humble and hearty confession of his sins. It cannot be doubted, however often he may have received the Blessed Eucharist, that he will earnestly long for a last reception of the holy Mysteries. It may be taken for granted that, in his final conflict with the powers of evil, he will thankfully receive the supernatural aid which the Church supplies in Holy Anointing.

If this be so, for the last time the faithful Christian will receive absolution, perhaps after a life-long confession made not out of necessity but from humility, perhaps only after a penitent recital of his yet unforgiven transgressions. For the last time he will receive the sacred Species and be made one with Him as a Saviour, Whom he is so shortly to see as his Judge. For the only time, as a rule, in fulfilment of S. James' words and in accordance with the tradition of the Church he will receive the Unction of the SPIRIT'S power. Absolution will relieve him of the last remains of the guilt of sin ; and will free the soul from the burden of all earthly anxieties and fears. Viaticum will more than fulfil him with support for his journey ; and will supply him Angels' food for the soul's flight with Angels. Anointing will furnish him with spiritual power and strength for his final agony ; and will afford supernatural defence for the soul's last and fiercest attack by the ghostly foe.

Indeed, in a manner, the sacrament of Unction combines and gathers into one the spiritual effects of the other two mysteries by which it is preceded, and fulfils them with its own direct purpose in the Sacramental system of the Church. It removes the stain of past sin, and specially of the stain caused by the misuse of the five senses of the mortal frame; remedies the languor and infirmity entailed by sin which has been absolved; and remits all venial sin and lighter offences. It renews the oneness which we have attained, for the last time and imperfectly on earth, with the sacred, sinless Humanity of JESUS; and fortifies us thereby, in proportion as the sacrament is worthily received and as the oneness is complete, against the last violent assaults of Satan. But, it effects more of its own inherent power and virtue, as the last of the Sacraments of the Church. It calms the natural dread and terror of approaching dissolution. It quiets our fear of impending judgment. It illumines the gloom which has already begun to surround us. It produces a supernatural atmosphere of light in which, to some extent but not yet fully, we see things as they are, and not as they appear; we see ourselves not as man sees us, but as GOD beholds. And lastly, it fills our soul with resignation, with patience, with pious and holy joy; and it enables us to await with confidence the coming of our Divine LORD to us and our approach to Him, prepared to yield, nay, desirous and anxious to yield into His hand all we are and all we have received, as into the hands of an Almighty Father and a most merciful Saviour.

The three-fold constitution of the Last Sacraments of the Church—Confession, Communion, Unction—to a large extent indicates the relation which they collectively bear to the two cardinal dogmas, CHRIST'S Incarnation and Sacrifice. The relationship which the two earlier sacraments individually bear to them has been already dwelt upon. The relationship of Unction of course suffers, to a degree, from the obscurity, before observed, which surrounds the sacrament. But, if we remember the influence which human sin has been permitted to exert upon the one dogma, and the acknowledged antagonism which exists between human sin and the other dogma, we shall not fail to perceive the relationship in question. If Holy Unction supplies strength for the last conflict with man's great enemy, Satan, to separate him for ever from divine incorporation, and to cause him to fall for ever from divine grace, it clearly extends one degree further the mystery which unites the creature with the Creator ; it certainly applies in a seventh and final way the mystery by which the sins of the world are atoned to the Justice of GOD. Devout meditation will show how these several elements when combined affect, or are affected by, the dogmas to which they are thus individually related.

Such, in theological language, is my apology, in a brief and superficial form, for the seven-fold Sacramental system of GOD'S Church. In spite of the inadequacy of its treatment, I am bold to enquire—Can any system be more perfect ? Can any be more complete ? What may be absent ? What has been overlooked ? Is any period of human life forgotten ? Is any position in man's complicated existence left unprovided for ? Is any spiritual want, under any temporal emergency, not supplied ? So far as man can see—there is none.

It is the seven-fold system by which sin in the soul of man is in course of expiation and atonement, under the divine Power of GOD the HOLY GHOST. In course of expiation, thus: 1. Baptism, negatively, places man in a position not to displease GOD ; and hence, in a position not to sin. 2. Confirmation, positively, infuses power and ability to do good ; and hence, to resist future attacks of sin ? 3. Communion makes us one with the Pattern and Representative Man ; makes our doings His work ; makes us, so far as we are united to Him, sinless. 4. Confession conquers and uproots old sins, directly ; and indirectly, imparts grace to prevent the soul relapsing into sin. 5. Marriage gives a religious sanction to GOD'S Will in social life ; imparts the Church's blessing ; and removes temptation to sin. 6. Orders give power and authority to their recipients to forgive past sin, and to impart grace to withstand future sin to those to whom they minister. 7. The Last Sacraments afford supernatural strength for the soul's final conflict with sin and death and hell, in her last dread agony. Infancy, youth, manhood, old age are thus all and each provided for. Entrance into the world, and the soul's flight from the world, are both remembered. Sin is dealt with negatively and positively: retrospectively in the past, prospectively in the future. A single estate is equally regarded with married life. The expulsion of sin from the soul is not less an object of care than the infusion of grace. Man not only is relieved of self and Satan, but is made one with GOD. I ask again: Is any position in man's many-sided life forgotten? Is any want in his endless needs left unsupplied? There is none. The Sacramental system of the Catholic Church, in its seven-fold form of extending CHRIST'S Incarnation and applying His Sacrifice to the individual soul, man by man, is perfect, unique and exhaustive.

Of course, the spiritual interpretation which may inhere in the Sacramental system has afforded a wide field of treatment to mystical writers. Such a view can only be glanced at here, from two authors. Taking the Sacraments in the order in which they have been above considered, namely, 1. Baptism, 2. Confirmation, 3. Eucharist, 4. Penance, 5. Matrimony, 6. Orders, 7. Unction: The one writer perceives in the first, seventh and third Sacraments, an adumbration of the three Theological Virtues, Faith, Hope and Charity; and in the second, fourth, sixth and fifth, the representation of the four Cardinal Virtues, Fortitude, Justice, Prudence and Temperance. The other sees in the first Sacrament a mystic allusion to the natural act of birth; in the second, bodily growth and development; in the third, earthly nourishment; in the fourth, the cure of disease; in the fifth, the preservation and increase of the human race; in the sixth, public rule and government; and in the last, with a view of course to the original institution, restoration to health—perhaps we may venture to suggest, as an alternative, the restitution of all things at the last Great Day. Whilst a third Schoolman (whom I quote at third hand) gives the following exposition of the sacraments, without making any reference to the theoretic import of the Holy Eucharist :—

"The Sacraments are conducive to three benefits, which, however cannot be received without faith, namely, 1. the humiliation, 2. the instruction, and 3. the exercise of the soul. 1. They conduce to humiliation, inasmuch as they subject us to material things. Our soul is higher in dignity than matter; but we must learn to submit ourselves to a lower nature as a punishment for our sin; having yielded up ourselves to sensual desires, we must confess in all humility that we have become dependent on the sensual. 2. The Sacraments conduce to instruction; because by their means we are called from our worldly distractions to a remembrance of the Divine. Man, weakened by sin and prone to the sensual, can only by a sensible symbol be reminded of GOD, and summoned to reflect upon Him. 3. The Sacraments also serve as an exercise. Of such exercise we stand in perpetual need, for we cannot remain in this life without activity. We are directed to action as to that in which we exercise our forces, and learn to distinguish good from evil. Here, however, is the danger that we may allow ourselves to be enticed by the good things of a worldly practical life, so as to be lured away from the thought of GOD and His Commandments. This danger is anticipated by the Sacraments, inasmuch as they constantly remind us of the higher destination of our souls, and to the enjoyment of the divine presence, and give us a foretaste of the Divine. Thus, they afford a sufficient employment and exercise of our forces, that we may not be tempted to yield to worldly pleasures."

IV.

In meditating on the Sacramental system of the Church in relation to sin, there are three points, more or less affecting each of the divine modes for its expiation, which demand consideration. 1. The sacraments must be duly administered. 2. They must be worthily received. 3. They must be honestly acted up to. We will take these points in their order, and in as brief a manner as may be compatible with clearness.

I. The sacraments must be duly administered. This is the first essential in regard to their superhuman effect upon sin. For, however worthily the sacraments may be received, and however honestly they may be acted up to, if they be not duly administered, all is lost, all is invalid. This result is of necessity from the nature of things—the sacraments being divine agencies for dealing with human sin. If the agency be not perfect, the result of its action must fall short of perfection.

What, then, are the conditions under which the sacraments are duly administered? Three elements are required for their perfection. They must be performed, 1. by a competent person; 2. in the right way; 3. with a proper intention. The intention, the way, and the person are decided by Holy Church. 1. The person, as a rule, must be a priest, whom the Church appoints as her representative in the administration of the sacrament. Baptism indeed may be performed by a lay person in cases of emergency: and Orders can only be conferred by a Bishop. A Priest is needed for the other extensions of the Incarnation, or applications of the Sacrifice, even in the one which elevates social marriage into the sacrament of Holy Matrimony. 2. The way, mode, or manner, as the next element of sacramental perfection, is the manner, mode or way which the Church has ordained : the contemporary combination of the matter of each sacrament respectively with its form of words. The matter not less than the form of words, of course, vary in each case. Both may be learnt from the offices of the Church. It is only necessary to say, in this place, that the matter of the sacraments, speaking generally, consists, either separately or in combination, of actions on the part of the priest, or of words on the part of the penitent, or of the elements of water, flour and water, wine and water, or the creature of oil. 3. The intention, as

U

the last element of perfection, consists simply in the will or wish which the Church feels or desires to carry into effect, in the administration of each sacrament, according to its object. The wish or will of the Church, must be the wish or will of the administrator; and the intention of the Church is supposed to exist in the mind of the celebrant by the fact of his ministration.

These three requisites for the due administration of the sacraments we obtain in the Church of GOD. All of them are more or less essential to a due and valid administration.

II. The sacraments must be worthily received. However valid and regular may be their ministration, if they be not received by the penitent, as a rule, with due preparation, with good disposition at the time, and with a right intention for the future, they are valueless as a means of extending CHRIST'S Incarnation and of applying His Sacrifice to the individual soul.

Take the single case of Confession, which illustrates all the requirements. The sacrament of Penance, in order to be efficacious, must be administered by a Priest of the Church, in a form of absolution sanctioned by the Church, with the intention of the Church. Suppose all this to be done. In the case of a worthy reception, all is valid. A sin-forgiving absolution is the result. But, suppose the last element to be wanting. Suppose the reception to be not worthy, to be unworthy; a sin-forgiving absolution is not the result. Rather, the result is sacrilegious. For instance: granted the person, the form, the intention; if the penitent be not worthy of pardon, from the nature of the case, GOD'S absolution cannot ensue, even though man's authorized word of pardon be pronounced. And observe: the penitent is not worthy if he be not contrite, for the love of GOD; if he make not a full, humble and hearty confession of sin; if he be not prepared to forsake his sin in the future. In such a case the sacrament is unworthily received. The conditions have been violated. Absolution is null and void in grace.

III. The sacraments must be honestly acted up to. Due and valid administration, so far as the individual soul is concerned, is nothing ; worthy and good reception, so far as the individual soul is concerned, is nothing—if, after their reception, the individual soul fails honestly to live in conformity with them. For instance : Of what practical use is Baptism, if a layman lives the life of a cultivated heathen, of an unbeliever, of an atheist ; and if he dies the death of a vegetable or animal ? Of what benefit to himself or others are Orders to a Priest, or self-dedication to a Religious, if either of them live like a layman ; a life of pleasure, ease and self-seeking ; the life of a man of the world, not of a man of GOD ? The character in both cases remains ! No doubt. But in regard to the individual soul, and with a view to human sin, the result is not the same. The recipient is not in the same position. He is in a worse. Even if he repent at the last, his repentance must be far more deep, his guilt will be far greater—as one who has received grace and has fallen from it, as one who has been received into covenant with GOD and has done despite unto the SPIRIT of His grace.

V.

The last question for our consideration is a personal one : How do these three points in the divine method of expiating human sin affect us personally ? How are we individually concerned with the due administration of the sacraments, with their worthy reception at the present, with their honest after-use ?

(i.) The inquiry touching the due administration of the sacraments, hardly affects us individually, being one which is altogether external to oneself, being one upon which the Church alone can pronounce. Yet, the unhealthy instinct of some persons sometimes import this external element into their meditations at wrong times and inconvenient occasions ; which is only equivalent to saying, that there are occasions and times in which the inquiry is neither inconvenient nor wrong. Hence, this result ensues. Instead of using these means of grace, such persons dispute over them. But, such an inquiry does not necessarily enter into the line of argument adopted in this Retreat. And a Retreat, in the ordinary use of all the terms, is no fitting time or occasion to discuss religious difficulties of this description. Thus much, however, may be said, that we may not be supposed to avoid any real difficulty. The question of the due administration of the sacraments is one with which the Church alone is concerned, or in truth is alone competent to deal. Of course, this question is liable to be raised in our minds at any period of our spiritual career; and being raised, must be settled by the use of such helps as GOD is pleased to place within our reach. If we be persuaded, in our inmost conscience, that where we spiritually live and move and have our being the sacraments are not duly administered—in GOD'S holy Name, we must depart whither there is no doubt of their administration. The soul cannot be spiritually starved. But, if we be persuaded that they are duly given and may be duly taken; that the authority on which they are offered is sufficient; that such authority is expressive of GOD'S will—then, in such a case, it is our duty not to discuss the sacraments but to use them. The soul must be spiritually nourished.

There is, indeed, no more fatal obstacle to growth in holiness, than to cavil where we should adore. It places us in a false position in relation to grace; in the position of critic, instead of that of suppliant. It places us above, instead of below, the sacraments. Our main business in life is to save our souls. It tends more to this end that we use, than that we discuss the sacraments. If we were to bestow upon the use of the sacraments half the amount of religious energy which some persons give to the question of their validity, we should more certainly advance in godliness of life. If we were to become more loving, humble, patient, pure; less distracted in prayer, and more collected at all times; less irritable when thwarted, and less hard and intolerant in word and thought, we should be enabled to take a more just view even of controversial questions, and we should be more likely to arrive at a true estimate of the amount of authority on which are administered the Sacraments of the Church. Have we personally failed under either of these two conditions?

(ii.) Apart from the critical faculty in controversial questions, the sacraments must be worthily received. Have we personally fulfilled this condition? One test will suffice. There is no need to speak in general terms of good dispositions for receiving the sacraments. They vary, of course, with different means of grace, and cannot be summarized in a single clause. But, in the case of Holy Communion how do we stand? And the test I would offer is moral, not of faith, not of ceremonial. How do we prepare ourselves to come worthily to GOD'S Altar? Do we throw ourself, mind and heart and soul and strength, into our preparation? Do we remember, as between GOD and our soul alone in the universe, Whom we are to meet in the most Holy Eucharist, and whom GOD is to meet? Who GOD is, and who we are? Do we reflect, that it is not impossible, nay, in the uncertainty of life that it is not improbable, the next meeting of those two beings in the universe may take place before the great White Throne? may take place where the conditions of meeting will be changed, if not reversed—when the giver will be our Judge, as the Creator, and the receiver, as the creature, will be judged? Do we prepare ourselves accordingly? This is the test. I will specify no given sin. I will not even speak of deadly sin. I will only inquire : Do we venture to receive our Saviour now and our Judge hereafter, in both cases our GOD ; and do we deliberately, willingly, knowingly, consciously retain in our soul one single venial sin?

(iii.) If we prepare ourselves to receive the blessed sacraments by this test, there is every chance, there is almost a moral certainty that in their after-action they will be honestly employed. Yet, human nature, even when supernaturally strengthened, is weak. With every firm and good purpose to the contrary; after repeated and earnest self-assurance, promise to our confessor, determination before our Angel, vow to GOD; in spite of many opportunities not to fall again, and self-interest and the welfare of others being involved in our not falling again—yet, as a fact, we do. As a matter of sad, painful, bitter, humiliating, reiterated experience, we do fall again and again into the sin which doth so easily beset us. Here, also, we need specify no special sin. Here, also, one test only need be applied. It is this. Do we, after worthy reception of holy mysteries duly administered, do we honestly act up to the union which has been effected and the grace which has been imparted, in this one point, the occasion of sin? Is the person or place, is the time or season, is the thought or the sight, is the real pleasure or the supposed duty, is the occupation, trade, employment, or business—which once led to sin, scrupulously avoided for the future? Remember, what has been, in the spiritual life, may be again. Do we then deliberately, willingly, knowingly, consciously, place ourself in the way of the occasion of our sin? Or, do we rather avoid the occasion of sin as poison, as death to the soul?

End of the Retreat.
CONCLUDING ADDRESS.

TO one class of minds, perhaps to the average intellect, the great mystery which meets us in our earthly career is the end of it; the great mystery of life is death. To another class of minds, perhaps to the less common and more speculative, the mystery of origination appears to be the most marvellous: the great mystery of life is birth. But of three chief mysteries in the present state of existence—birth, life, death; whence we come, and what we actually are, and whither we go—the central mystery, to thoughtful men, for depth, interest and importance, is unsurpassed and unsurpassable. The all-engrossing mystery is that of life.

Naturally, we think more of the mystery of birth, because we have no recollection of it, and speculation has free scope for argument and theory: and of death, because we are powerless to anticipate it, and the possibilities which may follow must be, in any case, momentous. Naturally, we think less of the mystery of life, simply because we have experience of it, daily and hourly, for months and years together—whenever we will we may realize it. Yet, a mystery with which we are familiar is not less mysterious than one we know not of, or one we cannot personally realize. And, if we apply our minds to the mystery of life, we shall see, probably, even more and deeper reasons to wonder at its marvels, than at the mystery either of birth or of death.

The very continuance of this state of existence—which began with birth—for threescore-and-ten years, adds only not infinity to the mystery of life: and the certitude we possess of another condition of being—of which death alone is the portal—adds positive infinity to the marvel. Origination and decease are instantaneous in their operation. GOD spake and man was created; He summons and man ceases to exist. GOD breathed into his nostrils, and man became a living soul; He withholds His inspiration, and the work of His hands yields up the ghost. Simple, sovereign and efficient acts are these of divine volition on the part of GOD'S Majesty, in relation to human birth and human death. But life—can any single word convey a more complex and complicated system of being, than the one which describes man's present mode of existence? Can any word express more in relation to our inmost selves, than life?

We are wont to think and speak of GOD, as the Maker, Redeemer and Inspirer of men. Few thoughts are more becoming for a Christian to entertain, than those which unite him in meditation to the several Persons of the Holy TRINITY, in their respective relations to man's creation, to man's purchase, to man's sanctification. But there is another aspect of the GODHEAD, which we should contemplate, that intimately affects the question of life—life in the abstract; life, as it will now again present itself to us; the renewed life, after a time of retreat, for men and women living in the world. And this aspect is revealed through the medium of the words, GOD the Preserver of man. These words disclose also the presence of two hostile and contradictory theories of life, to one of which we must become pledged. If we accept them, in their integrity, the words place us in accord with a ceaseless stream of inspired tradition, from the very first. If we reject their plain meaning, we find ourselves in harmony with the teaching of a pagan and anti-Christian philosophy. Preservation is an expression of the attribute of GOD which alone explains the mystery that we are about to consider—the mystery of life. It is at once the justification of Catholic tradition, and a defence against the fallacies of falsehood.

II.

GOD the Preserver of man. This formula supplies a key to the mystery of man's life—of the life of man, the image of GOD, in whom the eternal counsels of the divine decrees was fulfilled, in the union of the creature with the Creator. Apart from this attribute of the DEITY—Preservation—it is not too much to say, that the work of creation would be imperfect; that the work of redemption would be imperfect; that the work of inspiration would be imperfect. And why? Because, in each case the means would be inadequate to the end: because the final cause of all three operations of the GODHEAD being the increase of accidental glory, such increase of GOD'S glory could not occur without the co-operation of the attribute of Preservation. The ultimate salvation of man—whether there be many that be saved or whether there be few—is a necessary element in the greater glory of GOD: and towards such ultimate salvation, the preservation of man by GOD directly tends. Apart from this attribute, man, made in the image of GOD-MAN, could not exist to realize his creation and to become one with his Creator: man, bought with the precious Blood of JESUS, could not benefit by the purchase and work out his own salvation with fear and trembling: man, sanctified by the Holy SPIRIT of CHRIST, could not bring forth fruit unto holiness and in the end everlasting life. Apart from the preservation of GOD, towards the work of His Almighty hand, none of these results could ensue to man. And the failure of any one of them, of any two, or of all three, ensures the failure of the end for which human nature was first made, was then made anew, and is again and again re-made God-like.

Certain so-called philosophic theories, widely held at the present time under various hard names, deny all this; deny that GOD, a Personal GOD, is the Preserver of His own creation in general, and in particular of man, as the highest act of creative power. They affirm that creation, once an accomplished fact—though by what agency, they cannot agree amongst themselves to determine—or the principle of development or evolution once organized, GOD'S work in the universe was left either to its own inherent power, or even to the imperious and unbending laws of nature, stamped upon matter by the great First Cause.

This, to speak plainly, is a pagan, a non-Catholic opinion: if for no further reason, at least for this, that it ignores and denies the Christian dogma, that GOD is the Preserver of creation. But, upon this false system we need not dwell further, beyond saying thus much. Of late, the opinion has advanced from the realm of nature, where little could be said on its behalf, to the empire of grace, where nothing can be said, at least by a believer in Revelation. Not content with limiting the attributes of the Eternal FATHER, in the fact of creation, falsehood has advanced into the domain of Redemption and Sanctification. It denies the continuous work of the Everlasting SON, in man's purchase by the Sacrifice of Calvary, and His ceaseless intercession in Heaven. It denies the continuous labour of the Con-substantial and Co-equal SPIRIT, in man's individual sanctification, through the Sacramental system of the Church. It denies both: denies them, not perhaps in set terms, for it affects to ignore the Christian Religion as a philanthropic though unintelligent superstition, which is now out of date; but denies them in its logical results, when perfected from the teaching of the Despised Galilean. But the Church believes in both, believes in all three dogmas. The Church believes in GOD the Protector, as well as in, though not as distinct from GOD the Creator, GOD the Saviour, GOD the Inspirer. And it is in the realization of this attribute of DEITY, Preservation, that the mystery of man's life consists.

Let us endeavour to estimate this position clearly, even at the cost of repetition. GOD is not only our Creator, Redeemer, Sanctifier. He is also our Preserver. This, in the order of grace, GOD not only decrees our first beginning and determines our last end. He also ceaselessly wills our support and continuance at each instant of our being, through the whole course of our earthly career. This, in the order of nature. Such is the Christian view of man's existence in life. In this overpowering thought consists the mystery—GOD ever-present with man : the Creator ever protecting the result of His creation ; the Redeemer ever preserving the object of His Passion ; the Sanctifier ever sustaining the being whom He is pleased to inspire.

No wonder the ancient heathen world declined to contemplate an ever-present DEITY ; although it failed to see beyond the relation of the Creator to the created, and knew not at all of the attributes of redemption and inspiration. No wonder the civilized paganism of to-day—although living in an atmosphere of Christianity of which it cannot really be unconscious and by which it is influenced in spite of itself—declines to conceive such intimate union as exists between the Redeemer and the redeemed, between the Inspirer and whom He is pleased to sanctify. The nameless vices of old, which we know or know of, hardened the heart of the elder heathenism. The scarcely less vicious state of modern society, in almost every relation of life—now and then exposed when, as lately, the thinly curtained picture is unveiled in the courts of law and the moral leprosy is exhibited—deadens the baptized, even if the apostate conscience of the younger paganism. Both are utterly and hopelessly inconsistent with the Christian belief in GOD, the Protector of man. They rightly admit that light and darkness, holiness and sin, have and can have no concord. Un-regenerate nature and nature regenerated indeed, but fallen into a depth of iniquity even more profound than before, combine to deny the absolute, perfect and constant intercourse between GOD and man. From their own point of view, holding the opinion which they profess, living the life which they now lead—they are right, undeniably right. The intercourse which they can alone realize were impossible. Yet, the attribute of preservation is of faith. In spite of sin—

sin resisted not indulged ; sin committed but absolved—a Christian humbly believes what is inconceivable to a heathen. He believes, on sufficient authority, that the Source of Light is pleased to illumine a darkness which is not self-created, and the All-pure is pleased to protect the non-pure, if not the impure ; that GOD is the ever-present Preserver of man from birth to life, in life to death, through death to life eternal.

GOD'S protectorate over man in life is only one instance of a general law of universal application ; namely, that GOD is the living Preserver of all created things. What men call Law, the law of nature or science, only means the expression of GOD'S irresistible will and pleasure. It does not mean an invariable result of cause and effect, apart from an Almighty and Ever-present Divine Personality—at least, it does not mean this to a Christian. But, of this matter we have before spoken. The position is only re-asserted in order to allow the human race to be included in the world-wide truth. Man is not outside such protectorate. It might even be said, in view of his origination and destiny, that man stands in the centre of the divine scheme ; that in view of the earthly career of the Incarnated GOD, the universal protectorate existed on behalf of man, was developed specially for man, is continued only for man's sake.

For instance : It is a law of nature that man is born, lives, dies. Yes : but only under the consent of GOD the Preserver. Man might have lived without being born. He need not die because he has lived. And of these three conditions of humanity, Science can tell us, after a fashion, why man was born—how he originated. Philosophy can learnedly discourse of life—how he exists. Medicine can explain why he dies—how he ceases to exist—to its own satisfaction. But Theology alone satisfies a Christian consciousness on the mystery of man's existence. Theology teaches that man's existence, from the cradle to the grave, is but the expression of the divine Will of GOD the Preserver. It is by GOD'S almighty Will alone that man, the unit of the race, each individual soul, emerges from his original and abysmal nothingness. It is by His Will that man's spirit returns to GOD Who gave it. It is by His Will, in the intermediate time of life, between man's beginning and his end, that he lives and moves and has his being. It is GOD the Preserver Who decides upon the birth, the life, the death of man.

The mystery of human existence, therefore, is only the expression of the Will of GOD the Preserver. Consider, then, some few of the facts of life, upon a single side only of its complicated being, its natural side. In the familiarity which life-long experience produces, the marvel has lost much of its mysteriousness. But enough remains to absorb our attention.

Take, in the first place, the mere extent of human life, at any given moment; a numerical extent, observe, over and above the existences which have been in the past, and will be in the future. Try to realize the fact, that something like twelve-hundred millions of intelligent beings people our planet at the present time. Try to realize that these myriads are beings who have their own personal individualities, of which we are types: who are endowed with a three-fold nature, of body, soul and spirit, such as we are endowed with: of whom, to speak of one side only of their composite existence, each one is possessed of his own hopes and fears; his own feelings and affections; his own memory, understanding and will; his own pains and joys; his own blessings, trials, sympathies and sorrows. Try to realize this initial and elemental fact in human life, stupendous as it is to grasp; and then pass on in thought to another fact of nature.

As Christians we believe in a particular Providence: that is to say, we believe in GOD the Preserver of all the creatures of His hand. What does this belief involve with regard to the initial fact we have considered, the fact that twelve-hundred millions of GOD'S accountable creatures people this earth? I answer, it involves many truths, of which some may be named. It involves the fact, that it is only of the ceaseless energizing power of the great First Cause which preserves each unit of these millions from returning instantly to its original abyss of nothingness. It involves the fact, that every individual unit exists in the mind of GOD the Preserver, as if it alone existed in the universe ; and that nothing happens to any one created being without the foreknowledge of GOD in the past, without the assent of GOD in the present, without the permission of GOD in the future. It involves the fact, that not one human personality was born apart from His permissive Will ; that none lives without His constant supervision ; that none dies except after His sovereign decree and sentence. It involves the fact, that no created individuality can act or speak or think in this life, unseen by or unknown to His Omniscience ; and to us at least who are Christians, it necessitates the conclusion that in the next life all will be brought to judgment, man by man, by His Omnipotence, and all will receive judgment from His unerring Wisdom.

These are further mysteries of human life in relation to GOD the Preserver.

Again : Pass from the sum total of human life, and what affects the aggregate ; and consider never so superficially the life of any unit of these created myriads—your life and mine. Try to realize the truth, that it is due to a particular Providence that you and I were so much as called out of our original nothingness ; that being born, we lived ; that living, we have not died—you and I, personally and individually, apart from the greatness of created humanity : you and I, under the never-ceasing care of an Almighty First Cause, under the ever-present protection of GOD the Preserver of man. Try to realize that this is true, not only in general terms, but in every particular instance, and in all the events of life.

Take a few cases for consideration on one side only of the mystery of existence. To what cause do we attribute the fact, that each day, as it comes, we are permitted to pass in our wonted health and usual manner ; that at night we lie down to sleep in confidence which is not disappointed; that in the morning we awake with renewed vigour for the work of a fresh daily term of vitality? I answer: whether we allow it or not—to the personal, living Will of a particular Providence, of GOD the Preserver. To what cause, again, is it due, that each respiration of the lungs enables us to breathe; that every palpitation of the heart circulates the blood; that the power of mind over matter is exercised every minute of the day, in the muscular and other movements of our members; and that all the organs in our highly intricate bodily mechanism duly perform their proper functions, escape disorder, and continue our course of life? I reply: to the ever-present Personality of a particular Providence, of GOD the Preserver.

Or, once more, to speak of the very commonest matters, yet not so common but that we may perform them to the greater glory of GOD—to what cause can we assign the result that day by day and many times a day, what we eat does not choke us, and what we drink does not suffocate us; that appetite and digestion precede and follow respectively the reception of food; that in health sustenance nourishes, whilst in sickness it injures us; and that, in any case, substances external to ourselves become assimilated with our nature, when received inwardly, and affect, for good or ill, every component part of man's complex system, even to our intellectual and spiritual forces? Once more, the same explanation only can be given—to a particular Providence, to GOD the Preserver of His people.

Nor, if we pass to another class of life's mysteries, is the supporting protectorate of the First Cause less obvious to a thoughtful mind. Take a single case on which to exercise devout thought: Why do we—you and I—escape a thousand accidents, even if we fall into the thousand-and-first, in this age of accidents, hourly, daily, year after year: accidents by danger and speed of travel; by carelessness and recklessness in others or oneself; by scamped labour and other deliberate wickedness; by fire, flood, explosion, lightning on land, tempest by sea; by murder from anger, jealousy, envy; by direct judgment of GOD for the sins we have committed, or intended, or wished to commit; or by causes beyond the control of human agency.

Or: Take another class, in a different field of the mysteries of life, and a single instance in the class: Why do we enjoy and continue to enjoy those faculties which we share in common with the Angelic Intelligences—our mental and intellectual faculties; faculties which raise man above his natural tendencies, in their perfection; but apart from which, in their withdrawal or decay, man becomes a mere wreck of his former God-like self, and sinks beneath the level of the animal creation, in common with which he shares his bodily organization? Why, I ask, do we continuously enjoy consciousness of existence, of being, of life; of feeling, moving acting, thinking? Why do we enjoy the power of self-introspection, of retrospection in the past, of anticipation in the future, of realization in the present? Why do we enjoy the faculty of passing moral judgment on ourselves or others, the gifts of reason and argument, talents natural or acquired, the genius of intellect, instincts of discovery or invention, the power of determination or will which can make us do or suffer anything? The like answer must be made. It is only at the pleasure of a Personal DEITY. It is solely by the Will of GOD the Preserver of man.

Hitherto, we have contemplated only the natural mysteries of life, those that are common to all the sons of Adam. But how great is the additional mystery of our supernatural existence, over and above the marvels of creation, viewed in the light of the divine support of GOD the Preserver! Who can explain, I will not say the higher mysteries of the GODHEAD in relation to Himself, but the lower mysteries of grace in relation to man, when their effects severally are estimated upon the new creation in the Church of CHRIST? Take but a single case, though undoubtedly a wide one, the case of the holy Sacraments; and take it not in detail, but in broad outline: and who can explain the Sacramental system, in its principle, in its agency, in its operation, or in its result, apart from the truth which we are considering, the protectorate over man by GOD? Even Catholics do not understand although they accept what non-Catholics reject, equally without understanding, the sacramental principle, agency, operation and result. No. Yet, we firmly believe the superhuman cause and consequence. We believe in the spiritual effects produced by ceremonial form and material substance and human agency in conjunction with spoken words and simple acts, said or done either alone or together with a given intuition, either to the outward form of man, or even to his inmost self. We believe in the results of the Sacraments of the Church on the bodies and souls of men, by the power of the HOLY GHOST. And we adore in consequence of our belief. We adore in the presence of spiritual effects which we, Catholics, are assured ensue; of effects which the world, through its authorized organs of opinion, sneers at as magical, and depreciates as superstition; of effects which we know to be those of the seven-fold sacramental system. We adore, I say, because here, equally with the case of natural results in daily life, we are enabled to perceive the actual interposition of a particular Providence in a supernatural kingdom; we can see the agency, whether direct or mediate, of GOD the Preserver of man.

Into this mystery of life, in both its aspects, natural and supernatural, and as affecting both the soul and body of man, we are again on the point of re-entering. In retreat, although we have not been actually outside or apart from the mystery; yet, in thought we have placed ourselves there, by the contemplation of co-ordinate truths. After retreat, although we must not forget the truths which are external, but not in opposition to the mystery; yet, practically we shall be surrounded by it, and its claims will continually force themselves upon our notice. We are about to return, after more or less severance for a time from its absorbing cares, to our life in the world. To men and women living in the world, the mystery of a divine protectorate in creation is all-important. We are thankful to believe in the truth, that GOD is the Preserver of man.

III.

We now approach the conclusion of our Retreat. To-day we come to our last address. Let us shortly retrace the steps which have led us to this end. The subject-matter of our meditations has been certain first principles of divine faith in relation to human sin; to sin in the soul of man, in your soul and in mine; to man's sin under various conditions and from different points of view, theoretic and practical. It has divided itself into these three heads: I. GOD, the Creator, the Redeemer, the Sanctifier, in relation to sin; II. Man, made, purchased, made again, in relation to sin; III. GOD in union with Man, in the Incarnation, on Calvary, through the Sacraments, in relation to sin. Such are the simple, elementary truths of our holy Religion, dogmatically, which have been placed before you in regard to the most practical of all questions to men and women on the path of life which leads to death, and after death to judgment. Such are the truths which we have now to work out in our lives in the world, under the supporting and protecting care of GOD the Preserver.

At the outset you were warned that two objects would be kept in view during retreat: 1. to recall to mind old, perhaps half-forgotten truths in regard to the sin of man; in order, 2. to place before the conscience old, perhaps half-forgotten sins in regard to the truth of GOD. My part it was to treat these divine common-places as simply as might be, and as plainly as possible. It was your part to choose one or more points in each address; to meditate upon them, and work them out for yourself; to apply them to your own case, and to become self-acquitted or self-condemned ; and to make such resolutions as you might be prompted to make by GOD the HOLY GHOST. In whatever way the part of either has been performed, its performance is now a matter of history, the practical effect of which is concentrated on the concluding feature—the resolutions which we have been moved to form.

These resolutions in regard to sin would naturally include a reference to the past, to the present, and to the future.

1. As to the past, they would be suggestive of such thoughts as these : Have I realized what sin actually is, and the amount of sin within the soul ? Have I grasped my ruling passion or master-sin, and learned in what it consists, and how it has mastered me ? Have I, by self-examination, discovered what my faults may be which do not rise to sins, or which in character are accounted only as venial sins ? Have I fully repented of my sin—as fully as if assured that no future opportunity would be afforded me for penitence ? Have I repented as I once hoped and still hope to repent before I die, with a repentance not to be repented of, and as GOD, my Guardian Angel, my spiritual guide, my own conscience bid me repent ? Have I repented, as the Church commands, by a humble submission to the discipline of penance, under the protection of GOD the Preserver of man ?

2. As to the present, our resolutions could hardly fail to suggest these further thoughts : Am I quite sure that my self-searching has been effective, and that my repentance has been accepted ? Am I persuaded that I am actually freed from the burden of past sin, and that I have not so much as a stain of guilt upon my soul ? Am I satisfied with the means which I have taken for my freedom from sin and freedom from guilt, and with the authority on which the means have been adopted ? Am I content—having done all, all that I know I ought to have done, all that I believe I ought to have done to be freed from sin—am I content, so far as the present is concerned and duty calls, to await my summons before the great

White Throne and the judgment to follow by GOD the Preserver of man?

3. As to the future, our resolutions must in no wise fail to suggest these final thoughts: Shall I adhere to my self-made promises when the Retreat is over; when I leave behind its influence, and the influence of the world surrounds me; when its thoughts gradually fade and worldly thoughts imperceptibly take their place; and when I look forward to a fresh Retreat, which GOD the Preserver of man may not in His goodness vouchsafe? And if, as a fact, I shall thus adhere in the future, why do I think so now? Was my penitence in the past so earnest and deep; is my assurance of forgiveness in the present so positive and absolute—that I have reasonable hopes, as a rational being as well as a Christian, for my resolutions in the future, that in due time they will become promises fulfilled?

However imperfectly in the case of both, I assume that we have attempted, under the protection of GOD the Preserver, to do our duty. The question, then, which arises for the soul to answer, at the close of a Retreat, is this: Granted that, in the course of these meditations, I have done all that I ought to have done, what lack I yet? The reply, in regard to the practical aspect of the Retreat is plain and decided: After penitence in the past and assurance at the present, I must avoid sin in the renewed life in the world, on which, by GOD'S grace, I am now about to enter.

Our concluding Retreat-thoughts may be given to this subject. They will be three-fold in form. For there are three ways of avoiding sin in the renewed life in the world after retreat, under the support of GOD the Preserver. In the first place, we must be ever watchful against our besetting sin. In the next place, we must be always jealous of falling into little faults. In the last place, we must never cease to be persevering in good works. We will take these ways of avoiding sin in their order.

IV.

1. We must be watchful against our besetting sin.

It is no figure of speech, but indicates a stern reality, to say, that life is a warfare. It is, in truth, a ceaseless, wearisome, harassing, dangerous strife between sin and the soul. As such, the strife is fiercer and more intense, in the life under the divine protectorate, after Retreat than it was before. Observe—I do not say that we are not better prepared for the fight, that we are not possessed of more within us to support the attack, that the chances of success are not greater in our favour than before. GOD forbid: it would be unfaithful thus to assert. It is a similar case to the position which we occupy after a devout reception of Holy Communion. Everything is really in our favour, if only we would believe such to be the case, and would act in accordance with our belief. GOD is certainly nearer. Our Angel is more than ever our guardian. Special Retreat-aids and blessings have been lavishly afforded; or have been granted in proportion to our needs. Perhaps the holy Sacrifice has been offered on our behalf; and certainly the director has been anxious and careful for us, and zealous and urgent with us. And as to ourself—you and I personally—if we have not been more jealous than before of falling into venial sins, as we ought to have been; if we have not been more persevering than before in good works, as we ought to have been; at least, we have been more watchful against the sin of which we are mainly conscious and by which we are chiefly assailed, our masterpassion or besetting sin. But in spite of all, perhaps in consequence of all, our warfare, as a fact, is more intense; Satan is more active; we are more assailed.

What may be the reason of this increased activity on the part of Satan? Why have we to act more on the defensive, in the life of protection after a Retreat, than before? Perhaps, for four reasons, natural or supernatural. For instance:

1. Our warfare is more intense, from the nature of things in our human life. We have been brought nearer to GOD, in retreat, in some one definite way, possibly in more than one. We have been enabled to settle some moral or religious doubt which perplexed us. We have at last come to a definite understanding with a sluggish or rebellious conscience. We have broken the tyranny of some one evil habit; or we have become servant to some good and holy custom. We have once and for all accepted a higher standard in faith or works; and submitted to some principle or discipline to which previously we could not or would not submit. We have been blessed with some special gift or grace; and in generous self-surrender we have promised to live less for self, and more for others, and wholly for GOD. In short, as before said, we have been led nearer to GOD: and GOD is pleased to will that we should remain closer to His Majesty. From the nature of things, the effort to approach GOD is far less than the effort to remain in union with Him; and hence, our warfare becomes more intense in order to retain the spiritual position which we have gained.

This is the first reason; and this arises from ourselves. But

2. Our warfare is more intense from the action of Satan, in consequence of our nearer approach to GOD. With the infernal wisdom which the experience of human nature during four-thousand years has secured, he is little likely to witness our renewed efforts for self-dedication without making fresh attempts to counteract them. In fact, his Satanic power and ingenuity is practically defied, and he exercises his office of tempter accordingly. He subjects us to endless temptations, direct and indirect; it may be, to take but one kind of attack, to doubtfulness and distrust—in our sincerity and earnestness, or GOD'S faithfulness Who leads us onward; in our wisdom and discretion, or the judgment of others who advise with us; in our own power, will, constancy; in the possibility of living in the world, and yet not being of it; in the advantage and gain, after all, of a godly, righteous and sober life; in the

probability, at the end, of positive failure to secure happiness, and of making shipwreck of both worlds, this and the next, when one at least is now within our grasp. No effort of temptation is too great for him to make. No success in temptation is too small for him to welcome. If only Satan can succeed in sowing distrust between the soul and GOD, or instilling a doubt into the inner conscience of man; if only he can detach us from GOD, or even place some obstacle between GOD and us; if only he can inspire us with some evil of which we were before unconscious, or secure our falling again into a snare from which we have once been freed— Satan's work is done : the work of the Retreat is marred.

This is the second cause; it arises from our malicious enemy.

3. Our warfare is more intense now, because in a state of ordinary quietude Satan can afford to allow us to remain in peace. Why should he not? He is capable of preaching peace when there is none, as well as false prophets; and he does so. He is capable of letting well alone in a soul self-prepared for temptation without his aid; and he does so. What more, indeed, can he require—to take, again, a single specimen of human existence—than the life of average respectability with which the world is thronged? What more can he desire, than the life of nine-tenths of persons of this class living in the world, who are outwardly conforming to, or at least are not obviously at issue with, a nominal Christian standard?

Here we have no need to judge the lives of others. Only let our past life be self-judged in this estimate—if indeed it be not repudiated, as no reflection of ourselves. Can we imagine a life made up to a large extent of self-pleasing and self-devotion—objectless towards man, without enthusiasm towards GOD; careless even of the acts of temporal mercy, and indifferent to those which are spiritual; content with the *minimum*, instead of seeking a level above the lowest of religious duty; absorbed in its own hopes, fears, pleasures; working only for its own end and object in life; without power or energy to resist temptation when it comes, and safe from grave falls only because an opportunity to fall does not present itself; neglectful of meditation, distracted in prayer, superficial in self-examination, perfunctory in confession, tepid at communion, and satisfied for itself with contemplating the higher life and with admiring it in others, instead of bravely walking in it? If we are able to conceive of such an existence in another, if we feel that such an existence bears any relation to our own, we must allow that, in his work of temptation to actual, definite wickedness, Satan has here but little cause to use active efforts. He may fairly leave the actor in such a life to the inevitable course of his own chosen career. The end will surely come, without interference, sooner or later. But a Retreat checks this inevitable course, this self-chosen career. And it is only in the after-effects of a Retreat, or of some other equally decided change in life, when a man is inspired with the will and is furnished with the means to abandon such a worthless existence, that he can be said to offer any obstacle to Satan's wiles, much less that his warfare has become intensified.

4. But, there is yet another cause for the intensity of our present warfare—our warfare, that is, who are emerging from our annual Retreat. It is a law, not only of nature but of grace, that re-action follows action; that relaxation follows tension; that fatigue is the result of exertion. Hence, in our renewed life after a Retreat, tepidity succeeds fervour, and a greater exertion is now demanded than in retreat to prevent our devotion to GOD and sanctity from becoming lukewarm. This position is equally true, whether during our Retreat we have conquered the causes which led to our life of selfishness, or whether after our Retreat we shall be tempted with doubts and difficulties—both of which have been above described. In both cases, the law is so obvious that it is needful only to be stated. In both cases, as the warfare is intensified, so must our watchfulness, also, become more keen.

Watchfulness against our besetting sin may be exercised in three ways: i. in the occasion of sin; ii. under temptation to sin; iii. after falling into sin.

i. In the occasion of sin.

If we avoid the occasion of sin, we seldom fall into temptation, and still more seldom fall into sin. The occasion oftentimes proves to be a crisis in our spiritual career; the actual point of departure from GOD to Satan; the obstacle which Satan introduces between us and GOD. It stands in the same relation to temptation, that temptation stands towards sin. It is the predisposing cause. But it differs from temptation, in the majority of cases, in an important point. Generally speaking, temptation reaches us from without. Ordinarily, the occasion of sin meets us by our own act and deed. We will the occasion; and the occasion finds us, or rather, we find ourselves in the midst of the occasion. It is, as a rule, within our power to accept or to reject the occasion of sin. If we avoid that, in most cases, we escape temptation. If we disregard that, in most cases, we fall into sin; we fall, perhaps, deeply; after our Retreat, its discipline and its blessings, we fall, it may be, fatally into sin. On this topic we have before dwelt; and therefore it is only necessary to remind ourselves of the forms which the occasion of sin may take in our own lives, and which are almost endless, in regard to our besetting sin.

ii. Under temptation to sin.

If unhappily we have been unwatchful in the occasion of sin: if from tepidity, or from selfishness, or from doubtfulness, or from the nature of things in human life; if in the permissive Will of GOD, or by the policy of Satan; if we have failed in our promises to GOD, our Angel, our director, our soul; or indeed, if we have not failed, and yet have been led into temptation—what is then to be done? Of course, the answer to this question can only be made in outline, or in general terms, the details must be added or changed to suit individual cases. But this may be done literally, or in figure.

Act exactly as you would act if you were surprised into temptation when the Divine Master was at your side, or our Blessed Lady, or your Guardian Angel, or even your confessor, or yet again, one whom you love or fear or respect. Flee from it, if you be men, as Lot fled from Sodom, albeit led thence by Angel-hands. Look not behind you, if you be women, as Lot's wife looked, and was powerless to flee further. Turn from the thought or idea. Break off half-way in the act or word. Keep silence; or check the deed. Say or do just the opposite of your intention. Utter an ejaculatory prayer. Sign yourself with the sign of the holy Cross. Exorcise yourself, in the Holy Name, from the temporary possession of the Evil One. Place yourself under the protection of your Guardian Angel, or patron Saint, or the LORD of both. Place yourself, by an act of your will, in the immediate presence of Almighty GOD. I do not say that these efforts will deliver you from evil. There is no infallible specific against sin. But they will tend to lead you out of temptation. And the sooner they are made, and the more faithfully and simply they are made, the greater will be the probability of their success.

iii. After falling into sin.

Have you been unwatchful in the occasion of sin, or under the trial of temptation. Or, have you been careful in both; and yet, have you fallen? Even then, be not unwatchful; be more than ever cautious. It is not too late—you know it well from experience—to arise again. Only, be careful to rise as quickly as possible. Do not remain prostrate in sin, like a child who has fallen to the ground and remains there, lamenting indeed its fall, but making no efforts to regain its feet. You know what steps must be taken, again from experience, to arise and go to your FATHER Who is in Heaven, in order, as the Church wills, that you should repent. And in so doing, be specially careful in one point. Do not be surprised at your fall, nor angry, nor irritable, nor fault-finding—with GOD, or with Satan, or with others, or with circumstances, or even with yourself. Only be sorry; be extremely, heartily, quietly sorry for your fall. Be sorry for GOD'S loss of glory in your sin, and for your loss of grace. Be sorry: and then do three things, as calmly and as completely and as fervently as the matter permits: 1. Instantly make a mental act of contrition, and if possible an act of reparation to GOD, or your neighbour. 2. Confess the sin to GOD, verbally, in actual words and not only as a mental remembrance, at the earliest moment, either on the spot, or in your chamber, or in church, or in the presence of the Blessed Sacrament. 3. Make a full, humble and hearty confession of the sin to GOD'S minister, at the first opportunity which is afforded you; an act of confession, with a mental recollection of your act of reparation for sin, and of your informal acknowledgment of it.

These words may afford a few hints in regard to the first way of avoiding sin in the renewed life after retreat, by the exercise of the spirit of watchfulness against our besetting sin.

V.

II. We must be jealous of falling into little faults.

Few greater dangers, perhaps, exist in the renewed life after the discipline of a Retreat than this. Those who, by GOD'S grace, have conquered deadly sin, or who have subdued their besetting sin, often retain an attraction to a venial fault, which they cannot subdue, or which declines to allow itself to be conquered. Nay, more: it sometimes happens, that the attraction will not be surrendered, it is almost cultivated. With such little faults, after a profitable Retreat, a large part of the spiritual warfare consists. Persons will not altogether and at once part with them. They play with them; dally with them; indulge them in secret, if not avowedly; view them with partiality, if not with the fondness of possession; and if they do not actually encourage them, yet they are patient with them. But this is exactly what we should not be; this is the attitude we should not take. We should not be patient with little faults. In a downright fall into sin we ought to be patient, even with ourselves, as being so frail; and patient with GOD, Who, in our penitence, is so forbearing towards us. But, we ought not to be patient with sin, and least of all with little faults.

Why should we not be patient with little faults? I might reply; because, without actually placing us outside a state of grace, they predispose the soul to withdraw itself from grace, they predispose GOD (if we may so speak with reverence) to withdraw grace from us. I might answer; they tend to sever us from the fear of GOD, from the love of JESUS, from the inspiration of the COMFORTER. But, I will take a lower level of spirituality; and in return, will ask one who dallies with a little fault: Why is he assured that a little fault will remain little? How can he tell when little sins will become large? Who can venture to say in sin,—be it venial or deadly,—thus far shalt thou go and no further? Who can decide with certainty when sins of ignorance may become sins of knowledge; when sins of infirmity may become sins of design; when occasional sins may become habitual; when venial sins may become deadly, or presumptuous, or against the HOLY GHOST, and so unpardonable? One reply to these questions is beyond controversy certain: The man who voluntarily indulges in little faults, is one of the last persons who can supply a satisfying answer. He cannot be self-assured when small faults become great. He cannot by his own power assign the boundaries to sin. He cannot of himself declare when sins of ignorance develop into sins which may not be, or can with difficulty be, forgiven. And the man whose answer will be in the next degree less satisfactory, is the one who so indulges after the discipline of a Retreat.

Take three strict rules for guidance, in regard to devout jealousy against falling into little sins.

i. Never to allow self-indulgence in any known fault, however small.

People, in relation to this rule, may be heard to say, "Yes; it is not right; it is even wrong; but, still, I do allow myself in such and such a liberty." Do we say this, or anything comparable to this? Do we act in the spirit of these words, or in any way comparable to them? If so, we are certainly not jealous with a Godly jealousy. These little infidelities, these actual unfaithfulnesses, these doubtful proprieties, these nameless dangers—they sap the spiritual life; they make it hard and cold and dry; they make it dead and stone-like. Here, there is no need to specify any definite fault. There may be a besetting venial sin, as well as a deadly master-passion, in the spiritual life. But, after retreat, the soul will be conscious of the lesser evil, as well as of the graver wickedness; and an allusion to a besetting venial fault will find a responsive echo in the hearts of all. Hence, it will be needful only to be urgent in general terms against positive sin of any kind. We must be honest and true and open and loyal and loving to our Blessed LORD on leaving a Retreat; and we must never consciously permit ourselves to indulge in any known fault.

ii. Always to be in opposition to some definite fault.

Here is one open secret of perfection: ever to strive after it even in small matters in some one definite way. If we always fight against minor faults, we seldom fall into major ones. Few checks are so instantaneous and powerful in the spiritual existence, against temptation to possible sins, as a conscious antagonism towards actual wickedness. We are in possession of an agency which always obeys our will, and ever strengthens with the increased strength of our will, in proportion as it is employed. This, by a law of the natural life. Nothing, again, so predisposes the Holy SPIRIT to help us to avoid deadly sin as our own voluntary co-operation with Him in fighting against some specified venial fault. He is pleased to supply us with power in the future according as we avail ourselves of His assistance in the present. This, by a law of the supernatural life. As money inevitably attracts money in the world, so grace attracts grace. "To him that hath," it is a distinct promise, "shall be given." But, on the other hand, there is a threat equally distinct: "From him that hath not shall be taken even that which he hath." By not being in active opposition to sin, we forfeit the divine grace which we otherwise would enjoy.

iii. Not to despair when we fall into any given fault.

Despair is the last and most fatal of Satan's weapons. It is one which he uses with the deadliest effect. Only let him secure this, and he gains all. It is the one sin which successfully defies grace and ensures our eternal loss; and therefore it is at once foolish and wicked to indulge in it. It is wicked, because it does despite unto one of the chiefest of GOD's attributes—it doubts His love. It is foolish, because it is forgetful of past experience. Life-long experience in the spiritual world teaches us, that what has been, may be again. Whenever we have fallen, we have had power given us to rise. If such power were given formerly when we were tempted, why should it not be again given? If it were once bestowed, why not now, when we have fallen? No doubt the conflict is beyond words wearisome. The daily fight, the daily fall, the daily confession of sin and amendment, the daily absolution and renewal of strength, the daily trial and daily temptation —over and over and over again—are indescribably painful. But, life is a warfare from which we cannot escape. Yet, in spite of all, our Blessed LORD awaits us at the end of life with a beautiful crown in His hand. Remember the case of Judas. The soul of Judas is the one lost soul in divine history; is the one soul lost by despair.

These words may suggest a few further hints in regard to the second way of avoiding sin in the renewed life after retreat, by the exercise of the spirit of jealousy in falling into little faults.

VI.

III. We must persevere in good works.

It may be taken for granted that each soul has settled with itself to do some one thing for GOD and its own salvation more than, and over and above that which it was wont to do before the beginning of our Retreat. What that one thing may be, each one will have settled with GOD, his director, and his own soul. It is of less importance what it may be, than that it be something definite, something which deserves the appellative, good. It must be some positive action, moral or religious, in faith or practice. We must avoid, in such a case, a merely negative attitude. Watchfulness is not enough. Jealousy is not enough. Religion is not a matter of negations only or chiefly. It is one of positive, actual duty. But, whatever good work be taken up, it must be continued perseveringly. This, please GOD, it shall be our duty to perform. We have settled what may be our Retreat-work to accomplish for our soul, or for GOD. Never mind the definite form which this work may take. We will only say, that it will take some form beyond that of conquering our besetting sin and of abstaining from minor faults: for to these we are already pledged. But knowing as we do, each one his own need, and each one his own determination, it is now our part to take action.

In order to assist our determination to persevere in good-works, consider three points, common-place though they may be.

i. No great work was ever done without perseverance.

Although this is almost a truism in words, it might well be a doubtful proposition if it were weighed by the manner in which it is practically neglected. It becomes, theoretically, a necessary truth to be enforced. It is in practice a difficult one to be followed. The commonest examples of the results of perseverance are equally good with the most unusual. Ploughing a field of many acres, with an old-fashioned, picturesque plough, may suffice as one instance. Furrow after furrow, a few inches of land at a time, backwards and forwards, slowly and surely, is turned by the team of the patient, plodding plough-man—and the broad acres are made ready for the fruitful seed. Building a house of many stories, with courses of hard-burned brick, may suffice as another. Brick after brick, in ever increasing layers; course after course, ever growing upwards; a few inches of material at a time, are laid with the trowel of the skilled and persevering artizan—and the ground is covered with a human habitation. Not otherwise is it in our religious life. The great work of securing our salvation cannot be done without perseverance. We must plough the field here; and GOD will sow the seed for the harvest of the next life. We must build the house here; and when our earthly house of this tabernacle is dissolved, we shall have a building of GOD, an house not made with hands, eternal in the heavens.

ii. Holiness in this life is dependent upon perseverance.

It is so dependent from the nature of things. In one aspect, holiness is simply the habit of doing good works. And a habit implies perseverance. For, if a good work well done be only done once and again, be done now and then, be done one day and omitted the next, be not done with regularity—it ceases to be done habitually, it ceases to be a habit. How would earthly matters prosper, which are done after this fashion? Not less ill do things heavenly prosper, which are done with the like want of perseverance; and amongst others, the cultivation of personal holiness. Again, the commonest examples of a want of perseverance are equally valid with the most uncommon. How would a tradesman's business prosper, whose accounts were irregularly kept? How could the sailor depend upon the course he was steering, if he failed continually to consult his compass? How were it possible for the watchmaker to regulate a time-piece, which he only occasionally keeps duly wound-up? How can the politician be conversant with the order of public events, if he reads his journal only at intervals of two or three days? How can we —you and I—do any one thing well, that is worth doing at all, without regularity? It is not otherwise, in the spiritual life, with holiness. It is not irregular, inconsistent, occasional, spasmodic, accidental service which our Divine Master requires at our hands ; but the opposite of all these. Holiness, equally with success in every department of human life, cannot be secured without the ceaseless efforts which render it habitual. In a word, it is dependent upon perseverance.

iii. Salvation is pledged to follow after perseverance.

It is so pledged by GOD. Hence, there is no question about the result : the only question to be considered is the cause. It is indeed a mighty work to be accomplished by so small a means. Eternal salvation is the necessary product of holiness persevered in during our short span of life. Salvation, then, depends upon our own efforts. It is, actually, in our hands. A truth not less blessed than assured—it is. In union with the sacred Humanity and divine Personality of our Blessed LORD—it is. Only persevere in good works, and they will lead to holiness of life. Only persevere in holiness of life, and salvation will follow. Indeed, salvation is merely holiness of life under fresh conditions—perpetual, instead of intermittent ; without effort, instead of after many and great efforts ; perfect, instead of wanting in perfection. Only say—I will ; in union with the Person of JESUS CHRIST, I will ; I will persevere in holiness of life, in thought, word and deed ; I will be saved— and the promised result will ensue. The power is self-willed, self-applied, self-completed—in union with JESUS CHRIST. His words may serve as our motto, as they assure us of His divine will : " He that endureth unto the end, the same shall be saved."

These words, once again, may furnish a few final hints in regard to the last method of avoiding sin in the renewed life after retreat, by the exercise of the spirit of perseverance in good works.

VII.

These practical hints may fitly form the concluding advice of a Retreat. They may suitably be followed by us, in regard to the avoidance of evil for the future in the renewed life, under the protectorate of GOD the Preserver of man. In brief, they may bear repetition: Be watchful against besetting sin; in the occasion of, under temptation to, after falling into sin. Be jealous of falling into little faults; never allowing a single fault, always opposing some one fault, and being despairing under no circumstances. Be persevering in good works; because no great work is done without perseverance, holiness depends upon it, salvation follows after it. Therefore, be watchful, jealous, persevering.

This three-fold counsel is applicable to two classes of persons: 1. to those who, by GOD'S mercy, are more or less devout; and 2. to those who, by Satan's power, are more or less indifferent. Perhaps, both may be found amongst those who are gathered together in retreat. Certainly, thank GOD, one of the two classes is present—the more devout. Let us shortly consider both classes of persons.

1st. Are there, amongst those who have joined in this Retreat, any who may be self-condemned as more or less indifferent? GOD knoweth: it is possible.

What may be, amongst others, the marks of indifference, without seeking to exhaust them? The indifferent are disposed to question whether or not GOD loves them, cares for them, thinks of them, remembers them, hears them. They are disposed to think that GOD tries them hardly; afflicts them heavily; visits them too often; punishes them overmuch, more than others, more than they deserve, more than they can bear. They are disposed to complain, because they cannot become Saints all at once; because they fall again and again; because they are tempted time after time; because they are not given the gift or grace which they need so much, and ask for so fervently and so often. They are disposed, lastly, and herein consists the awful danger of indifferentism, to give up religion, for any excuse or for no reason, at the call of friendship, to secure a position in the world, to continue in a certain employment or business, for the attractions of married life, or under the mild persecution which this age can alone inflict. For these and the like results, men and women living in the world will forego their devotion, will abandon their meditation, will neglect their communion, will omit their confession. For these, they will minimise public religious duties, give up retreats, overlook the seasons of the Church, care no longer for early celebrations, deny the obligation of fasting reception, be ashamed of the sign of the holy Cross. For these, they will fail to take the highest line, when a lower course is open to them; will advocate expediency, when principles are at stake; will compromise their opinions and practice, when firmness would have secured a moral triumph; and will not follow the dictates of conscience, when such dictates appear to lead to evils, real or supposed, which they are not bold enough to face, or in which they cannot see the hand or the will of GOD. For these, they are content to be almost, but not altogether persuaded to be Christian; they congratulate themselves on having had a narrow escape of being made Catholic; they stifle all doubts which may be implanted by GOD in their minds, of their real position in religion, decline to re-consider it, and condemn all lines of action more consistent than their own with the conclusive and unanswerable verdict of being "extreme." For these, they dismiss all like questions to a convenient season, which never comes; to a time when they feel more devout, which they never feel; and to a period of less indifference, whilst indifference is flooding the soul like poison tainting the blood, or like paralysis creeping through the nervous system.

What may be, amongst others, a remedy? It is difficult to say—beyond the single word which is common to many questions of divine faith in relation to human sin, penitence, and all that word conveys; beyond a renewed conversion to GOD in the way which He has appointed, through the threefold portal of contrition, confession and satisfaction; beyond the common-place precepts of doing our duty to GOD and our neighbour, of leaving undone what we have formerly done and doing what we have formerly left undone, and of doing unto all men as we would they should do unto us; beyond the suggestions, in relation to sin in the life of protection which we now lead, of watchfulness, of jealousy and of perseverance. But, lest this advice should be considered too vague to be of value, suffer me to offer one further practical counsel. In addition to other efforts against the spirit of indifference, strive after conformity of the human will to the Will Divine, in some of the affairs of life, in many, in all. Strive after it, positively, if you have not before sought for it. Strive more earnestly to secure it, if it has been to some extent attained. Strive zealously and intensely, under any circumstances. In proportion to our conformity with the Divine Will our indifference will be sensibly diminished; and in proportion as our indifference is diminished, shall we be free for, shall we attain to, a more intimate and close union with the Person of JESUS CHRIST.

2nd. Are there, amongst those who have joined in this Retreat, any who are more or less devout? Thank GOD, there are; there are some, whom GOD knows, whom their Guardian Angel knows, whom their director knows, even if their own conscience will not allow them thus to be self-called. A Retreat should be enabled to do something for these also. There are three failings into which the more or less devout are liable to fall. Suffer me to point to their symptoms as well as to their cure.

Firstly. Some persons are apt to give to feeling in religion too prominent a place. It is not, in their case that they fear GOD does not love them: but, they do not love GOD, do not believe in Him, hope in Him, fear Him, recognize His presence, worship, serve and obey Him, as they ought; at least, they are powerless to feel that they do. Secondly. Some persons are wont to assign to motive in religion too important a position. In any given word or work they doubt whether they act from a high motive ; or, whether they act from any motive at all, and not from chance ; or, if they act from some motive, whether it be not a low, or a bad motive. In short, they are more concerned with the motive than with the action—an exaggeration of a true principle in morals. Thirdly. Some persons, again, are too introspective. They carry self-examination too far. They can do nothing, they are able to take no action, without self-accusation and self-condemnation. They are forgetful of the theological fact, I would rather say of the blessed truth, that we are able to do, we can do good works, works absolutely good, in union with the Person of JESUS CHRIST. They fail to use the balance fairly, between self and sin ; they do not judge themselves honestly, as they ought, as GOD judges them, with just judgment ; they seldom speak or act or think or even feel, without a fear of evil and a dread of sin.

Little as these three classes of devout minds may believe it, hard as it may be to convince them of the fact, they are all more or less victims of morbidness, under the forms of sentiment, scrupulosity and self-consciousness. Such is the disease from which they suffer. The cure consists in the realization of the sacred Humanity of JESUS, of the divine Personality of CHRIST ; of the fact that He both was and is a living, acting, feeling, thinking Person, human and divine, MAN and GOD. It consists in the realization that, as Perfect MAN, He absolutely sympathizes in all we have to bear in deadness and hardness of feeling, in doubtfulness of motive, in the accusations of an ill-balanced conscience. It consists in the realization that, as Perfect GOD and in union with His sacred Manhood, He is pleased in His Mercy to accept all that is done for His sake, feel what we may ; in His Wisdom to solve all difficulties of motive, though they may be full of doubt in our judgment ; and in His Omniscience to judge justly of our actions, in spite of self-accusation however apparently free from all doubt. Believe in Him as a Person, with Whom we are sacramentally united, Who is One with us, and with

Whom we are one—and unreal and unworthy sentiment will give way to pure and intense devotion, notwithstanding the natural feeling of unworthiness; scrupulosity will flee before the spirit of single-mindedness, even in the presence of motives which are not always plainly discerned; and self-consciousness will be conquered in a simple abandonment of self to Another, by our incorporation into the sacred and sinless Humanity, and by our personal union with our LORD GOD and Saviour JESUS CHRIST.

A. M. D. G.

BY THE SAME EDITOR.

IN THE PRESS.

THE SACRAMENT OF PENANCE: Essays on Confession of Sin in the Church of England. *By various Authors.*

LITURGICAL.

RITUAL OF THE ALTAR: The Order of the Holy Communion, with Introits, Collects, Epistles, Graduals, Gospels, Offertories, Secrets, Communions and Postcommunions throughout the year, according to the Use of the Church of England; the Office of Benediction of the Most Holy Sacrament, Order of Ceremonies for Candlemas, Lent and Easter, the Asperges, and various Benedictions; together with Rubrical Directions, Secret Prayers, Ritual Music, and the General Rubrics; illustrated with 70 Woodcuts and a Plate of the Crucifixion.

THE LITURGIES OF 1549 AND 1662: The Office of Holy Communion of the First Book of Edward VI. and our own Prayer Book; printed in parallel pages.

COLLECTS, EPISTLES AND GOSPELS: For various Days and Occasions not provided for in the Book of Common Prayer.

THEOLOGICAL AND ECCLESIASTICAL ESSAYS.

By various Authors.

THE CHURCH AND THE WORLD: Three Series; 1866, 1867, 1868.
TRACTS FOR THE DAY; 1867.
ECCLESIASTICAL REFORM; 1873.
STUDIES IN MODERN PROBLEMS: Two Series; 1874.

SERIAL LITERATURE.

THE ENGLISHMAN'S MAGAZINE: Of Literature, Religion, Science and Art. Two Volumes. 1865.

THE ASCETIC LIBRARY.

A Series of Translations, from Catholic Sources, of Books for Devotional Reading.

MYSTERIES OF CALVARY: On the Passion. *From the Latin of Guevara.*

PREPARATION FOR DEATH; For Advent. *From the Italian of Liguori.*

HOLINESS OF LIFE: First Part of the Sinner's Guide. *From the Spanish of Luis of Granada.*

EXAMINATION OF CONSCIENCE: For Laity and Clergy, on Special Subjects. *From the French of Tronson.*

RELIGIOUS VERSE.

Translated and Original.

LYRA EUCHARISTICA: Hymns and Verses on the Holy Communion.
LYRA MESSIANICA: Hymns and Verses on the Life of our Lord.
LYRA MYSTICA: Hymns and Verses on Sacred Subjects.

BIOGRAPHY.

THE FEMALL GLORY: Life of the Holy Virgin Mary. *By Anthony Stafford.* A.D. 1635. With facsimiles of the original Engravings.

BY THE SAME EDITOR (*continued*).

COMMENTARY.

DEVOTIONAL COMMENTARY: On the Gospel according to S. Matthew.
From the French of Quesnel.

GLOSSARY.

GLOSSARY OF ECCLESIASTICAL TERMS: Brief Explanation of Words used in Antiquities, Architecture, Ecclesiology, Greek Hierology, Heresies, Hymnology, Law, Liturgiology, Mediæval Latin Works, Symbolism, Theology, and Miscellaneous Subjects. *By various Authors.*

SERMONS AND LECTURES.

PRINCIPLES OF THE FAITH IN RELATION TO SIN. Topics for Thought in Times of Retreat. Eleven Addresses delivered during a Retreat of Three Days to Persons living in the World: With an Introduction on the Neglect of Dogmatic Theology in the Church of England.

A THEORY ABOUT SIN: In relation to some facts of daily life; Lectures on the Seven Deadly Sins—Pride, Envy, Anger, Sloth, Avarice, Gluttony and Lust. With an Analysis and Summary.

SIX SHORT SERMONS ON SIN: On the Nature, Effect, Remedy and Removal, etc., of Sin.

THE FOUR CARDINAL VIRTUES: In relation to the public and private life of Catholics; with an Appendix on the Dissolution of Church and State, Episcopal Authority not unlimited, etc.

SPIRITUAL AND DEVOTIONAL MANUALS.

AVRILLON: On the Holy Spirit. For Ascension and Whitsuntide.
AVRILLON: Meditations for a Month. On the Holy Communion.
BOURDALOUE: Spiritual Exercises. For a Retreat.
CHALLONER: Short Meditations. For a Month.
DAILY SACRIFICE: A Manual for Spiritual Communion; for daily use. From Ancient Sources.
DIVINE LITURGY: A Manual of Holy Communion for Communicants; together with the Office of Holy Communion. From Ancient Sources.
EUCHARISTIC LITANIES: From Ancient Sources.
IGNATIUS, S.: Spiritual Exercises; Newly translated, with a Preface on the use of the Book.
INVOCATION OF SAINTS AND ANGELS: From Greek, Latin and English Sources. For Members of the English Church.
LUIS OF GRANADA: Considerations on the Four Last Things, etc.
MEDITATIONS: From Advent to Lent. Short daily Meditations.
RODRIGUEZ: Of the Virtue of Humility.

PAMPHLETS, ETC.

OUGHT WE TO OBEY the New Court created by the Public Worship Regulation Act, 1874?
CAN CHURCHMEN RECOGNIZE the New Judge?
SECULAR JUDGMENTS in Spiritual Matters.
ON THE ESTABLISHMENT of an Oratory in London.
SUNDAY MORNING in Leather Lane.
THE ORDER OF Unction.
RESURRECTION: An Easter Sermon of Luis of Granada.
TRACTS OF CHRISTIAN Faith, Fact, and Duty.

A LIST OF

C. KEGAN PAUL & CO.'S PUBLICATIONS.

THE

NINETEENTH CENTURY.

A Monthly Review.

EDITED BY JAMES KNOWLES.

Price 2*s*. 6*d*.

VOLS. I. & II. PRICE 14*s*. EACH, VOL. III. 17*s*., CONTAIN CONTRIBUTIONS
BY THE FOLLOWING WRITERS :—

RABBI HERMANN ADLER.
THE DUKE OF ARGYLL.
ARTHUR ARNOLD.
MATTHEW ARNOLD.
REV. DR. GEORGE PERCY BADGER, D.C.L.
REV. CANON BARRY.
DR. H. CHARLTON BASTIAN.
SIR T. BAZLEY, M.P.
MR. EDGAR BOWRING.
MR. THOMAS BRASSEY, M.P.
REV. J. BALDWIN BROWN.
PROFESSOR GEORGE VON BUNSEN.
DR. W. B. CARPENTER.
PROFESSOR CLIFFORD.
PROFESSOR COLVIN.
REV. R. W. DALE.
MR. EDWARD DICEY.
M. E. GRANT DUFF, M.P.
ARCHIBALD FORBES.
JAMES ANTHONY FROUDE.
THE RIGHT HON. W. E. GLADSTONE, M.P.
THE BISHOP OF GLOUCESTER AND BRISTOL.
MR. W. R. GREG.
MR. FREDERIC HARRISON.
MR. GEORGE J. HOLYOAKE.
MR. R. H. HUTTON.
PROFESSOR HUXLEY.
HENRY IRVING.
SIR JOHN LUBBOCK.

REV. MALCOLM MACCOLL.
REV. A. H. MACKONOCHIE.
CARDINAL MANNING.
REV. DR. MARTINEAU.
HIS HIGHNESS MIDHAT PASHA.
PROFESSOR HENRY MORLEY.
RIGHT HON. LYON PLAYFAIR, M.P.
MR. GEORGE POTTER.
W. R. S. RALSTON.
VISCOUNT STRATFORD DE REDCLIFFE.
PROFESSOR CROOM ROBERTSON.
REV. J. GUINNESS ROGERS.
PROFESSOR RUSKIN.
THE VERY REV. THE DEAN OF ST. PAUL'S.
LORD SELBORNE.
PROFESSOR GOLDWIN SMITH.
JAMES SPEDDING.
RIGHT HON. JAMES STANSFELD, M.P.
SIR JAMES FITZJAMES STEPHEN.
ALFRED TENNYSON.
PROFESSOR TYNDALL.
SIR JULIUS VOGEL.
SIR THOMAS WATSON, M.D.
DR. WARD.
MR. FREDERICK WEDMORE.
THE VERY REV. THE DEAN OF WESTMINSTER.
MAJOR-GEN. SIR GARNET WOLSELEY.
THE RIGHT HON. CHAS. WORDSWORTH,
&c. &c.

1 Paternoster Square,
London.

A LIST OF
C. KEGAN PAUL & CO.'S PUBLICATIONS.

ABDULLA (*Hakayit*)—AUTOBIOGRAPHY OF A MALAY MUNSHI. Translated by J. T. THOMSON, F.R.G.S. With Photo-lithograph Page of Abdulla's MS. Post 8vo. price 12s.

ADAMS (*A. L.*) *M.A., M.B., F.R.S., F.G.S.*—FIELD AND FOREST RAMBLES OF A NATURALIST IN NEW BRUNSWICK. With Notes and Observations on the Natural History of Eastern Canada. Illustrated. 8vo. price 14s.

ADAMS (*F. O.*) *F.R.G.S.*—THE HISTORY OF JAPAN. From the Earliest Period to the Present Time. New Edition, revised. 2 volumes. With Maps and Plans. Demy 8vo. price 21s. each.

A. K. H. B.—A SCOTCH COMMUNION SUNDAY, to which are added Certain Discourses from a University City. By the Author of 'The Recreations of a Country Parson.' Second Edition. Crown 8vo. price 5s.

FROM A QUIET PLACE. A New Volume of Sermons. Crown 8vo. cloth.

ALBERT (*Mary*).—HOLLAND AND HER HEROES TO THE YEAR 1585. An Adaptation from 'Motley's Rise of the Dutch Republic.' Small crown 8vo. price 4s. 6d.

ALLEN (*Rev. R.*) *M.A.*—ABRAHAM; HIS LIFE, TIMES, AND TRAVELS, 3,800 years ago. With Map. Second Edition. Post 8vo. price 6s.

ALLEN (*Grant*) *B.A.*—PHYSIOLOGICAL ÆSTHETICS. Large post 8vo. 9s.

ANDERSON (*Rev. C.*) *M.A.*—NEW READINGS OF OLD PARABLES. Demy 8vo. price 4s. 6d.

CHURCH THOUGHT AND CHURCH WORK. Edited by. Second Edition. Demy 8vo. price 7s. 6d.

THE CURATE OF SHYRE. Second Edition. 8vo. price 7s. 6d.

ANDERSON (*R. C.*) *C.E.*—TABLES FOR FACILITATING THE CALCULATION OF EVERY DETAIL IN CONNECTION WITH EARTHEN AND MASONRY DAMS. Royal 8vo. price £2. 2s.

ARCHER (*Thomas*)—ABOUT MY FATHER'S BUSINESS. Work amidst the Sick, the Sad, and the Sorrowing. Crown 8vo. price 5s.

ARNOLD (*Arthur*)—SOCIAL POLITICS. Demy 8vo. cloth.

BAGEHOT (Walter)—THE ENGLISH CONSTITUTION. A New Edition, Revised and Corrected, with an Introductory Dissertation on Recent Changes and Events. Crown 8vo. price 7s. 6d.

LOMBARD STREET. A Description of the Money Market. Seventh Edition. Crown 8vo. price 7s. 6d.

SOME ARTICLES ON THE DEPRECIATION OF SILVER, AND TOPICS CONNECTED WITH IT. Demy 8vo. price 5s.

BAGOT (Alan)—ACCIDENTS IN MINES : Their Causes and Prevention. Crown 8vo. price 6s.

BAKER (Sir Sherston, Bart.)—HALLECK'S INTERNATIONAL LAW ; or, Rules Regulating the Intercourse of States in Peace and War. A New Edition, revised, with Notes and Cases. 2 vols. Demy 8vo. price 38s.

BALDWIN (Capt. J. H.) F.Z.S. Bengal Staff Corps.—THE LARGE AND SMALL GAME OF BENGAL AND THE NORTH-WESTERN PROVINCES OF INDIA. 4to. With numerous Illustrations. Second Edition. Price 21s.

BARNES (William)—AN OUTLINE OF ENGLISH SPEECHCRAFT. Crown 8vo. price 4s.

BARTLEY (G. C. T.)—DOMESTIC ECONOMY : Thrift in Every-Day Life. Taught in Dialogues suitable for children of all ages. Small Cr. 8vo. price 2s.

BAUR (Ferdinand) Dr. Ph., Professor in Maulbronn.—A PHILOLOGICAL INTRODUCTION TO GREEK AND LATIN FOR STUDENTS. Translated and adapted from the German. By C. KEGAN PAUL, M.A. Oxon., and the Rev. E. D. STONE, M.A., late Fellow of King's College, Cambridge, and Assistant Master at Eton. Crown 8vo. price 6s.

BAYNES (Rev. Canon R. H.)—AT THE COMMUNION TIME. A Manual for Holy Communion. With a preface by the Right Rev. the Lord Bishop of Derry and Raphoe. Cloth, price 1s. 6d.

BECKER (Bernard H.)—THE SCIENTIFIC SOCIETIES OF LONDON. Crown 8vo. price 5s.

BELLINGHAM (Henry) Barrister-at-Law—SOCIAL ASPECTS OF CATHOLICISM AND PROTESTANTISM IN THEIR CIVIL BEARING UPON NATIONS. Translated and adapted from the French of M. le Baron de Haulleville. With a preface by His Eminence Cardinal Manning. Crown 8vo price 6s.

BENNIE (Rev. J. N.) M.A.—THE ETERNAL LIFE. Sermons preached during the last twelve years. Crown 8vo. price 6s.

BERNARD (Bayle)—SAMUEL LOVER, HIS LIFE AND UNPUBLISHED WORKS. In 2 vols. With a Steel Portrait. Post 8vo. price 21s.

BISCOE (A. C.)—THE EARLS OF MIDDLETON, Lords of Clermont and of Fettercairn, and the Middleton Family. Crown 8vo. price 10s. 6d.

BISSET (A.)—HISTORY OF THE STRUGGLE FOR PARLIAMENTARY GOVERNMENT IN ENGLAND. 2 vols. Demy 8vo. price 24s.

BLANC (H.) M.D.—CHOLERA : HOW TO AVOID AND TREAT IT. Popular and Practical Notes. Crown 8vo. price 4s. 6d.

BONWICK (J.) F.R.G.S.—PYRAMID FACTS AND FANCIES. Crown 8vo. price 5s.

EGYPTIAN BELIEF AND MODERN THOUGHT. Large Post 8vo. cloth, price 10s. 6a.

BOWEN (H. C.) M.A., *Head Master of the Grocers' Company's Middle Class School at Hackney.*
   STUDIES IN ENGLISH, for the use of Modern Schools. Small crown 8vo. price 1s. 6d.

BOWRING (L.) C.S.I.—EASTERN EXPERIENCES. Illustrated with Maps and Diagrams. Demy 8vo. price 16s.

BOWRING (Sir John).—AUTOBIOGRAPHICAL RECOLLECTIONS OF SIR JOHN BOWRING. With Memoir by LEWIN B. BOWRING. Demy 8vo. price 14s.

BRADLEY (F. H.) — ETHICAL STUDIES. Critical Essays in Moral Philosophy. Large post 8vo. price 9s.
   MR. SIDGWICK'S HEDONISM: an Examination of the Main Argument of 'The Methods of Ethics.' Demy 8vo. sewed, price 2s. 6d.

BROOKE (Rev. S. A.) M.A., *Chaplain in Ordinary to Her Majesty the Queen, and Minister of Bedford Chapel, Bloomsbury.*
   LIFE AND LETTERS OF THE LATE REV. F. W. ROBERTSON, M.A., Edited by.
      I. Uniform with the Sermons. 2 vols. With Steel Portrait. Price 7s. 6d.
      II. Library Edition. 8vo. With Two Steel Portraits. Price 12s.
      III. A Popular Edition. In 1 vol. 8vo. price 6s.
   THE FIGHT OF FAITH. Sermons preached on various occasions. Third Edition. Crown 8vo. price 7s. 6d.
   THEOLOGY IN THE ENGLISH POETS.—Cowper, Coleridge, Wordsworth, and Burns. Third Edition. Post 8vo. price 9s.
   CHRIST IN MODERN LIFE. Eleventh Edition. Crown 8vo. price 7s. 6d.
   SERMONS. First Series. Ninth Edition. Crown 8vo. price 6s.
   SERMONS. Second Series. Third Edition. Crown 8vo. price 7s.
   FREDERICK DENISON MAURICE: The Life and Work of. A Memorial Sermon. Crown 8vo. sewed, price 1s.

BROOKE (W. G.) M.A.—THE PUBLIC WORSHIP REGULATION ACT. With a Classified Statement of its Provisions, Notes, and Index. Third Edition, revised and corrected. Crown 8vo. price 3s. 6d.
   SIX PRIVY COUNCIL JUDGMENTS—1850–72. Annotated by. Third Edition. Crown 8vo. price 9s.

BROUN (J. A.)—MAGNETIC OBSERVATIONS AT TREVANDRUM AND AUGUSTIA MALLEY. Vol. I. 4to. price 63s.
   The Report from above, separately sewed, price 21s.

BROWN (Rev. J. Baldwin) B.A.—THE HIGHER LIFE. Its Reality Experience, and Destiny. Fourth Edition. Crown 8vo. price 7s. 6d.
   DOCTRINE OF ANNIHILATION IN THE LIGHT OF THE GOSPEL OF LOVE. Five Discourses. Second Edition. Crown 8vo. price 2s. 6d.

BROWN (J. Croumbie) LL.D.—REBOISEMENT IN FRANCE; or, Records of the Replanting of the Alps, the Cevennes, and the Pyrenees with Trees, Herbage, and Bush. Demy 8vo. price 12s. 6d.
   THE HYDROLOGY OF SOUTHERN AFRICA. Demy 8vo. price 10s. 6d.

BROWNE (Rev. M. E.)—UNTIL THE DAY DAWN. Four Adven Lectures. Crown 8vo. price 2s. 6d.

BURCKHARDT (Jacob)—THE CIVILIZATION OF THE PERIOD OF THE RENAISSANCE IN ITALY. Authorised translation, by S. G. C. Middlemore. 2 vols. Demy 8vo. price 24s.

BURTON (Mrs. Richard)—THE INNER LIFE OF SYRIA, PALESTINE, AND THE HOLY LAND. With Maps, Photographs, and Coloured Plates. 2 vols. Second Edition. Demy 8vo. price 24s.

BURTON (Capt. Richard F.)—THE GOLD MINES OF MIDIAN AND THE RUINED MIDIANITE CITIES. A Fortnight's Tour in North Western Arabia. With numerous illustrations. Second Edition. Demy 8vo. price 18s.

CARLISLE (A. D.) B.A.—ROUND THE WORLD IN 1870. A Volume of Travels, with Maps. New and Cheaper Edition. Demy 8vo. price 6s.

CARNE (Miss E. T.)—THE REALM OF TRUTH. Crown 8vo. price 5s. 6d.

CARPENTER (W. B.) LL.D., M.D., F.R.S., &c.—THE PRINCIPLES OF MENTAL PHYSIOLOGY. With their Applications to the Training and Discipline of the Mind, and the Study of its Morbid Conditions. Illustrated. Fourth Edition. 8vo. price 12s.

CHILDREN'S TOYS, and some Elementary Lessons in General Knowledge which they Teach. With Illustrations. Crown 8vo. price 5s.

CHRISTOPHERSON (The Late Rev. Henry) M.A.
  SERMONS. With an Introduction by John Rae, LL.D., F.S.A. Second Series. Crown 8vo. price 6s.

CLODD (Edward) F.R.A.S.—THE CHILDHOOD OF THE WORLD: a Simple Account of Man in Early Times. Third Edition. Crown 8vo. price 3s.
  A Special Edition for Schools. Price 1s.

  THE CHILDHOOD OF RELIGIONS. Including a Simple Account of the Birth and Growth of Myths and Legends. Third Thousand. Crown 8vo. price 5s.
  A Special Edition for Schools. Price 1s. 6d.

COLERIDGE (Sara)—PHANTASMION. A Fairy Tale. With an Introductory Preface by the Right Hon. Lord Coleridge, of Ottery St. Mary. A New Edition. Illustrated. Crown 8vo. price 7s. 6d.

  MEMOIR AND LETTERS OF SARA COLERIDGE. Edited by her Daughter. With Index. 2 vols. With Two Portraits. Third Edition, Revised and Corrected. Crown 8vo. price 24s.
  Cheap Edition. With one Portrait. Price 7s. 6d.

COLLINS (Rev. R.) M.A.—MISSIONARY ENTERPRISE IN THE EAST. With special reference to the Syrian Christians of Malabar, and the Results of Modern Missions. With Four Illustrations. Crown 8vo. price 6s.

COOKE (Prof. J. P.) of the Harvard University.—SCIENTIFIC CULTURE. Crown 8vo. price 1s.

COOPER (T. T.) F.R.G.S.—THE MISHMEE HILLS: an Account of a Journey made in an Attempt to Penetrate Thibet from Assam, to open New Routes for Commerce. Second Edition. With Four Illustrations and Map. Post 8vo. price 10s. 6d.

CORY (Lieut.-Col. Arthur)—THE EASTERN MENACE ; OR, SHADOWS OF COMING EVENTS. Crown 8vo. price 5s.

COX (Rev. Sir George W.) M.A., Bart.—A HISTORY OF GREECE FROM THE EARLIEST PERIOD TO THE END OF THE PERSIAN WAR. 2 vols. Demy 8vo. price 36s.

THE MYTHOLOGY OF THE ARYAN NATIONS. 2 vols. Demy 8vo. price 28s.

A GENERAL HISTORY OF GREECE FROM THE EARLIEST PERIOD TO THE DEATH OF ALEXANDER THE GREAT, with a sketch of the subsequent History to the present time. Crown 8vo. price 7s. 6d.

TALES OF ANCIENT GREECE. Third Edition. Small crown 8vo. price 6s.

SCHOOL HISTORY OF GREECE. With Maps. Fcp. 8vo. price 3s. 6d.

THE GREAT PERSIAN WAR FROM THE HISTORY OF HERODOTUS. New Edition. Fcp. 8vo. price 3s. 6d.

A MANUAL OF MYTHOLOGY IN THE FORM OF QUESTION AND ANSWER. Third Edition. Fcp. 8vo. price 3s.

COX (Rev. Samuel)—SALVATOR MUNDI ; or, Is Christ the Saviour of all Men? Fifth Edition. Crown 8vo. price 5s.

CROMPTON (Henry) — INDUSTRIAL CONCILIATION. Fcap. 8vo. price 2s. 6d.

CURWEN (Henry)—SORROW AND SONG ; Studies of Literary Struggle. Henry Mürger—Novalis—Alexander Petöfi—Honoré de Balzac—Edgar Allan Poe—André Chénier. 2 vols. crown 8vo. price 15s.

DANCE (Rev. C. D.)—RECOLLECTIONS OF FOUR YEARS IN VENEZUELA. With Three Illustrations and a Map. Crown 8vo. price 7s. 6d.

DAVIDSON (Rev. Samuel) D.D., LL.D. —THE NEW TESTAMENT, TRANSLATED FROM THE LATEST GREEK TEXT OF TISCHENDORF. A New and thoroughly revised Edition. Post 8vo. price 10s. 6d.

CANON OF THE BIBLE : Its Formation, History, and Fluctuations. Second Edition. Small crown 8vo. price 5s.

DAVIES (G. Christopher)—MOUNTAIN, MEADOW, AND MERE : a Series of Outdoor Sketches of Sport, Scenery, Adventures, and Natural History With Sixteen Illustrations by Bosworth W. Harcourt. Crown 8vo. price 6s.

DAVIES (Rev. J. L.) M.A.—THEOLOGY AND MORALITY. Essays on Questions of Belief and Practice. Crown 8vo. price 7s. 6d.

DAWSON (Geo.), M.A.—PRAYERS, WITH A DISCOURSE ON PRAYER. Edited by his Wife. Fifth Edition. Crown 8vo. 6s.

SERMONS ON DISPUTED POINTS AND SPECIAL OCCASIONS. Edited by his Wife. Second Edition. Crown 8vo. price 6s.

SERMONS ON DAILY LIFE AND DUTY. Edited by his Wife. Second Edition. Crown 8vo. price 6s.

DE LESSEPS (Ferdinand)—THE SUEZ CANAL : Letters Descriptive of its Rise and Progress in 1854-1856. Translated by N. R. D'ANVERS. Demy 8vo. price 10s. 6d.

DE REDCLIFFE (Viscount Stratford) P.C., K.G., G.C.B.—WHY AM I A CHRISTIAN? Fifth Edition. Crown 8vo. price 3s.

DESPREZ (Philip S.) B.D.—DANIEL AND JOHN. Demy 8vo. cloth.

DE TOCQUEVILLE (A.)—CORRESPONDENCE AND CONVERSATIONS OF, WITH NASSAU WILLIAM SENIOR, from 1834 to 1859. Edited by M. C. M. SIMPSON. 2 vols. post 8vo. price 21s.

DOWDEN (Edward) LL.D.—SHAKSPERE: a Critical Study of his Mind and Art. Third Edition. Post 8vo. price 12s.

STUDIES IN LITERATURE, 1789–1877. Large Post 8vo. price 12s.

DREW (Rev. G. S.) M.A.—SCRIPTURE LANDS IN CONNECTION WITH THEIR HISTORY. Second Edition. 8vo. price 10s. 6d.

NAZARETH: ITS LIFE AND LESSONS. Third Edition. Crown 8vo. price 5s.

THE DIVINE KINGDOM ON EARTH AS IT IS IN HEAVEN. 8vo. price 10s. 6d.

THE SON OF MAN: His Life and Ministry. Crown 8vo. price 7s. 6d.

DREWRY (G. O.) M.D.—THE COMMON-SENSE MANAGEMENT OF THE STOMACH. Fourth Edition. Fcp. 8vo. price 2s. 6d.

DREWRY (G. O.) M.D., and BARTLETT (H. C.) Ph.D., F.C.S. CUP AND PLATTER: or, Notes on Food and its Effects. Small 8vo. price 2s. 6d.

EDEN (Frederick)—THE NILE WITHOUT A DRAGOMAN. Second Edition. Crown 8vo. price 7s. 6d.

ELSDALE (Henry)—STUDIES IN TENNYSON'S IDYLLS. Crown 8vo. price 5s.

ESSAYS ON THE ENDOWMENT OF RESEARCH. By Various Writers.

List of Contributors.—Mark Pattison, B.D.—James S. Cotton, B.A.—Charles E. Appleton, D.C.L.—Archibald H. Sayce, M.A.—Henry Clifton Sorby, F.R.S.—Thomas K. Cheyne, M.A.—W. T. Thiselton Dyer, M.A.—Henry Nettleship, M.A. Square crown 8vo. price 10s. 6d.

EVANS (Mark)—THE STORY OF OUR FATHER'S LOVE, told to Children. being a New and Cheaper Edition. With Four Illustrations. Fcp. 8vo. price 1s. 6d.

A BOOK OF COMMON PRAYER AND WORSHIP FOR HOUSEHOLD USE, compiled exclusively from the Holy Scriptures. Fcp. 8vo. price 2s. 6d.

THE GOSPEL OF HOME LIFE. Crown 8vo. cloth, price 4s. 6d.

EX-CIVILIAN.—LIFE IN THE MOFUSSIL: or Civilian Life in Lower Bengal. 2 vols. Large post 8vo. price 14s.

FAVRE (Mons. J.)—THE GOVERNMENT OF THE NATIONAL DEFENCE. From the 30th June to the 31st October, 1870. Translated by H. CLARK. Demy 8vo. price 10s. 6d.

FINN (The late James) M.R.A.S.—STIRRING TIMES ; or, Records from Jerusalem Consular Chronicles of 1853 to 1856. Edited and Compiled by his Widow ; with a Preface by the Viscountess STRANGFORD. 2 vols. Demy 8vo. price 30s.

FLEMING (James) D.D.—EARLY CHRISTIAN WITNESSES; or, Testimonies of the First Centuries to the Truth of Christianity. Small Crown 8vo. cloth.

FOLKESTONE RITUAL CASE : the Arguments, Proceedings, Judgment, and Report. Demy 8vo. price 25s.

FOOTMAN (Rev. H.) M.A.—FROM HOME AND BACK ; or, Some Aspects of Sin as seen in the Light of the Parable of the Prodigal. Crown 8vo. price 5s.

FOWLE (Rev. Edmund)—LATIN PRIMER RULES MADE EASY. Crown 8vo. price 3s.

FOWLE (Rev. T. W.) M.A.—THE RECONCILIATION OF RELIGION AND SCIENCE. Being Essays on Immortality, Inspiration, Miracles, and the Being of Christ. Demy 8vo. price 10s. 6d.

FOX-BOURNE (H. R.) — THE LIFE OF JOHN LOCKE, 1632–1704. 2 vols. demy 8vo. price 28s.

FRASER (Donald)—EXCHANGE TABLES OF STERLING AND INDIAN RUPEE CURRENCY, upon a new and extended system, embracing Values from One Farthing to One Hundred Thousand Pounds, and at rates progressing, in Sixteenths of a Penny, from 1s. 9d. to 2s. 3d. per Rupee. Royal 8vo. price 10s. 6d.

FRISWELL (J. Hain)—THE BETTER SELF. Essays for Home Life. Crown 8vo. price 6s.

FYTCHE (Lieut.-Gen. Albert) C.S.I. late Chief Commissioner of British Burma. BURMA PAST AND PRESENT, with Personal Reminiscences of the Country. With Steel Portraits, Chromolithographs, Engravings on Wood, and Map. 2 vols. Demy 8vo. cloth, price 30s.

GAMBIER (Capt. J. W.) R.N.—SERVIA. Crown 8vo. price 5s.

GARDNER (J.) M.D.—LONGEVITY : THE MEANS OF PROLONGING LIFE AFTER MIDDLE AGE. Fourth Edition, revised and enlarged. Small crown 8vo. price 4s.

GILBERT (Mrs.)—AUTOBIOGRAPHY AND OTHER MEMORIALS. Edited by Josiah Gilbert. Third and Cheaper Edition. With Steel Portrait and several Wood Engravings. Crown 8vo. price 7s. 6d.

GILL (Rev. W. W.) B.A.—MYTHS AND SONGS FROM THE SOUTH PACIFIC. With a Preface by F. Max Müller, M.A., Professor of Comparative Philology at Oxford. Post 8vo. price 9s.

GODKIN (James)—THE RELIGIOUS HISTORY OF IRELAND : Primitive, Papal, and Protestant. Including the Evangelical Missions, Catholic Agitations, and Church Progress of the last half Century. 8vo. price 12s.

GODWIN (William)—WILLIAM GODWIN: HIS FRIENDS AND CONTEMPORARIES. With Portraits and Facsimiles of the Handwriting of Godwin and his Wife. By C. KEGAN PAUL. 2 vols. Large post 8vo. price 28s.

THE GENIUS OF CHRISTIANITY UNVEILED. Being Essays never before published. Edited, with a Preface, by C. Kegan Paul. Crown 8vo. price 7s. 6d.

GOODENOUGH (*Commodore J. G.*) R.N., C.B., C.M.G.—Memoir of, with Extracts from his Letters and Journals. Edited by his Widow. With Steel Engraved Portrait. Square 8vo. cloth, 5s.

*** Also a Library Edition with Maps, Woodcuts, and Steel Engraved Portrait. Square post 8vo. price 14s.

GOODMAN (*W.*) Cuba, the Pearl of the Antilles. Crown 8vo. price 7s. 6d.

GOULD (*Rev. S. Baring*) *M.A.*—The Vicar of Morwenstow: a Memoir of the Rev. R. S. Hawker. With Portrait. Third Edition, revised. Square post 8vo. 10s. 6d.

GRANVILLE (*A. B.*) *M.D., F.R.S., &c.*—Autobiography of A. B. Granville, F.R.S., &c. Edited, with a Brief Account of the Concluding Years of his Life, by his youngest Daughter, Paulina B. Granville. 2 vols. With a Portrait. Second Edition. Demy 8vo. price 32s.

GREY (*John*) *of Dilston.*—Memoirs. By Josephine E. Butler. New and Revised Edition. Crown 8vo. price 3s. 6d.

GRIFFITH (*Rev. T.*) *A.M.*—Studies of the Divine Master. Demy 8vo. price 12s.

GRIFFITHS (*Capt. Arthur*)—Memorials of Millbank, and Chapters in Prison History. With Illustrations by R. Goff and the Author. 2 vols. post 8vo. price 21s.

GRIMLEY (*Rev. H. N.*) *M.A., Professor of Mathematics in the University College of Wales, and sometime Chaplain of Tremadoc Church.*

Tremadoc Sermons, chiefly on the Spiritual Body, the Unseen World, and the Divine Humanity. Second Edition. Crown 8vo. price 6s.

GRÜNER (*M. L.*)—Studies of Blast Furnace Phenomena. Translated by L. D. B. Gordon, F.R.S.E., F.G.S. Demy 8vo. price 7s. 6d.

GURNEY (*Rev. Archer*)—Words of Faith and Cheer. A Mission of Instruction and Suggestion. Crown 8vo. price 6s.

HAECKEL (*Prof. Ernst*)—The History of Creation. Translation revised by Professor E. Ray Lankester, M.A., F.R.S. With Coloured Plates and Genealogical Trees of the various groups of both plants and animals. 2 vols. Second Edition. Post 8vo. cloth, price 32s.

The History of the Evolution of Man. With numerous Illustrations. 2 vols. Post 8vo.

HAKE (*A. Egmont*)—Paris Originals, with Twenty Etchings, by Léon Richeton. Large post 8vo. price 14s.

HALLECK'S International Law; or, Rules Regulating the Intercourse of States in Peace and War. A New Edition, revised, with Notes and Cases, by Sir Sherston Baker, Bart. 2 vols. Demy 8vo. price 38s.

HARCOURT (*Capt. A. F. P.*)—The Shakespeare Argosy. Containing much of the wealth of Shakespeare's Wisdom and Wit, alphabetically arranged and classified. Crown 8vo. price 6s.

HAWEIS (*Rev. H. R.*) *M.A.*—CURRENT COIN. Materialism—The Devil — Crime — Drunkenness — Pauperism — Emotion — Recreation — The Sabbath. Third Edition. Crown 8vo. price 6s.

SPEECH IN SEASON. Fourth Edition. Crown 8vo. price 9s.

THOUGHTS FOR THE TIMES. Eleventh Edition. Crown 8vo. price 7s. 6d.

UNSECTARIAN FAMILY PRAYERS for Morning and Evening for a Week, with short selected passages from the Bible. Second Edition. Square crown 8vo. price 3s. 6d.

ARROWS IN THE AIR. Conferences and Pleas. Crown 8vo. cloth.

HAYMAN (*H.*) *D.D.*, *late Head Master of Rugby School.*—RUGBY SCHOOL SERMONS. With an Introductory Essay on the Indwelling of the Holy Spirit. Crown 8vo. price 7s. 6d.

HELLWALD (*Baron F. Von*)—THE RUSSIANS IN CENTRAL ASIA. A Critical Examination, down to the Present Time, of the Geography and History of Central Asia. Translated by Lieut.-Col. Theodore Wirgman, LL.B. With Map. Large post 8vo. price 12s.

HINTON (*J.*)—THE PLACE OF THE PHYSICIAN. To which is added ESSAYS ON THE LAW OF HUMAN LIFE, AND ON THE RELATIONS BETWEEN ORGANIC AND INORGANIC WORLDS. Second Edition. Crown 8vo. price 3s. 6d.

PHYSIOLOGY FOR PRACTICAL USE. By Various Writers. With 50 Illustrations. 2 vols. Second Edition. Crown 8vo. price 12s. 6d.

AN ATLAS OF DISEASES OF THE MEMBRANA TYMPANI. With Descriptive Text. Post 8vo. price £6. 6s.

THE QUESTIONS OF AURAL SURGERY. With Illustrations. 2 vols. Post 8vo. price £6. 6s.

LIFE AND LETTERS. Edited by ELLICE HOPKINS, with an Introduction by Sir W. W. GULL, Bart., and Portrait engraved on Steel by C. H. JEENS. Crown 8vo. price 8s. 6d.

CHAPTERS ON THE ART OF THINKING, and other Essays. Crown 8vo.

H. J. C.—THE ART OF FURNISHING. A Popular Treatise on the Principles of Furnishing, based on the Laws of Common Sense, Requirement, and Picturesque Effect. Small crown 8vo. price 3s. 6d.

HOLROYD (*Major W. R. M.*)—TAS-HIL UL KALAM ; or, Hindustani made Easy. Crown 8vo. price 5s.

HOOPER (*Mary*)—LITTLE DINNERS: HOW TO SERVE THEM WITH ELEGANCE AND ECONOMY. Thirteenth Edition. Crown 8vo. price 5s.

COOKERY FOR INVALIDS, PERSONS OF DELICATE DIGESTION, AND CHILDREN. Crown 8vo. price 3s. 6d.

EVERY-DAY MEALS. Being Economical and Wholesome Recipes for Breakfast, Luncheon, and Supper. Second Edition. Crown 8vo. cloth, price 5s.

HOPKINS (*Ellice*)—LIFE AND LETTERS OF JAMES HINTON, with an Introduction by Sir W. W. GULL, Bart., and Portrait engraved on Steel by C. H. JEENS. Crown 8vo. price 8s. 6d.

HOPKINS (*M.*)—THE PORT OF REFUGE ; or, Counsel and Aid to Shipmasters in Difficulty, Doubt, or Distress. Second and Revised Edition. Crown 8vo. price 6s.

HORNE (William) M.A.—REASON AND REVELATION: an Examination into the Nature and Contents of Scripture Revelation, as compared with other Forms of Truth. Demy 8vo. price 12s.

HORNER (The Misses)—WALKS IN FLORENCE. A New and thoroughly Revised Edition. 2 vols. Crown 8vo. Cloth limp. With Illustrations.
    VOL. I.—Churches, Streets, and Palaces. Price 10s. 6d.
    VOL. II.—Public Galleries and Museums. Price 5s.

HULL (Edmund C. P.)—THE EUROPEAN IN INDIA. With a Medical Guide for Anglo-Indians. By R. S. MAIR, M.D., F.R.C.S.E. Third Edition, Revised and Corrected. Post 8vo. price 6s.

HUTTON (James)—MISSIONARY LIFE IN THE SOUTHERN SEAS. With Illustrations. Crown 8vo. price 7s. 6d.

JACKSON (T. G.)—MODERN GOTHIC ARCHITECTURE. Crown 8vo. price 5s.

JACOB (Maj.-Gen. Sir G. Le Grand) K.C.S.I., C.B.—WESTERN INDIA BEFORE AND DURING THE MUTINIES. Pictures drawn from Life. Second Edition. Crown 8vo. price 7s. 6d.

JENKINS (E.) and RAYMOND (J.) Esqs.—A LEGAL HANDBOOK FOR ARCHITECTS, BUILDERS, AND BUILDING OWNERS. Second Edition, Revised. Crown 8vo. price 6s.

JENKINS (Rev. R. C.) M.A.—THE PRIVILEGE OF PETER and the Claims of the Roman Church confronted with the Scriptures, the Councils, and the Testimony of the Popes themselves. Fcap. 8vo. price 3s. 6d.

JENNINGS (Mrs. Vaughan)—RAHEL: HER LIFE AND LETTERS. With a Portrait from the Painting by Daffinger. Square post 8vo. price 7s. 6d.

JONES (Lucy)—PUDDINGS AND SWEETS; being Three Hundred and Sixty-five Receipts approved by experience. Crown 8vo. price 2s. 6d.

KAUFMANN (Rev. M.) B.A.—SOCIALISM: Its Nature, its Dangers, and its Remedies considered. Crown 8vo. price 7s. 6d.

KERNER (Dr. A.) Professor of Botany in the University of Innsbruck.—FLOWERS AND THEIR UNBIDDEN GUESTS. Translation edited by W. OGLE, M.A., M.B. With Illustrations. Square 8vo. cloth.

KIDD (Joseph) M.D.—THE LAWS OF THERAPEUTICS; or, the Science and Art of Medicine. Crown 8vo. price 6s.

KINAHAN (G. Henry) M.R.I.A., of H.M.'s Geological Survey.—THE GEOLOGY OF IRELAND, with numerous Illustrations and a Geological Map of Ireland. Square 8vo. cloth.

KING (Alice)—A CLUSTER OF LIVES. Crown 8vo. price 7s. 6d.

KINGSLEY (Charles) M.A.—LETTERS AND MEMORIES OF HIS LIFE. Edited by his WIFE. With Two Steel Engraved Portraits, and Illustrations on Wood, and a Facsimile of his Handwriting. Thirteenth Edition. 2 vols. Demy 8vo. price 36s.

    ALL SAINTS' DAY, and other Sermons. Edited by the Rev. W. HARRISON. Second Edition. Crown 8vo. price 7s. 6d.

    TRUE WORDS FOR BRAVE MEN. A Book for Soldiers' and Sailors' Libraries. Crown 8vo. price 2s. 6d.

LACORDAIRE (Rev. Père)—LIFE : Conferences delivered at Toulouse. A New and Cheaper Edition. Crown 8vo. price 3s. 6d.

LAMBERT (Cowley) F.R.G.S.—A TRIP TO CASHMERE AND LADAK. With Illustrations. Crown 8vo. price 7s. 6d.

LAURIE (J. S.)—EDUCATIONAL COURSE OF SECULAR SCHOOL BOOKS FOR INDIA :—

THE FIRST HINDUSTANI READER. Stiff linen wrapper, price 6d.

THE SECOND HINDUSTANI READER. Stiff linen wrapper, price 6d.

THE ORIENTAL (ENGLISH) READER. Book I., price 6d.; II., price 7½d.; III., price 9d.; IV., price 1s.

GEOGRAPHY OF INDIA ; with Maps and Historical Appendix, tracing the Growth of the British Empire in Hindustan. Fcap. 8vo. price 1s. 6d.

L. D. S.—LETTERS FROM CHINA AND JAPAN. With Illustrated Title-page. Crown 8vo. price 7s. 6d.

LEE (Rev. F. G.) D.C.L.—THE OTHER WORLD; or, Glimpses of the Supernatural. 2 vols. A New Edition. Crown 8vo. price 15s.

LENOIR (J.)—FAYOUM ; or, Artists in Egypt. A Tour with M. Gérome and others. With 13 Illustrations. A New and Cheaper Edition. Crown 8vo. price 3s. 6d.

LIFE IN THE MOFUSSIL ; or, Civilian Life in Lower Bengal. By an Ex-Civilian. Large post 8vo. price 14s.

LINDSAY (W. Lauder) M.D., F.R.S.E., &c.—MIND IN THE LOWER ANIMALS IN HEALTH AND DISEASE. 2 vols. Demy 8vo. cloth. Vol. I.—Mind in Health. Vol. II.—Mind in Disease.

LORIMER (Peter) D.D.—JOHN KNOX AND THE CHURCH OF ENGLAND. His Work in her Pulpit, and his Influence upon her Liturgy, Articles, and Parties. Demy 8vo. price 12s.

JOHN WICLIF AND HIS ENGLISH PRECURSORS. By GERHARD VICTOR LECHLER. Translated from the German, with additional Notes. 2 vols. Demy 8vo. price 21s.

LOTHIAN (Roxburghe)—DANTE AND BEATRICE FROM 1282 TO 1290. A Romance. 2 vols. Post 8vo. price 24s.

LOVER (Samuel) R.H.A.—THE LIFE OF SAMUEL LOVER, R.H.A. ; Artistic, Literary, and Musical. With Selections from his Unpublished Papers and Correspondence. By BAYLE BERNARD. 2 vols. With a Portrait. Post 8vo. price 21s.

LYONS (R. T.) Surg.-Maj. Bengal Army.—A TREATISE ON RELAPSING FEVER. Post 8vo. price 7s. 6d.

MACAULAY (J.) M.D. Edin.—THE TRUTH ABOUT IRELAND : Tours of Observation in 1872 and 1875. With Remarks on Irish Public Questions. Being a Second Edition of 'Ireland in 1872,' with a New and Supplementary Preface. Crown 8vo. price 3s. 6d.

MACLACHLAN (A. N. C.) M.A.—WILLIAM AUGUSTUS, DUKE OF CUMBERLAND ; being a Sketch of his Military Life and Character, chiefly as exhibited in the General Orders of His Royal Highness, 1745-1747. With Illustrations. Post 8vo. price 15s.

MACNAUGHT (Rev. John)—CŒNA DOMINI: An Essay on the Lord's Supper, its Primitive Institution, Apostolic Uses, and Subsequent History. Demy 8vo. price 14s.

MAIR (R. S.) M.D., F.R.C.S.E.—THE MEDICAL GUIDE FOR ANGLO-INDIANS. Being a Compendium of Advice to Europeans in India, relating to the Preservation and Regulation of Health. With a Supplement on the Management of Children in India. Second Edition. Crown 8vo. limp cloth, price 3s. 6d.

MANNING (His Eminence Cardinal) — ESSAYS ON RELIGION AND LITERATURE. By various Writers. Third Series. Demy 8vo. price 10s. 6d.

THE INDEPENDENCE OF THE HOLY SEE. With an Appendix containing the Papal Allocution and a translation. Crown 8vo. price 5s.

THE TRUE STORY OF THE VATICAN COUNCIL. Crown 8vo. price 5s.

MARRIOTT (Maj.-Gen. W. F.) C.S.I.—A GRAMMAR OF POLITICAL ECONOMY. Crown 8vo. price 6s.

MAUGHAN (W. C.)—THE ALPS OF ARABIA; or, Travels through Egypt, Sinai, Arabia, and the Holy Land. With Map. Second Edition. Demy 8vo. price 5s.

MAURICE (C. E.)—LIVES OF ENGLISH POPULAR LEADERS. No. 1.—STEPHEN LANGTON. Crown 8vo. price 7s. 6d. No. 2.—TYLER, BALL, and OLDCASTLE. Crown 8vo. price 7s. 6d.

MAZZINI (Joseph) — A Memoir. By E. A. V. Two Photographic Portraits. Second Edition. Crown 8vo. price 5s.

MEDLEY (Lieut.-Col. J. G.) R.E.—AN AUTUMN TOUR IN THE UNITED STATES AND CANADA. Crown 8vo. price 5s.

MICKLETHWAITE (J. T.) F.S.A.—MODERN PARISH CHURCHES: Their Plan, Design, and Furniture. Crown 8vo. price 7s. 6d.

MILLER (Edward)—THE HISTORY AND DOCTRINES OF IRVINGISM; or, the so-called Catholic and Apostolic Church. 2 vols. Large post 8vo. price 25s.

MILNE (James)—TABLES OF EXCHANGE for the Conversion of Sterling Money into Indian and Ceylon Currency, at Rates from 1s. 8d. to 2s. 3d. per Rupee. Second Edition. Demy 8vo. Cloth, price £2. 2s.

MIVART (St. George) F.R.S.—CONTEMPORARY EVOLUTION: An Essay on some recent Social Changes. Post 8vo. price 7s. 6d.

MOCKLER (E.)—A GRAMMAR OF THE BALOOCHEE LANGUAGE, as it is spoken in Makran (Ancient Gedrosia), in the Persia-Arabic and Roman characters. Fcap. 8vo. price 5s.

MOFFAT (R. S.)—ECONOMY OF CONSUMPTION: a Study in Political Economy. Demy 8vo. price 18s.

THE PRINCIPLES OF A TIME POLICY: being an Exposition of a Method of Settling Disputes between Employers and Employed in regard to Time and Wages, by a simple Process of Mercantile Barter, without recourse to Strikes or Locks-out. Reprinted from 'The Economy of Consumption,' with a Preface and Appendix containing Observations on some Reviews of that book, and a Re-criticism of the Theories of Ricardo and J. S. Mill on Rent, Value, and Cost of Production. Demy 8vo. price 3s. 6d.

MOLTKE (Field-Marshal Von)—LETTERS FROM RUSSIA. Translated by ROBINA NAPIER. Crown 8vo. price 6s.

MOORE (Rev. D.) M.A.—CHRIST AND HIS CHURCH. By the Author of 'The Age and the Gospel,' &c. Crown 8vo. price 3s. 6d.

MORE (R. Jasper)—UNDER THE BALKANS. Notes of a Visit to the District of Philippopolis in 1876. With a Map, and Illustrations from Photographs. Crown 8vo. price 6s.

MORELL (J. R.)—EUCLID SIMPLIFIED IN METHOD AND LANGUAGE. Being a Manual of Geometry. Compiled from the most important French Works, approved by the University of Paris and the Minister of Public Instruction. Fcap. 8vo. price 2s. 6d.

MORSE (E. S.) Ph.D.—FIRST BOOK OF ZOOLOGY. With numerous Illustrations. Crown 8vo. price 5s.

MUSGRAVE (Anthony)—STUDIES IN POLITICAL ECONOMY. Crown 8vo. price 6s.

NEWMAN (J. H.) D.D.—CHARACTERISTICS FROM THE WRITINGS OF. Being Selections from his various Works. Arranged with the Author's personal Approval. Third Edition. With Portrait. Crown 8vo. price 6s.

*** A Portrait of the Rev. Dr. J. H. Newman, mounted for framing, can be had price 2s. 6d.

NICHOLAS (T.)—THE PEDIGREE OF THE ENGLISH PEOPLE. Fifth Edition. Demy 8vo. price 16s.

NOBLE (J. A.)—THE PELICAN PAPERS. Reminiscences and Remains of a Dweller in the Wilderness. Crown 8vo. price 6s.

NORMAN PEOPLE (THE), and their Existing Descendants in the British Dominions and the United States of America. Demy 8vo. price 21s.

NOTREGE (John) A.M.—THE SPIRITUAL FUNCTION OF A PRESBYTER IN THE CHURCH OF ENGLAND. Crown 8vo. red edges, price 3s. 6d.

O'MEARA (Kathleen.)—FREDERIC OZANAM, Professor of the Sorbonne: His Life and Work. Second Edition. Crown 8vo. cloth.

ORIENTAL SPORTING MAGAZINE (THE). A Reprint of the first 5 Volumes, in 2 Volumes. Demy 8vo. price 28s.

PARKER (Joseph) D.D.—THE PARACLETE: An Essay on the Personality and Ministry of the Holy Ghost, with some reference to current discussions. Second Edition. Demy 8vo. price 12s.

PARSLOE (Joseph) — OUR RAILWAYS. Sketches, Historical and Descriptive. With Practical Information as to Fares and Rates, &c., and a Chapter on Railway Reform. Crown 8vo. price 6s.

PARR (Harriet)—ECHOES OF A FAMOUS YEAR. Crown 8vo. price 8s. 6d.

PAUL (C. Kegan)—WILLIAM GODWIN: HIS FRIENDS AND CONTEMPORARIES. With Portraits and Facsimiles of the Handwriting of Godwin and his Wife. 2 vols. Square post 8vo. price 28s.

THE GENIUS OF CHRISTIANITY UNVEILED. Being Essays by William Godwin never before published. Edited, with a Preface, by C. Kegan Paul. Crown 8vo. price 7s. 6d.

PAYNE (Prof. J. F.)—LECTURES ON EDUCATION. Price 6*d*. each.
  II. Fröbel and the Kindergarten System. Second Edition.
  A VISIT TO GERMAN SCHOOLS: ELEMENTARY SCHOOLS IN GERMANY. Notes of a Professional Tour to inspect some of the Kindergartens, Primary Schools, Public Girls' Schools, and Schools for Technical Instruction in Hamburgh, Berlin, Dresden, Weimar, Gotha, Eisenach, in the autumn of 1874. With Critical Discussions of the General Principles and Practice of Kindergartens and other Schemes of Elementary Education. Crown 8vo. price 4*s*. 6*d*.

PENRICE (Maj. J.) B.A.—A DICTIONARY AND GLOSSARY OF THE KO-RAN. With Copious Grammatical References and Explanations of the Text. 4to. price 21*s*.

PERCEVAL (Rev. P.) — TAMIL PROVERBS, WITH THEIR ENGLISH TRANSLATION. Containing upwards of Six Thousand Proverbs. Third Edition. Demy 8vo. sewed, price 9*s*.

PESCHEL (Dr. Oscar)—THE RACES OF MAN AND THEIR GEOGRAPHICAL DISTRIBUTION. Large crown 8vo. price 9*s*.

PIGGOT (J.) F.S.A., F.R.G.S.—PERSIA—ANCIENT AND MODERN. Post 8vo. price 10*s*. 6*d*.

PLAYFAIR (Lieut-Col.), Her Britannic Majesty's Consul-General in Algiers.
  TRAVELS IN THE FOOTSTEPS OF BRUCE IN ALGERIA AND TUNIS. Illustrated by facsimiles of Bruce's original Drawings, Photographs, Maps, &c. Royal 4to. cloth, bevelled boards, gilt leaves, price £3. 3*s*.

POOR (H. V.)—MONEY AND ITS LAWS: embracing a History of Monetary Theories &c. Demy 8vo. price 21*s*.

POUSHKIN (A. S.)—RUSSIAN ROMANCE. Translated from the Tales of Belkin, &c. By Mrs. J. Buchan Telfer (*née* Mouravieff). Crown 8vo. price 7*s*. 6*d*.

POWER (H.)—OUR INVALIDS: HOW SHALL WE EMPLOY AND AMUSE THEM? Fcp. 8vo. price 2*s*. 6*d*.

PRESBYTER—UNFOLDINGS OF CHRISTIAN HOPE. An Essay shewing that the Doctrine contained in the Damnatory Clauses of the Creed commonly called Athanasian is Unscriptural. Small crown 8vo. price 4*s*. 6*d*.

PRICE (Prof. Bonamy) — CURRENCY AND BANKING. Crown 8vo. price 6*s*.
  CHAPTERS ON PRACTICAL POLITICAL ECONOMY. Being the Substance of Lectures delivered before the University of Oxford. Large post 8vo. price 12*s*.

PROCTOR (Richard A.) B.A.—OUR PLACE AMONG INFINITIES. A Series of Essays contrasting our little abode in space and time with the Infinities around us. To which are added Essays on 'Astrology,' and 'The Jewish Sabbath.' Third Edition. Crown 8vo. price 6*s*.
  THE EXPANSE OF HEAVEN. A Series of Essays on the Wonders of the Firmament. With a Frontispiece. Third Edition. Crown 8vo. price 6*s*.

PROTEUS AND AMADEUS. A Correspondence. Edited by AUBREY DE VERE. Crown 8vo. price 5s.

PUNJAUB (THE) AND NORTH-WESTERN FRONTIER OF INDIA. By an Old Punjaubee. Crown 8vo. price 5s.

RAM (James)—THE PHILOSOPHY OF WAR. Small crown 8vo. price 3s 6d

RAVENSHAW (John Henry) B.C.S.—GAUR: ITS RUINS AND INSCRIPTIONS. Edited by his Widow. With 40 Photographic Illustrations, and 14 facsimiles of Inscriptions. Royal 4to.

READ (Carveth)—ON THE THEORY OF LOGIC: An Essay. Crown 8vo. price 6s.

RIBOT (Prof. Th.)—ENGLISH PSYCHOLOGY. Second Edition. A Revised and Corrected Translation from the latest French Edition. Large post 8vo. price 9s.

HEREDITY: A Psychological Study on its Phenomena, its Laws, its Causes, and its Consequences. Large crown 8vo. price 9s.

RINK (Chevalier Dr. Henry)—GREENLAND: ITS PEOPLE AND ITS PRODUCTS. By the Chevalier Dr. HENRY RINK, President of the Greenland Board of Trade. With sixteen Illustrations, drawn by the Eskimo, and a Map. Edited by Dr. Robert Brown. Crown 8vo. price 10s. 6d.

RODWELL (G. F.) F.R.A.S., F.C.S.—ETNA: A HISTORY OF THE MOUNTAIN AND ITS ERUPTIONS. With Maps and Illustrations. Square 8vo. cloth.

ROBERTSON (The late Rev. F. W.) M.A., of Brighton.—LIFE AND LETTERS OF. Edited by the Rev. Stopford Brooke, M.A., Chaplain in Ordinary to the Queen.

    I. Two vols., uniform with the Sermons. With Steel Portrait. Crown 8vo. price 7s. 6d.

    II. Library Edition, in Demy 8vo. with Two Steel Portraits. Price 12s.

    III. A Popular Edition, in 1 vol. Crown 8vo. price 6s.

SERMONS. Four Series. Small crown 8vo. price 3s. 6d. each.

NOTES ON GENESIS. Third Edition. Crown 8vo. price 5s.

EXPOSITORY LECTURES ON ST. PAUL'S EPISTLES TO THE CORINTHIANS. A New Edition. Small crown 8vo. price 5s.

LECTURES AND ADDRESSES, with other Literary Remains. A New Edition. Crown 8vo. price 5s.

AN ANALYSIS OF MR. TENNYSON'S 'IN MEMORIAM.' (Dedicated by Permission to the Poet-Laureate.) Fcp. 8vo. price 2s.

THE EDUCATION OF THE HUMAN RACE. Translated from the German of Gotthold Ephraim Lessing. Fcp. 8vo. price 2s. 6d.

    The above Works can also be had, bound in half-morocco.

⁎ A Portrait of the late Rev. F. W. Robertson, mounted for framing, can be had, price 2s. 6d.

RUTHERFORD (John)—THE SECRET HISTORY OF THE FENIAN CONSPIRACY: its Origin, Objects, and Ramifications. 2 vols. Post 8vo. price 18s.

SCOTT (W. T.)—ANTIQUITIES OF AN ESSEX PARISH; or, Pages from the History of Great Dunmow. Crown 8vo. price 5s.; sewed, 4s.

SCOTT (Robert H.)—WEATHER CHARTS AND STORM WARNINGS. Illustrated. Crown 8vo. price 3s. 6d.

SENIOR (N. W.)—ALEXIS DE TOCQUEVILLE. Correspondence and Conversations with Nassau W. Senior, from 1833 to 1859. Edited by M. C. M. Simpson. 2 vols. Large post 8vo. price 21s.

JOURNALS KEPT IN FRANCE AND ITALY. From 1848 to 1852. With a Sketch of the Revolution of 1848. Edited by his Daughter, M. C. M. Simpson. 2 vols. Post 8vo. price 24s.

SEYD (Ernest) F.S.S.—THE FALL IN THE PRICE OF SILVER. Its Causes, its Consequences, and their Possible Avoidance, with Special Reference to India. Demy 8vo. sewed, price 2s. 6d.

SHAKSPEARE (Charles)—SAINT PAUL AT ATHENS. Spiritual Christianity in relation to some aspects of Modern Thought. Five Sermons preached at St. Stephen's Church, Westbourne Park. With a Preface by the Rev. Canon FARRAR.

SHELLEY (Lady)—SHELLEY MEMORIALS FROM AUTHENTIC SOURCES. With (now first printed) an Essay on Christianity by Percy Bysshe Shelley. With Portrait. Third Edition. Crown 8vo. price 5s.

SHILLITO (Rev. Joseph)—WOMANHOOD : its Duties, Temptations, and Privileges. A Book for Young Women. Third Edition. Crown 8vo. price 3s. 6d.

SHIPLEY (Rev. Orby) M.A.—CHURCH TRACTS : OR, STUDIES IN MODERN PROBLEMS. By various Writers. 2 vols. Crown 8vo. price 5s. each.

PRINCIPLES OF THE FAITH IN RELATION TO SIN. Topics for Thought in Times of Retreat. Eleven Addresses delivered during a Retreat of Three Days to Persons living in the World. Demy 8vo.

SHUTE (Richard) M.A.—A DISCOURSE ON TRUTH. Large post 8vo. price 9s.

SMEDLEY (M. B.)—BOARDING-OUT AND PAUPER SCHOOLS FOR GIRLS. Crown 8vo. price 3s. 6d.

SMITH (Edward) M.D., LL.B., F.R.S.—HEALTH AND DISEASE, as Influenced by the Daily, Seasonal, and other Cyclical Changes in the Human System. A New Edition. Post 8vo. price 7s. 6d.

PRACTICAL DIETARY FOR FAMILIES, SCHOOLS, AND THE LABOURING CLASSES. A New Edition. Post 8vo. price 3s. 6d.

TUBERCULAR CONSUMPTION IN ITS EARLY AND REMEDIABLE STAGES. Second Edition. Crown 8vo. price 6s.

SMITH (Hubert)—TENT LIFE WITH ENGLISH GIPSIES IN NORWAY. With Five full-page Engravings and Thirty-one smaller Illustrations by Whymper and others, and Map of the Country showing Routes. Third Edition. Revised and Corrected. Post 8vo. price 21s.

SOME TIME IN IRELAND. A Recollection. Crown 8vo. price 7s. 6d.

STEPHENS (Archibald John), LL.D.—THE FOLKESTONE RITUAL CASE. The Substance of the Argument delivered before the Judicial Committee of the Privy Council on behalf of the Respondents. Demy 8vo. cloth, price 6s.

STEVENSON (Rev. W. F.)—HYMNS FOR THE CHURCH AND HOME. Selected and Edited by the Rev. W. Fleming Stevenson.
The most complete Hymn Book published.
The Hymn Book consists of Three Parts :—I. For Public Worship.—II. For Family and Private Worship.—III. For Children.
₊ Published in various forms and prices, the latter ranging from 8d. to 6s. Lists and full particulars will be furnished on application to the Publishers.

STEVENSON (*Robert Louis*)—AN INLAND VOYAGE. With Frontispiece by Walter Crane. Crown 8vo. price 7s. 6d.

SULLY (*James*) M.A. — SENSATION AND INTUITION. Demy 8vo. price 10s. 6d.

PESSIMISM : a History and a Criticism. Demy 8vo. price 14s.

SUPERNATURAL IN NATURE (THE). A Verification by Free Use of Science. Demy 8vo. price 14s.

SYME (*David*)—OUTLINES OF AN INDUSTRIAL SCIENCE. Second Edition. Crown 8vo. price 6s.

TELFER (*J. Buchan*) F.R.G.S., *Commander R.N.*—THE CRIMEA AND TRANS-CAUCASIA. With numerous Illustrations and Maps. Second Edition. 2 vols. Royal 8vo. medium 8vo. price 36s.

THOMPSON (*Rev. A. S.*)—HOME WORDS FOR WANDERERS. A Volume of Sermons. Crown 8vo. price 6s.

THOMSON (*J. Turnbull*)—SOCIAL PROBLEMS ; OR, AN INQUIRY INTO THE LAWS OF INFLUENCE. With Diagrams. Demy 8vo. cloth.

TRAHERNE (*Mrs. A.*)—THE ROMANTIC ANNALS OF A NAVAL FAMILY. A New and Cheaper Edition. Crown 8vo. price 5s.

VAMBERY (*Prof. A.*)—BOKHARA : Its History and Conquest. Second Edition. Demy 8vo. price 18s.

VILLARI (*Professor*)—NICCOLO MACHIAVELLI AND HIS TIMES. Translated by Linda Villari. 2 vols. Large post 8vo.

VYNER (*Lady Mary*)—EVERY DAY A PORTION. Adapted from the Bible and the Prayer Book, for the Private Devotions of those living in Widowhood. Collected and Edited by Lady Mary Vyner. Square crown 8vo. extra, price 5s.

WALDSTEIN (*Charles*) Ph.D.—THE BALANCE OF EMOTION AND INTELLECT ; an Introductory Essay to the Study of Philosophy. Crown 8vo. cloth.

WALLER (*Rev. C. B.*)—THE APOCALYPSE, reviewed under the Light of the Doctrine of the Unfolding Ages, and the Relation of All Things. Demy 8vo. price 12s.

WELLS (*Capt. John C.*) R.N.—SPITZBERGEN—THE GATEWAY TO THE POLYNIA ; or, a Voyage to Spitzbergen. With numerous Illustrations by Whymper and others, and Map. New and Cheaper Edition. Demy 8vo. price 6s.

WETMORE (*W. S.*)—COMMERCIAL TELEGRAPHIC CODE. Second Edition. Post 4to. boards, price 42s.

WHITE (*A. D.*) LL.D.—WARFARE OF SCIENCE. With Prefatory Note by Professor Tyndall. Crown 8vo. price 3s. 6d.

WHITNEY (*Prof. William Dwight*)—ESSENTIALS OF ENGLISH GRAMMAR, for the Use of Schools. Crown 8vo. price 3s. 6d.

WHITTLE (*J. L.*) A.M.—CATHOLICISM AND THE VATICAN. With a Narrative of the Old Catholic Congress at Munich. Second Edition. Crown 8vo. price 4s. 6d.

WILBERFORCE (*H. W.*)—THE CHURCH AND THE EMPIRES. Historical Periods. Preceded by a Memoir of the Author by John Henry Newman, D.D. of the Oratory. With Portrait. Post 8vo. price 10s. 6d.

WILKINSON (T. L.)—SHORT LECTURES ON THE LAND LAWS. Delivered before the Working Men's College. Crown 8vo. limp cloth, price 2s.

WILLIAMS (A. Lukyn)—FAMINES IN INDIA; their Causes and Possible Prevention. The Essay for the Le Bas Prize, 1875. Demy 8vo. price 5s.

WILLIAMS (Chas.)—THE ARMENIAN CAMPAIGN. A Diary of the Campaign of 1877 in Armenia and Koordistan. Large post 8vo. price 10s. 6d.

WILLIAMS (Rowland) D.D.—LIFE AND LETTERS OF; with Extracts from his Note-Books. Edited by Mrs. Rowland Williams. With a Photographic Portrait. 2 vols. large post 8vo. price 24s.

PSALMS, LITANIES, COUNSELS, AND COLLECTS FOR DEVOUT PERSONS. Edited by his Widow. New and Popular Edition. Crown 8vo. price 3s. 6d.

STRAY THOUGHTS COLLECTED FROM THE WRITINGS OF THE LATE ROWLAND WILLIAMS, D.D. Edited by his Widow.

WILLIS (R.) M.D.—SERVETUS AND CALVIN: a Study of an Important Epoch in the Early History of the Reformation. 8vo. price 16s.

WILLIAM HARVEY. A History of the Discovery of the Circulation of the Blood: with a Portrait of Harvey after Faithorne. Demy 8vo. cloth.

WILSON (H. Schütz)—STUDIES AND ROMANCES. Crown 8vo. price 7s. 6d.

WILSON (Lieut.-Col. C. T.)—JAMES THE SECOND AND THE DUKE OF BERWICK. Demy 8vo. price 12s. 6d.

WINTERBOTHAM (Rev. R.) M.A., B.Sc.—SERMONS AND EXPOSITIONS. Crown 8vo. price 7s. 6d.

WOLLSTONECRAFT (Mary)—LETTERS TO IMLAY. New Edition with Prefatory Memoir by C. KEGAN PAUL, author of 'William Godwin: His Friends and Contemporaries,' &c. Crown 8vo.

WOOD (C. F.)—A YACHTING CRUISE IN THE SOUTH SEAS. With six Photographic Illustrations. Demy 8vo. price 7s. 6d.

WRIGHT (Rev. David) M.A.—WAITING FOR THE LIGHT, AND OTHER SERMONS. Crown 8vo. price 6s.

WYLD (R. S.) F.R.S.E.—THE PHYSICS AND THE PHILOSOPHY OF THE SENSES; or, the Mental and the Physical in their Mutual Relation. Illustrated by several Plates. Demy 8vo. price 16s.

YONGE (C. D.)—HISTORY OF THE ENGLISH REVOLUTION OF 1688. Crown 8vo. price 6s.

YOUMANS (Eliza A.)—AN ESSAY ON THE CULTURE OF THE OBSERVING POWERS OF CHILDREN, especially in connection with the Study of Botany. Edited, with Notes and a Supplement, by Joseph Payne, F.C.P., Author of 'Lectures on the Science and Art of Education,' &c. Crown 8vo. price 2s. 6d.

FIRST BOOK OF BOTANY. Designed to Cultivate the Observing Powers of Children. With 300 Engravings. New and Enlarged Edition. Crown 8vo. price 5s.

YOUMANS (Edward L.) M.D.—A CLASS BOOK OF CHEMISTRY, on the Basis of the New System. With 200 Illustrations. Crown 8vo. price 5s.

THE INTERNATIONAL SCIENTIFIC SERIES.

I. FORMS OF WATER: a Familiar Exposition of the Origin and Phenomena of Glaciers. By J. Tyndall, LL.D., F.R.S. With 25 Illustrations. Seventh Edition. Crown 8vo. price 5s.

II. PHYSICS AND POLITICS; or, Thoughts on the Application of the Principles of 'Natural Selection' and 'Inheritance' to Political Society. By Walter Bagehot. Fourth Edition. Crown 8vo. price 4s.

III. FOODS. By Edward Smith, M.D., LL.B., F.R.S. With numerous Illustrations. Fifth Edition. Crown 8vo. price 5s.

IV. MIND AND BODY: the Theories of their Relation. By Alexander Bain, LL.D. With Four Illustrations. Sixth Edition. Crown 8vo. price 4s.

V. THE STUDY OF SOCIOLOGY. By Herbert Spencer. Seventh Edition. Crown 8vo. price 5s.

VI. ON THE CONSERVATION OF ENERGY. By Balfour Stewart, M.A., LL.D., F.R.S. With 14 Illustrations. Fifth Edition. Crown 8vo. price 5s.

VII. ANIMAL LOCOMOTION; or, Walking, Swimming, and Flying. By J. B. Pettigrew, M.D., F.R.S., &c. With 130 Illustrations. Second Edition. Crown 8vo. price 5s.

VIII. RESPONSIBILITY IN MENTAL DISEASE. By Henry Maudsley, M.D. Third Edition. Crown 8vo. price 5s.

IX. THE NEW CHEMISTRY. By Professor J. P. Cooke, of the Harvard University. With 31 Illustrations. Fourth Edition. Crown 8vo. price 5s.

X. THE SCIENCE OF LAW. By Professor Sheldon Amos. Third Edition. Crown 8vo. price 5s.

XI. ANIMAL MECHANISM: a Treatise on Terrestrial and Aerial Locomotion. By Professor E. J. Marey. With 117 Illustrations. Second Edition. Crown 8vo. price 5s.

XII. THE DOCTRINE OF DESCENT AND DARWINISM. By Professor Oscar Schmidt (Strasburg University). With 26 Illustrations. Third Edition. Crown 8vo. price 5s.

XIII. THE HISTORY OF THE CONFLICT BETWEEN RELIGION AND SCIENCE. By J. W. Draper, M.D., LL.D. Eleventh Edition. Crown 8vo. price 5s.

XIV. FUNGI: their Nature, Influences, Uses, &c. By M. C. Cooke, M.D., LL.D. Edited by the Rev. M. J. Berkeley, M.A., F.L.S. With numerous Illustrations. Second Edition. Crown 8vo. price 5s.

XV. THE CHEMICAL EFFECTS OF LIGHT AND PHOTOGRAPHY. By Dr. Hermann Vogel (Polytechnic Academy of Berlin). Translation thoroughly revised. With 100 Illustrations. Third Edition. Crown 8vo. price 5s.

XVI. THE LIFE AND GROWTH OF LANGUAGE. By William Dwight Whitney, Professor of Sanscrit and Comparative Philology in Yale College, Newhaven. Second Edition. Crown 8vo. price 5s.

XVII. MONEY AND THE MECHANISM OF EXCHANGE. By W. Stanley Jevons, M.A., F.R.S. Fourth Edition. Crown 8vo. price 5s.

XVIII. THE NATURE OF LIGHT. With a General Account of Physical Optics. By Dr. Eugene Lommel, Professor of Physics in the University of Erlangen. With 188 Illustrations and a Table of Spectra in Chromo-lithography. Second Edition. Crown 8vo. price 5s.

XIX. ANIMAL PARASITES AND MESSMATES. By Monsieur Van Beneden, Professor of the University of Louvain, Correspondent of the Institute of France. With 83 Illustrations. Second Edition. Crown 8vo. price 5s.

XX. FERMENTATION. By Professor Schützenberger, Director of the Chemical Laboratory at the Sorbonne. With 28 Illustrations. Second Edition. Crown 8vo. price 5s.

XXI. THE FIVE SENSES OF MAN. By Professor Bernstein, of the University of Halle. With 91 Illustrations. Second Edition. Crown 8vo. price 5s.

XXII. THE THEORY OF SOUND IN ITS RELATION TO MUSIC. By Professor Pietro Blaserna, of the Royal University of Rome. With numerous Illustrations. Second Edition. Crown 8vo. price 5s.

XXIII. STUDIES IN SPECTRUM ANALYSIS. By J. Norman Lockyer. F.R.S. With six photographic Illustrations of Spectra, and numerous engravings on Wood. Crown 8vo. Second Edition. Price 6s. 6d.

Forthcoming Volumes.

Prof. W. KINGDON CLIFFORD, M.A. The First Principles of the Exact Sciences explained to the Non-mathematical.

W. B. CARPENTER, LL.D., F.R.S. The Physical Geography of the Sea.

Sir JOHN LUBBOCK, Bart., F.R.S. On Ants and Bees.

Prof. W. T. THISELTON DYER, B.A., B.Sc. Form and Habit in Flowering Plants.

Prof. MICHAEL FOSTER, M.D. Protoplasm and the Cell Theory.

H. CHARLTON BASTIAN, M.D., F.R.S. The Brain as an Organ of Mind.

P. BERT (Professor of Physiology, Paris). Forms of Life and other Cosmical Conditions.

Prof. A. C. RAMSAY, LL.D., F.R.S. Earth Sculpture: Hills, Valleys, Mountains, Plains, Rivers, Lakes; how they were Produced, and how they have been Destroyed.

Prof. T. H. HUXLEY. The Crayfish: an Introduction to the Study of Zoology.

The Rev. A. SECCHI, D.J., late Director of the Observatory at Rome. The Stars.

Prof. J. ROSENTHAL, of the University of Erlangen. General Physiology of Muscles and Nerves.

Prof. A. DE QUATREFAGES, Membre de l'Institut. The Human Race.

Prof. THURSTON. The Steam Engine. With numerous Engravings.

FRANCIS GALTON, F.R.S. Psychometry.

J. W. JUDD, F.R.S. The Laws of Volcanic Action.

Prof. F. N. BALFOUR. The Embryonic Phases of Animal Life.

J. LUYS, Physician to the Hospice de la Salpétrière. The Brain and its Functions. With Illustrations.

Dr. CARL SEMPER. Animals and their Conditions of Existence.

Prof. WURTZ. Atoms and the Atomic Theory.

GEORGE J. ROMANES, F.L.S. Animal Intelligence.

ALFRED W. BENNETT. A Handbook of Cryptogamic Botany.

MILITARY WORKS.

ANDERSON (Col. R. P.)—VICTORIES AND DEFEATS: an Attempt to explain the Causes which have led to them. An Officer's Manual. Demy 8vo. price 14s.

ARMY OF THE NORTH GERMAN CONFEDERATION: a Brief Description of its Organisation, of the Different Branches of the Service and their *rôle* in War, of its Mode of Fighting, &c. Translated from the Corrected Edition, by permission of the Author, by Colonel Edward Newdigate. Demy 8vo. price 5s.

BLUME (Maj. W.)—THE OPERATIONS OF THE GERMAN ARMIES IN FRANCE, from Sedan to the end of the War of 1870-71. With Map. From the Journals of the Head-quarters Staff. Translated by the late E. M. Jones, Maj. 20th Foot, Prof. of Mil. Hist., Sandhurst. Demy 8vo. price 9s.

BOGUSLAWSKI (Capt. A. von)—TACTICAL DEDUCTIONS FROM THE WAR OF 1870-1. Translated by Colonel Sir Lumley Graham, Bart., late 18th (Royal Irish) Regiment. Third Edition, Revised and Corrected. Demy 8vo. price 7s.

C. Kegan Paul & Co.'s Publications. 23

BRACKENBURY (*Lieut.-Col.*) C.B., R.A., A.A.G. MILITARY HANDBOOKS FOR REGIMENTAL OFFICERS. I. Military Sketching and Reconnaissance, by Lieut.-Col. F. J. Hutchison, and Capt. H. G. MacGregor. With 15 Plates. Small 8vo. cloth, price 6s. II. The Elements of Modern Tactics, by Major Wilkinson Shaw. With numerous Plates.

BRIALMONT (*Col. A.*)—HASTY INTRENCHMENTS. Translated by Lieut. Charles A. Empson, R.A. With Nine Plates. Demy 8vo. price 6s.

CLERY (*C.*) *Capt.*—MINOR TACTICS. With 26 Maps and Plans. Third and revised Edition. Demy 8vo. cloth, price 16s.

DU VERNOIS (*Col. von Verdy*)— STUDIES IN LEADING TROOPS. An authorised and accurate Translation by Lieutenant H. J. T. Hildyard, 71st Foot. Parts I. and II. Demy 8vo. price 7s.

GOETZE (*Capt. A. von*)—OPERATIONS OF THE GERMAN ENGINEERS DURING THE WAR OF 1870-1. Published by Authority, and in accordance with Official Documents. Translated from the German by Colonel G. Graham, V.C., C.B., R.E. With 6 large Maps. Demy 8vo. price 21s.

HARRISON (*Lieut.-Col. R.*) — THE OFFICER'S MEMORANDUM BOOK FOR PEACE AND WAR. Second Edition. Oblong 32mo. roan, elastic band and pencil, price 3s. 6d. ; russia, 5s.

HELVIG (*Capt. H.*)—THE OPERATIONS OF THE BAVARIAN ARMY CORPS. Translated by Captain G. S. Schwabe. With Five large Maps. In 2 vols. Demy 8vo. price 24s.

TACTICAL EXAMPLES : Vol. I. The Battalion, price 15s. Vol. II. The Regiment and Brigade, price 10s. 6d. Translated from the German by Col. Sir Lumley Graham. With nearly 300 Diagrams. Demy 8vo. cloth.

HOFFBAUER (*Capt.*)—THE GERMAN ARTILLERY IN THE BATTLES NEAR METZ. Based on the Official Reports of the German Artillery. Translated by Captain E. O. Hollist. With Map and Plans. Demy 8vo. price 21s.

LAYMANN (*Capt.*) — THE FRONTAL ATTACK OF INFANTRY. Translated by Colonel Edward Newdigate. Crown 8vo. price 2s. 6d.

NOTES ON CAVALRY TACTICS, ORGANISATION, &c. By a Cavalry Officer. With Diagrams. Demy 8vo. cloth, price 12s.

PAGE (*Capt. S. F.*)—DISCIPLINE AND DRILL. Cheaper Edition. Crown 8vo. price 1s.

PUBLIC SCHOOLBOY : the Volunteer, the Militiaman, and the Regular Soldier. Crown 8vo. cloth, price 5s.

RUSSELL (*Major Frank S.*)—RUSSIAN WARS WITH TURKEY, PAST AND PRESENT. With Maps. Second Edition. Crown 8vo. price 6s.

SCHELL (*Maj. von*)—THE OPERATIONS OF THE FIRST ARMY UNDER GEN. VON GOEBEN. Translated by Col. C. H. von Wright. Four Maps. demy 8vo. price 9s.

THE OPERATIONS OF THE FIRST ARMY UNDER GEN. VON STEINMETZ. Translated by Captain E. O. Hollist. Demy 8vo. price 10s. 6d.

SCHELLENDORF (*Major-Gen. B. von*) THE DUTIES OF THE GENERAL STAFF. Translated from the German by Lieutenant Hare. Vol. I. Demy 8vo. cloth, 10s. 6d.

SCHERFF (*Maj. W. von*)—STUDIES IN THE NEW INFANTRY TACTICS. Parts I. and II. Translated from the German by Colonel Lumley Graham. Demy 8vo. price 7s. 6d.

SHADWELL (*Maj.-Gen.*) C.B.—MOUNTAIN WARFARE. Illustrated by the Campaign of 1799 in Switzerland. Being a Translation of the Swiss Narrative compiled from the Works of the Archduke Charles, Jomini, and others. Also of Notes by General H. Dufour on the Campaign of the Valtelline in 1635. With Appendix, Maps, and Introductory Remarks. Demy 8vo. price 16s.

SHERMAN (*Gen. W. T.*)—MEMOIRS OF GENERAL W. T. SHERMAN, Commander of the Federal Forces in the American Civil War. By Himself. 2 vols. With Map. Demy 8vo. price 24s. *Copyright English Edition.*

STUBBS (*Lieut.-Col. F. W.*) — THE REGIMENT OF BENGAL ARTILLERY. The History of its Organisation, Equipment, and War Services. Compiled from Published Works, Official Records, and various Private Sources. With numerous Maps and Illustrations. 2 vols. demy 8vo. price 32*s.*

STUMM (*Lieut. Hugo*), *German-Military Attaché to the Khivan Expedition.* — RUSSIA'S ADVANCE EASTWARD. Based on the Official Reports of. Translated by Capt. C. E. H. VINCENT, With Map. Crown 8vo. price 6*s.*

VINCENT (*Capt. C. E. H.*) — ELEMENTARY MILITARY GEOGRAPHY, RECONNOITRING, AND SKETCHING. Compiled for Non-commissioned Officers and Soldiers of all Arms. Square crown 8vo. price 2*s.* 6*d.*

WHITE (*Capt. F. B. P.*) — THE SUBSTANTIVE SENIORITY ARMY LIST — MAJORS AND CAPTAINS. 8vo. sewed, price 2*s.* 6*d.*

WARTENSLEBEN (*Count H. von.*) — THE OPERATIONS OF THE SOUTH ARMY IN JANUARY AND FEBRUARY, 1871. Compiled from the Official War Documents of the Head-quarters of the Southern Army. Translated by Colonel C. H. von Wright. With Maps. Demy 8vo. price 6*s.*

THE OPERATIONS OF THE FIRST ARMY UNDER GEN. VON MANTEUFFEL. Translated by Colonel C. H. von Wright. Uniform with the above. Demy 8vo. price 9*s.*

WICKHAM (*Capt. E. H., R.A.*) — INFLUENCE OF FIREARMS UPON TACTICS : Historical and Critical Investigations. By an OFFICER OF SUPERIOR RANK (in the German Army). Translated by Captain E. H. Wickham, R.A. Demy 8vo. price 7*s.* 6*d.*

WOINOVITS (*Capt. I.*) — AUSTRIAN CAVALRY EXERCISE. Translated by Captain W. S. Cooke. Crown 8vo. price 7*s.*

POETRY.

ABBEY (*Henry*) — BALLADS OF GOOD DEEDS, and other Verses. Fcp. 8vo. cloth gilt, price 5*s.*

ADAMS (*W. D.* — LYRICS OF LOVE, from Shakespeare to Tennyson. Selected and arranged by. Fcp. 8vo. cloth extra, gilt edges, price 3*s.* 6*d.*

Also, a Cheaper Edition. Fcp. 8vo. cloth, 2*s.* 6*d.*

ADAMS (*John*) *M.A.* — ST. MALO'S QUEST, and other Poems. Fcp. 8vo. price 5*s.*

ADON — THROUGH STORM AND SUNSHINE. Illustrated by M. E. Edwards, A. T. H. Paterson, and the Author. Crown 8vo. price 7*s.* 6*d.*

A. J. R. — TOLD IN TWILIGHT ; Stories in Verse, Songs, &c. Fcp. 8vo. price 3*s.* 6*d.*

AUBERTIN (*J. J.*) — CAMOENS' LUSIADS. Portuguese Text, with Translation by. Map and Portraits. 2 vols. Demy 8vo. price 30*s.*

AURORA : a Volume of Verse. Fcp. 8vo. cloth, price 5*s.*

BARING (*T. C.*) *M.A., M.P.* — PINDAR IN ENGLISH RHYME. Being an Attempt to render the Epinikian Odes with the principal remaining Fragments of Pindar into English Rhymed Verse. Small 4to. price 7*s.*

BAYNES (*Rev. Canon R. H.*) *M.A.* — HOME SONGS FOR QUIET HOURS. Fourth Edition. Fcp. 8vo. price 2*s.* 6*d.*
This may also be had handsomely bound in morocco with gilt edges.

BENNETT (*Dr. W. C.*) — NARRATIVE POEMS AND BALLADS. Fcp. 8vo. sewed, in Coloured Wrapper, price 1*s.*

SONGS FOR SAILORS. Dedicated by Special Request to H.R.H. the Duke of Edinburgh. With Steel Portrait and Illustrations. Crown 8vo. price 3*s.* 6*d.*
An Edition in Illustrated Paper Covers, price 1*s.*

SONGS OF A SONG WRITER. Crown 8vo. price 6*s.*

BOSWELL (*R. B.*) *M.A. Oxon.* — METRICAL TRANSLATIONS FROM THE GREEK AND LATIN POETS, and other Poems. Crown 8vo. price 5*s.*

BRYANT (W. C.)—POEMS. Red-line Edition. With 24 Illustrations and Portrait of the Author. Crown 8vo. cloth extra, price 7*s*. 6*d*.
   A Cheap Edition, with Frontispiece. Small crown 8vo. price 3*s*. 6*d*.

BUCHANAN (Robt.)—POETICAL WORKS. Collected Edition, in 3 vols. with Portrait. Crown 8vo. price 6*s*. each.
   MASTER-SPIRITS. Post 8vo. price 10*s*. 6*d*.

BULKELEY (Rev. H. J.)—WALLED IN, and other Poems. Crown 8vo. price 5*s*.

CALDERON'S DRAMAS: the Wonder-Working Magician—Life is a Dream—the Purgatory of St. Patrick. Translated by Denis Florence MacCarthy. Post 8vo. price 10*s*.

CARPENTER (E.)—NARCISSUS, and other Poems. Fcp. 8vo. price 5*s*.

COLLINS (Mortimer)—INN OF STRANGE MEETINGS, and other Poems. Crown 8vo. cloth, price 5*s*.

CORY (Lieut.-Col. Arthur)—IONE: a Poem in Four Parts. Fcp. 8vo. cloth, price 5*s*.

COSMOS: a Poem. Fcp. 8vo. price 3*s*. 6*d*.

CRESSWELL (Mrs. G.)—THE KING'S BANNER: Drama in Four Acts. Five Illustrations. 4to. price 10*s*. 6*d*.

DENNIS (J.)—ENGLISH SONNETS. Collected and Arranged. Elegantly bound. Fcp. 8vo. price 3*s*. 6*d*.

DE VERE (Aubrey)—ALEXANDER THE GREAT: a Dramatic Poem. Small crown 8vo. price 5*s*.

   THE INFANT BRIDAL, and other Poems. A New and Enlarged Edition. Fcp. 8vo. price 7*s*. 6*d*.

   THE LEGENDS OF ST. PATRICK, and other Poems. Small crown 8vo. price 5*s*.

   ST. THOMAS OF CANTERBURY: a Dramatic Poem. Large fcp. 8vo. price 5*s*.

   ANTAR AND ZARA: an Eastern Romance. INISFAIL, and other Poems, Meditative and Lyrical. Fcp. 8vo. price 6*s*.

   THE FALL OF RORA, THE SEARCH AFTER PROSERPINE, and other Poems, Meditative and Lyrical. Fcp. 8vo. 6*s*.

DOBSON (Austin)—VIGNETTES IN RHYME, and Vers de Société. Third Edition. Fcp. 8vo. price 5*s*.

   PROVERBS IN PORCELAIN. By the Author of 'Vignettes in Rhyme.' Second Edition. Crown 8vo. price 6*s*.

DOWDEN (Edward) LL.D.—POEMS. Third Edition. Fcp. 8vo. price 5*s*.

DOWNTON (Rev. H.) M.A.—HYMNS AND VERSES. Original and Translated. Small crown 8vo. cloth, price 3*s*. 6*d*.

DURAND (Lady)—IMITATIONS FROM THE GERMAN OF SPITTA AND TERSTEGEN. Fcp. 8vo. price 4*s*.

EDWARDS (Rev. Basil) — MINOR CHORDS; or, Songs for the Suffering: a Volume of Verse. Fcp. 8vo. cloth, price 3*s*. 6*d*.; paper, price, 2*s*. 6*d*.

ELLIOT (Lady Charlotte)—MEDUSA and other Poems. Crown 8vo. cloth, price 6*s*.

ELLIOTT (Ebenezer), The Corn Law Rhymer.—POEMS. Edited by his son, the Rev. Edwin Elliott, of St. John's, Antigua. 2 vols. crown 8vo. price 18*s*.

EPIC OF HADES (THE). By the Author of 'Songs of Two Worlds.' Fifth and finally revised Edition. Fcp. 8vo. price 7*s*. 6*d*.

EROS AGONISTES: Poems. By E. B. D. Fcp. 8vo. price 3*s*. 6*d*.

EYRE (Maj.-Gen. Sir V.) C.B., K.C.S.I., &c.—LAYS OF A KNIGHT-ERRANT IN MANY LANDS. Square crown 8vo. with Six Illustrations, price 7*s*. 6*d*.

FERRIS (Henry Weybridge) — POEMS. Fcp. 8vo. price 5*s*.

GARDNER (H.)—SUNFLOWERS: a Book of Verses. Fcp. 8vo. price 5*s*.

G. H. T.—VERSES, mostly written in India. Crown 8vo, cloth, price 6*s*.

GOLDIE (Lieut. M. H. G.)—HEBE: a Tale. Fcp. 8vo. price 5*s*.

HARCOURT (Capt. A. F. P.)—THE SHAKESPEARE ARGOSY. Containing much of the wealth of Shakespeare's Wisdom and Wit, alphabetically arranged and classified. Crown 8vo. price 6*s*.

HEWLETT (Henry G.)—A SHEAF OF VERSE. Fcp. 8vo. price 3s. 6d.

HOLMES (E. G. A.)—POEMS. Fcp. 8vo. price 5s.

HOWARD (Rev. G. B.)—AN OLD LEGEND OF ST. PAUL'S. Fcp. 8vo. price 4s. 6d.

HOWELL (James)—A TALE OF THE SEA, Sonnets, and other Poems. Fcp. 8vo. price 5s.

HUGHES (Allison)—PENELOPE, and other Poems. Fcp. 8vo. price 4s. 6d.

INCHBOLD (J. W.)—ANNUS AMORIS: Sonnets. Fcp. 8vo. price 4s. 6d.

KING (Mrs. Hamilton)—THE DISCIPLES: a New Poem. Third Edition, with some Notes. Crown 8vo. price 7s. 6d.
ASPROMONTE, and other Poems. Second Edition. Fcp. 8vo. price 4s. 6d.

KNIGHT (A. F. C.)—POEMS. Fcp. 8vo. price 5s.

LADY OF LIPARI (THE): a Poem in Three Cantos. Fcp. 8vo. price 5s.

LOCKER (F.)—LONDON LYRICS. A New and Revised Edition, with Additions and a Portrait of the Author. Crown 8vo. cloth elegant, price 6s.
Also, an Edition for the People. Fcp. 8vo. price 2s. 6d.

LUCAS (Alice)—TRANSLATIONS FROM THE WORKS OF GERMAN POETS OF THE 18TH AND 19TH CENTURIES. Fcp. 8vo. price 5s.

MAGNUSSON (Eirikr) M.A., and PALMER (E. H.) M.A.—JOHAN LUDVIG RUNEBERG'S LYRICAL SONGS, IDYLLS, AND EPIGRAMS. Fcp. 8vo. cloth, price 5s.

MIDDLETON (The Lady)—BALLADS. Square 16mo. cloth, price 3s. 6d.

MILLER (Robert)—THE ROMANCE OF LOVE. Fcp. cloth, price 5s.

MORICE (Rev. F. D.) M.A.—THE OLYMPIAN AND PYTHIAN ODES OF PINDAR. A New Translation in English Verse. Crown 8vo. price 7s. 6d.

MORSHEAD (E. D. A.)—THE AGAMEMNON OF ÆSCHYLUS. Translated into English Verse. With an Introductory Essay. Crown 8vo. cloth, price 5s.

NEW WRITER (A)—SONGS OF TWO WORLDS. Third Edition. Complete in One Volume. With Portrait. Fcp. 8vo. price 5s.
THE EPIC OF HADES. By the Author of 'Songs of Two Worlds.' Fourth and finally revised Edition. Fcp. 8vo. price 7s. 6d.

NICHOLSON (Edward B.) Librarian of the London Institution—THE CHRIST CHILD, and other Poems. Crown 8vo. cloth, price 4s. 6d.

NOAKE (Major R. Compton)—THE BIVOUAC; or, Martial Lyrist. With an Appendix: Advice to the Soldier. Fcp. 8vo. price 5s. 6d.

NORRIS (Rev. Alfred)—THE INNER AND OUTER LIFE POEMS. Fcp. 8vo. cloth, price 6s.

PAUL (C. Kegan)—GOETHE'S FAUST. A New Translation in Rhyme. Crown 8vo. price 6s.

PAYNE (John)—SONGS OF LIFE AND DEATH. Crown 8vo. cloth, price 5s.

PEACOCKE (Georgiana)—RAYS FROM THE SOUTHERN CROSS: Poems. Crown 8vo. with Sixteen Full-page Illustrations by the Rev. P. Walsh. Crown 8vo. cloth elegant, price 10s. 6d.

PENNELL (H. Cholmondeley)—PEGASUS RESADDLED. By the Author of 'Puck on Pegasus,' &c. &c. With Ten Full-page Illustrations by George Du Maurier. Second Edition. Fcp. 4to. cloth elegant, 12s. 6d.

PFEIFFER (Emily)—GLAN ALARCH: His Silence and Song: a Poem. Crown 8vo. price 6s.
GERARD'S MONUMENT and other Poems. Second Edition. Crown 8vo. cloth, price 6s.
POEMS. Crown 8vo. cloth, price 6s.

POWLETT (Lieut. N.) R.A.—EASTERN LEGENDS AND STORIES IN ENGLISH VERSE. Crown 8vo. price 5s.

RHOADES (James)—TIMOLEON: a Dramatic Poem. Fcp. 8vo. price 5s.

ROBINSON (A. Mary F.)—A HANDFUL OF HONEYSUCKLE. Fcp. 8vo. cloth, price 3s. 6d.

SCOTT (Patrick)—THE DREAM AND THE DEED, and other Poems. Fcp. 8vo. price 5*s*.

SONGS OF TWO WORLDS. By the Author of 'The Epic of Hades.' Fourth Edition. Complete in one Volume, with Portrait. Fcp. 8vo. cloth, price 7*s*. 6*d*.

SONGS FOR MUSIC. By Four Friends. Containing Songs by Reginald A. Gatty, Stephen H. Gatty, Greville J. Chester, and Juliana Ewing. Square crown 8vo. price 5*s*.

SPICER (H.)—OTHO'S DEATH WAGER: a Dark Page of History Illustrated. In Five Acts. Fcp. 8vo. cloth, price 5*s*.

STAPLETON (John)—THE THAMES: a Poem. Crown 8vo. price 6*s*.

STONEHEWER (Agnes)—MONACELLA: a Legend of North Wales. A Poem. Fcp. 8vo. cloth, price 3*s*. 6*d*.

SWEET SILVERY SAYINGS OF SHAKESPEARE. Crown 8vo. cloth gilt, price 7*s*. 6*d*.

TAYLOR (Rev. J. W. A.) M.A.—POEMS. Fcp. 8vo. price 5*s*.

TAYLOR (Sir H.)—Works Complete in Five Volumes. Crown 8vo. cloth, price 30*s*.

TENNYSON (Alfred) — Works Complete:—

THE IMPERIAL LIBRARY EDITION. Complete in 7 vols. demy 8vo. price 10*s*. 6*d*. each; in Roxburgh binding, 12*s*. 6*d*. (*See p.* 32.)

AUTHOR'S EDITION. In Six Volumes. Post 8vo. cloth gilt; or half-morocco. Roxburgh style. (*See p.* 32.)

CABINET EDITION. 12 Volumes. Each with Frontispiece. Fcp. 8vo. price 2*s*. 6*d*. each. (*See p.* 32.)

CABINET EDITION. 12 vols. Complete in handsome Ornamental Case. (*See p.* 32).

POCKET VOLUME EDITION. 13 vols. in neat case, price 36*s*. Ditto, ditto. Extra cloth gilt, in case, price 42*s*. (*See p.* 32.)

THE GUINEA EDITION OF THE POETICAL AND DRAMATIC WORKS, complete in 12 vols. neatly bound and enclosed in box. Cloth, price 21*s*.; French morocco, price 31*s*. 6*d*.

TENNYSON (Alfred)—cont.

SHILLING EDITION OF THE POETICAL WORKS. In 12 vols. pocket size, 1*s*. each, sewed.

THE CROWN EDITION. Complete in 1 vol. strongly bound in cloth, price 6*s*.; cloth, extra gilt leaves, price 7*s*. 6*d*.; Roxburgh, half-morocco, price 7*s*. 6*d*.

*** Can also be had in a variety of other bindings.

Original Editions:—

POEMS. Small 8vo. price 6*s*.

MAUD, and other Poems. Small 8vo. price 3*s*. 6*d*.

THE PRINCESS. Small 8vo. price 3*s*. 6*d*.

IDYLLS OF THE KING. Small 8vo. price 5*s*.

IDYLLS OF THE KING. Complete. Small 8vo. price 6*s*.

THE HOLY GRAIL, and other Poems. Small 8vo. price 4*s*. 6*d*.

GARETH AND LYNETTE. Small 8vo. price 3*s*.

ENOCH ARDEN, &c. Small 8vo. price 3*s*. 6*d*.

IN MEMORIAM. Small 8vo. price 4*s*.

HAROLD: a Drama. New Edition. Crown 8vo. price 6*s*.

QUEEN MARY: a Drama. New Edition. Crown 8vo. price 6*s*.

SELECTIONS FROM THE ABOVE WORKS. Super royal 16mo. price 3*s*. 6*d*.; cloth gilt extra, price 4*s*.

SONGS FROM THE ABOVE WORKS. 16mo. cloth, price 2*s*. 6*d*.; cloth extra, 3*s*. 6*d*.

TENNYSON'S IDYLLS OF THE KING, and other Poems. Illustrated by Julia Margaret Cameron. 2 vols. folio. half-bound morocco, cloth sides, price £6. 6*s*. each.

TENNYSON FOR THE YOUNG AND FOR RECITATION. Specially arranged. Fcp. 8vo. 1*s*. 6*d*.

THE TENNYSON BIRTHDAY BOOK. Edited by Emily Shakespear. 32mo. cloth limp, 2*s*.; cloth extra, 3*s*.

THOMPSON (*Alice C.*)—PRELUDES : a Volume of Poems. Illustrated by Elizabeth Thompson (Painter of 'The Roll Call'). 8vo. price 7s. 6d.

THOUGHTS IN VERSE. Small crown 8vo. price 1s. 6d.

THRING (*Rev. Godfrey*), *B.A.*—HYMNS AND SACRED LYRICS. Fcp. 8vo. price 5s.

TODD (*Herbert*) *M.A.*—ARVAN ; or, the Story of the Sword. A Poem. Crown 8vo. price 7s. 6d.

TODHUNTER (*Dr. J.*)—LAURELLA, and other Poems. Crown 8vo. price 6s. 6d.

TURNER (*Rev. C. Tennyson*)—SONNETS, LYRICS, AND TRANSLATIONS. Crown 8vo. cloth, price 4s. 6d.

WATERFIELD (*W.*) — HYMNS FOR HOLY DAYS AND SEASONS. 32mo. cloth, price 1s. 6d.

WAY (*A.*) *M.A.*—THE ODES OF HORACE LITERALLY TRANSLATED IN METRE. Fcp. 8vo. price 2s.

WILLOUGHBY (*The Hon. Mrs.*)—ON THE NORTH WIND—THISTLEDOWN : a Volume of Poems. Elegantly bound, small crown 8vo. price 7s. 6d.

LIBRARY NOVELS.

BLUE ROSES ; or, Helen Malinofska's Marriage. By the Author of 'Véra.' Fifth Edition. 2 vols. cloth, gilt tops, 12s.

CHAPMAN (*Hon. Mrs. E. W.*)— A CONSTANT HEART : a Story. 2 vols. cloth, gilt tops, 12s.

HOCKLEY (*W. B.*)—TALES OF THE ZENANA ; or, a Nuwab's Leisure Hours. By the Author of 'Pandurang Hari.' With a Preface by Lord Stanley of Alderley. 2 vols. crown 8vo. cloth, price 21s.

MASTERMAN (*J.*)—WORTH WAITING FOR : a New Novel. 3 vols. crown 8vo. cloth.

MORLEY (*Susan*)—MARGARET CHETWYND : a Novel. 3 vols. crown 8vo.

PAUL (*Margaret Agnes*)—GENTLE AND SIMPLE : a Story. 2 vols. Crown 8vo. gilt tops, price 12s.

SHAW (*Flora L.*)—CASTLE BLAIR : a Story of Youthful Lives. 2 vols. crown 8vo. cloth, price 12s.

STRETTON (*Miss Hesba*)—THROUGH A NEEDLE'S EYE. 2 vols. crown 8vo. gilt tops, price 12s.

TAYLOR (*Colonel Meadows*) *C.S.I.*, *M.R.I.A.*—SEETA : a Novel. 3 vols. crown 8vo.

A NOBLE QUEEN. 3 vols. crown 8vo.

WITHIN SOUND OF THE SEA. By the Author of 'Vera,' &c. &c. 2 vols. Crown 8vo. gilt tops, price 12s.

WORKS OF FICTION IN ONE VOLUME.

BETHAM-EDWARDS (*Miss M.*) KITTY. With a Frontispiece. Crown 8vo. price 6s.

BLUE ROSES ; or, Helen Malinofska's Marriage. By the Author of 'Véra.' New and Cheaper Edition. With Frontispiece. Crown 8vo. cloth, price 6s.

CLERK (*Mrs. Godfrey*)—'ILÂM EN NÂS : Historical Tales and Anecdotes of the Times of the Early Khalifahs. Translated from the Arabic Originals. Illustrated with Historical and Explanatory Notes. Crown 8vo. cloth, price 7s.

GARRETT (*E.*)—BY STILL WATERS : a Story for Quiet Hours. With Seven Illustrations. Crown 8vo. price 6s.

HARDY (*Thomas*)—A PAIR OF BLUE EYES. Author of 'Far from the Madding Crowd.' New Edition. Crown 8vo. price 6s.

HOWARD (*Mary M.*)—BEATRICE AYLMER, and other Tales. Crown 8vo. price 6s.

IGNOTUS—CULMSHIRE FOLK: a Novel. New and Cheaper Edition. Crown 8vo. price 6s.

MACDONALD (G.)—MALCOLM. With Portrait of the Author engraved on Steel. Fourth Edition. Crown 8vo. price 6s.

THE MARQUIS OF LOSSIE. Second Edition. With Frontispiece. Crown 8vo. cloth, price 6s.

ST. GEORGE AND ST. MICHAEL. Second Edition. With Frontispiece. Crown 8vo. cloth, 6s.

MEREDITH (George) — ORDEAL OF RICHARD FEVEREL. New Edition. Crown 8vo. cloth, price 6s.

PALGRAVE (W. Gifford)—HERMANN AGHA: an Eastern Narrative. Third Edition. Crown 8vo. cloth, price 6s.

PANDURANG HARI; or, Memoirs of a Hindoo. With an Introductory Preface by Sir H. Bartle E. Frere, G.C.S.I., C.B. Crown 8vo. price 6s.

PAUL (Margaret Agnes)—GENTLE AND SIMPLE: A Story. New and Cheaper Edition, with Frontispiece. Crown 8vo. price 6s.

SAUNDERS (John) — ISRAEL MORT, OVERMAN: a Story of the Mine. Crown 8vo. price 6s.

SAUNDERS (Katherine) — GIDEON'S ROCK, and other Stories. Crown 8vo. price 6s.

SAUNDERS (Katherine)—cont.

JOAN MERRYWEATHER, and other Stories. Crown 8vo. price 6s.

MARGARET AND ELIZABETH: a Story of the Sea. Crown 8vo. price 6s.

SHAW (Flora L.)—CASTLE BLAIR; a Story of Youthful Lives. New and Cheaper Edition, with Frontispiece. Crown 8vo. price 6s.

TAYLOR (Col. Meadows) C.S.I., M.R.I.A. THE CONFESSIONS OF A THUG. Crown 8vo. price 6s.

TARA: a Mahratta Tale. Crown 8vo. price 6s.

CORNHILL LIBRARY of FICTION (The). Crown 8vo. price 3s. 6d. per volume.

HALF-A-DOZEN DAUGHTERS. By J. Masterman.

THE HOUSE OF RABY. By Mrs. G. Hooper.

A FIGHT FOR LIFE. By Moy Thomas.

ROBIN GRAY. By Charles Gibbon.

ONE OF TWO; or, The Left-Handed Bride. By J. Hain Friswell.

GOD'S PROVIDENCE HOUSE. By Mrs. G. L. Banks. New Edition.

FOR LACK OF GOLD. By Charles Gibbon.

ABEL DRAKE'S WIFE. By John Saunders.

HIRELL. By John Saunders.

CHEAP FICTION.

GIBBON (Charles)—FOR LACK OF GOLD. With a Frontispiece. Crown 8vo. Illustrated Boards, price 2s.

ROBIN GRAY. With a Frontispiece. Crown 8vo. Illustrated boards, price 2s.

SAUNDERS (John) — HIRELL. With Frontispiece. Crown 8vo. Illustrated boards, price 2s.

ABEL DRAKE'S WIFE. With Frontispiece. Illustrated boards, price 2s.

BOOKS FOR THE YOUNG.

AUNT MARY'S BRAN PIE. By the Author of 'St. Olave's.' Illustrated. Price 3s. 6d.

BARLEE (Ellen)—LOCKED OUT: a Tale of the Strike. With a Frontispiece. Royal 16mo. price 1s. 6d.

BONWICK (J.) F.R.G.S.—THE TASMANIAN LILY. With Frontispiece. Crown 8vo. price 5s.

MIKE HOWE, the Bushranger of Van Diemen's Land. With Frontispiece. Crown 8vo. price 5s.

BRAVE MEN'S FOOTSTEPS. By the Editor of 'Men who have Risen.' A Book of Example and Anecdote for Young People. With Four Illustrations by C. Doyle. Third Edition. Crown 8vo. price 3s. 6d.

CHILDREN'S TOYS, and some Elementary Lessons in General Knowledge which they teach. Illustrated. Crown 8vo. cloth, price 5s.

COLERIDGE (Sara)—PRETTY LESSONS IN VERSE FOR GOOD CHILDREN, with some Lessons in Latin, in Easy Rhyme. A New Edition. Illustrated. Fcp. 8vo. cloth, price 3s. 6d.

D'ANVERS (N. R.)—LITTLE MINNIE'S TROUBLES : an Every-day Chronicle. With 4 Illustrations by W. H. Hughes. Fcp. cloth, price 3s. 6d.

PIXIE'S ADVENTURES; or, the Tale of a Terrier. With 21 Illustrations. 16mo. cloth, price 4s. 6d.

NANNY. With numerous Illustrations. Square 16mo. cloth.

DAVIES (G. Christopher)—MOUNTAIN, MEADOW, AND MERE: a Series of Outdoor Sketches of Sport, Scenery, Adventures, and Natural History. With Sixteen Illustrations by Bosworth W. Harcourt. Crown 8vo. price 6s.

RAMBLES AND ADVENTURES OF OUR SCHOOL FIELD CLUB. With Four Illustrations. Crown 8vo. price 5s.

DRUMMOND (Miss)—TRIPP'S BUILDINGS. A Study from Life, with Frontispiece. Small crown 8vo. price 3s. 6d.

EDMONDS (Herbert) — WELL SPENT LIVES: a Series of Modern Biographies. Crown 8vo. price 5s.

EVANS (Mark)—THE STORY OF OUR FATHER'S LOVE, told to Children; being a New and Enlarged Edition of Theology for Children. With Four Illustrations. Fcap. 8vo. price 3s. 6d.

FARQUHARSON (M.)
I. ELSIE DINSMORE. Crown 8vo. price 3s. 6d.
II. ELSIE'S GIRLHOOD. Crown 8vo. price 3s. 6d.
III. ELSIE'S HOLIDAYS AT ROSELANDS. Crown 8vo. price 3s. 6d.

HERFORD. (Brooke)—THE STORY OF RELIGION IN ENGLAND : a Book for Young Folk. Cr. 8vo. cloth, price 5s.

INGELOW (Jean) — THE LITTLE WONDER-HORN. With Fifteen Illustrations. Small 8vo. price 2s. 6d.

KER (David) — THE BOY SLAVE IN BOKHARA: a Tale of Central Asia. With Illustrations. Cr. 8vo. price 5s.

THE WILD HORSEMAN OF THE PAMPAS. Illustrated. Crown 8vo. price 5s.

LEANDER (Richard) — FANTASTIC STORIES. Translated from the German by Paulina B. Granville. With Eight Full-page Illustrations by M. E. Fraser-Tytler. Crown 8vo. price 5s.

LEE (Holme)—HER TITLE OF HONOUR. A Book for Girls. New Edition. With a Frontispiece. Crown 8vo. price 5s.

LEWIS (Mary A.)—A RAT WITH THREE TALES. With Four Illustrations by Catherine F. Frere. Price 5s.

LITTLE MINNIE'S TROUBLES : an Everyday Chronicle. With Four Illustrations by W. H. Hughes. Fcap. price 3s. 6d.

MC CLINTOCK (L)—SIR SPANGLE AND THE DINGY HEN. Illustrated. Square crown 8vo. price 2s. 6d.

MAC KENNA (S. J.)—PLUCKY FELLOWS. A Book for Boys. With Six Illustrations. Fourth Edition. Crown 8vo. price 3s. 6d.

AT SCHOOL WITH AN OLD DRAGOON. With Six Illustrations. Third Edition. Crown 8vo. price 5s.

MALDEN (H. E.)—PRINCES AND PRINCESSES : Two Fairy Tales. Illustrated Small crown 8vo. price 2s. 6d.

MASTER BOBBY. By the Author of "Christina North." With Six Illustrations. Fcp. 8vo. cloth.

NAAKE (J. T.)—SLAVONIC FAIRY TALES. From Russian, Servian, Polish, and Bohemian Sources. With Four Illustrations. Crown 8vo. price 5s.

PELLETAN (E.)—THE DESERT PASTOR. JEAN JAROUSSEAU. Translated from the French. By Colonel E. P. De L'Hoste. With a Frontispiece. New Edition. Fcap. 8vo. price 3s. 6d.

REANEY (Mrs. G. S.)—WAKING AND WORKING; or, From Girlhood to Womanhood. With a Frontispiece. Crown 8vo. price 5s.

BLESSING AND BLESSED: a Story of Girl Life. Crown 8vo. cloth, price 5s.

ENGLISH GIRLS: Their Place and Power. With Preface by the Rev. R. W. Dale.

SUNBEAM WILLIE, and other Stories. Three Illustrations. Royal 16mo. price 1s. 6d.

SUNSHINE JENNY and other Stories. 3 Illustrations. Royal 16mo. cloth, price 1s. 6d.

ROSS (Mrs. E.), ('Nelsie Brook')— DADDY'S PET. A Sketch from Humble Life. With Six Illustrations. Royal 16mo. price 1s.

SADLER (S. W.) R.N.—THE AFRICAN CRUISER: a Midshipman's Adventures on the West Coast. With Three Illustrations. Second Edition. Crown 8vo. price 3s. 6d.

SEEKING HIS FORTUNE, and other Stories. With Four Illustrations. Crown 8vo. price 3s. 6d.

SEVEN AUTUMN LEAVES FROM FAIRY LAND. Illustrated with Nine Etchings. Square crown 8vo. price 3s. 6d.

STORR (Francis) and TURNER (Hawes). —CANTERBURY CHIMES; or, Chaucer Tales retold to Children. With Six Illustrations from the Ellesmere MS. Fcap. 8vo. cloth.

STRETTON (Hesba), Author of 'Jessica's First Prayer.'

MICHEL LORIO'S CROSS and other Stories. With Two Illustrations. Royal 16mo. price 1s. 6d.

THE STORM OF LIFE. With Ten Illustrations. Twenty-first Thousand. Roy. 16mo. price 1s. 6d.

STRETTON (Hesba)—cont.
THE CREW OF THE DOLPHIN. Illustrated. Fourteenth Thousand. Royal 16mo. price 1s. 6d.

CASSY. Thirty-eighth Thousand. With Six Illustrations. Royal 16mo. price 1s. 6d.

THE KING'S SERVANTS. Forty-third Thousand. With Eight Illustrations. Royal 16mo. price 1s. 6d.

LOST GIP. Fifty-ninth Thousand. With Six Illustrations. Royal 16mo. price 1s. 6d.

₊ Also a handsomely bound Edition, with Twelve Illustrations, price 2s. 6d.

STRETTON (Hesba)—cont.
DAVID LLOYD'S LAST WILL. With Four Illustrations. Royal 16mo. price 2s. 6d.

THE WONDERFUL LIFE. Thirteenth Thousand. Fcap. 8vo. price 2s. 6d.

A NIGHT AND A DAY. With Frontispiece. Twelfth Thousand. Royal 16mo. limp cloth, price 6d.

FRIENDS TILL DEATH. With Illustrations and Frontispiece. Twenty-fourth Thousand. Royal 16mo. price 1s. 6d.; limp cloth, price 6d.

TWO CHRISTMAS STORIES. With Frontispiece. Twenty-first Thousand. Royal 16mo. limp cloth, price 6d.

MICHEL LORIO'S CROSS, AND LEFT ALONE. With Frontispiece. Fifteenth Thousand. Royal 16mo. limp cloth, price 6d.

OLD TRANSOME. With Frontispiece. Sixteenth Thousand. Royal 16mo. limp cloth, price 6d.

₊ Taken from 'The King's Servants.'

THE WORTH OF A BABY, and How Apple-Tree Court was Won. With Frontispiece. Nineteenth Thousand. Royal 16mo. limp cloth, price 6d.

SUNNYLAND STORIES. By the Author of 'Aunt Mary's Bran Pie.' Illustrated. Small 8vo. price 3s. 6d.

WHITAKER (Florence)—CHRISTY'S INHERITANCE. A London Story. Illustrated. Royal 16mo. price 1s. 6d.

ZIMMERN (H.)—STORIES IN PRECIOUS STONES. With Six Illustrations. Third Edition. Crown 8vo. price 5s.

CONTENTS OF THE VARIOUS VOLUMES

IN THE COLLECTED EDITIONS OF

MR. TENNYSON'S WORKS.

THE IMPERIAL LIBRARY EDITION,

COMPLETE IN SEVEN OCTAVO VOLUMES.
Cloth, price 10s. 6d. per vol.; 12s. 6d. Roxburgh binding.

CONTENTS.

Vol. I.—MISCELLANEOUS POEMS.
II.—MISCELLANEOUS POEMS.
III.—PRINCESS, AND OTHER POEMS.

Vol. IV.—IN MEMORIAM and MAUD.
V.—IDYLLS OF THE KING.
VI.—IDYLLS OF THE KING.
VII.—DRAMAS.

Printed in large, clear, old-faced type, with a Steel Engraved Portrait of the Author, the set complete, cloth, price £3. 13s. 6d.; or Roxburghe half-morocco, price £4. 7s. 6d.
*** *The handsomest Edition published.*

THE AUTHOR'S EDITION,

IN SIX VOLUMES. Bound in cloth, 38s. 6d.

CONTENTS.

Vol. I.—EARLY POEMS and ENGLISH IDYLLS. 6s.
II.—LOCKSLEY HALL, LUCRETIUS, and other Poems. 6s.
III.—THE IDYLLS OF THE KING, complete. 7s. 6d.

Vol. IV.—THE PRINCESS and MAUD. 6s.
V.—ENOCH ARDEN and IN MEMORIAM. 6s.
VI.—QUEEN MARY and HAROLD 7s.

This Edition can also be had bound in half-morocco, Roxburgh, price 1s. 6d. per vol. extra.

THE CABINET EDITION,

COMPLETE IN TWELVE VOLUMES. Price 2s. 6d. each.

CONTENTS.

Vol. I.—EARLY POEMS. Illustrated with a Photographic Portrait of Mr. Tennyson.

II.—ENGLISH IDYLLS, and other POEMS. Containing an Engraving of Mr. Tennyson's Residence at Aldworth.

III.—LOCKSLEY HALL, and other POEMS. With an Engraved Picture of Farringford.

IV.—LUCRETIUS, and other POEMS. Containing an Engraving of a Scene in the Garden at Swainston.

V.—IDYLLS OF THE KING. With an Autotype of the Bust of Mr. Tennyson by T. Woolner, R.A.

Vol. VI.—IDYLLS OF THE KING. Illustrated with an Engraved Portrait of 'Elaine,' from a Photographic Study by Julia M. Cameron.

VII.—IDYLLS OF THE KING. Containing an Engraving of 'Arthur,' from a Photographic Study by Julia M. Cameron.

VIII.—THE PRINCESS. With an Engraved Frontispiece.

IX.—MAUD and ENOCH ARDEN. With a Picture of 'Maud,' taken from a Photographic Study by Julia M. Cameron.

X.—IN MEMORIAM. With a Steel Engraving of Arthur H. Hallam, engraved from a picture in possession of the Author, by J. C. Armytage.

XI.—QUEEN MARY: a Drama. With Frontispiece by Walter Crane.

XII.—HAROLD: a Drama. With Frontispiece by Walter Crane.

*** *These Volumes may be had separately, or the Edition complete, in a handsome ornamental case, price 32s.*

THE MINIATURE EDITION,

IN THIRTEEN VOLUMES.

CONTENTS.

Vol. I.—POEMS.
II.—POEMS.
III.—POEMS.
IV.—IDYLLS OF THE KING.
V.—IDYLLS OF THE KING.
VI.—IDYLLS OF THE KING.

Vol. VII.—IDYLLS OF THE KING.
VIII.—IN MEMORIAM.
IX.—PRINCESS.
X.—MAUD.
XI.—ENOCH ARDEN.
XII.—QUEEN MARY.

Vol. XIII.—HAROLD.

Bound in imitation vellum, ornamented in gilt and gilt edges, in case, price 42s.
This Edition can also be had in plain binding and case, price 36s.

Spottiswoode & Co., Printers, New-street Square, London.

www.ingramcontent.com/pod-product-compliance
Lightning Source LLC
Chambersburg PA
CBHW051728300426
44115CB00007B/505